10155440

G000071359

The Postwar Legacy of Appeasement

FOR SALE BY
SURREY COUNTY COUNCIL
WITH ALL FAULTS

S

The Postwar Legacy of Appeasement

British Foreign Policy Since 1945

R. GERALD HUGHES

BLOOMSBURY

LONDON · NEW DELHI · NEW YORK · SYDNEY

Bloomsbury Academic

An imprint of Bloomsbury Publishing Plc

50 Bedford Square	1385 Broadway
London	New York
WC1B 3DP	NY 10018
UK	USA

www.bloomsbury.com

Bloomsbury is a registered trademark of Bloomsbury Publishing Plc

First published 2014

© R. Gerald Hughes, 2014

R. Gerald Hughes has asserted his right under the Copyright, Designs and Patents Act, 1988, to be identified as Author of this work.

All rights reserved. No part of this publication may be reproduced or transmitted in any form or by any means, electronic or mechanical, including photocopying, recording, or any information storage or retrieval system, without prior permission in writing from the publishers.

No responsibility for loss caused to any individual or organization acting on or refraining from action as a result of the material in this publication can be accepted by Bloomsbury or the author.

British Library Cataloguing-in-Publication Data
A catalogue record for this book is available from the British Library.

ISBN: HB: 978-1-7809-3825-7
PB: 978-1-7809-3583-6
ePDF: 978-1-7809-3645-1
ePub: 978-1-7809-3545-4

Library of Congress Cataloging-in-Publication Data
A catalog record for this book is available from the Library of Congress

Typeset by Newgen Knowledge Works (P) Ltd., Chennai, India
Printed and bound in Great Britain

SURREY LIBRARIES

Askews & Holts	15-Jan-2014
327.41 GOV	£22.99

I fy nheulu
Nolle timere

In international politics . . . you must either be ready to practice appeasement indefinitely, or at some point you must be ready to fight.

George Orwell, 1947

It will be enough for me . . . if these words of mine are judged useful by those who want to understand clearly the events which happened in the past and which (human nature being what it is) will, at some time or other and in much the same ways, be repeated in the future. My work is not a piece of writing designed to meet the taste of an immediate public, but was done to last forever.

Thucydides, The History of the Peloponnesian War

Mae'r hen delynau genid gynt,
Ynghrog ar gangau'r helyg draw,
A gwaedd y bechgyn lond y gwynt,
A'u gwaed yn gymysg efo'r glaw.

Hedd Wyn, Rhyfel

CONTENTS

ILLUSTRATIONS

ACKNOWLEDGEMENTS

I should like to thank all of the staff of the libraries and archives consulted during the preparation of this book. *Great people all.* I am especially grateful to the National Archives (Public Record Office) in Kew, which is a wonderful place, and to the Thatcher Foundation Archive at the Churchill Archives Centre in Cambridge. My thanks to Aberystwyth University for granting a period of leave that was very helpful in writing this book. Many thanks to Thomas Robb for his great assistance and advice in the preparation of this book. I have known Thomas since he was an undergraduate student of mine and I take great pride in his success. I should like to acknowledge the helpful advice of Len Scott. My very best wishes to my old mate Martin Alexander (a gent of the 'Old School'). Thanks to Peter Jackson for his long-standing interest in my history. My sincere thanks to Peter Alan Lambert and Björn Udo Weiler for making their criticism of my history so much fun. I am grateful to Jan Ruzicka (*Masaryk*) for his knowledgeable insights – *Děkuji!* Thanks to Whitelegg (aka Spear), Kris Lovell, Gregory Moore, Bobby 'Bayern' Kammel and Oliver Dodd for their help. I am very grateful to Chikara Hashimoto (橋本力 -万歳!) for his assistance with the index. Thanks to Rhodri Mogford, Claire Lipscomb, Giles Herman at Bloomsbury for their professionalism and good humour; similar to Toby Hopkins at Corbis; and thanks to Srikanth Srinivasan at Newgen Imaging Systems for his hard work and for his unfailing patience. Best wishes to Gibson & Christine, Gegs (ac O2), Rab, Dav, Lindy, Babar, Tom Lewis, Owen K, Aled, Magnus Synge, Matt, Tony, Bryan (Mr. Lloyd's friend), Terry John, Tom and Percy. Thanks to the Owain the 'Ozone' and Simon for Friday lunches and laughter at the *Rheidol.* I have long appreciated the support of Toxy over the years – *Go raibh maith agat.* My salutations to all my brothers and sisters at Bangor City FC; a happy hundredth to dear old Anglesey GC; and my best wishes and thanks to all my friends in Rhosneigr. Finally, my thanks to my family – Arnie, Ma, Dave, Owen and Rachel – for all of their support over the years. *Hwyl i bawb!*

FOREWORD

The two words 'Munich' and 'Appeasement' are scored more deeply than any foreign policy concept into the Velcro of the national collective memory. Part stain, part shadow they lurk in the British consciousness ready to burst forth, floodlit, whenever a British government is confronted by the question of peace or war or even to intervene or not to intervene in circumstances short of war.

This is a book for which we have been waiting for years. R. Gerald Hughes is a consummate calibrator of the force and reach of the Munich/Appeasement spasm on the occasions it has pulsed through the national political conversation. Not for him what Edward Thompson called 'the enormous condescension of posterity'. He judges each case on its merits and in the context of its own time. From his pen flows the sensitivity of the historian and the discipline of the international relations scholar.

In a rational world, any minister or parliamentarian itching to reach for the 'Munich' analogy should pause, reach for Hughes on the bookshelf and think twice. This is a book of high utility and a real pleasure to read.

Lord Hennessy of Nympsfield, FBA
Attlee Professor of Contemporary British History
Queen Mary, University of London

INTRODUCTION

Present histories and past follies: the legacy of appeasement and British foreign policy since 1945

On another occasion when the Emperor Alexander, referring
to the King of Saxony, spoke bitterly of 'those who have
betrayed the cause of Europe', Talleyrand replied with
justice, 'that, Sire, is a question of dates'.

ALFRED DUFF COOPER, *Talleyrand*[1]

The day may come when my much cursed visit to
Munich will be understood.

NEVILLE CHAMBERLAIN TO MARGOT ASQUITH, 11 May 1940[2]

Chamberlain would have made a good Lord Mayor
of Birmingham in a lean year.

LLOYD GEORGE[3]

This is a book about the impact of one past upon another, more recent, past. It deals with how the framers of British foreign policy sought to negotiate and manipulate what are often crudely termed the 'lessons of history'. The 'lessons' I am referring to here are specifically those derived from the policies of appeasement employed by the British governments of the 1930s (during the premiership of Neville Chamberlain (1937–9) in particular). Many of the figures that feature in subsequent pages tried to learn from history or, more often, have sought to ensure that their view prevailed by invoking history. In the endless debates about the 'lessons of history', people are wont to fall back upon what Hegel wrote in 1837:

> Rulers, Statesmen, Nations, are wont to be emphatically commended to the teaching which experience offers in history. But what experience and history teach is this – that peoples and governments never have learned anything from history, or acted on principles deduced from it. Each period is involved in such peculiar circumstances, exhibits a condition of things so strictly idiosyncratic, that its conduct must be regulated by considerations connected with itself, and itself alone. Amid the pressure of great events, a general principle gives no help. It is useless to revert to similar circumstances in the Past. The pallid shades of memory struggle in vain with the life and freedom of the Present.[4]

The widespread currency achieved by Hegel's quote has never, alas, prevented the past being invoked by policy makers, historians, journalists and others to demonstrate the rectitude of a particular point of view or of a certain policy option. With regard to the present study, interpretations of the history of postwar British foreign policy are intimately associated with international relations between the two world wars, in what has come to be known as the 'era of appeasement'. And yet appeasement, as famously argued by Paul Kennedy in 1976, was very much in line with earlier manifestations of British policy towards Europe.[5] Kennedy traced the influence of the concept of appeasement from 1865 up until 1939. This book takes this forward and likewise demonstrates that throughout the Cold War and after appeasement was a constant factor in British foreign policy. In the post-1945 world it is important to note that policy makers, be they pro- or anti-appeasement, paid due reference to the frameworks of foreign policy debates created by the Chamberlainite appeasement of the 1930s. In this regard, of paramount importance was the distinction that arose between the *real* meaning of the word appeasement and the negative connotations that it has acquired because of its intimate association with the attempts to avoid war in the 1930s.[6] In 1976, Kennedy asserted that he understood appeasement as being *'the policy of settling international (or, for that matter, domestic) quarrels by admitting and satisfying grievances through rational negotiation and compromise, thereby avoiding the resort to an armed conflict which would be expensive, bloody, and possibly very dangerous'*. Importantly, Kennedy notes: 'It is in essence a *positive* policy.'[7] In 1925, Austen Chamberlain had thus commended the Locarno Pact to the House of Commons by stating that 'the work of Locarno will not be complete until it is followed up by further steps of general pacification and appeasement . . . we regard Locarno, not as the end of the work of appeasement and reconciliation, but as its beginning'.[8] The British appeasers of the 1930s certainly saw, and used, the term appeasement *in this sense* but, in the opinion of their defenders, after 1945 the 'appeasers' have been as misunderstood as was 'appeasement' itself. Robert Rhodes James noted that, when Anthony Eden had been foreign secretary in the 1930s, '[i]n his own words, his purpose was to secure "the appeasement of Europe",[9] by which he meant the maintenance of peace: it was only later that [appeasement] became synonymous with a very different policy of unilateral concessions to the Fascist Governments'.[10]

In 1994, the historian and Conservative peer Lord Beloff was accused of impugning his political opponent's motives by employing the word appeasement to describe them. Beloff replied that he did 'not regard the word "appeasement" as pejorative.' After all, '"[a]ppeasement" was used in the 1920s by those who wished to achieve a peaceful settlement at the time of Locarno, for instance. It is an honourable word. It means that you think that you cannot resist some external force which is too great and therefore you recommend getting the best deal possible.'[11] Beloff was being provocative, and possibly deliberately obtuse,[12] but his point was no less valid for that. One of his challengers nevertheless responded: '[D]oes the noble Lord agree that the word "appeasement", whatever it may have meant in the 1920s, acquired an unfavourable interpretation in 1939?'[13] This was a legitimate point for, by June 1939, even Neville Chamberlain was avoiding the word with which he had previously been so readily associated.[14] That alone says a great deal about the inflammatory and contested nature of a word whose dictionary definition had been so thoroughly subverted by historical developments.

In 1993, Donald Cameron Watt identified the manner in which appeasement evolved from what was originally 'a technique for conflict resolution'. In 1934 'the recognition . . . of the threat from a rearmed Germany [meant that] it evolved through stages of conflict avoidance, conflict limitation (Ethiopia, Spanish Civil War), conflict management (1938), to deterrence (1939)'.[15] An awareness of this process remains important in assessing the notion of a British 'tradition' of appeasement, despite the almost uniquely negative connotations it has acquired since 1939, which employed a variety of political, diplomatic, economic, military and social means in order to attain policy ends identified as being in the national interest.[16] British policy makers had long accepted the necessity of employing such means in order to avert war with another power or with other powers. In the long term, the continental interventions of the Napoleonic era, and of the First World War, were exceptional in terms of British policy. Even in such cases British foreign policy could still revert to form. And, in this vein, it is of note the ministry of Henry Addington sought to appease Napoleon in 1802–3.[17] Historically, appeasement was thus a favoured option for British policy makers, but only so long as vital interests were not at stake.[18] The foreign policy of the Earl of Aberdeen (foreign secretary, 1841–6), for instance, employed appeasement to a degree that made it highly controversial domestically (as it was when used by Chamberlain).[19] Appeasement was almost a natural option for British policy makers as prosperity was dependent upon free trade and war was, and is, bad for business. Thomas Otte has argued convincingly that the appeasement of the 1930s was thus rooted in the evolution of official British attitudes in the 50 years before the First World War.[20] In the century or so before 1914, the pragmatic diplomacy of appeasement was of great utility in avoiding wars against other industrialized states.[21] And, above all, the conceptual model of appeasement fitted in very well with Lord Palmerston's famous exposition of Britain's world role.

> I hold that the real policy of England – apart from questions which involve her own particular interests, political or commercial – is to be the champion of justice and right; pursuing that course with moderation and prudence, not becoming the Quixote of the world, but giving the weight of her moral sanction and support wherever she thinks that justice is, and wherever she thinks that wrong has been done. Sir, in pursuing that course, and in pursuing the more limited direction of our own particular interests, my conviction is, that as long as England keeps herself in the right – as long as she wishes to permit no injustice – as long as she wishes to countenance no wrong – as long as she labours at legislative interests of her own – and as long as she sympathises with right and justice, she never will find herself altogether alone. She is sure to find some other State, of sufficient power, influence, and weight, to support and aid her in the course she may think fit to pursue. Therefore I say that it is a narrow policy to suppose that this country or that is to be marked out as the eternal ally or the perpetual enemy of England. We have no eternal allies, and we have no perpetual enemies. Our interests are eternal and perpetual, and those interests it is our duty to follow.[22]

If we accept the accuracy, and longevity, of Palmerston's characterisation of British foreign policy as virtuous and self-serving it is clear why Chamberlainite appeasement has been so long excoriated. The policy's virtue, doubtful from the outset, was forever discredited by the horrors inflicted upon Europe after 1939. As a policy of self-interest, appeasement's damnation was completed as it had signally failed to prevent the precipitate decline of the British Empire. The appeasers of the 1930s, epitomized by Neville Chamberlain, have long been derided for making one-sided concessions to the dictatorships (and, worst of all, to Nazi Germany). Chamberlain's 'guilt' was apparent to contemporary observers. One such figure was Friedrich Kellner, a German Social Democrat opponent of Nazism, who made a number of remarkably prescient observations in his diary. In May 1940, one day after Chamberlain resigned, Kellner reflected on the consequences of the appeasement of Hitler. 'Mr. Chamberlain has laid down his office at last. With that, an unbelievably sad dunce has disappeared for good. Now the Nazi folk with their burned-out brains will finally be shown what it means to make an enemy of the whole world. It will cost many sacrifices before reason, coming out of a better past, slowly begins to make an impact again.'[23] Such sentiments were shared by the majority of the British people, while the anti-appeasers of the 1930s, led by Winston S. Churchill, came to stand for all that Britain sees as being best in its own national self-image: free, honourable and defiant.

The black-and-white view of the history of the appeasement of the 1930s[24] that emerged after the Second World War was due, not least, to the fact that one of the champions of those who decried appeasement and its proponents most loudly was Winston S. Churchill. Churchill was but the most noted proponent of the interpretation of appeasement that dominated the early post-1945 period (and heavily influenced British policy during the Cold War) namely: the 'Guilty Men' theory of British appeasement policy in the 1930s. While this term was derived from a passionate polemic penned under the pseudonym of 'Cato' (actually Michael Foot, Peter Howard and Frank Owen),[25] it is Churchill who is most readily associated with the indictment of the appeasement of Hitler. As Kellner noted in his diary in June 1940: 'In my opinion, there was only one man among the [Third Reich's 1930s] opponents who recognised the danger, and that was Churchill.'[26] Churchill has been, and is, invoked more than any other single figure by politicians seeking to decry appeasement. In the context of Britain and the United States, Richard Toye notes that 'the rhetorical uses to which his memory has been put' since 1945 demonstrate how Churchill 'continues to hold such power over the collective Anglo-American imagination'.[27]

After Hitler occupied Prague in March 1939, British policy makers assiduously sought to avoid the label of appeaser. After the war, the necessity of doing so was underlined by the appearance of the first volume of Churchill's history of the Second World War (which appeared in 1948).[28] Churchill's discrediting of appeasement was achieved not least through his characterisation of Chamberlain. For although Chamberlain was 'an upright, competent, well-meaning man' whose premiership was typified by 'a narrow, sharp edged efficiency within the limits of the policy in which he believed', Churchill portrayed him as naïve, inexperienced, over-confident and out of his depth in his European policy.[29] Upon the death of Chamberlain in November 1940, Kellner observed:

> Were I an Englishman, then it is true that I would certainly also lay a heavy burden of guilt onto Chamberlain . . . [as] Chamberlain and the whole of the previous government bear the guilt of having failed to allow England to keep pace in face of the monstrous rearmament of Germany. A world empire must always be armed in order to fend off every attack, wherever it may fall.

> It is plain for everyman to see that England was not adequately armed. Even the Navy does not appear to be strong enough to undertake anything decisive. Maybe it is holding itself back. But that is an error.

> It had to be put into action immediately. Neither in Africa (Somaliland, Eritrea) nor in the Mediterranean did the Engl. *[sic]* Navy take sufficient advantage of the opportunity [afforded].[30]

The passage of time and hindsight did little to rehabilitate the dead man's reputation. As Robert Self notes: 'Poor Neville did come badly out of history – and to a very considerable degree this was precisely because Churchill wrote that history in order to ensure that his carefully crafted version of the 1930s would be the one which became indelibly etched upon the national consciousness.'[31] Thus, partly as a result of Churchill's efforts, it was the case, as Watt later noted, that '"appeasement" and "Munich" acquired a pejorative association with ignominious surrender of principle and the purchase of peace . . . which they will never lose'. Appeasement was now defined as 'purchasing peace for one's own interests by sacrificing the interests of others'.[32] In the postwar years the great majority of professional historians (and the British public) duly embraced the 'Guilty Men' thesis.[33] Despite the rise of a revisionist historiography,[34] and then a counter-revisionist historiography,[35] the 'Guilty Men' thesis continues to exert a powerful influence to this day. Of course, while the debates on appeasement have continually evolved,[36] this is not a linear process whereby any given school of thought is entirely supplanted.[37] Revisionism, for example, was never going to achieve even a semblance of intellectual hegemony with ease. As Robert Skidelsky noted in 1972: 'To challenge the existing interpretations is . . . to challenge in a sense everything that came out of the War – as well as to deprive ourselves [the British] of our last true moment of glory.'[38] Or, as John Charmley later noted, to accept the tradition of appeasement in British foreign policy directly challenges the 'bold and heroic' Churchillian version of British history.[39]

In late 1940, Kellner noted: 'The former *Ministerpräsident* [Chamberlain] died a few days ago. It was clear to me that the falsifiers of history are now going to work anew and quickly push the guilt for the war into this old man's shoes.'[40] In referring to 'falsifiers of history' Kellner was talking about the Nazis, but he was uncannily accurate in his prediction that Chamberlain was going to have guilt and blame heaped upon his grave (albeit by *all* sides). In the popular imagination, and in the populist rhetoric of politicians, the clarity of the 'Guilty Men' thesis remains powerful to this day. One reason for this is the clarity of Churchill's message. 'One day President Roosevelt told me that he was asking publicly for suggestions about what the war should be called. I said at once "the Unnecessary War." There never was a war more easy to stop than that which has just wrecked what was left of the world from the previous struggle.'[41] Notably, and almost uniquely, Churchill argued his case from a position of almost unique moral, political and scholarly strength derived from his longevity as a leading politician and as an author historian of some repute.[42]

Churchill's six-volume history of the Second World War was the crowning glory of all his historical writing, which was recognized by the Nobel Prize in Literature in 1953.[43] It was the first of these volumes, published in 1948, in which Churchill relayed the story of appeasement. Peter Clarke notes that 'The Gathering Storm instantly became the classic post-war vindication of Churchill's pre-war prophetic stance.'[44] Of Churchill's quip, 'History will be kind to me, for I intend to write it',[45] we might thus legitimately answer: 'You did, and it was.' Churchill was never slow to highlight his own virtues (Lloyd George observed that he 'would make a drum out of the skin of his own mother in order to sound his own praises').[46] But Labour's Clement Attlee was probably correct when, in 1939, he told Churchill: 'It must be a melancholy satisfaction to see how right you were.'[47] Watt correctly notes: 'Churchill's parliamentary attack on Munich made him the central figure in all eyes, including those of Hitler, in British opposition to Nazism and its leader.'[48] Churchill's version of history has certainly always attracted very eminent and powerful adherents. In 2000, Alastair Parker wrote: 'Churchill could have prevented the Second World War. If Churchill had controlled British foreign policy, he would have made a "Grand Alliance", grouping other European countries around a firm Anglo-French alliance . . . Churchill might even have managed to make Britain and France to seem to Stalin to be safer collaborators than Nazi Germany.'[49] That an eminent historian could posit such a counterfactual[50] says much for the reputation forged by Churchill's opposition to appeasement. Thus, while appeasement as a diplomatic tactic was commonplace in the formulation of British foreign policy in the nineteenth century, policy makers who pursued it in the 1930s have been excoriated.[51]

Churchill was the first historian to win the Nobel Prize in Literature since 1902,[52] and David Reynolds argues with some justification that Churchill was not only at the helm of the British state during the 'finest hour' he was also 'in command of history'.[53] In 1938, Churchill observed: 'Words are the only thing that last forever' and his own literary legacy means that he is now remembered as the opponent of Hitler in the 1930s and 1940s, and of the 'Iron Curtain' and Stalinist domination after 1945. (Convinced, as he was, that he could maintain a workable partnership with Stalin until the end of the war). In addition, the four volumes of The History of the English Speaking Peoples meant that Churchill will forever be associated with cementing the 'Special Relationship' as the cornerstone of British foreign policy. (In fact, Churchill (half-American as he was) could barely tolerate the United States for long periods of his life and his wife even remarked upon his 'known hostility to America').[54]

The intimate relationship of power and history, personified by Churchill as author *and* statesman, meant that the latter felt morally justified in pursuing détente with the Soviet Union in order to ameliorate the Cold War in Europe.[55] Thus, thanks in large part to Churchill's influence, the notion of the 'Guilty Men', and their weakness in allowing the breakout of the 'unnecessary war', was both powerful and enduring. In popular terms this holds true for Britain right down until the present day. In 1995, Wesley K. Wark noted how 'appeasement continues to enjoy mythic status as a foreign policy of catastrophic failure – out of the folly of appeasement came the destruction of the Second World War, the loss of Britain's superpower status, and the end of empire'.[56] After 1939, appeasement certainly became a policy option that politicians sought to disassociate themselves from as a domestically unpopular policy, and a pejorative term.[57] Typically, in debates over the war in Bosnia (1992–5) the word 'appeasement' was invoked constantly by interventionists,[58] while their opponents, by contrast, avoided the use of the word assiduously as association with appeasement was political poison. In 1993, the Conservative MP Peter Tapsell recalled:

> When I first entered the House [in 1939] a considerable number of hon. Members, particularly Conservative Members [had] sat in the Chamber throughout all the debates on Neville Chamberlain's appeasement policies. I never spoke to one such Member who could recall in his heart ever having been a supporter of those policies. I sometimes used to wonder whether the Munich agreement had been carried single-handed by Neville Chamberlain and the Conservative Whips Office.

Walter Elliot MP told Tapsell that he had voted in favour of Munich out of personal loyalty to Chamberlain but, alas, 'he had never ceased to reproach himself for that vote as events unfolded'.[59] The wider interpretation of history that this recollection feeds was immeasurably strengthened by the myth and symbolism of the Munich conference of 1938, which saw the 'betrayal' of democracy and Czechoslovakia in a vain attempt to appease Hitler. Robert J. Beck rightly notes that 'few episodes of diplomatic history have attracted as much scholarly attention as the Munich conference'.[60] The central role of Britain at Munich meant that its policy makers wrestled with the legacy of Munich for many years, despite its repudiation by Anthony Eden on 5 August 1942.[61] Immediately after Munich, the American journalist Edgar A. Mowrer wrote: 'A little people . . . has been betrayed . . . by a state reputed friendly and by a sworn ally. By the United Kingdom and the French Republic. By Englishmen deliberately and after calm reflection; by Frenchmen in an hour of panic.'[62] The shame felt by what Mowrer termed 'any right-minded person' in both Britain and France only increased after Hitler tore up the Munich Agreement when he marched into Prague in March 1939. It is no exaggeration to state that, within British society, this shame extends to the present day.

The enduring shame attached to Munich meant that Communist historians, and other figures with an axe to grind, continued to make capital from Chamberlainite appeasement at Britain's expense for many years.[63] Even the robustly patriotic Margaret Thatcher, an ardent opponent of appeasement and whose formative years took in the 1930s and the

Second World War, conceded that 'British foreign policy is at its worst when it is engaged in giving away other people's territory'.[64] Yet, although anti-appeasers, in the 1930s and since, always tend to stress the moral strength of their case, the underlying rationale for criticism had to lie in traditional notions of national self-interest. Alfred Duff Cooper, who had resigned as First Lord of the Admiralty because of Munich, later candidly admitted that war in 1938 would not have been for Czechoslovakia any more than it had been for Belgium in 1914. Rather, any war against Hitler would have been 'in accordance with the sound, traditional foreign policy of England, to prevent any Great Power, in defiance of treaty obligations, of the laws of nations and the decrees of morality, dominating by brute force the continent of Europe'.[65] In a similarly 'pragmatic' vein, Sir Robert Vansittart (permanent under-secretary at the Foreign Office (FO), 1930–8) had supported the Hoare-Laval Plan of 1935, while vigorously opposing Munich in 1938.[66] Thus, Vansittart, widely identified as being an arch anti-appeaser would be better cast as an arch anti-Hitlerite. As he stated: 'We shall have to compromise with *Mussolini*, for we can never compromise securely or even live safely with *Dictator Major* [Hitler], if we are at loggerheads with *Dictator Minor* [Mussolini].'[67]

Leo Amery typified the Conservative MPs who had favoured appeasement up until 1938 and then became alarmed at the threat to British interests arising from 'the blundering and humiliation of our first backing Czechoslovakia . . . and then suddenly climbing down . . . [at] Munich.' Those who had supported appeasement often resorted to the defence that they had done so to buy time for Britain to re-arm, hence ensuring the ultimate destruction of Nazism. Much of this was disingenuous and retrospective, designed to ensure that association with appeasement affected careers as little as possible. R.A. ('Rab') Butler (FO under-secretary in September 1938) is a prime example here, and even sympathetic biographers have highlighted the misleading nature of his memoirs.[68] Butler, described by Henry 'Chips' Channon, as Chamberlain's 'blue-eyed boy', never escaped his intimate association with appeasement and his career was undoubtedly tainted as a result.[69] Despite this, more discreet associations with appeasement proved not to be politically fatal and Alec Douglas-Home, parliamentary private secretary to Neville Chamberlain at Munich, became prime minister in 1963. Home, indeed, continued to defend Munich to the end of his life, writing in his memoirs: 'In the House of Commons . . . Churchill said "England has been offered a choice between war and shame. She has chosen shame and will get war". True [in 1939] we got war; but also final victory, whereas war in 1938 would have meant not victory but defeat.'[70]

In 2002, the British-based German academic Beatrice Heuser asserted: 'I was surprised to hear that the British associated a feeling of guilt with [the Munich Agreement] . . . until then [I had] never imagined that anybody other than the Germans felt responsible for what happened in Europe between 1933 and 1945.'[71] And if one phrase eternally damned Chamberlain and Munich it was Churchill's taunting prophesy: 'You were given the choice between war and dishonour. You chose dishonour, and you will have war.'[72] The longevity of such epithets reflects the fact that Munich has remained a defining moment in modern British history. In 1956, Hugh Trevor-Roper asked:

> How shall I ever forget Munich? My friends were divided, families were divided, social life was forced into new patterns. The cleavage cut society into novel forms: it did not correspond with any of the old cleavages of political party, economic activity, social class. And while the virtuous Left uttered pacifist nonsense, the Chamberlainites declared, in ever more strident tones, that Chamberlain was the greatest leader we ever had, a genius, an immortal, a Messiah.[73]

Noel Annan later similarly recalled: 'No event in our lifetime so divided the country as Munich. Families were divided, friendships were severed and shame vied with relief as the ruling emotion.'[74] Such commonly held, and widely expressed, sentiments meant that the overwhelming pre-1939

ILLUSTRATION I.1 *The Munich Conference, 1938. (l–r) Neville Chamberlain, Édouard Daladier, Adolf Hitler, Benito Mussolini and Galeazzo Ciano. Jan Masaryk, the Czechoslovak ambassador in London, told Chamberlain and Halifax: 'If you have sacrificed my nation to preserve the peace of the world, I will be the first to applaud you. But if not, gentlemen, God help your souls.'*

public approval of British policy is sometimes forgotten or, more often, rejected as unrepeatable as a policy option in *moral* terms.[75] In 1945, George Orwell noted: 'In England the fiercest tirades against Quislings are uttered by Conservatives who were practising appeasement in 1938 and Communists who were advocating it in 1940.'[76] The intensity of the feelings generated by the memory of the 1930s is heightened by the inevitability of increasingly frequent invocations of the past during national crises, such as those over Suez or the Falklands. David Chuter rightly observes that the 'myth of Munich' was the most enduring and potent political myth of the second half of the twentieth century.[77] Such myths matter because, 'history is about cognition and knowledge, [while] collective memory is about experience and feeling. If history is a matter of the past, collective memory is most definitely a phenomenon of the present'.[78] That said, Geoffrey Cubitt is right to criticise attempts to promote 'memory as an alternative to historiographical discourse' as attempts to reconcile history and memory are detrimental to the former.[79] Certainly, the history underpinning the British collective memory of appeasement led to an unbridled hostility towards adopting similar policies ever again. This manifested itself in long-standing, if vague, popular sympathy for the Czechoslovak case over Munich.[80] Czechoslovak policy makers and historians obviously sought to maximize such sentiments,[81] but with limited success with regard to British policymaking circles. What is certain is that views of the Munich Agreement were, and are, entwined with collective memory in Britain and its institutions.

From the start, the historical meaning of Munich represented a contested and highly politicized area of dispute in debates about Britain's recent past.[82] This was the case for professional historians, policy makers and the general public. This is hardly surprising for, as Enoch Powell once observed, typically by means of a rhetorical question, 'What is history except a nation's collective memory?'[83] On a visit to the Soviet Union in 1989, Powell opined: 'What an important thing memory is, collective memory. It's really collective memory that makes a nation, its memory of what its past was, what is has done, what is has suffered and what it has endured.'[84] And, as Maurice Halbwachs observed: 'It is in society that people normally acquire their memories. It is also in society that they recall, recognize, and localize their memories.'[85] The collective memory of those serving in the British FO derived from their nationality *and* their institution. To invoke 'memory' in this body, as elsewhere, highlights 'connections between the cultural, the social, and the political, between representation and social experience.'[86] Zara Steiner has suggested that that history offers the policy maker an antidote to short-term thinking and the loss of institutional memory.[87] This may be a truism, but here one immediately runs up against the problems of seeking to integrate, and demarcate, history and memory.[88] Jan-Werner Müller points out that collective memory is often 'ahistorical, even anti-historical', oversimplifying the 'ambiguities of the past' and possessing 'moral messages . . . which most historians cannot accept'.[89] Such messages often appear as in the guise of the analogy. In discussing the British appeasement of Napoleon (in 1802–3) and of Hitler (in 1938–9), Paul Schroeder rightly reflected: 'The problem with this analogy is . . . that it breaks down at certain points, as historical analogies always do.'[90] Sir William Strang, permanent undersecretary at the FO between 1949 and 1953, noted that historical analogies were thus unsuitable for policy ends, as '[d]ecisions on foreign policy have often to be taken at short notice on incomplete information and with not much time for thought'.[91] Of course, the historical record (and/or the need to make amends for it) is not always supportive of the contemporary national interest. In any case, attitudes towards the status of the Munich Agreement, and appeasement generally, were (and are) always tailored to contemporary policy imperatives.[92]

Churchill's status as arch advocate of the 'Guilty Men' thesis was wholly apposite: and his dual persona as statesman and historian was mirrored in all manner of attempts to derive lessons from Munich beyond simple moral fables.[93] Blind adherence to this narrative suited many politicians. Indeed, it was usually an essential element in the continuation of their careers. To be cast as appeaser certainly meant political and career death. This was certainly the case with Chamberlain's last foreign secretary, Lord Halifax, who was demoted to the post of ambassador to Washington by Churchill in 1940. Yet, although Halifax had enjoyed a harmonious relationship with Chamberlain, when appeasement seemed to him to be doomed to failure, he began to oppose the prime minister and appeasement with increasing effectiveness.[94] Conversely, the fact that Eden's resignation from office in February 1938 was primarily caused by Chamberlain's interference in the conduct of foreign affairs, as opposed to any disagreement over appeasement, was glossed over for many years.[95] Eden's resignation lay at the heart of his reputation as an anti-appeaser. Much of this image was constructed retrospectively and validated only by virtue of his opposition to Munich and his time as Churchill's wartime foreign secretary. But Eden was to learn that being typecast in a supposedly positive role could have as many consequences as being cast in an opposite mould. Thus, despite the fact that Halifax's opposition to appeasement had undermined Chamberlain far more than Eden's sulking had ever done, it was the latter whose career blossomed. One of the reasons for this undoubtedly lay in Eden's befitting from the myth of his being an arch anti-appeaser. After Munich, Eden joined Churchill in enjoying the veneration of a group of acolytes now ranged against appeasement. Churchill's followers included the Conservative MPs Robert Boothby, Harold Macmillan and Duncan Sandys (Churchill's son-in-law). All of these men were to enjoy long careers built, at least in part, upon the kudos of having behaved 'honourably' in the era of 1930s appeasement. The more numerous, but also more restrained, members of the 'Eden Group' had sought to derive the benefits of association with Churchillian anti-appeasement rhetoric, while avoiding antagonizing the hierarchy of the Conservative Party by indulging in excessive protest that might, conceivably, be deemed as being disloyal (and thus harmful to their political careers and the cause of all who opposed Chamberlain's policies).[96] This was important for, as Maurice Cowling noted in 1971, 'high politics' *is* 'a matter of rhetoric and manoeuvre' by statesmen.[97] This necessitates a particular focus on the language of politics. Party political interests were *always* a factor in where one stood on appeasement – in the 1930s as much as in the postwar era. Richard Toye argues that, given its importance, scholars should engage in rather more analysis of the rhetoric of British prime ministers since 1945.[98] This book duly pays due attention to the use of words (the *rhetoric*) in the public utterances of policy makers in the postwar era (not least as reported in *Hansard*) and seeks, where possible, to utilize both public and confidential statements in order to establish *how* discourses on appeasement were constructed for political ends.[99]

Reflecting the broader ambiguity inherent in much of the course, and legacies, of appeasement, nothing was straightforward with regard to the influence that their actions in the 1930s had upon any number of the 'Guilty Men' or their opponents. In 2010, Terrance L. Lewis traced the post-Munich legacies of a number of British politicians by focusing on their memoirs and their biographies.[100] From it we can see that opponents of the appeasement of Hitler (or, at least, those who claimed to be so) did not necessarily derive the political benefits that they might have expected. For in truth, the legacy of appeasement limited and hampered, to some degree or other, *all* British politicians in their pursuit of postwar foreign policy goals. Even Harold Macmillan, a staunch opponent of 1930s appeasement, was equivocal and sympathetic in his assessment of just how the British people had come to support the ceding of a portion of Czechoslovakia to Nazi Germany.[101]

In the years after the Second World War, authors such as Sir Lewis Namier, John Wheeler-Bennett, A.L. Rowse, and Margaret George all subscribed to the 'Guilty Men' school.[102] Such was the power of the anti-appeasement message after Munich, it was some years before the simplistic vision of casting Chamberlain and acolytes as hapless weaklings was challenged by a powerful (so-called) Revisionist school which, in the words of Paul Schroeder, held: 'If one begins to tot up all the plausible motivations for appeasement . . . one sees that these are far more than enough to explain it. It was massively over-determined.'[103] The Revisionist position was epitomised by a positive reappraisal of the character and career of Neville Chamberlain.[104] One of the crucial factors in the rise of Revisionism was the introduction of the 'Thirty-year rule' for the release of public records in 1967.[105] This shaped the historiography of appeasement in the 1970s and 1980s in particular. Historians now became more sympathetic towards Chamberlain as, for the first time, they fully appreciated the constraints placed upon him. By 1989, one Revisionist, John Charmley, went so far as to argue that Chamberlain's appeasement policy had, in actual fact, been the only option that could *possibly* have avoided war *and* preserved the British Empire.[106]

In popular terms, the seeds for the revision of the postwar orthodox interpretation of appeasement were laid when A.J.P. Taylor's *The Origins of the Second World War* was published in 1961.[107] Contrary to popular misconceptions, Taylor did not make excuses for Hitler. And the orthodox version of appeasement survived his book intact, in the short term at least. Thus, books very much in line with the 'Guilty Men' thesis – such as Gilbert and Gott's *The Appeasers* – continued to appear.[108] Sensationalism meant that Taylor caused outrage by some statements that seemed to certain critics (and an often ill-informed public) to 'normalize' Hitler. But Taylor also attracted opprobrium from some of the most eminent men of letters then alive. Isaac Deutscher, for instance, dismissed *The Origins of the Second World War*, saying that it had 'nothing in common with historical scholarship' and 'only provided a pseudo-academic justification for a prevalent trend of official history'.[109]

In truth, Taylor's style, his eminent readability and accessible prose meant that his work lent itself to easy quotation. Thus, the infamous line 'In principle and doctrine, Hitler was no more wicked than many other contemporary statesmen' was much quoted while the sentence that followed it was not ('In wicked acts he outdid them all').[110] Yet, such was its impact, historians have debated Taylor's book ever since.[111] The fact that many of the reading public were not of an age to remember first-hand the deeds of Hitler (and the guilt of the appeasers) undoubtedly allowed those challenging the orthodoxy the chance to receive a fairer hearing than they had received hitherto. As Alan Taylor noted: 'The second world War has ceased to be "today" and has become "yesterday."'[112] Hugh Trevor-Roper, reviewing *The Origins of the Second World War*, echoed Taylor's thoughts on the passing of the wartime generation.

> A generation has grown up which never knew the 1930's, never shared its passions and doubts, was never excited by the Spanish civil war, never boiled with indignation against the 'appeasers', never lived in suspense from Nuremberg Rally to Nuremberg Rally, awaiting the next hysterical outburst, the next clatter of arms, from the megalomaniac in Berlin . . . How can we communicate across such a gulf the emotional content of those years, the mounting indignation which finally convinced even the 'appeasers' themselves that there could be no peace with Hitler, and caused the British people, united in pacifism in 1936, to go, in 1939, united into war? . . . And even across the gulf such a mood must be conveyed by those who teach history to those who learn it: for it is an element in history no less important than the mere facts. [113]

Trevor-Roper was right in as much as time had ensured that there was a less personal dimension to the history of the Second World War. Taylor noted that the Second War was no longer 'contemporary history'. And 'there comes a time when the historian can stand back and review events that were once contemporary with the detachment that he would show if he were writing of . . . [for example] the English civil war. At least, he can try.'[114] The challenge to the orthodox view in the appeasement debates was assessed, and boosted, by D. C. Watt in 1965. This effort was designed to address the fact that appeasement 'has taken to itself the status of a myth – loaded with implication, undertones, and overtones'.[115] In 1966, Martin Gilbert took a more sympathetic view of the 'Guilty Men' (although he still maintained a distinction between appeasement before and up to Munich and the unacceptable advocacy of appeasment subsequent to that time). This fitted with the Churchillian view of history, as it was Munich that had caused Churchill's decisive break with the National Government.[116] In 1972, David Dilks was emboldened to mount a defence of Munich that invoked Maitland's First Law[117] when he warned historians about 'the perils of reading the past in terms of later events' because of their own personal prejudices.[118]

In 1975, Maurice Cowling's seminal *The Impact of Hitler* added a muscular intellectual edge to the Revisionist case. With his insistence upon the study of 'high politics', Cowling's was an innovative work. Broadly speaking, such interpretations were supported by adhering to the notion of a tension between the *Primat der Aussenpolitik* and the *Primat der Innenpolitik*. Cowling's work was characteristic of an era where historians now began to seriously discuss and evaluate the limitations imposed by internal national politics on the formulation of international policy. Cowling phrased it thus: 'The politics of the Powers must be seen through the filtering effect by the politics of the parties.' Cowling further asserted that: 'In the late thirties, foreign policy was the form that party conflict took. Politicians conducted it in the light of party considerations; it can only be understood if these considerations are reconstructed.' This was unapologetic history, freed of the constraints of a postwar era that paid homage to Cato and Churchill. 'To history, until yesterday, Halifax was the arch-appeaser. This, it is now recognised, was a mistake. His role, however, was complicated. In these pages he is not the man who stopped the rot, but the embodiment of Conservative wisdom who decided that Hitler must be obstructed because Labour could not otherwise be resisted.' Furthermore, a realistic evaluation of the appeasement debates of the 1930s 'demands a language as dispassionate about Chamberlain (and Nevile Henderson) as in writing about Churchill (or [Robert] Vansittart). Above all it demands the assumption that it was neither morally obligatory nor prudential self-evident that Hitler should be obstructed in Eastern Europe.'[119]

In an assessment that any postwar politician could relate to, the Revisionists stressed that Britain was limited to a policy of appeasement because of internal weakness (primarily military[120] and economic).[121] This, as Watt had predicted, was confirmed by a number of official histories.[122]

It was also confirmed in a number of archive-based accounts: on British military and naval shortcomings;[123] on British Imperial overstretch;[124] on the British relationship with the English-speaking dominions;[125] and on the British relationship with the United States.[126] From the perspective of those historians who were broadly sympathetic to Chamberlain, the economic constraints of the 1930s meant that the policy of appeasement was virtually inevitable. This was the case regardless of who was in government; and regardless of which opponents the British state faced. George Peden has repeatedly demonstrated – in forensic detail – the economic constraints, and heightened influence of the Treasury, upon British foreign policy formulation in the 1930s.[127] This established the direct link between economic weakness and appeasement and, as Peden shows elsewhere, this link was magnified (along with, logically enough, Treasury influence over foreign policy) by the great strains imposed by the Second World War.[128] These factors, above all, ensured that those same forces driving appeasement before 1939 played an even greater role in foreign policy formulation since 1945.[129]

A number of historians have argued that further constraints on British foreign policy were imposed by public opinion.[130] For these writers, the appeasement of the 1930s was undeniably 'rooted in the British conscience'.[131] If one was seeking reasons to rescue the reputation of Chamberlain and his acolytes, one must concede that any foreign policy based, in any part, on appeasement will always be partly a result of the increasing vulnerability of policy makers to 'public opinion' (hence Henry Kissinger's distaste for the interaction of diplomacy and mass politics).[132] As Keith Robbins noted, appeasement was both a 'domestically generated initiative and an externally generated response'.[133] Crucially, successive extensions of the political franchise, and the growth in the popular press, meant that politicians increasingly had to justify their policies a great deal more than in previous eras.[134] And, during the 1920s and 1930s, in the wake of the slaughter of the First World War, politicians became ever increasingly aware that 'public opinion' was firmly against an aggressive foreign policy.[135] Even amongt those who believed that Revisionism went too far, an appreciation of Chamberlain's *motives*, at least, now permeated debates. Margaret Thatcher, perhaps the fiercest prime ministerial critic of appeasement, observed that Chamberlain 'was a very honourable man . . . I thought he knew that in 1938 he must gain time to get us ready. I believe he gained more in that last year than Hitler . . . It may be that we owe Chamberlain a great debt of gratitude for what happened during those years. And it brought Winston forward that much more.'[136]

The rise of Revisionism was by no means the end of the story of the historiography of appeasement (this is hardly surprising, given that 'History is an argument without end').[137] The proponents of the 'Guilty Men' thesis returned – reinvigorated, more sophisticated and equipped with ever more raw material for scholarly reassessment. Thus, a new school of thought emerged. The so-called Counter-Revisionists held that the Second World

War was Chamberlain's fault because '[h]e would shortly find that he had no gift for prophecy – only a penchant for unwarranted optimism'.[138] Alastair Parker argued that the Chamberlain government choose appeasement despite viable 'alternative policies' and, moreover, the prime minister's 'powerful, obstinate personality and his skill in debate probably stifled serious chances of preventing the Second World War'.[139] For the Counter-Revisionists, the outbreak of war in 1939 proved that Chamberlain's policies had been wrong and 'his failure was pervasive and personal'.[140] In this fashion, the historiography of appeasement came full circle. Chamberlain had gone from 'Guilty Man' to embattled leader valiantly pursuing the best possible course of action for his country to 'Guilty Man' (but with rather less emotion, and rather more footnotes attached to the assessments of his performance). If the weight of historical evidence is on the side of the Counter-Revisionists, as a verdict of history it also has the advantage of absolving many of Chamberlain's accomplices of blame. The excessive focus on Chamberlain as the villain of the piece has masked the fact that the vast majority of the policy-making elite supported appeasement (as did the overwhelming majority of the general public). The Second World War may well have been 'Hitler's War', but in no sense was it simply Chamberlain's 'lost peace'. As Sir Samuel Hoare observed of Chamberlain: '[He] was not an autocrat who imposed his views upon doubting or hostile colleagues. Appeasement was not his personal policy. Not only was it supported by his colleagues; it expressed the general desire of the British people.'[141] Civil servants,[142] newspaper magnates, journalists, academics and even members of the Royal family, most notably Edward VIII and, to a lesser degree, his brother and successor, George VI, all championed appeasement. All of this meant that A. J. P. Taylor could write, with typically mischievous intent, that Munich was 'a triumph for all that was best and most enlightened in British life; a triumph for those who had preached equal justice between peoples: a triumph for those who had courageously denounced the harshness and short-sightedness of Versailles'.[143] Appeasement, in short, was nothing less than the foreign policy of the Establishment.[144]

In terms of history, the lessons of the 1930s were relatively limited as is the nature of all such instruction. Inasmuch as there were any they could be boiled down to: first, do not appease those who cannot be appeased and, second, ensure that the international security architecture is favourable towards your fall-back plan for restraint should appeasement fail. But the effects of the foreign policy failures of 1938–9 meant that the postwar restrictions imposed upon policy makers were usually far more stringent than was implied by this model. What the appeasement of the 1930s had ensured was that, in future, appeasement would be regarded as an unacceptable way of conducting the foreign policy of any state. This state of affairs effectively introduced a moral element specifically attached to appeasement into international relations even if, in reality, this was maintained for purely self-serving political purposes. That being so, it is important to recall that, as E.H. Carr once noted: 'The place of morality in international politics is the most obscure and difficult problem in the whole range of international studies.'[145] Yet, just as appeasement in British policy pre-dated the 1930s, so too did the idea of moral constraints in the conduct of international relations. This gave greater weight to John Bright's 1858 assertion: 'I do most devoutly believe, that the moral law was not written for men alone in their individual character, but that it was written as well for nations, and for nations great as this of which we are citizens.'[146] The introduction of such supposedly ethical, and often deeply personal, codes of morality into the business of statecraft was to have profound effects for British policy making for the remainder of the twentieth century and beyond. Ironically, Churchill, having done so much to demonise the appeasers of the 1930s, found his room for manoeuvre limited by the manner in which society now equated the specific (i.e. British foreign policy in the 1930s) with the universal (i.e. the conduct of *all* foreign policy) by drawing upon the lessons of Chamberlainite appeasement. In *The Gathering Storm*, published in 1948, Churchill had encouraged such thinking when he sought to warn against repeating the errors of the 1930s.

> In their loss of purpose, in their abandonment even of the themes they most sincerely espoused, Britain, France and most of all, because of their immense power and impartiality, the United States allowed conditions to be gradually built up to the very climax they dreaded most. They have only to repeat the same well-meaning, short-sighted behaviour towards the new problems which in singular resemblance confront us today to bring about a third convulsion from which none may live to tell the tale.[147]

Churchill, however, was convinced that he could have his cake and eat it. For, despite his anti-appeasement rhetoric, on which his reputation rests, Churchill had been no stranger to appeasement himself, when *he* deemed it *necessary*.[148] E. H. Carr was not imperceptive when he wrote of Churchill's opposition to appeasement: 'The realist will have no difficulty in recognizing the pragmatic, through no doubt unconscious adjustment of Mr. Churchill's judgments to his policy of the moment.'[149] In 1950, Churchill stated in the House of Commons:

> The declaration of the Prime Minister [Clement Attlee] that there will be no appeasement also commands almost universal support. It is a good slogan for the country. It seems to me, however, that in this House it requires to be more precisely defined. What we really mean, I think, is no appeasement through weakness or fear. Appeasement in itself may be good or bad according to the circumstances. Appeasement from

weakness and fear is alike futile and fatal. Appeasement from strength is magnanimous and noble and might be the surest and perhaps the only path to world peace.[150]

Alas, Churchill had done his job well over the previous fifteen years or so. Appeasement *was* anathema thanks, in no small part, to him. When, at the outset of the Second World War, Neville Chamberlain reflected on the fact that '[e]verything that I have worked for, everything that I have believed in during my public life has crashed into ruins', it signalled a moment where, henceforth, the concept of appeasement was damned almost beyond redemption.[151] Perhaps it is unfair to Churchill to blame him for the transformation of appeasement into a dirty word.[152] But that was a fact of life that he, and his successors, would have to live with. By 1968, William Norton Medlicott was moved to write, despairingly, that the word appeasement had 'been so stretched and distorted since 1939 that it is now used to cover almost ever manifestation of British diplomacy in the interwar years'.[153]

For all this, appeasement, as a *tactic*, a diplomatic approach, still had a place in the formulation of foreign policy after 1945. The absolutist position adopted towards Chamberlainite appeasement could hardly be sustained with regard to policy formulation; this, after all, would have meant that every postwar dispute in which Britain found itself would have led to armed conflict. In the immediate postwar years, however, the backlash against appeasement had been difficult to resist in policymaking (at least publicly). Nevertheless, from the early 1960s onwards, the Revisionist historiography of appeasement made a powerful case for the motivating factors of British economic weakness and the weight of anti-war feeling in public opinion. This indicated that, with the financial cataclysm of the Second World War and the advent of nuclear weapons, the rationale for appeasement had not diminished. The history of the 1930s, and the manner in which that history had been portrayed, meant that the *good* in appeasement had been entirely obliterated by the *bad*. Those conducting diplomacy could never admit to the utility of appeasement in *any* situation. In terms of the conduct of foreign policy, especially with regard to diplomacy with those deemed opponents, this was to prove highly restrictive. It is against this background, and within these parameters, that this book examines how policy makers sought freedom of manoeuvre in their pursuit of British interests.

CHAPTER ONE

In the footsteps of Cromwell: an empire against two evils, 1941–53

Winston S. Churchill: 'Cromwell was a great man, wasn't he?'
Harold Macmillan: 'Yes, sir, a very great man.'
Winston S. Churchill: 'Ah, but he made one terrible mistake.
Obsessed in his youth by the fear of the power of Spain he failed to observe the rise of France. Will that be said of me?'

LATE NIGHT CONVERSATION IN CAIRO, 1943[1]

Militarily not very desirable. Psychologically inevitable.

EMANUEL 'MANNY' SHINWELL, SECRETARY OF STATE FOR DEFENCE, on the decision to send British troops to Korea, 25 July 1950[2]

On the eve of the Nazi invasion of the Soviet Union in 1941 Churchill memorably told his private secretary Jock Colville: 'If Hitler invaded hell he would at least make a favourable reference to the devil!'[3] In such circumstances was the 'Grand Alliance' born. Thus, as the German invasion proceeded, the British government sought to ingratiate itself with Moscow.[4] Lothar Kettenacker observed that the approach of anti-appeasers like Churchill and Eden to Stalin resembled nothing so much as Chamberlain's earlier diplomacy towards Hitler.[5] This alliance entailed forgetting about the 'bad blood', which was considerable, accrued in Anglo-Soviet relations since 1917.[6] This was manageable while Nazi Germany represented a supreme danger, and presented a common enemy,[7] but it would be virtually impossible to maintain in the long term.[8] Once the war had ended, and the Cold War had descended, the Soviets and British both sought to make political capital out of the others' dealings with Hitler. The Soviets thus made repeated references to Munich, while the British periodically cited the Nazi–Soviet Pact. Unsurprisingly, both sides remained extraordinarily sensitive to any reference to these two agreements.[9] In 1973, a Foreign and Commonwealth Office (FCO) brief for the then–foreign secretary, Alec Douglas-Home, stressed that 'the right to say that responsibility for the terms of the Munich Agreement is shared by all four signatories. Mr. Chamberlain, for his part, believed at the time that he secured an honourable settlement.'[10] Meanwhile as late as 1988, a leading Soviet historian wrote, in hypersensitive fashion, that: 'The Soviet-German Non-Aggression Pact fully corresponded to all ethical and legal norms.'[11]

In April 1943, the discovery at Katyń of the mass graves of 22,000 Poles, murdered by the Soviet NKVD in 1940, threatened the fragile unity of the anti-Hitler coalition.[12] The Germans, predictably, had revealed Katyń to the world in the hope of sowing disharmony within the 'United Nations',[13] while the Soviets, equally predictably, immediately denied the killings and blamed them on the Germans.[14] Eden had pleaded with the Polish prime minister-in-exile, General Władysław Sikorski, to effectively set aside the Soviet crime. He refused and Moscow inevitably denounced the government-in-exile and broke off diplomatic relations.[15] Whatever the truth of the charges emanating from Berlin, attempts to sow discord between London and Moscow were doomed to failure as a policy of appeasement was now firmly directed at Stalin by Churchill and the British government. At a meeting with Sikorski, Churchill identified the affair as a German plot, although he added: 'I may observe, however, that the facts are pretty grim.'[16] Although absent from the official British record, at that same meeting Churchill admitted to Sikorski: 'Alas, the German revelations are probably true. The Bolsheviks can be very cruel.'[17] Alas, *Realpolitik* dictated that the British did nothing. After an international commission seemed to have confirmed Soviet guilt, Sir Owen O'Malley, ambassador to the Polish Government-in-Exile, reflected bitterly on matters.

> If, then, morals have become involved with international politics, if it be the case that a monstrous crime has been committed by a foreign Government – albeit a friendly one – and that we, for however valid reasons, have been obliged to behave as if the deed was not theirs, may it not be that we now stand in danger of bemusing not only others but ourselves . . . If so, and since no remedy can be found in an early alteration of our public attitude towards the Katyn affair, we ought, maybe, to ask ourselves how, consistently with the necessities of our relations with the Soviet Government, the voice of our political conscience is to be kept up to concert pitch.[18]

If O'Malley expected the crusade that Britain had undertaken against Hitler to yield a new international politics of morality he was to be sorely disappointed. In the autumn of 1943, George Orwell was particularly scathing of the manner in which the Left's sycophancy towards Moscow was increasingly emulating the Right's attitude towards Berlin and Rome during the heyday of appeasement. He noted how 'the intellectuals of the Left' defended the Nazi-Soviet Pact of August 1939 for being ' "realistic", like Chamberlain's appeasement policy, and with similar consequences.' For Orwell the solution was clear: 'If there is a way out of the moral pigsty we are living in, the first step towards it is probably to grasp that "realism" does *not* pay, and that to sell out your friends and sit rubbing your hands while they are destroyed is not the last word in political wisdom.'[19] By this stage, the ascendancy of Soviet arms increasingly portended the substitution of German hegemony with Soviet dominion. In March 1944, Foreign Secretary Anthony Eden confessed to a 'growing apprehension that Russia has vast aims, and that these may include the domination of Eastern Europe and even the Mediterranean and the "communizing" of much that remains.'[20] Yet, as Chamberlain had concluded in the 1930s, the British government decided it had no option but to parley with the strongest power on the continent. On 9 October 1944, Churchill, acting rather less officially than Chamberlain had done at Munich, attempted to divide the states of Eastern Europe with Stalin by means of crude percentages.[21] Of this extraordinary agreement, Henry Kissinger notes: 'Never before had spheres of influence been defined by percentages.' Yet, by the time of the Yalta Conference in early 1945, the 'percentages agreement' was dead. It had been rendered so by the physical control of much of Eastern and South-Eastern Europe by the Red Army.[22]

Sometime after Munich a politician who had opposed the agreement supposedly asked Chamberlain how he could trust Hitler after the latter had broken so many promises since 1933. The prime minister, then at the height of his popularity, supposedly replied: 'Ah, but this time he promised me.'[23] Churchill attacked such naïveté with regard to Hitler, although he was also prone to the very same brand of wishful thinking when it came to Stalin, and when it was in his interest. Churchill's attempt to appease Stalin peaked at the Yalta Conference of February 1945, after which he asserted: 'Poor Neville Chamberlain believed he could trust Hitler. He was wrong. But I don't think I'm wrong about Stalin.'[24] Frank Roberts, a British diplomat at Yalta, recalled that Churchill bitterly regretted his public professions of faith in Stalin, just as Chamberlain had lamented flouting the 'piece of paper' (both symptomatic of what John Charmley termed 'post-conference optimism syndrome'). In Churchill's case, Nikolai Tolstoy noted that this marked the culmination of a journey from bitter foe of Stalinism to active connivance with Soviet dominion over Eastern Europe: a 'bitter irony of history' brought about by political neccessity.[25] On the eve of Yalta, MP Sir Duncan McCallum warned Eden: 'While most reasonably-minded people agree that appeasement was necessary at the time of Munich . . . H.M. Government is acting on the lines of "peace at any price" with Russia.'

Walter Lippmann noted that the decisions to confirm Stalin's control of much of Europe reflected the fact that 'the West paid the political price for having failed to deter Hitler in the 1930s, for having failed to unite and rearm against him'.[26] A. J. P. Taylor later wrote: 'This was exactly what the opponents of Churchill had feared, and even he hardly foresaw all that was involved. Victory, even if this meant placing the British empire in pawn to the United States; victory, even if it meant Soviet domination of Europe; victory at all costs.'[27] Lord Dunglass (Alec Douglas-Home) gave voice to 'certain misgivings about certain sections of this Yalta Agreement' in the Commons, opining: 'We could never be a party to a process under which a whole range of the smaller countries of Europe was drawn, by a mixture of military pressure from without and political disruption from within, into the orbit of another and a greater Power.'[28] The Conservative MP Harold Nicolson observed: 'Winston is as amused as I am that the warmongers of the Munich period have now become appeasers, while the appeasers have become the warmongers.'[29] A. J. P. Taylor later noted how '[t]he men of Munich began to re-form' as twenty-five MPs voted against the motion to approve Yalta, whilst one minister (Henry Strauss) resigned.[30] While A. L. Rowse viewed the decision to allow the Soviet Union into 'the middle of Europe . . . as an historic mistake for which we have to endure the gravest consequences', British diplomats remained unapologetic. For Gladwyn Jebb, Hitler's war meant: 'If there hadn't been any Yalta conference at all, the result would have been much the same. I think history would have fulfilled itself, Yalta or no Yalta.'[31]

As well as signalling the demise of the 'Grand Alliance', the end of the war also meant the end of political collaboration between the major political parties in Britain. Early in 1945 Konni Zilliacus, who hailed from Labour's Far Left, wrote: 'The Second World War is in a very real sense the price paid for the preservation of the capitalist system and almost uninterrupted Tory rule after the First World War.'[32] Labour's campaign for the general election in July of that year developed this theme further and sought to use the legacy of appeasement to undermine the Conservative Party at every turn.[33] This involved the repeated invocation of Neville Chamberlain, shameful events such as the betrayal of the League of Nations and the Hoare-Laval Pact and digging up the numerous favourable references to Mussolini and Hitler made by Conservative politicians (including Churchill) in the 1930s.[34] Such events were recounted in publications like the Labour Party's pamphlet, *The Guilty Party*, as the MP Sir William Jowitt urged his constituents to 'recall the awful pre-war mess the Tories had made of things . . . Think of "Munich"; appeasement of Hitler; shortage of war weapons; hatred of Russia'.[35] The Conservative MP Quentin Hogg argued that the Labour Party hierarchy ignored a whole range of issues in 1945 and concentrated, instead, on Munich.

If there be such a thing as a High Command among the Left, it is evident that the order has gone forth that the word 'Munich' should become a

ILLUSTRATION 1.1 *Opening session of the Potsdam Conference in Potsdam, Germany, 17 July 1945. Cadogan, Eden, Churchill, Attlee et al. face Stalin and Truman. On the same day the conference opened Eden minuted Churchill: 'I am deeply concerned about the pattern of Russian policy, which becomes clearer as they become more brazen every day.'*

legend, a battlecry, or scalping knife for Tories, anything but a subject for sober reflection . . . To be a member of the party of Churchill and Eden is to be a Man of Munich, and to be a Man of Munich is to commit political suicide.[36]

The Labour Party duly went on to win the general election of July 1945 with a huge overall majority of 146 seats. Harold Macmillan later famously lamented: 'It was not Churchill who lost the 1945 election; it was the ghost of Neville Chamberlain.'[37] Attlee himself later asserted that the memory of Munich had played a significant role in the crushing Conservative defeat.[38] Nevertheless, whatever the effectiveness of the invocation of appeasement in the campaign of 1945, its prominence foreshadowed any number of postwar debates on foreign policy.

After the Potsdam Conference ended in early August 1945, the new Labour government of Clement Attlee found itself increasingly unable and unwilling to continue the appeasement of the Soviet Union.[39] The traumatic experience of Chamberlainite appeasement made the decision to stand firm against the Soviets a very natural one for most policy makers.[40] This was especially the case with Ernest Bevin, the new foreign secretary, who had talked of 'left speaking to left in comradeship and confidence',[41] but who now embraced anti-Sovietism with all the zeal of the convert. Such attitudes were encouraged by the rapid hardening of US attitudes as the likes of Secretary of the Navy James Forrestal dismissed the idea of approaching Stalin with 'understanding and sympathy' as '[w]e tried that once with Hitler. There are no returns on appeasement.'[42] The lesson of the recent past only underlined the need to reject appeasement given the pattern of Soviet expansion in Eastern Europe as Stalin, like Hitler, was seen to have broken his word repeatedly while expanding his dominion state-by-state.[43] The idea that the USSR had to be opposed resolutely was accompanied in London by a belief that Britain remained a global power to be reckoned with. After all, Stalin was but the latest tyrant seeking hegemony on the continent of Europe (following Charles V, Philip II, Louis XIV, Napoleon, Wilhelm II and Hitler).[44] It had been resistance to such a pattern of domination that had laid the foundations for the modern European state system.[45] Policy makers in London therefore maintained that Britain, traditionally in the lead in the denial of the notion of a continental hegemon, still had a role to play. Ernest Bevin outlined matters thus in 1947:

> We regard ourselves as one of the Powers most vital to the peace of the world, and we still have our historic part to play. The very fact that we have fought so hard for liberty, and paid such a price, warrants our retaining this position; and, indeed, it places a duty upon us to continue to retain it. I am not aware of any suggestion seriously advanced, that, by a sudden stroke of fate, as it were, we have overnight ceased to be a great Power.[46]

As a corollary of this belief in the continuing relevance of British power, and following an awkward and humbling meeting with US Secretary of State James Byrnes,[47] Bevin famously declared that he wanted to see the atomic bomb 'with a bloody Union Jack on it'.[48] And, although Bevin did not live to see it, Britain duly tested its first atomic bomb in 1952 (and its first H-bomb in 1957). The drive for nuclear weapons signified that appeasement was but a distant memory. Negotiation itself was now seen as dangerous and General Sir Brian Robertson, military governor in Germany, warned: 'if we keep on talking indefinitely, we might wake up some fine morning to find the Hammer and Sickle already on the Rhine.'[49] The resolution demonstrated by the West, and by the United States and the United Kingdom in particular, in its confrontation over Berlin in 1948–9[50] led directly to the establishment of the North Atlantic Treaty Organisation (NATO). This secured a permanent American commitment to the defence of Western Europe,[51] and institutionalized the rejection of a policy of appeasement towards Moscow.

In 1972, Robert Skidelsky noted the 'transatlantic motive for buttressing the conventional wisdom' on appeasement. This arose because, after 1945, the United States had inherited Britain's world position 'and with it a Commitment to preserve the status quo against a new challenger, Russia'. And, in both the United States and Britain, '"Munich" became synonymous with "appeasing Communism"'.

> The opprobrium attached to appeasing the dead dictator in Berlin was [now] attached to appeasing the living dictator in Moscow; to affirm Munich was to deny NATO. In this way the lessons of the 1930s were drawn in the context of the Cold War; and it was essential to these lessons to portray Hitler as bent on world conquest, and appeasement as a fatal mistake which had almost enabled him to achieve it.[52]

As noted above, one of the leading proponents of a firm policy towards the USSR was Ernest Bevin. The foreign secretary played a crucial role in the process of constructing the Western security architecture with which to resist the Soviets. This represented a decisive repudiation of the diplomatic methods that had characterized the era of appeasement.[53] As Alan Bullock later noted: 'The Berlin experience . . . confirmed [Bevin's] view that there would be no recovery in Europe until confidence that neither a Russian occupation nor a war was inevitable was restored.'[54] Another historian similarly noted that, from the start of the Berlin Crisis, Bevin 'set his face firmly against any retreat under Soviet pressure and any compromise which smacked of appeasement. The lessons of Munich a decade earlier conditioned his whole approach to the Berlin crisis.'[55]

In a speech that is often heralded as one of the landmarks in the foundation of NATO, Bevin told the House of Commons in 1948 that Yalta had made sense at the time, although subsequent Soviet actions had transformed the situation. 'It therefore matters little how we temporise, and maybe appease, or try to make arrangements . . . all the evidence is that [Moscow] is not satisfied with this tremendous expansion.'[56] Once the Berlin Blockade was underway Bevin therefore declared that 'His Majesty's Government and the Western allies can see no alternative between that and surrender, and none of us can accept surrender.'[57] The shadow foreign secretary, Anthony Eden, concurred: 'If ever there was a time to stand firm, it is now: if ever there was a cause in which to stand firm it is this.'[58] In Cabinet Bevin made it clear in an obvious reference to Munich that further concessions would lead 'to further withdrawals . . . and in the end war'.[59]

The disillusion with the notion of appeasing the Soviet Union, which had rapidly accelerated from 1945 onwards, was finally completed when Communist North Korea invaded its southern neighbour on 25 June 1950. The Cabinet resolved that '[i]t was the clear duty of the United Kingdom Government to do everything in their power, in concert with other members of the United Nations, to help the South Koreans to resist this aggression'.[60]

This time, in contrast to the 1930s, 'aggression' was to be resisted. Churchill's argument that, in the 1930s, 'the weakness of the virtuous' had been exploited by the 'malice of the wicked'[61] was particularly popular with those US policy makers who had embraced a policy of 'Containment' towards the global Soviet threat.[62] This policy sought to avoid the mistakes of the past and steer a middle way between appeasement and war.[63] In this climate, the outbreak of the Korean War immediately led US President Harry S. Truman to reflect on the lessons of the 1930s.[64]

> In my generation, this was not the first occasion when the strong had attacked the weak. I recalled some earlier instances: Manchuria, Ethiopia, Austria. I remembered how each time that the democracies failed to act, it had encouraged the aggressors to keep going ahead. Communism was acting in Korea just as Hitler, Mussolini and the Japanese had acted ten, fifteen and twenty years earlier . . . If the Communists were permitted to force their way into the Republic of Korea without opposition from the free world, no small nation would have the courage to resist threats and aggression by stronger Communist neighbors. If this was allowed to go unchallenged it would mean a third world war, just as similar incidents had brought on a second world war.[65]

Regardless of his personal feelings, Truman would have had little option but to adopt a hard-line over Korea, as his Republican opponents in Congress, already demanding an answer to their mantra 'Who lost China?'[66] now engaged in populist outbursts about the necessity of avoiding appeasement. On 26 June 1950 Senator William F. Knowland (R-CA) told the Senate: 'Korea today stands in the same position as did Manchuria, Ethiopia, Austria and Czechoslovakia of an earlier date. In each of those instances a firm stand by the law-abiding nations of the world might have saved the peace.'[67] Such rhetoric and historical references resonated with British policy makers. The British prime minister, Labour's Clement Attlee, had been a staunch opponent of Munich from the start (and, unlike Churchill – who abstained – Attlee had actually voted against the agreement in the Commons).[68] Attlee, in common with Bevin, had long harboured suspicions of the Soviet Union.[69] The British government therefore committed British forces to the UN operation to defend South Korea (indeed it was a British resolution, carried by the UN general Assembly on 7 October 1950, that called on UN forces to cross the 38th parallel, restore 'stability throughout Korea' and hold elections).[70] Attlee and Bevin embarked upon this path in the belief that it was Britain's destiny, in common with the United States, to safeguard democracy against the global threat from Moscow. In any case, the sending of troops to Korea would surely enhance British influence over

American policy in the Far East.[71] Churchill, now in Opposition, stood foursquare behind the decision to fight in Korea.[72]

The British government's actions in defence of South Korea were not, however, enough for many in the United States who, having stood by while Hitler sought to undermine the European state system in the 1930s, had embraced anti-appeasement (albeit of Communism) with great enthusiasm. *Life* magazine criticized the fact that the Attlee government, which had recognized Red China, 'was publicly on its knees to the Communist aggressors of Peking'.[73] Although Bevin would hardly agree that he was obsequious in its dealings with Red China, he had told Cabinet that:

> The Nationalist Government were our former allies in the war and since the war they have been a useful friend . . . [but] they are no longer representative of anything . . . British interests can reap no advantage from continued recognition of this shadowy Government, since they lie almost entirely within Communist control . . . For the time being the Communist Government of the People's Republic of China [PRC] is the only alternative. The Communists are now the rulers of most of China. The fall of Canton has brought them to the Hong Kong frontier.[74]

Although the British had essentially pursued Washington's line while the Chinese Civil War raged,[75] the aftermath saw a divergence of policy between London and Washington.[76] Once Chiang had been defeated, the British priority was the security of Hong Kong. Such self-interested logic would have been familiar to those who had supported British recognition of the Franco government in 1939.[77] After all, for the British government Hong Kong was the equivalent of Berlin in Asia. Attlee had told the Cabinet in May 1949 that a failure to ensure Hong Kong's security would seriously damage British prestige in Asia. In order to achieve this a policy of mutual tolerance with Red China was essential.[78] The British felt even more justified in pursuing this because of their belief that the United States was erroneous in simply regarding Red China as a puppet of Moscow.[79] But the realities of power nevertheless meant that the United Kingdom would have to appease Mao Zedong without alienating the United States to an unacceptable degree. The British goal was to avoid escalation in Korea at all costs – for that would necessitate adhering to US policy to the bitter end.[80] In London the secretary of state for war, John Strachey, warned Bevin that any escalation would be nearly as ruinous to Britain as a lost war. Strachey feared that aggressive 'recent American policies . . . threaten to involve us in early and general war [that would be] almost certainly fatal, in the most literal sense of that term, to this country . . . [as no] degree of rearmament which is humanly possible to achieve in two years [could] alter this situation'.[81] The Korean War therefore exerted a paradoxical effect

on Anglo-American relations whereby the unity of purpose engendered by
the Communist threat was matched by very real differences in strategy.[82]
Indeed, in the same Cabinet where it had been agreed to commit fully to the
defence of South Korea, the British government asked

> whether it was expedient publicly to attribute responsibility for this
> aggression . . . The announcement which the United States Government
> were proposing to make, by linking this up with Communist threats
> in other parts of Asia, would present a major challenge to the Soviet
> Government; it would bring into controversy other issues which had
> not yet been brought before the Security Council; and its reference to
> Formosa might . . . even provoke that Government to attack Hong Kong
> or to foment disorder there.[83]

In a curious exercise in psychological second-guessing, the *Life* editorial
of 4 December 1950 carried an imaginary question and answer session
with General Douglas MacArthur in which 'his' opinions were stated in the
third person.[84] Thus, '[h]istory demonstrates unmistakably that yielding
to unjustified international pressure leads inevitably to war. A recent
precedent is the Munich settlement of 1938 and the German expansion
which followed.' It was noted that the State Department's publication
Postwar Foreign Policy Planning had asserted: 'The Crisis occasioned by
the German occupation [of Austria] in March 1938 was followed by the
Munich Crisis in September, when the weakness of peaceful efforts toward
just settlements on the face of determined aggression was unmistakably
demonstrated.'[85] And, in spite of the recent policy of the United States,
'General MacArthur feels that this concept is as valid now as when the
State Department formulated it. There is no reason to doubt its validity.'[86]
Life's editorial was right inasmuch as British policy towards the Far East
was cautious. And this was, indeed, anathema to MacArthur as he viewed
even the 'limited' war in Korea as an act of appeasement.[87] Attlee famously
flew to Washington to seek an undertaking from Truman that the United
States would not use nuclear weapons in Korea.[88] The US Joint Chiefs
of Staff duly recommended that Attlee be told that Washington had 'no
intention' of using nuclear weapons in Korea (except in the event of a forced
evacuation by UN forces or to stave off a 'major military disaster').[89] Attlee
was therefore given an assurance that the United States would not use
nuclear weapons without consulting the United Kingdom and Canada.[90]
Attlee appreciated the pressures under which Truman was operating.[91]
When visiting Washington in December 1950 Attlee stressed that the British
were dead against concessions in Korea, as '[w]e all know from our own
bitter experience that appeasement does not pay'.[92] Attlee nevertheless had
no problem simultaneously defending his government's recognition of the
PRC on the grounds that the Reds already ruled the mainland![93] In contrast

with the British position, US policy explicitly linked the defence of South Korea with a refusal to recognize Red China. On 27 June Truman stated:

> The attack upon Korea makes it plain beyond all doubt that communism has passed beyond the use of subversion to conquer independent nations and will now use armed invasion and war . . . In these circumstances the occupation of Formosa by Communist forces would be a direct threat to the security of the Pacific area and to United States forces performing their lawful and necessary functions in that area.[94]

This heralded the beginning of a new phase of uncompromising American anti-Communism. Appeasement was out as a policy option – even where it made sense to recognize the strength of an opponent and compromise. Of course, there was far less incentive for the Americans, as opposed to the British, to do this given the huge power disposed of by the United States after 1945. One of the bitter ironies of the Korean War was that the MiG-15, which was used in large numbers against the UN forces in Korea, powered the VK-1 engine, a composite copy of the Rolls Royce Nene and Derwent engines – which the Labour government had authorized for export to the USSR in 1946.[95] This attempt to boost exports and improve relations with the Soviets by this aeronautical diplomacy by trusting Moscow's assurance that they would not copy the British engine was, to say the least, rather naïve. (When Stalin was first told that the engines were advertised for sale, and should be bought, he supposedly exclaimed: 'What kind of fool will sell you his secrets?')[96] It certainly induced consternation in Washington – whose aviators (and, indeed, those of the Fleet Air Arm) had come to greatly respect the MiG-15 in the skies over Korea.[97] The episode foreshadowed one of the great on-going debates of the Cold War: namely at what level did trade with the Soviet bloc cease to be profitable and of utility in promoting understanding?[98] These debates flared up at intervals during the Cold War (over, for instance, the sale of British Leyland trucks to Cuba in the 1960s,[99] and the construction of the Siberian gas pipeline in the 1980s).[100]

Attlee's reasoning vis-à-vis the recognition of Red China was not at all the way the Americans saw things. The issue of the recognition of China, the export of jet engines to the USSR and Attlee's concerns regarding nuclear weapons foreshadowed one of the central justifications for British 'pragmatism' (or appeasement') during the Cold War: namely the idea that one should go to almost any length to avoid major war because of the existence of nuclear weapons. Yet, as Campbell Craig notes, the fact that thermonuclear war can end life on earth plays a very small role in the history of US thinking about international politics.[101] This, no doubt, was part of the process whereby policy makers and military figures thought 'about the unthinkable'.[102] This was often the case in Britain with one notable exception – when the threat of nuclear war was employed as de facto justification for appeasement.

The vision of a nuclear war causing catastrophic damage at a global level was the atomic age equivalent of the interwar maxim: 'the bomber will always get through' (derived from a 1932 speech by British Prime Minister Stanley Baldwin).[103] This line reflected a widespread belief that war would bring cataclysmic levels of destruction upon civilization.[104] This was derived from a fear that modern science was the harbinger of doom for humanity. The pacifist cleric Norman Maclean wrote in 1934 of the 'fear of poison gas; [the] fear of bombing planes; [the] fear of bacilli; [and the] fear of blight that will blacken the harvest fields'.[105] Once Ernest Rutherford had split the atom in 1917, the potential of the 'mighty atom' developed none of the positive connotations associated with nuclear energy and the like. Indeed, Rutherford himself wrote in 1933: 'Anyone who says that with the means at present at our disposal and with our present knowledge we can utilize atomic energy is talking moonshine.' Even prior to Hiroshima and Nagasaki, a 'nuclear culture' of quite extraordinary pessimism existed in Britain. As the geneticist J. B. S. Haldane opined: 'If we could utilize the forces which we now know to exist inside the atom, we should have such capacities for destruction that I do not know of any agency other than divine intervention which would save humanity from complete and peremptory annihilation.'[106]

Of course, to advocate avoiding nuclear war (or mass bombing, for that matter) is an entirely rational and morally laudable course. Yet, such ambiguous British attitudes to the use of force (in the guise of bombers, atom bombs or whatever) were at variance with the deterrence theories that successive governments effected to subscribe to. That is, deterrence would only work if the enemy believed that you had every intention of using the ultimate weapon. Thomas Schelling, an American economist and scholar, termed this 'the threat that leaves something to chance'. Schelling posited that: 'The key to these threats, is that, though one may or may not carry them out, the final decision is not altogether in the threatener's control'. This would mean that any weakening of resolve, if communicated or detected by the enemy, would lead to a situation where war was *more* and not *less* likely. This would lead to a situation where 'only the enemy's withdrawal' would remove the danger to both sides.[107] Given this, it is small wonder that the *doublethink* involved in deterrence theory was something that British politicians sought to avoid being scrutinized upon, although the 1930s had taught them to avoid speeches employing language in the vein of Chamberlain's infamous reference to quarrels in far-off places between peoples 'of whom we know nothing'.[108] But the core of Chamberlain's appeal had been his ability to place the pursuit of peace at the heart of his agenda. Towards the end of his life A. J. P. Taylor recalled that even he was rendered rhetorically impotent during the Czechoslovakian crisis of 1938.

I suppose I addressed half a dozen meetings on the theme of stand up to Hitler. They were terrible. I tried every argument: national honour, anti-Fascism, Hitler's weakness and the certainty he would back down. Always came the reply, 'What you are advocating means war. We want peace'.

Those who think the British people were ready for a strong stand in 1938 were very mistaken, at any rate to judge from their feelings around Manchester.[109]

In the nuclear age, the word 'peace' was an even more powerful rhetorical device than it had been in the interwar era.[110] Its invocation represented a powerful and emotive lever against opponents. Only days after the atomic bomb attacks on Japan in 1945, the Royal Navy's Rear-Admiral Robert D. Oliver, Assistant Chief of Naval Staff, noted 'that the price worth paying for peace is now very much higher, and . . . the main function of our armed forces should be the prevention of war, rather than the ability to fight it on purely military grounds'.[111] Bernard Brodie, the first and perhaps the greatest of all nuclear strategists,[112] summarized the logic of deterrence: 'Thus far the chief purpose of our military establishment has been to win wars. From now on its chief purpose must be to avert them. It can have almost no other useful purpose.'[113] The mistaken impression that Attlee had stopped the United States using nuclear weapons in Korea nevertheless proved a very valuable one for the Labour Party in the 1951 general election. The Labour Party peddled the nuclear myth relentlessly, and simultaneously tried to paint the Conservative Party as being the party of war via a campaign slogan asking: 'Whose finger is on the trigger?'[114] Churchill and Eden, naturally objecting to being cast as warmongers,[115] inserted a clause in the Conservative manifesto that proposed safeguards against profiteering in military contracts. Ironically, this was very close to Chamberlain's abortive 1937 National Defence Contribution, which sought to tax excessive profits from military contracts, and of which Churchill had been a vocal critic.[116] Churchill, like Chamberlain before him, was learning that the maxim 'blessed are the peacemakers' had electoral, as well as spiritual, benefits. During the 1951 election campaign, Churchill was thus robust in his rebuttal of the warmonger charge that had been made against him repeatedly.

This is a cruel and ungrateful accusation. It is the opposite of the truth. If I remain in public life at this juncture it is because, rightly or wrongly, but sincerely, I believe that I may be able to make an important contribution to the prevention of a Third World War and to bringing nearer that lasting peace settlement which the masses of the people of every race and in every land fervently desire.[117]

Such arguments reflected the manner in which the fear of nuclear war now vied with the detestation of appeasement in the popular mind. The danger that a fear of war might now reinvigorate appeasement caused veterans of the campaign against its Chamberlainite variety to take a hand in matters. No less a personage than Lord Vansittart[118] told the House of Lords in 1951:

> Litvinov said that Peace is indivisible. That sounded very clever, and the phrase caught on. But, like a great many of the clichés that have come prancing and rumbling down to us, it is not true. There are many kinds of peace, including the brand that we are now enduring, and many of them are highly divisible . . . I think that the minds of the Government and the Foreign Office . . . seem to be assuming that all Communists are not our inveterate enemies. But, in fact, they are. Thus, the Chinese Communists have never had any intention of coming to a settlement in Korea until they had satisfied themselves that they could get the better of us by no other means . . . it is our duty to prove to them that they cannot get the better of us by any means. It therefore follows, logically, that peace, if and when it does come, must not be too easy, otherwise it will prove deceptive.[119]

The invocation of Litvinov (whose former master, Stalin, was now the West's leading antagonist) was designed to indicate the ascendancy of morality in international affairs. Lord Jowitt, the lord chancellor, welcomed Vansittart's intervention in the House of Lords stating 'that there must be no appeasement, if by appeasement is meant weakening on this particular issue . . . we are not fighting Communism or Communist China; we are fighting aggression . . . We are perfectly ready to have a cease-fire – and that is not appeasement at all.'[120] In October 1951 Churchill was returned to power by the electorate and found the war in Korea as intractable as had his predecessor.[121] By 1953 the populations of the United States and Britain were tired of the Korean War which, once the People's Republic of China had become involved, seemed likely to drag on in bloody stalemate. In the event, the death of Stalin in March 1953 paved the way for the signing of an armistice agreement on 27 July (although the British acceded to an American demand that it be made clear that any violation of the armistice by the Communists would lead to a resumption of hostilities).[122] The British had committed nearly 100,000 men to the war and cemented the 'Special Relationship' with the United States as the cornerstone of Britain's global foreign and security policies. Yet, despite initial hopes in London that it could act as the 'guide' to American policy,[123] by the war's end it was clear that the British had exerted very little influence over the Americans.[124] The anti-appeasement model was in the ascendancy in Washington and flexibility was in short supply as President Dwight D. Eisenhower warned the British that if Red China ever got control of Formosa, 'that would be a real Munich'.[125] At Bermuda in December 1953 Churchill, recognizing the dominant mood of US policy makers, even conceded to Eisenhower that the US government would be well within its rights to use nuclear weapons if the Chinese and the North Koreans abrogated the ceasefire![126] Despite their possession of nuclear weapons, in matters of war and peace it was now clear that the British were no longer masters of their own destiny.

In 2008, Michael Lumbers concluded that 'if the lessons of Munich demonstrated the imperative of *containing* the PRC, the example of Chinese intervention in the Korean War underlined the risks of *confronting* the mainland'.[127] Thus, a delicate balance between simultaneously avoiding major war and desisting from being seen to engage in appeasement had come about. The Korean War demonstrated that there could be no absolute victory for even such a result could well lead to disaster for the victors as well as the defeated. Nuclear weapons meant that there could be no victors in total (nuclear) war, and '[t]he living would envy the dead'. And yet, for all this, the business of international politics and brinkmanship continued apace in a manner that would have been wholly familiar to any nineteenth-century statesman. This, more than any other single factor, would present the supreme challenge to British policy makers.

CHAPTER TWO

Churchill and Locarno, Eden and Geneva: the limits and possibilities of diplomacy

'Appeasement', where it is not a device to gain time, is the result of an inability to come to grips with a policy of unlimited objectives.

HENRY KISSINGER[1]

The world has achieved brilliance without conscience. Ours is a world of nuclear giants and ethical infants. We know more about war than we know about peace, more about killing than we know about living.

GENERAL OMAR BRADLEY, 1948[2]

To jaw-jaw is better than to war-war.

WINSTON CHURCHILL SPEECH, Washington DC, 26 June 1954[3]

Churchill had returned to office as prime minister on 25 October 1951 with Eden, his heir apparent, as foreign secretary. Since the two had left office in July 1945, the substance of British power had eroded further and the rising costs of Britain's global commitments were particularity unyielding. Eden, as foreign secretary between 1935 and 1938, had known of the weaknesses in the British economy that had been such a factor in the appeasement of the dictators. Eden had attempted to blame his Labour successors for the wartime concessions to Stalin (confirmed by Attlee and Bevin at Potsdam) but there was now no place to hide. Away from the glamour of international diplomacy, in which he was well versed, Eden was candid with the Cabinet as to the limitations within which Britain found itself in the early 1950s (with a war in Korea, an emergency in Malaya, unrest in the Empire and a fading economy at home).

> The essence of a sound foreign policy is to ensure that a country's strength is equal to its obligations. If this is not the case, then either the obligations must be reduced to the level at which resources are available to maintain them, or a greater share of the country's resources must be devoted to their support. It is becoming clear that rigorous maintenance of the presently-accepted policies of Her Majesty's Government at home and abroad is placing a burden on the country's economy which it is beyond the resources of the country to meet. A position has already been reached where there is no reserve and therefore no margin for unforeseen additional obligations.[4]

Eden recognized that abandoning commitments, however necessary, would have four major drawbacks. First, it would grant an opportunity to the Soviet Union. Second, it would undermine the world power status of the United Kingdom necessary for the maintenance of relations with the Commonwealth, Western Europe and the United States. Third, it would hurt British trade and commerce. And, finally, it would lead to a great 'loss of prestige'. While it was not possible to 'assess in concrete terms the consequences . . . of our drastically and unilaterally reducing our responsibilities; the effects of a failure of will and relaxation of grip in our overseas commitments are incalculable. But once the prestige of a country has started to slide there is no knowing where it will stop.'[5] In addition to the general inability of the United Kingdom to meet its global obligations, it was clear that the Korean War had imbued war weariness in the British people. Churchill thus intended to make good on his electoral peace pledge. All he awaited was the moment and, in 1953, he believed that it had arrived when, on 5 March, Stalin died.[6] On May 11, Churchill made a major foreign policy speech announcing his belief that the time was right for détente.

> The supreme event which has occurred since we last had a debate on foreign affairs is, of course, the change of attitude and, as we all hope, of mood which has taken place in the Soviet domains and particularly in the Kremlin since the death of Stalin. We, on both sides of the House, have watched this with profound attention. It is the policy of Her Majesty's Government to avoid by every means in their power doing anything or saying anything which could check any favourable reaction that may be taking place and to welcome every sign of improvement in our relations with Russia.

It was thus vital 'that a conference on the highest level should take place between the leading powers without delay. This conference should not be overhung by a ponderous or rigid agenda.' Churchill did not 'believe the immense problem of reconciling the security of Russia with the freedom and safety of Western Europe is insoluble'.[7] The prime minister therefore proposed a summit to address the issues, including the matter of the 'provisional' nature of German frontiers in Eastern Europe. In doing this, Churchill invoked a spirit of détente from another era.

> The Locarno Treaty of 1925 has been in my mind. It was the highest point we reached between the wars. As Chancellor of the Exchequer in those days I was closely acquainted with it. It was based upon the simple provision that if Germany attacked France we should stand with the French, and if France attacked Germany we should stand with the Germans.

> The scene today, its scale and its factors, is widely different, and yet I have a feeling that the master thought which animated Locarno might well play its part between Germany and Russia in the minds of those whose prime ambition it is to consolidate the peace of Europe as the key to the peace of mankind. Russia has a right to feel assured that as far as human arrangements can run the terrible events of the Hitler invasion will never be repeated, and that Poland will remain a friendly Power and a buffer, though not, I trust, a puppet State.[8]

Churchill's initiative was bold. It was also doomed from the outset. For a start, Churchill's own Foreign Office (FO), acutely aware of the danger of being tarred as appeasers, were highly sensitive to charges of horse-trading over German frontiers (a fear shared by Foreign Secretary Eden).[9] The FO warned the prime minister that he risked neutralizing Germany, wrecking NATO's posture of forward defence (which was based on the Elbe River) and even driving the Americans out of Europe.[10] Harold Macmillan, then minister of housing, and a staunch anti-appeaser in the 1930s, lamented: 'Does Churchill know what he wants from a settlement with Russia? Will Central and Eastern Europe be "sold out" in a super Munich? All these things are very worrying. At present I can do nothing in the Cabinet. But I shall not stay if we are now to seek "appeasement" and call it Peace.'[11] Although Eden, too, had disliked Churchill's initiative, not least for its public and vulgar method, the foreign secretary had effectively pointed the way for his prime minister.

> A special factor which may . . . compel us to consider some reduction in our forces in Germany is the fact that after June, 1953, we must be prepared to pay in addition to our present expenditure a sum probably amounting to about £100 million a year in foreign exchange in respect of

the local costs hitherto borne on the German occupation budget. These should be fully covered by Germany as part of her defence contribution only until June, 1953.[12]

In avoiding such a hike in costs, Churchill's 'Eastern Locarno', whether the foreign secretary liked it or not, would yield instant benefits for the British. It was no coincidence that Churchill's initiative was launched just months before costs in Germany would rocket. Without détente, any reduction of forces in Germany was impossible: 'Psychologically the reduction and still more the complete withdrawal of United Kingdom forces from the Continent, even if kept in being in the United Kingdom, would have a serious effect on the will of all our European allies to resist aggression.'[13] In the event, the 'Eastern Locarno' proposal was a stillborn one. While he was no 'hawk' on foreign policy, US President Dwight D. Eisenhower rejected Churchill's proposal as 'untimely'.[14] One of the reasons for this was apparently lost on Churchill: Munich had made all democratic leaders slaves to the electoral slavery of anti-appeasement. He could never accept anything like the 'Eastern Locarno' proposals. Instead, Eisenhower put his name to a draft resolution that rejected 'any interpretations or applications of any international agreements or understandings, made during the course of World War II, which have been perverted to bring about the subjugation of free peoples'.[15] Such rhetoric was nothing less than a feeble attempt to wrap the Anglo-American appeasement of Stalin at Yalta in high-sounding verbiage.[16] In truth, Eisenhower was a prisoner of his own hard line, imposed by his own electoral rhetoric which had declared the Democrats to be irresolute in the face of Communism.[17] The attitude of the United States came as a relief to the West's Cold Warriors, not least West German Chancellor Konrad Adenauer (for it was German territory that Churchill proposed being effectively renounced via any 'Eastern Locarno'). Adenauer, recently returned from preaching the gospel of anti-Communism in the USA,[18] was diplomatic about the proposed 'Eastern Locarno' in conversation with Churchill. Publicly, however, the chancellor made it clear that the question of Germany's eastern frontiers was the exclusive business of a future all-German government and a 'free' Poland.[19] Wholly aware of the propaganda value of pursuing détente, Adenauer called for East–West negotiations in July 1953. But this was mere rhetoric and Washington colluded with the charade for the benefit of world opinion.[20]

Churchill bemoaned the loss of the opportunity afforded by the demise of the Soviet dictator,[21] although in reality there was little chance of his prevailing in the face of such determined opposition.[22] But his initiative had attracted a great deal of support from many quarters in Britain. The feeling that the death of Stalin was a major opportunity was genuinely felt in Britain. Sir William Hayter (British ambassador to Moscow, 1953–7) recalled that Soviet Premier Georgy Malenkov, one of the collective leadership who had succeeded Stalin, was a man with whom 'business could be done'.[23]

Labour's popular maverick MP Aneurin Bevan went so far as to make wild claims about Malenkov's alleged willingness to negotiate the withdrawal of Soviet troops from Germany.[24] In a series of *Tribune* articles, published in July 1953 and entitled 'In Place of the Cold War', Bevan advocated a conciliatory policy in order to capitalize upon the opportunity afforded by Stalin's death. Bevan believed that 'in the short run or in the long run Russia will get her Reformation. It is for us to see that she is enabled to get it without fear of attack from the outside and to give her every reason to believe that her search for more urbane ways of life are watched with eager sympathy by hundreds of millions of people outside her frontiers.'[25]

Harold Macmillan later defended Churchill's 'efforts to prevent a third world war' stating that there was no 'question of "appeasement", as some people tried to read into his words. This was neither implicit nor explicit in his speech. He wished to move from strength, which the West undoubtedly had, not from weakness, as had been our mistake in the fatal days before the Second World War.'[26] But the *Economist* was perhaps nearer the mark when it commented acidly that Churchill's 'musings on Locarno ignore the tragedy of the East' and had been made in an insensitive 'spirit of appeasement'.[27] During a debate on a proposed treaty with Egypt in 1954, which many Tories viewed as appeasement, Viscount Hinchingbrooke, a right-wing Conservative, referred to

> the sea-change in his thinking on foreign policy which began with that great watershed speech of 11th May, 1953; and after which we have had – not 'appeasement' because that word has sinister connotations[28] – Realism, if the hon. Gentleman likes – pacification; the lowering of tension; ending in the accepted policy of co-existence with the Communist world which now rules the day.

How, pondered Hinchingbrooke, did Churchill square this appeasement with the thermonuclear deterrence he was so passionately advocating?[29] In truth, there was no answer (or at least not one that was intellectually coherent). Indeed, and certainly by the standards that he had imposed on other people, Churchill could certainly sound like an appeaser on occasion. The prime minister reacted with a callous fury to an FO protest against the Soviets' crushing of the East German workers' rising of 17 June 1953: 'Is it suggested that the Soviets should have allowed the Eastern Zone to fall into anarchy and riot? I had the impression that they acted with considerable restraint in the face of mounting disorder.'[30] Such insensitive attitudes did little to dispel the widespread belief that the British would sell out Germany's national interests in order to achieve a settlement with Moscow (a view confirmed by British behaviour at the Berlin conference of foreign ministers in January and February of 1954).[31] Any such deal would effectively implement the Carthaginian peace that Potsdam had seemed a prelude to.[32] From the perspective of the West German government this was no way to treat an ally and was fundamentally at odds with the view from Bonn.[33] For Adenauer, Soviet Communism was an irreconcilable enemy and he made little secret of this: 'The conditioning factor of our policy and the root of historical developments of the past several years has been the aggressive expansionist policy of Soviet Russia.'[34] By the mid-1950s, disgruntled Cold Warriors in Bonn, Washington and Paris charged that London remained wedded to the concept of appeasement. This state of mind was even equated with an affliction, unofficially dubbed the 'English disease'.[35] This attitude was regarded as ridiculous by British policy makers, particularly by those with seemingly impeccable credentials as anti-appeasers in the 1930s. Chief of these were, of course, three successive Conservative prime ministers: Churchill, Eden and Macmillan.

At this juncture Eden achieved a series of diplomatic coups. First, he managed to ensure a smooth aftermath to the fall of Mosaddeq in Iran (which had been engineered by SIS and the CIA). Second, the Italian–Yugoslav dispute over Trieste was settled when, on 5 October 1954, representatives of the United States, United Kingdom, Italy and Yugoslavia initialled the so-called London Memorandum. Third, between April and July 1954, the British government played a leading role in the Geneva Conference that ended France's war in Indochina (although, as Macmillan noted, certain observers compared Eden's role at Geneva to Chamberlain's at Munich).[36] Fourth, a collective defence organization for Southeast Asia was established by the Manila Treaty of 8 September 1954 (SEATO). Fifth, on 19 October 1954 the Suez Canal Base Agreement was concluded with Egypt (this involved the withdrawal of Britain's troops from the region, in exchange for the maintenance of the Canal as a British base). Sixth, a treaty of 11 December 1954 associated Britain with the newly created European Coal and Steel Community (ECSC). Seventh, in response to the French Assembly's decision to 'set aside' the proposed European Defence Community (EDC) on 31 August 1954, Eden came up with the ingenious idea of extending the Brussels Pact to include the Federal Republic of Germany (FRG) in a Western European Union (WEU) and, in May 1955, for that state to accede to NATO. And, finally, May 1955 saw the signing of the Austrian State Treaty, which ended the Allied military occupation of that country and secured a neutral future for a free Austria. Eden's private secretary termed the year capped by this achievement as an *annus mirabilis*.[37] Given this, Eden was understandably overwhelmed by hubris, and he later recalled that '[p]eace is not something that just happens. At times it is necessary to take risks and even to increase the immediate danger to win a lasting agreement. Trieste was one of those occasions.'[38]

In 1955, an ailing Churchill finally conceded that it was time to resign as prime minister. In Cabinet on 14 March, the possibility of a four-power summit was discussed.[39] Such a meeting would have provided a fitting swansong for Churchill. Alas, superpower disinterest killed off any such hopes and Churchill quietly stepped down on 5 April 1955.[40] The ten years

ILLUSTRATION 2.1 *Churchill and Eden: The elder statesman and his successor. Prime Minister Winston Churchill and Foreign Secretary Anthony Eden in the United States, 5 January 1952. When Eden became foreign secretary in 1935, Churchill had written: 'Eden's appointment does not inspire me with confidence, I expect the greatness of his office will find him out.'*

since the Second World War had seen three British governments make a significant contribution to the construction of a viable anti-Soviet global alliance. The embrace of containment as a 'third way' between war and appeasement, while led by the United States, had been adopted with skill and alacrity by the British. In his last years as foreign secretary, Eden had demonstrated, by his adroit negotiating strategy, a degree of diplomatic competence that fully justified his reputation. Yet, the high-profile successes of Eden's diplomacy in the mid-1950s were, to some degree, misleading. Just as he was handing the premiership over to Eden, Churchill, at the end of one evening, had told his private secretary: 'I don't believe Anthony can do it.'[41] The challenges Britain was to face, with its international status ever more imperilled, called for skilled leadership. But, as the Conservative MP Walter Elliot perceptively observed upon the resignation of Churchill, Eden was 'a diplomat but Prime Ministers have to give orders'.[42] Eden nevertheless seemed at the height of his powers. This meant that, when it came, his fall from grace would be all the more tragic and dramatic.

CHAPTER THREE

'I have never thought Nasser a Hitler': Suez and the shadow of Munich

You may gain temporary appeasement by a policy of concession to violence, but you do not gain lasting peace that way. It is a grave delusion to suppose that you can.

ANTHONY EDEN, May 1938 [1]

All my life, I've been a man of peace, working for peace, striving for peace, negotiating for peace. I've been a League of Nations man and a United Nations man and I'm still the same man with the same convictions, the same devotion to peace. I couldn't be other even if I wished. But I'm utterly convinced that the action we have taken is right.

SIR ANTHONY EDEN, address to the nation, BBC, 3 November 1956

Sir Anthony Eden became prime minister on 6 April 1955. His elevation to the highest office was long overdue, as Eden had waited years for the aged Churchill to relinquish the reins of power.[2] In less than two years his career was in ruins.[3] As Munich destroyed Chamberlain, so Suez did for Eden. This was appropriate for they were the two most notoriously divisive episodes in the history of British foreign policy in the twentieth century. As D. R. Thorpe noted in 2006: '[T]he Suez Crisis . . . was, for the Fifties generation, what Munich had been for that of the Thirties, dividing families and crossing party lines.'[4] In the postwar era, the Suez affair of 1956 was the occasion when all of the appeasement chickens came home to roost with a vengeance.[5] Eden was widely thought (wrongly) to have resigned from Chamberlain's government over appeasement. Henceforth, Eden was inextricably identified with anti-appeasement (a stance popular with many young Conservative MPs who believed that 'their elders had lost their nerve' at Munich). As David Dutton noted: 'The lessons of the 1930s and their supposed application to later decades developed into a near obsession, and [Eden] bitterly assailed those who offered even a moderately charitable interpretation of the rationale behind appeasement'. Yet, Eden was a diplomat who believed in compromise and, prior to its being tainted by Munich, he had no problem with the word 'appeasement'. In 1933, he had told the Commons: 'We have to appreciate that the situation is that, unless, as the result of the Disarmament Conference, we can secure a Convention which all the nations will sign, we cannot secure for Europe that period of appeasement which it needs.'[6] Sir Alexander Cadogan even opined that Eden had been largely responsible for 'appeasement' by 'not reacting' to the re-militarization of the Rhineland in 1936. Eden's flaws remained largely hidden after 1945, and while a skilled diplomat, it was the attempt to morph into a warrior that lay at the root of the Suez disaster. The final crisis laid bare Eden's tortured character – which R. A. Butler summed up thus: 'Anthony's father was a mad baronet and his mother a very beautiful woman. That's Anthony – half mad baronet, half beautiful woman.'[7]

If we wish to draw parallels between Eden's undoing and the path trodden by the British governments of the 1930s, we might observe that the saga of Suez was German conscription, the Rhineland, the *Anschluß*, Munich and the occupation of Prague all rolled into one. What is certain is that, in the summer and autumn of 1956, Eden and his colleagues convinced themselves that they had to take a stand against Egypt's leader, President Gamal Abdel Nasser, over the Suez Canal. In 1952, Eden had advised his Cabinet colleagues: 'The basic assumption of this paper . . . is that steps must be taken to safeguard the free transit of the Suez Canal irrespective of whether or not current bilateral discussions with Egypt make headway and irrespective of the decision taken in regard to a Middle East Defence Organisation.'[8] In the 1950s, those in the Conservative Party who feared 'another Munich' believed that they had learned that appeasement could not possibly further the British interest. Chief among these were the members of the so-called Suez Group – a faction of Conservative MPs formed after the débâcles in Palestine (which ended in 1948)[9] and at Abadan in 1951.[10] In the latter case, despite the advice of the chiefs of staff that a quick and surgical military operation was both feasible and necessary,[11] the Attlee government had prevaricated and resorted to a legalistic insistence on Britain's rights and done no more than protest mildly.[12] Attlee later wrote that force would, no doubt, have been used in the past 'but would in the modern world have outraged opinion at home and abroad'.[13] Attlee's forecast, made in 1954, turned out to be very prescient.

The CIA-SIS arranged *coup d'état* in Iran in 1953, which overthrew the nationalist Prime Minister Mosaddeq, was very much to the taste of those who favoured no appeasement in the Middle East.[14] In Iran, a populist leader whose demands seemed outrageous had confronted the West and had been deposed by British and American power. Yet, and not for the first time, the British had initially viewed the Americans as naïve on the question of Mosaddeq's Iran. In September 1951, Herbert Morrison (Bevin's successor as foreign secretary)[15] had welcomed the fact that the United States was now interested in the Middle East 'even though the crudeness of American thinking had its embarrassments.'[16] The US Assistant Secretary of State George McGhee was accused of appeasement by elements in the Foreign Office (FO) who fretted that Washington had no conception of exactly what Mosaddeq's aggressive nationalism was all about.[17] The British, to be fair, had a point. McGhee was very much out of sympathy with the British, later criticizing them for their obstinacy and for the government's decision to leave key decisions in the hands of the Anglo-Iranian Oil Company.

> Anglo-Iranian was run by William Frasier, a Scotch *[sic]* accountant who didn't understand the modern world . . . [and his] failure to understand the political forces in Iran helped create a very difficult problem for them. The company and the U.K. faced the possibility of a grave loss at a time when they badly needed the income from Iranian oil; so they played their hand pretty close. They missed a great opportunity. We warned them that we were offering fifty-fifty. They could perhaps have had a settlement at fifty-fifty, but they wouldn't offer it.[18]

The morale of the British had been raised by Truman's replacement as president by Eisenhower in 1953. The British believed that they now had a staunch and loyal friend in the White House, a man who could be relied on to back their policies in Iran.[19] This misconception, along with the notion that Nasser would keep his word, would cost Eden dear.[20] Nevertheless, there were grounds for optimism. Even prior to the deposition of Mosaddeq, British economic muscle had yielded results: 'Britain warned the Iranians that their action would bring them nothing but bankruptcy, that they could not operate the refineries without British technical assistance and that they could not sell their oil without British tankers and marketing facilities. For the past year the British have been proving their point – with a vengeance.'[21] The lessons for anyone, and anywhere, else in the Middle East seemed clear: Britain would not tolerate any attempt to usurp its ascendancy. Yet, in a portent for the future and Nasser, the CIA noted that if Mosaddeq should succeed in overcoming the British sanctions against Iran's exporting of oil his 'prestige would be greatly enhanced'.[22] Nevertheless, even after the ousting of Mosaddeq, Eden remained convinced that the United States would play only a supporting role to the British in the Middle East.

With regard to Britain's position in Egypt, Eden was under pressure from many even in his own party including, worst of all, the prime minister. In 1953 Churchill, exasperated with what he saw as Eden's appeasement of Nasser, had exclaimed: 'he never knew ... that Munich was situated on the Nile'![23] In truth, Eden's negotiation of British withdrawal from the Canal Zone had been rendered long overdue by Churchill's lethargy. Churchill knew this, but he preferred to put it about that the idea of an agreement with Egypt was all Eden's doing, even telling the 1922 Committee 'I'm not sure I'm on our side!'.[24] Nevertheless, Eden, now backed by the Cabinet and a reassured and repentant Churchill,[25] commended the détente treaty with Egypt to the Commons on 29 July 1954 in masterly fashion. The Suez Group, frustrated and isolated, was rendered impotent.[26] Eden struck a statesmanlike pose.

> Everybody knows the history of our relations with the Arab States in recent years and that these have been largely bedevilled by the actions of Egypt, whose influence in this respect is very powerful. If we can improve our relations, it might be possible to do something to reduce in its turn tension between the Arab States and Israel and to try to obtain agreement and final peace. Truly, short of warlike action, I do not believe that it is possible to do anything effective in this particular situation unless we can reduce this tension between the Arab States and Israel.[27]

If the thorny problem of the Suez Canal had been addressed, the British government could concentrate on the Soviet threat. This would allow the British government to shift their diplomatic attention and over-stretched military resources away from Egypt. Jo Grimond, the Liberal MP, had sounded a note of caution: '[S]urely what we are faced with very often is not a world war or a hydrogen bomb war, but local aggression at secondhand such as we have seen in Indo-China and Korea – such as we may see in the Middle East. It is against that sort of attack that we have to provide defences just as much as for a full-scale world war with hydrogen bombs.'[28] Grimond was, alas, ignored. In October 1954, Britain and Egypt concluded the Suez Canal Base Agreement. This provided for the phased evacuation of British troops from the Suez base, to be completed within twenty months, Britain maintaining civilian workers in the zone and reserving the right to return until 1961.[29] In October 1955, six months after becoming prime minister, Eden confided to Cabinet that the importance of the reported Soviet bloc arms sales to Europe lay in their repercussions for the whole British position in the Middle East.

> Our interests in the Middle East [are] greater than those of the United States because of our dependence on Middle East oil, and our experience

was greater than theirs. We should not therefore allow ourselves to be restricted overmuch by reluctance to act without full American concurrence and support. We should frame our own policy in light of our interests in the area and get the Americans to support it to the extent we could induce them to do so. Our policy should be based on the need to help our acknowledged friends and allies, such as Iraq, and on the Trucial States whom our oil [supply] depended.

Eden saw the prevention of further Soviet penetration as vital and he did not see any advantage in bringing pressure to bear on the Nasser regime by economic threats or by 'obstructing Egyptian policies in regard to the [Aswan] High Dam'.[30] Eden had believed that his appeasement of Nasser would ensure his cooperation. Others were not so sure. Selwyn Lloyd, appointed foreign secretary in December 1955, later recalled: 'I felt that we probably had to go in the long run, but I would have preferred a much slower process.'[31] Such fears were well founded as Nasser came increasingly to be seen as the root of British troubles in the Middle East. After King Hussein of Jordan dismissed Sir John Glubb as the commander of the Jordanian Arab Legion Eden, convinced that Nasser had orchestrated this humiliation, asserted: 'It's either him or us, don't forget that.'[32] Henceforward, Eden's policy often seemed to be somewhat detached from reality. In this he was hardly alone and French Premier Guy Mollet told Eden that France faced a Soviet-backed threat from Islam: 'All this [is] the work of Nasser, just as Hitler's policy [was] written down in *Mein Kampf*. Nasser [has] the ambition to recreate the conquests of Islam. But his present position is largely due to the policy of the West in building up and flattering him.'[33] At the same time, the United States was growing weary of the Egyptian leader's bombastic style. Nasser's official recognition of Red China (on 16 May 1956) greatly angered a US government that was also increasingly convinced that the Aswan project was beyond Egypt's capabilities.[34] In March 1956 Eisenhower had already confidently predicted: 'If Egypt finds herself . . . with no ally in sight except Soviet Russia, she would very quickly get sick of the prospect and would join us in the search for a just and decent peace in the region.'[35] Convinced that Nasser was not worth the expense, the United States withdrew all American financial aid for the Aswan project on 19 July (with the British tamely following suit). On 26 July Nasser nationalized the Suez Canal. The die was cast. One member of the Suez Group later compared Eden's failure with that of Chamberlain. Nasser could not be trusted any more than Hitler, and Eden's policy was, thus, in ruins.[36] Eden now saw matters in terms of a re-run of the 1930s.

There has been an increasing tendency to condone breaches of international agreement. To take the easy way, to put off decisions, to fail even to record a protest when international undertaking are broken on which the ink is scarcely dry, can lead only one way. It is all so much more difficult to do later on, and so we come full circle. The insidious appeal of appeasement leads to deadly reckoning.[37]

Eden's hard line during the Suez Crisis was prompted, at least in part, by the actions of US policy makers who had initially encouraged him in his appeasement of Egypt (and who had themselves then broken off aid to Nasser for his Aswan High Dam). Alas, the same US policy makers later refused to back Anglo-French military action against Nasser's Egypt. It seemed that Chamberlain had been right when he wrote (in 1937): 'One should count on nothing from the Americans except words.'[38] US policy makers were nevertheless well aware of the dilemma in which Nasser's actions had placed Eden and his government. In September 1956 the CIA reported that Anglo-French military action was, at that time, unlikely although both countries were militarily prepared and politically resolute.

> The majority of the British cabinet, especially Prime Minister Eden, and virtually all the members of the French cabinet, are convinced that the elimination of Nasser is essential to the preservation of vital Western interests in the Middle East and North Africa. They are gravely concerned with the dangers of *appeasement* and . . . believe that forceful action against Nasser offers the only real hope of arresting the decline of their positions.

While the CIA report concluded that the UK and France would not act without US support, the truth was that the Suez Group was remorselessly driving Eden towards war. The Conservative MP Nigel Nicolson feared that any attempt at moderation 'will mean a row like Munich'.[39] Such tensions naturally intensified Labour's desire to make political capital out of the Tory 'appeasement complex'. The MP Sydney Silverman taunted one Conservative opponent thus: 'Does the hon. and gallant Member attach no significance at all to the fact that those who, in 1935, took the view of appeasement which he did not take then but does take now, are the very people who think the Government today are wrong, whereas those who supported appeasement in 1935 are the very ones who now think that the Government are right?'[40] Yet, as Douglas Hurd asserts, Eden certainly allowed his memories of the 1930s to 'distort his judgement' and caused him to attack Egypt in order to 'humiliate and overthrow Nasser without any serious concept of what or who would take his place'.[41] Eden's reaction against appeasement meant that he was largely impervious to the fact that, while the British public deeply disapproved of Nasser's action, there was no majority in favour of military action.[42] But nothing succeeds like success and, since public opinion is volatile, and was particularly so over Suez,[43] the divisions in British society would have mattered less if Eden had taken military action immediately after the Canal's nationalization, and ensured that when military action came it would be swift and decisive. In the event he did neither.

Although the invoking of Munich during Suez is usually associated with Eden it was, in fact, his domestic opponents who first made such references.[44] On 2 August Hugh Gaitskell, the Labour Party leader, saw things as being 'all very familiar. It is exactly the same that we encountered from Mussolini and Hitler in those years before the war.'[45] But the Labour Party soon backed away from such rhetoric and placed its faith in an international settlement. The international London 22-Power Conference, held between 16 and 23 August, proposed an International Board to run the Canal. Nasser, alas, dismissed this proposal out of hand. Eden told the Commons that 'Colonel Nasser rejected the proposals without weighing their merits or listening to reason'.[46] Eden's options were, nevertheless, limited (not least due to the military unpreparedness of the British and the French).[47]

Although Eden was correct when, on 13 September, he made the point that 'it was the Leader of the Opposition who first made the comparison [between the current situation and the 1930s]',[48] the domestic consensus was evaporating. The Labour MP Alfred Robens rejected Eden's invocation of the 1930s, stating that 'the comparison between Hitler and Nasser as such, or between Germany and Egypt, is obviously not a fair one'.[49] Labour's faith in 'internationalism' (and in the UN in particular) unfortunately ignored the fact that the USSR would inevitably veto any meaningful indictment of Nasser. In an attempt to demonstrate the exhaustion of diplomatic options the British government duly went to the United Nations. Nothing was achieved.[50] Despite Nasser's intransigence, the British followed the US lead and supported a proposal, made by US Secretary of State John Foster Dulles, for a Suez Canal Users' Association (SCUA). This, too, foundered.[51] Lord Salisbury, the lord president of Council, summed up British frustration when he told Cabinet: 'The lessons of the 1930s should not be forgotten. Experience with Italy and Germany had surely shown that if the encroachments of a dictator were not checked at the outset, when comparatively little strength was needed to check them, the ultimate reckoning involved a far greater convulsion and much greater sacrifice.'[52] Aware of the numerous charges of weakness that had been made against his person in recent years by the Suez Group and Churchill, Eden himself obviously regarded the historical lessons of the 1930s as a 'trump card' that he might play in moments of extremity. But Eden had staked all on what he saw as a determination to avoid the mistakes of the 1930s.

> Of course, there are those who say that we should not be justified and are not justified in reacting vigorously unless Colonel Nasser commits some further act of aggression. That was the argument used in the 1930s to justify every concession that was made to the dictators. It has not been my experience that dictators are deflected from their purpose

because others affect to ignore it. This reluctance to face reality led to the subjugation of Europe and to the Second World War. We must not help to reproduce, step by step, the history of the thirties. We have to prove ourselves wiser this time, and to check aggression by the pressure of international opinion, if possible; but, if not, by other means before it has grown to monstrous proportions.[53]

The 'lesson' of history at such junctures was that resolution was all and Eden was, therefore, suitably unambiguous in his language: '[T]he Government are not prepared to embark on a policy of abject appeasement – nor, I think, would the House – or most of it – ask them to, because the consequences of such a policy are known to us.'[54] In fact, Eden's rhetoric was often rather more conciliatory than it might have been (not least as could rely on his own party's right-wingers and the press to make a more hysterical case for him). Nevertheless, Eden was unwavering in his insistence upon the necessity of avoiding any repetition of past mistakes.

I do not think I have ever inflicted a quotation of my own upon the House, but I am going to do so tonight, from something which I said when I parted with my Cabinet colleagues in 1938, because I think it still applies . . . What I said then was this: 'I do not believe that we can make progress in European appeasement' – Europe is still there – '. . . if we allow the impression to gain currency abroad that we yield to constant pressure . . . progress depends above all on the temper of the nation, and that temper must find expression in a firm spirit. That spirit, I am confident, is there. Not to give voice to it is, I believe, fair neither to this country nor to the world.'[55] I do not think that that is menacing language in the temper of the situation in which we are now. It is what many of us feel. The majority of the country did not agree with me then. My right hon. Friend the Member for Woodford (Sir W. Churchill) agreed with me, and he tells me he agrees with me now. But we have, I believe, all of us in all parties learned our lesson since then. Do not let us, I implore the House and I implore the country, unlearn that lesson now.[56]

Harold Macmillan, the chancellor of the exchequer and a hardliner over Suez, angrily noted the defeatism in the Commons, even among 'a good many Tories, mostly young and mostly sons of "Munichites"' who had begun to 'rat' on the government.[57] Such thinking reflected the manner in which the moral rejection of appeasement had, once again, obliterated the necessity of turning to the ugly pragmatism of compromise as an option in an international crisis. By the early autumn of 1956, Eden and the war party were the ones driving government policy. Macmillan noted that about a third of the Conservatives in the Commons were opposed to using force, even as a 'last resort'. But he cheerfully noted that the 'P.M. seemed, however quite determined. It was 1938 all over again, and he could not be a party to it.'[58] The heady brew of pride, hurt and indignity in the government encouraged a unilateralism (disguised as resolution) that would have made Disraeli blush. One of Eden's greatest miscalculations over Suez was the attitude and actions of the United States in the event of a decision on the part of the British and the French to undertake military action. Alas, the patronizing British attitude towards the United States, and to which Eden was particularly prone, was one of the main reasons for this. The influence of what had come to be known as the 'Greeks and Romans' model[59] is clear in the language employed by Eden in his advice to the Cabinet. 'Our aim should be to persuade the United States to assume the real burdens in such organisations, while retaining for ourselves as much political control – and hence prestige and world influence – as we can.' This unfortunate attitude was even less forgivable in light of the fact that Eden had been so very accurate with regard to the attitude of the policy-making elite of the United States, and British need for Washington's support.

> [In the United States] distrust of the British and fear of becoming an instrument to prop up a declining British Empire are still strong. (This is truer among Republicans than Democrats, but we – must-clearly prepare ourselves to deal with either Government.) As regards the United Kingdom part, a policy of this kind will only be successful with the United States in so far as we are able to demonstrate that we are making the maximum possible effort ourselves, and the more gradually and inconspicuously we can transfer the real burdens from our own to American shoulders, the less damage we shall do to our position and influence in the world.[60]

Eden thus recognized the British dependence upon American goodwill and power while simultaneously thinking he could manipulate the US government. Eden (the learned Greek) resorted to lecturing Eisenhower (the barbarian Roman) on the parallels with the 1930s. The prime minister thus warned the president on 27 July 1956: 'If we do not [take a firm stand against Nasser], our influence and yours throughout the Middle East will, we are convinced, be finally destroyed.'[61] On 1 August Eden informed the president: 'I have never thought Nasser a Hitler, he has no warlike people behind him. But the parallel with Mussolini is close. Neither of us can forget the lives and treasure he cost us before he was finally dealt with.'[62] Henry Kissinger later reflected that when Eden and Mollet 'nailed their flag to the anti-appeasement mast' it should have been obvious that they would not go back. 'They belonged to the generation . . . that viewed appeasement as a cardinal sin, and Munich as a permanent reproach. Comparing a leader to Hitler or even to Mussolini meant that they had moved beyond then possibility of compromise. They would either have to prevail or lose all.'[63] Eden thus rejected any idea of compromise and, instead, looked to Britain's 'finest hour' for inspiration as the country's situation was 'certainly the most hazardous that has faced our country since 1940'.[64] In an attempt to bring the United States onside, Eden paired the appeasement of the 1930s with the contemporary Communist threat: 'There is no doubt in our minds that Nasser, whether he likes it or not, is now effectively in Russian hands, just as Mussolini was in Hitler's. It would be as ineffective to show weakness to Nasser now in order to placate him as it was to show weakness to Mussolini.'[65] At home, Eden's appeasement analogies were too much for Labour's Richard Crossman, a sceptical opponent of Eden's reputation as an anti-appeaser of long-standing.[66] Crossman railed against 'the Prime Minister's dangerous mistake of drawing political parallels . . . I think that Nasser in certain ways is a dangerous man, but if we are to have parallels we ought to have them in some relation to perspective'. Crossman, warming to his theme, then deployed his famously caustic wit:

> It is quite ridiculous to compare Nasser with either Hitler or Mussolini, and those who do so are rather like the person who supposed that Goliath thought he was the fellow who was in danger and the likely victim of aggression and got it into his head that David, with his sling, was a dangerous little fellow and that one had really got to deal with him before he brought his sling into operation.[67]

Eden was not to be deflected and the military option to topple Nasser was embraced. After the Anglo-French attack on Egypt, agreed upon after secret collusion with Israel (which had already initiated hostilities),[68] began on 31 October 1956, Eden saw history being invoked *against* him. The *Daily Mirror* thundered:

> Tory spokesmen in the Commons and some Tory newspapers claim that Eden's action against Egypt is a triumph for the rule of law. That is claptrap. *The truth is this: There is NO treaty, NO international authority, NO moral sanction for this desperate action.* This is Eden's War. Unlike some newspapers which are whooping with joy at this grave news, the Mirror has no shameful record of appeasement to live down.[69]

Scenting blood, Labour MPs made comparisons between the Anglo-French action in Egypt and the contemporary Soviet crushing of the Hungarian Rising. Arthur Henderson told the Commons on 5 November: 'The action of Her Majesty's Government in using force against the people and Government of Egypt offered a direct encouragement to the Government of Russia to employ the brutal force that they did yesterday in Budapest to suppress the struggle of the Hungarian people for freedom and independence.'[70] The Anglo-French intervention in Egypt may not have precipitated the invasion of Hungary, but it certainly heightened the diplomatic problem of condemning Soviet action for the United States

ILLUSTRATION 3.1 *The empires strike back: Port Said under Allied attack, 1956.*
'What should we do? We put the matter to the Security Council. Should we have left
it to them? Should we have been content to wait and see whether they would act?
How long would this have taken? And where would the forest fire have spread in the
meantime?' Sir Anthony Eden, broadcast to the nation, 3 November 1956.

and the West.[71] Although recent scholarship demonstrates that the Soviets
would have crushed the Hungarians regardless of events on the Middle
East,[72] the charges against Eden and Mollet remain amongst the most
potent of the popular myths surrounding Suez. Yet, even as the 'Old
World' of the British and French empires sought to topple Nasser, the
'New World' of Eisenhower and Dulles brought the whole Suez adventure
to a shuddering halt by targeting British economic weakness.[73] Although,
Eisenhower and Dulles later regretted their hamstringing of their British
ally, this was of little comfort to Eden – who was to leave office a sick
man in January 1957.[74] Upset by American 'betrayal', Eden continued to
invoke the lessons of the past to the end. On 5 November Eden wrote to
Eisenhower stating:

> I am convinced that, if we had allowed things to drift, everything would
> have gone from bad to worse. Nasser would have become a kind of
> Moslem Mussolini and our friends in Iraq, Jordan, Saudi Arabia and
> even Iran would gradually have been brought down. His efforts would

have spread westwards, and Libya and all North Africa would have been brought under his control.[75]

Richard Crossman once wrote that '[m]emory is always an improvement on the facts, a story with a moral'.[76] While this was certainly true, the events of 1956 did real damage to the respectability of invoking Munich and the appeasement of the 1930s as an absolute evil in order to justify policy. Donald Watt later concluded that Suez, 'besides the personal disaster which overtook Lord Avon's career', had resulted in a change of attitude which was 'to discredit the conduct of foreign policy by the light of historical analogy in Britain'.[77] Such a shift in attitudes to the 'memory' of Munich and the 1930s undoubtedly facilitated the rise of the 'Revisionist' school in the study of Chamberlainite Appeasement. Of course, as with Chamberlain and Munich, charges of appeasement did not really hurt Eden until his agreement with Nasser was invalidated by the Egyptian leader's actions. The whole picture changed when Nasser nationalized the Suez Canal in July 1956. Hitler's violation of Munich enraged and undermined Chamberlain. It also spurred him to action. Nasser's nationalization of the Suez Canal did the same to Eden. As Robert Skidelsky later observed, 'for a mad intoxicating moment, Talleyrand saw himself as Napoleon'.[78] Yet, despite the disaster that overtook the British, Harold Macmillan remained defiant.

> Every interest of mine, every private, every personal interest that I had, would be in favour of leading me to oppose what we have done. Why, then, have I supported it? I will tell the House. All my interests would have been to follow what we used to call a policy of appeasement. Why have I not followed that? I will tell the House frankly and sincerely. It is because I have seen it all happen before.[79]

After the failure of the Suez adventure Eden continued to justify his actions by recourse to the lessons of 1930s. With his career in ruins, Eden now sought his place in history by asserting that no one would ever know what he had achieved by fighting Nasser: 'I noticed that the *Washington Post* commented that I had learnt too well the lessons of Munich. I feel quite sure that if anyone had attempted to scotch Hitler & Mussolini early in their careers, there would have been plenty to proclaim that they did not deserve it. It would have been better if the attempt had been made all the same.'[80] Harold Macmillan, who would have to pick up the pieces after Eden was gone, argued that 'we have stopped the small war, which might have led to the big war . . . a third world war'.

> History alone will prove whether what we did was right or wrong. Ministers, if they are fortunate, can go through a period of office with the ordinary debates and the ordinary discussions – and they are plentiful, and

quite agreeable – and never be faced with decisions like these, but when we are faced with them there are only two courses: one is to run away from them, and the other is to make the right decisions. I am sincerely convinced, having seen this happen twice in my lifetime, that the events of this period may prevent a third disaster coming to the world.[81]

Having celebrated the Sèvres Protocol, the secret agreement to attack Egypt, as 'the highest form of statesmanship', Eden was similarly unrepentant.[82] But, hubris aside, one of the obvious lessons to be drawn from Suez was that international isolation was to be avoided at all costs. After all, even Lord Salisbury's last government had concluded that 'Splendid Isolation' was too precarious (and this, around 1900, was at a time when Britain was far stronger). Eden's failure to understand the Americans had led to disaster at Suez. Of Enoch Powell, Eden reflected:

> Ah, Enoch, dear Enoch! He once said something to me I never understood. He said, 'You know, I've told you all I know about housing, and you can make your speech accordingly. Can I talk to you about something that you know all about and I know nothing? I want to tell you that in the Middle East our great enemies are the Americans'. You know, I had no idea what he meant. I do now.[83]

Senior figures in the British military, never entirely happy with their role in Eden's adventure, did not shrink from drawing lessons. The commander of the Suez intervention (Operation *Musketeer*), General Sir Charles Keightley, opined: 'The one overriding lesson of the Suez operations is that world opinion is now an absolute principle of war and must be treated as such. However successful the pure military operations may be they will fail in their object unless national, Commonwealth and Western World opinion is sufficiently on our side.' Above all, it was concluded that the ditching of the alliance with the United States was simply not an option for *any* British government.

> [I]t was the action[s] of the [US] which really defeated us in attaining our object. Her action in the United Nations is well known, but her move of the 6th Fleet, which is not so generally known, was a move which endangered the whole of our relations with that country. It is not difficult to appreciate the effect of the shooting down of a United States aircraft or the sinking of a United States submarine, but both these might easily have happened if Egypt had obtained certain practical support from outside which she tried to get or our Commanders had not shown patience and care of the highest order . . . Conversely a united Anglo-American position [over Suez] would have assured a complete success of all our political objects with the minimum of military effort . . . [therefore although the] achievement of this is a political matter but the effects on military operations are vital.[84]

The old proverb 'The road to hell is paved with good intentions' is insufficient explanation for Suez – even when added to a catalogue of Eden's shortcomings. The central causes of the Suez disaster were myriad but the pressures on policy makers caused by the legacies of appeasement were central to many of the miscalculations made by decision makers between July and November 1956. If – in the light of the experience of the 1930s – we take anti-appeasement as being a good thing, and we take the professions of the central protagonists at face value, this was rarely so true as was the case during the Suez affair of 1956. This does not, of course, excuse any of the central protagonists in this sorry saga. Typifying the disgust of many of the old anti-Munich Establishment figures was Harold Nicolson, who thundered in his diary:

> The analogy with the Munich crisis is curiously close. Even as people then said, 'Chamberlain has saved us from war', now people say, 'Eden has saved us from war', forgetting that we have been humiliated in the face of the world and broken our word. The sad thing is that whereas at the time of Munich, we who opposed Chamberlain were proved right in six months, it will never become utterly apparent how bad Eden's action was.[85]

In truth, the British people preferred to think of Suez as an aberration. A. J. P. Taylor later reflected of the whole affair: 'The moral for British governments is clear. Like most respectable people, they will make poor criminals and had better stick to respectability. They will not be much good at anything else.'[86]

In undertaking the path they took in 1956, Eden and the British government had convinced itself that it was right, not least because it was repudiating appeasement. This was an act of self-delusion. It was also a grave miscalculation. As Hans J. Morgenthau has written:

> We cannot conclude from the good intentions of a statesman that his foreign policies will be either morally praiseworthy or politically successful. Judging his motives, we can say that he will not intentionally pursue policies that are morally wrong, but we can say nothing about the probability of their success. If we want to know the moral and political qualities of his actions, we must know them, not his motives. How often have statesmen been motivated by the desire to improve the world, and ended by making it worse? And how often have they sought one goal, and ended by achieving something they neither expected nor desired?[87]

In 1986, Kenneth Morgan reflected that 'Anthony Eden's career was the supreme personal tragedy of post-war British politics'. In the 1930s 'he established a rare charisma as the *jeune* premier of the League of Nations at Geneva who apparently resigned as Foreign Secretary in protest at Britain's failure to stand up to the European dictators. During the war, he emerged as an international diplomat of the first rank.' Between 1951 and 1955, he was a foreign secretary 'of distinguished achievement'. But his time as prime minister was 'brief and inglorious', culminating with 'the utter debacle and national humiliation of Suez'. After this, 'Eden's reputation, especially in his chosen field of foreign affairs, was totally discredited. There had been no real recovery. Eden had been raised up and struck down with classical finality.'[88] Eden had determined to live up his (somewhat misleading) image as an anti-appeaser, had reacted to the forces in British life let loose and a paradigm rampant since the Nazi occupation of Prague on 15 March 1939. Yet, ironically, his opponents used the same rhetoric against him that he had done for his opponents in 1940. Michael Foot, now in cooperation with Mervyn Jones, indicted the government as the 'Guilty Men' thesis was resurrected: and this time, of course, Eden was a central figure amongst the guilty[89] (although the obvious party political bias of the *Guilty Men, 1957* lessened its impact).[90] The recognition of Cato's longevity even led to attempts by supporters of Eden's Suez policy to seek to emulate its success. One such attempt was made by Frank Verity whose polemic sought to demonstrate the disgraceful failures of leading figures in the Labour Party ('Britain's Left-wing politicians [are] the Guilty Men of Suez'). Verity left the reader in no doubt that 'Nasser is Guilty Man of Suez No. 1'. And, in opposing Nasser, 'Once again' the British had 'done the world a service'.[91] Such attacks did little to rescue the government's reputation and did not prevent others on the Left seeking to make capital at the expense of the Tories. In another polemic Paul Johnson wrote:

> It is possible that . . . as events proved the fallacies of the Munich policy, Eden reproached himself for not opposing it more actively. In this he had a great deal in common with other Tory politicians. Munich had left a scar on the Tory Party, a scar which will not heal until a new generation takes over. Many of its members, believing that the Second World War could have been prevented if Britain had opposed the dictators earlier, vowed that their party would never again be guilty of weakness. Eden was foremost among them. Gradually they succumbed to what might be called a 'Munich psychosis', with a resultant tendency to draw false analogies from contemporary facts.[92]

Yet, scar or no scar, the Conservative Party knew how to maintain a façade of unity and absolute firmness in the face of external scrutiny. This fitted together with the worldview of the FO. The pragmatic tradition and the belief in the essential rectitude of the British diplomacy would have allowed for nothing else.

CHAPTER FOUR

'I will be no Mr. Chamberlain': Harold Macmillan and Berlin, 1958–62

Yesterday . . . was the anniversary of the 1st war . . . from which fatal
date spring all our troubles – the beginning of the end of Empire's
supremacy; the predominance of the White man in the world. From this
date began the end of the British Empire & the capture of the greatest
Euro/ Asian country – Russia – by the strange doctrines of a German
Jew Intellectual – Karl Marx. Happily we did not realise all
this when we were young.

HAROLD MACMILLAN, 5 August 1961[1]

In all of the shapers of postwar British foreign policy and appeasement
no figure is as complex as that of Eden's successor, Harold Macmillan.
Macmillan's attitude towards appeasement was rooted in the history of
his own times, as a participant in the greatest cataclysm of the modern
age, the Great War.[2] In the 1930s he had risked his own political career
by opposition to his own party hierarchy over Chamberlain's policy of
appeasement.[3] To his own mind Macmillan could never be labelled as an
appeaser because of his steadfast opposition to the Chamberlainite variety.[4]
The Macmillan premiership saw many of the bit-part political players of
Munich at the height of their powers. For, in addition to Macmillan, Rab
Butler was home secretary and Lord Home was foreign secretary (after
1960). In 1961, Anthony Eden wrote:

The Munich Agreement left a trauma from which hardly anyone in Britain over forty years of age may hope to be free, no matter whether he then, or since, thought the agreement good or bad, necessary or avoidable, a gainer of time or a loser of opportunity . . . The passions have died. Although the debate lives on the disputants can by now share some common ground on the lessons Munich taught.[5]

It was against this backdrop, that Macmillan's policy during the Berlin Wall Crisis of 1958–62[6] drew many to charge him with appeasement. Macmillan, although an opponent of Munich, was also haunted by a fear of war and believed that the best way for it to be avoided was for British 'pragmatism' to guide a path through the international crises afflicting the globe. As a corollary of this, Macmillan believed the 'Special Relationship' with the United States was the key to Britain's international position. Following the Suez debacle Macmillan, drawing the opposite conclusion from his French counterparts, believed that the closer his government was to United States, the better for his international position. Macmillan therefore steered his government rapidly back into the American orbit.[7] Macmillan handled this skilfully and the restoration of the 'Special Relationship' meant that Britain's international position improved rapidly during 1957.[8] During the presidency of John F. Kennedy (1961–3) the relationship reached new heights, which Macmillan utilized to good effect for his diplomacy over Berlin.[9]

In common with Neville Chamberlain, Macmillan saw the role of peacemaker as being the best way for Britain to stay in the front rank of global powers while, simultaneously, assuring his own role in history. The Geneva summit of 1955 was, thus, 'never far from his thoughts'.[10] Macmillan's Foreign Secretary Selwyn Lloyd remarked: 'Summiting is an occupational weakness of any incumbent of No. 10 . . . Since the war Winston was the principle advocate. Eden disapproved when Foreign Secretary, but not when P.M.'[11] Home Secretary Rab Butler recalled that Macmillan, like Churchill, suffered from a surfeit of enthusiasm for the possibilities afforded by 'Summitry'.[12] That the central issues to be pursued were Berlin and Germany was of no surprise given that, as long ago as 1946, Macmillan had warned: 'Unless an accommodation can be found . . . between the eastern and western hemispheres, you can have no sound policy regarding Germany.' By the time Macmillan became prime minister, matters had deteriorated into stalemate as West German Chancellor Adenauer, maintaining an uncompromising *Politik der Stärke* ('Policy of Strength'), insisted that East Germany must not to be recognized and that the West refuse to negotiate over Berlin.[13]

In the late 1950s Soviet leader Nikita Khrushchev, following the logic of Stalinist statecraft, sought to place pressure on the West by means of Berlin[14] (stating, in typically crude terms: 'Berlin is the testicles of the West. Every time I want to make the West scream, I squeeze on Berlin').[15] In November 1958, Khrushchev threatened to sign a separate peace treaty with the East

Germans and hand all access rights to West Berlin over to them.[16] While this deadline passed without incident, and Khrushchev failed to implement his threats, Macmillan remained vocal in calling for negotiations over Berlin.[17] Macmillan was not as blatant in his 'appeasement' as his 1930s predecessors but he was prepared to conciliate East Germany and the Soviet Union as he feared that any escalation could have catastrophic implications. Philip de Zulueta, Macmillan's private secretary, asserted:

> The rigid Allied position is dangerous because it is unreal; a nuclear war over Berlin would be absurd . . . But if we were to say this or even indicate our desire for realism there would be a real danger of the other allies blaming us for weakness. We may have to accept such blame but should only do so in the last resort. We have, therefore, two objectives here: (i) To prevent a war over Berlin, (ii) To prevent our allies blaming us for any settlement worse (or alleged to be worse) than the status quo.[18]

Macmillan told Eisenhower that 'World War I – the war which nobody wanted – came because of the failure of the leaders at the time to meet at the Summit'. When Eisenhower pointed out that summitry (presumably a pointed reference to Munich) prior to the Second World War had been employed (and failed), Macmillan stated that that had been the exception as 'we were dealing with a mad man [in] Hitler' and war was therefore unavoidable.[19] That said, and personalities aside, nuclear weapons had transformed the utility of force. Macmillan believed that the Soviets were rational, if undemocratic, and he was insistent that they shared his fear of a major,[20] a view shared by the US State Department and Eisenhower.[21] The American president, who had opposed dropping the atom bomb on Japan in 1945,[22] thus made common cause with Macmillan in seeking to ensure that Berlin must not become a *causus belli*.[23]

Macmillan was well aware that it was difficult to negotiate when under pressure 'as we were then accused of "appeasement"'.[24] It was, however, certainly the case that Macmillan was no great fan of the Germans. And such sentiments were shared by many of his countrymen and women. In 1959, the US ambassador in Bonn noted: 'The Germans, so desirous of being liked, have realised that the British have long memories, and ineradicable pride and prejudice.'[25] This only reinforced Adenauer's belief that the British, possessed of an 'appeasement spirit',[26] were preparing to 'sell out' German interests to the Communists.[27] President Eisenhower noted Adenauer's 'psychopathic fear of British weakness'[28] (a fear shared, moreover, by US Secretary of State John Foster Dulles and the Joint Chiefs of Staff).[29] The US embassy in London was more sympathetic, arguing that 'there is no parallel between emphasis given by Macmillan to negotiation with Soviet and Chamberlain's efforts of "appeasement"'.[30] Macmillan himself stated: 'We want a negotiated settlement because we do *not* believe that the allies will face war over . . . Berlin. However, we must not get into the position we got into at Munich. I will be no Mr. Chamberlain . . . What would be the worst thing for the West would be a humiliating climb-down *after* talking big.'[31] There was something in this and Anthony Nicholls has argued that Macmillan's policy was designed to keep control of events and retained an element of flexibility throughout lest diplomatic intransigence should lead to disaster.[32] Such arguments were strengthened in 2011 when newly released documents revealed that Adenauer, too, regarded West Berlin's position as untenable and had approached the US government, before the construction of the Wall, to propose 'swapping' West Berlin for other parts of East Germany.[33]

In February 1959, Macmillan went to Moscow where he demonstrated a willingness to discuss proposals involving East Germany, the Oder-Neiße line and Berlin that were, to say the least, far short of the agreed minimum Western positions. Macmillan did not reveal, even to Cabinet, the level of British appeasement that he justified by asserting that the Berlin Crisis was 'likely to compel the West to give increasing de facto recognition of the DDR'.[34] In the Commons, Macmillan misleadingly declared: '[O]ur purpose was not to negotiate. It was to try and seek a better understanding of our respective views . . . The main point is that . . . we reached agreement that the great issues which separate East and West must be settled by negotiation.'[35] The prime minister nevertheless remained vulnerable (and sensitive) to charges of appeasement. In the House of Commons, one opponent woundingly asserted:

> On his return from Moscow, the Prime Minister went round the capitals of the West trying, apparently, to mend the broken fences, but, judging from the foreign press, these visits were not a great success. The veritable 'giant of the Free World' . . . appeared more gigantic at home than abroad, more gigantic in the columns of the Tory Press than in those of the Press of Europe, where he was depicted, and I understand was recently described at a conference of Conservative women, as a 'man of Munich'.[36]

Possessed of a strong martyr complex, Macmillan hoped that the endurance of such abuse would be a price worth paying if war was avoided and if matters were settled peacefully. But the fates were against him.

The failure of the Paris Summit in May 1960[37] was a disaster for Macmillan personally, and for British foreign policy in general.[38] An embittered Macmillan concluded that matters were now 'pretty hopeless',[39] as '[a]nyone who talks sense is called a coward and a traitor'.[40] In any case Macmillan rejected the portrayal of his policy as appeasement because, to his mind, that would have been unpopular. And Macmillan's enthusiasm for negotiation arose from his fixation with public opinion[41] (and peacemaking undoubtedly played well at home and contributed to his attaining an absolute majority of 100 in the General Election of 1959).[42] Macmillan was right in

ILLUSTRATION 4.1 *Western powers' summit conference, final session, Palais de l'Élysée, Paris, 21 December 1959. (l-r) Prime Minister Harold Macmillan, President Dwight D. Eisenhower, President Charles de Gaulle and Chancellor Konrad Adenauer. '[T]he Americans have moved from their rigid position and are ready to consider various plans for the future of Berlin wh[ich] they were unwilling to discuss some time ago.' Macmillan diary entry, 20 December 1959.*

recognizing that there existed, in Anglo-American policy-making circles at least, a consensus that Soviet restrictions upon East Berliners did not warrant a war.[43] Macmillan made clear to Dulles that he was determined that there would not be a war over whether it was Soviet or GDR personnel who manned the access routes to West Berlin.[44] For him, as he noted in his diary, a war over the issue of whether it is 'USSR or GDR police or customs officials [who] issue the necessary permits'[45] was simply unthinkable.

After January 1961, the administration of John F. Kennedy was even closer to Macmillan's thinking than Eisenhower's had been[46] and the new president conceded: 'On Berlin, we have no bargaining position.'[47] This was serious if, as former secretary of state Dean Acheson predicted, the 'Soviets would press the issue of Berlin this year'.[48] Acheson had thus recommended that the United States declare a national emergency and be placed on a war footing.[49] Although Kennedy did not implement all of the recommendations,[50] he initiated sufficient of them to alarm London (which had regarded Acheson's proposals as 'ostentatious' and 'threatening').[51]

The fact that the defence of West Berlin would involve nuclear weapons was of particular concern to both Kennedy and Macmillan.[52] Macmillan had been told that 'purely military arguments for more conventional forces in Europe are almost certainly invalid. If the Soviets wish, they can outfight us conventionally, and then we should still be faced with the decision whether to initiate a nuclear war.'[53] Articles in the British press alerted the general public to the danger (especially when the likes of Field Marshal Lord Montgomery set out matters in stark terms).[54] Sir Evelyn Shuckburgh, assistant secretary-general of NATO, thus asserted: '[W]e must work out a basis for negotiation because in none of the countries of the Alliance will public opinion be prepared to face preparations for a major war unless there has been some sort of negotiation.'[55]

Although Macmillan subscribed to the notion that war had broken out accidentally in 1914,[56] he was also a member of what was often termed the 'A. J. P. Taylor School of History', seeing malevolent continuity as the central characteristic of Germany history.[57] (And Macmillan believed himself to represent the 'man-in-the-street' in this matter.)[58] Macmillan's worldview was, not unnaturally, informed by history and personal experience.[59] This made him essentially anti-German, despite the reality of Cold War alignments.[60] Lord Home, Macmillan's foreign secretary after 1960, similarly perceived the Germans to be 'tiresome [and] over-sensitive'.[61] Resentful of West German economic success,[62] Macmillan expressed reservations about fighting for West Berlin: 'Do you want the British to go to war for two million of the people we twice fought wars against and who almost destroyed us?'[63] In any case, '[i]f nuclear war takes place over Berlin, we shall all be dead, or nearly all. Therefore, whether we die in bankruptcy or affluence is of minor importance.'[64]

Macmillan had long since opted for a policy of inaction, believing it wise to placate Soviet grievances instead of risking war.[65] The prime minister believed that this could be attained because Khrushchev, unlike Hitler, genuinely wanted a settlement.[66] The prime minister, encouraged by reports that the Soviet leader shared his enthusiasm for peace,[67] therefore pursued a settlement with unseemly haste. Sir Frank Roberts (British ambassador in Moscow, 1960–2) affirmed that the Soviet Union's primary goal was to avoid armed conflict with the West,[68] and echoed Macmillan by asserting that Germany was seen by Moscow as the only real obstacle to détente.[69] Thus, 'behind his tough talk, Khrushchev might now be turning increasingly to the idea of serious negotiation'.[70]

If, indeed, Khrushchev and the Soviet leadership were genuinely seeking to take active measures to avoid a war the main danger of war would arise from a miscalculation or a misperception. It is here that Macmillan's take on the 'July Crisis' of 1914 came into its own as a *raison d'être* for the contemporary policy of avoiding an accidental war.[71] Macmillan did not 'want to get "morally" committed to foolish and dangerous plans'[72] by means of rigid defence plans that would set off a chain reaction (in the manner of the alliance system in 1914). In short, there would be no nuclear 'war by timetable' over Berlin. To ensure this, Macmillan recognized that the United

States must be brought onside.[73] Since Britain no longer enjoyed the kind of freedom of action that had been possible at its zenith in the mid-nineteenth century,[74] Macmillan warned that 'Britain – with all her experience – has neither the economic nor military power to take the leading role'.[75] Thus, '[t]he policies and personality of a President of the United States today are of deep importance to every Government'.[76] Macmillan was thus sensitive to the point of paranoia about the 'Special Relationship' with the United States, and his aides constantly sought to reassure him on this point.[77]

Macmillan's faith in the 'Special Relationship' was reinforced by his personal rapport with President Kennedy, which extended to their readings of history. Kennedy urged his senior national security officials to read Barbara Tuchman's *The Guns of August*, stating: 'I don't ever want to be in that position. We are not going to bungle into a war.' Robert Kennedy, the president's brother and attorney general, later recalled that, during the Cuban Missile Crisis, the president had stated: 'I am not going to follow a course which will allow anyone to write a comparable book about this time, *The Missiles of October*.'[78] Given its influence on Kennedy, Tuchman's book is thus lauded for what it tells us about the early 1960s, as well as the summer of 1914.[79]

Kennedy's remark that '[i]f there were to be any such war, we must know what it is for, and know what other steps we can take before such war comes'[80] is often subjected to scrutiny invoking an epic historical sweep. For 'Hawks' such statements betray the spirit of an appeaser. 'Doves', by contrast, can approvingly note that Kennedy – unlike Kaiser Wilhelm II – intended to keep control of events. Evidencing this was Kennedy's desire to move the United States away from its dependence upon nuclear weapons policy and the policy of 'Massive Retaliation'.[81] Kennedy certainly had little time for those who thought about the 'unthinkable' – that is, those who planned for nuclear war,[82] and National Security Advisor McGeorge Bundy later testified that the only thinking that Kennedy devoted to nuclear weapons was concerned with how not to use them.[83] The problem for Kennedy and his adherents was that 'Massive retaliation' was, in effect, the Schlieffen Plan of its day. The US strategic nuclear arsenal, like the German army in 1914, was the supreme instrument of state coercion available. Both recourses to overwhelming force were designed to address political and tactical shortcomings; both were designed to pre-empt the other side. Imperial Germany's *Kaiserheer* was supposed to do the job (i.e. achieving decisive strategic superiority) in six weeks; US Strategic Air Command in six hours. Yet the advent of nuclear weapons had fundamentally altered the threat and use of force in international relations. This was especially so with regard to the ever-increasing pace of technological change that, in turn, had a fundamental effect on the concepts and theories of 'deterrence'. Kennedy fretted that Moscow would never believe that the United States would risk itself to halt the Soviet Union in Europe.[84] In short, the question was usually boiled down to: 'Would the United States sacrifice Chicago to save Hamburg?'[85] Kennedy, naturally, wished to avoid being forced to choose between all-out nuclear war and diplomatic defeat.[86] After all, had not the Russian Empire, after humiliation in the Bosnian Annexation Crisis of 1908–9, staked all on standing by its allies in July 1914?[87] In the light of the need for flexibility, in early 1961 the CIA had strongly advocated that the president be given options short of all-out war in times of crisis.[88] But nuclear strategy had a dynamic and a logic all of its own. So even though Kennedy and his closest confidants deemed a nuclear war an unacceptably high price for Berlin,[89] they did debate the idea of a 'First Strike',[90] as they were forced, by virtue of the very existence of nuclear weapons, to 'think the unthinkable'. To even contemplate this – at however abstract a level – was fraught with danger. As it was, the high-level debate within the Kennedy administration frightened Soviet intelligence into believing the United States was planning a surprise nuclear attack.[91]

Macmillan, too, had reasons to fear the manner in which the doctrine of nuclear deterrence had evolved in the 1950s. The basing of US missiles in the United Kingdom had made the latter a prime target as soon as any conflict erupted with the USSR. The prime minister recognized the ambiguity that nuclear weapons had engendered. In 1959 he told Eisenhower that although 'nuclear weapons had served to defend Europe and to keep the peace in the world', 'it should [nevertheless] be regarded as a great misfortune for the world that these weapons had been discovered'.[92] After all, '[e]ight bombs . . . would mean 20 or 30 million Englishmen dead'.[93] This vulnerability was hardly a secret and, on 2 July 1961, Khrushchev told the British ambassador, Sir Frank Roberts, that six Soviet hydrogen bombs 'would be quite enough to annihilate the British Isles'.[94] The threat of nuclear attack increased after *Sputnik* in 1957,[95] and de Gaulle recalled that Macmillan feared a war in which Britain 'would be in danger of sinking with all hands' and was thus disinclined to back Adenauer over Berlin.[96] (Indeed, Macmillan privately even regarded the US Polaris system, which he was to purchase in 1962, as 'dangerous').[97] Macmillan, fully able to project the worst-case scenario when the mood took him, noted that '[i]n the military sphere, the overwhelming nuclear superiority of the West has been replaced by a balance of destructive power.'[98] This was nothing other than a nuclear age update of the maxim: 'The bomber will always get through.'[99] This was all the more alarming as the Soviets seemed to be forging ahead in the Space Race[100] and Macmillan informed Kennedy that '[a]gainst nuclear attack, we are huddled too close together and so all our people could do would be to carry on and grin and die.'[101]

The similarities in thinking between Macmillan and Kennedy on international affairs and nuclear weapons extended into their respective views of the path to the Second World War. This is clear from the book of Kennedy's Harvard dissertation, *Why England Slept*, which rather simplistically argued that democracies should equip themselves with sufficient arms and armaments to deter dictatorships from recourse to war.[102] (Kennedy was fond of invoking Churchill's maxim –'We arm to parley').[103] Yet, at a fundamental level, the book strikes one as a curio: not least because Kennedy's father was an anti-Semitic appeaser and a defeatist.[104] While hypocrisy was part-and-parcel of the whole Kennedy approach to politics, the president's lack of self-knowledge here is striking. In 1961 Macmillan was similarly self-assured, not least because of his own history of anti-appeasement.

> We and our allies have certain obligations in Germany, and we do not intend to abandon them. Among these obligations is the preservation of the freedom of the people of West Berlin. The Soviet Government must come to realise that we intend to defend this, and that we cannot countenance proposals inconsistent with it. If they wish to discuss the issue with us, we are prepared to do so, but they must understand that it can only be on the basis I have described. The House will appreciate from what I have said that there is no question whatever of any modification of British commitments in Berlin.[105]

Lord Home, dubbed by many as 'the arch-appeaser',[106] advocated 'quiet [i.e. secret] diplomacy' over Berlin in a Cabinet memorandum of July 1961. If this were done in consultation with the sympathetic figures of Kennedy and Rusk, the West Germans (and the French) would understand that their policy of 'talking simply of standing firm' while 'making no effective contribution' was unacceptable. Home had some sympathy for the Soviet goal of strengthening their East German ally and therefore proposed adopting a policy of appeasement.

> We could . . . accept the . . . Oder-Neisse line. Nor, in fact, do we really want German reunification, at least for the time being, though we cannot abandon the principle of self-determination for the Germans. The same is probably true of the rest of [NATO], including the Germans. German reunification now would upset what has been achieved in Western European integration since the war.[107]

Throughout the Berlin Wall Crisis, Lord Home called for negotiations and was willing to make concessions on crucial issues in order to get an agreement.[108] Home proposed placing Berlin under the jurisdiction of the UN, and proposed that the two German states – one of which the West did not even recognize – should settle the issue of Berlin between them in a set period of time.[109] Although US Secretary of State Dean Rusk dismissed these particular proposals,[110] Macmillan believed that the United States was coming round to the British point of view.[111] Rusk informed Home that in order to achieve 'a solution to the Berlin Crisis the West Germans were going to have to swallow a lot of things that they had hitherto maintained were entirely unacceptable to them'.[112] Home believed Rusk had been given express orders from the president to seek a negotiating platform with the Soviets.[113] This was confirmed when George F. Kennan suggested that some sort of settlement over Berlin could be reached if the West gave de facto recognition to the Oder-Neiße frontier and the GDR.[114]

If the West feared war over Berlin, it was increasingly clear that the Soviet leadership's patience was waning. The two main reasons for this were the West's use of Berlin for intelligence operations[115] and the unacceptable rate at which the East German state was losing people through the bolthole of West Berlin (200,000 in 1960).[116] Moscow was undoubtedly concerned by the fact that the population of the GDR had reduced by 1.2 million people since 1950.[117] Secretary of State Dean Rusk later described this flow of persons as representing nothing less than a 'haemorrhage'.[118] By the summer of 1961 it was clear that the Communists had to act. Rumours abounded but the reports that all holiday leave in East Germany was to be cancelled that year[119] were accurate. Home warned that Khrushchev was probably going to be forced into some sort of action by an increasingly agitated leadership in Pankow,[120] with GDR leader Walter Ulbricht demanding that it was 'high time for a peace treaty' to be signed.[121] West German Foreign Minister Heinrich von Brentano opined that the East Germans were bound to close the borders with West Berlin in order to staunch the loss of people from their state.[122] Thus, after repeatedly refusing Ulbricht requests, Khrushchev now finally assented to the construction of a permanent barrier.[123] On 12 August 1961 Macmillan presciently informed Home that they were on the 'eve of great perils in Europe'.[124]

In the six days after 13 August 1961, the East Germans sealed off West Berlin with a wall.[125] While the West German government viewed the Berlin Wall as an outrage, Macmillan saw it as lawful.[126] Seeking to calm matters, Macmillan rather over-did things when he stated that the whole thing had '[b]een got up by the Press' and that, in any case, '[n]obody is going to fight about it.'[127] While Macmillan was a little embarrassed, privately he conceded only that his remarks had lacked tact and, when discussing matters with Kennedy, he insisted that, on the substantive points, he was right.[128] Fortunately, Kennedy agreed: 'It's not a very nice solution, but a wall is a hell of a lot better than a war.'[129] The British ambassador in Bonn cynically advised that 'the Federal Government are not really interested in reunification and their attitude is all politics' as he confessed that he had 'always wondered [why] the East Germans . . . waited so long to seal this boundary.'[130] The fact that the US administration shared this view,[131] encouraged British hopes that Bonn (and Paris) would now embrace negotiations on Berlin.[132] This was reinforced by Yugoslav advice to the effect that it was extremely likely that Khrushchev would sign a separate peace treaty with the East Germans soon.[133] Macmillan optimistically noted that 'Khrushchev wants negotiation' while Home now predicted an agreement (so long as the agenda could be kept limited).[134] Adam Rapacki,

Poland's foreign minister, asserted: 'There will be no war for Berlin . . . there would be no reason.'[135] At such times it seemed Macmillan had more in common with his Communist opponents than with his West German allies. In Washington, DC, Kennan, having returned from Belgrade, urged restraint and advised Kennedy that Khrushchev had authorized the Wall only so as to avoid war.[136] Although elements in the US military urged stronger action,[137] Rusk stuck with his decision to keep 'shooting issues and non-shooting issues separate'.[138] On 30 August, Kennedy publicly reaffirmed his administration's belief that any outstanding matters would have to be resolved by negotiation.[139] Although Kennedy and Macmillan both wrote letters to Adenauer to reassure him of the West's willingness to defend West Berlin,[140] this was little more than a sop. The West had essentially embraced the pragmatic (British) approach and rejected the inflexible intransigence espoused by the Adenauer government.

At no point during the Berlin Wall Crisis had the British or the Americans been prepared to tear down the Wall.[141] The West would only fight if access routes were interfered with[142] as its 'moral position rested on the defence of the people of West Berlin'.[143] After the Wall's construction Kennedy made this abundantly clear to the mayor of West Berlin, Willy Brandt: 'Neither you nor we, nor any of our Allies, have ever supposed that we should go to war on this point.' Kennedy instead limited himself to enquiring as to how to exploit the Wall for propaganda purposes.[144] Neither the United States nor the British had ever sought to encourage a popular uprising against the USSR and were not going to support one if it did break out.[145] British and American policy makers had made a hard-headed assessment of the situation and decided that it was better to allow East Berlin to be sealed off rather than risk a nuclear confrontation.[146] At this juncture Eden waded into the fray, opining: 'It is not perhaps a happy time to bring out a defence of appeasement as it was practised by Mr. Chamberlain, because, whatever the opinions in this country about it, Europe has condemned that kind of appeasement, and in the present international situation it is certainly not a policy the West can pursue if it intends to survive.'[147] In deference to his successor, Eden did not refer directly to Berlin but, while the British government rarely viewed such interventions as helpful, by this time the diplomacy of Macmillan's government had made a great deal of headway. The embassy in Washington reported that the United States would adopt a joint negotiating platform with the United Kingdom, as the Kennedy administration had embraced the inevitability of a negotiated settlement over Berlin.[148] Kennedy wrote to Adenauer stating: 'I do not share the point of view that we should be reluctant to negotiate, on the grounds that to do so might be interpreted as a sign of weakness on our part.'[149] At the same time, Kennedy ordered Rusk to begin secret talks with Soviet Foreign Minister Andrei Gromyko over Berlin.[150] After Rusk professed a very serious desire for a negotiated settlement with the USSR, Home gleefully informed the Cabinet that he was 'amazed' at the degree to which Washington had accepted British proposals on the Oder-Neiße and the GDR.[151] In the Commons, Macmillan stated:

> Of course, there is danger, in connection with Berlin perhaps and the access to it, that there might arise a military incident leading to a clash between the opposing forces. It might be at first on a small scale. It might become something rather bigger. It is clear that in these events we must try to contain that clash by conventional means. The object of the strategy and planning of all the allies has been to ensure that in such a period there would be a pause during which one would hope that the statesmen of the different countries could get together and find some possibility of solution before the full horror of war was launched.

Having established his resolution, and horror of war, Macmillan now unveiled the progress made by means of Britain's unyielding promotion of negotiation.

> We have had talks with Mr. Gromyko, the [Soviet] Foreign Minister. We want a settlement by negotiation which will be satisfactory to all concerned. Unsuccessful negotiation would be very bad . . . [but the] Russians, I think, now realise the seriousness of the situation, the unwillingness of the allies to surrender and their determination not to do so. I think that they also recognise that we know it will be necessary to negotiate and guarantee the status and access and that that can best be done before any question of a Russian treaty with the D.D.R.[152]

Given Macmillan's personal history, this was a curious updating of Chamberlainite thinking. Kennedy and Macmillan agreed to prevail upon Adenauer and de Gaulle to accept the new reality – as Macmillan informed the Cabinet that 'it would be premature to despair since President de Gaulle, like other great men, never yield to argument but occasionally to facts. An argument which appears to be repelled at the moment might sink in later.'[153] At Bermuda in December 1961, Home told Kennedy that the West might have to make four concessions in order to get a settlement with the East: de facto recognition of the GDR; the recognition of the Oder-Neiße line; concessions on Western occupation rights in Berlin and diminished links between West Berlin and the Federal Republic of Germany (FRG).[154] Regardless of whether or not such concessions would work, Macmillan continued to insist that the West must 'never go to war unless there had been negotiations first . . . we must not allow ourselves to drift into war. Had appropriate action been taken at the time, World War One could have been avoided.'[155] Whether Macmillan knew it or not, his use of 1914 as a reference point in international affairs was reminiscent of nothing so much as the appeasers of the 1930s. This was largely lost on Macmillan, who assumed that his opposition to Chamberlain in the 1930s disbarred him from ever being accused of appeasement. Where Macmillan had been prescient in his judgement was in his assessment of the British electorate and of the prevailing mood in the Kennedy administration after 1961.

In 1945 Ernest Bevin had stated: 'There has never been a war yet which, if the facts had been put calmly before the ordinary folk, could not have been prevented. The fact is they are kept separated from one another.'[156] In the case of Berlin between 1958 and 1962 this was true as the British population, when faced with the possibility of nuclear war, preferred the diplomacy of Macmillan over any attempt to maintain a hard line. US policy makers drew much the same lesson. The increasing nuclear muscle of the Soviets, when combined with Khrushchev's belligerence, had led the West to embrace the possibility of compromise (much to the chagrin of Adenauer). Crucially, as Home noted, Gromyko had agreed to leave West Berlin alone if agreement were reached on the questions of German nuclear weapons, the Oder-Neiße and the GDR. That this was so was due, not least, to the fact that Khrushchev – unlike Hitler – was amenable to rational discourse. As Khrushchev himself later observed: 'We didn't want a military conflict. There was no necessity for one. We only wanted to conduct a surgical operation.' This was indicative of the fact that the diplomacy of all parties had, to a certain degree, recognized the changes wrought by nuclear weapons: sabre-rattling in a nuclear world was irresponsible and dangerous. As a CIA report noted in early 1961: 'The strategic situation does not make general nuclear war impossible, but it makes it a highly irrational response to international disputes.'[157] This let appeasement in by the back door inasmuch as it rehabilitated the notion of negotiating on fundamental issues as a respectable policy option. There had been no war over Berlin. A line in the sand had been drawn, a line drawn by British diplomacy. Appeasement, partly by the assiduous denial of its employment, had worked.

CHAPTER FIVE

Helsinki, 1975: Nuclear age Westphalia, Versailles or Munich?

Will the Prime Minister answer quite clearly whether the United States
Government were consulted? He will recognise the great dangers here
of any tendency towards appeasement in this matter. Were the United
States Government consulted before his hon. Friend left?

SIR ALEC DOUGLAS-HOME

Should there be any question of my wanting lessons
in appeasement, I know who to go to.

HAROLD WILSON[1]

We cannot buy our security, our freedom from the threat of the bomb
by committing an immorality so great as saying to a billion now in
slavery behind the Iron Curtain, 'Give up your dreams of
freedom because to save our own skin, we are willing
to make a deal with your slave masters'.

RONALD REAGAN, 1964 [2]

It is difficult to see any difference between appeasement and détente.

MARGARET THATCHER[3]

In 1976, an internal Foreign and Commonwealth Office paper reflected on the contested nature of the *zeitgeist* in contemporary international affairs.

> The word 'détente' has been much overworked and misused, but the gradual evolution of East/West relations . . . cannot conveniently be described by any other term . . . [following] the negotiation . . . of a modest *modus vivendi* based upon a common interest in the avoidance of military confrontation leading to nuclear war.

Détente had been constructed upon a shared recognition that both sides had core interests and, simultaneously, wished to avoid war. In 1961 the US ambassador in Moscow advised Secretary of State Rusk:

> I consider K[hrushchev] has so deeply committed his personal prestige and that of the Soviet Union to some action on [the] Berlin and German problems that if we take [a] completely negative stance . . . this would probably lead to developments in which chances of war or ignominious Western retreat are close to 50–50 . . . Both sides consider other would not risk war over Berlin. Danger arises from fact that if K[hrushchev] carries out his declared intentions, and we carry out ours, situation likely get out of control and military as well as political prestige would become involved making retreat for either side even more difficult.[4]

The sensitivity towards the question of prestige displayed by Kennedy during the Cuban Missile Crisis of October 1962 played no small role in its peaceful resolution. Indeed, the whole incident represented one of the more famous instances of politicians 'learning' from history, whereby John F. Kennedy's reading of Barbara Tuchman's *The Guns of August*,[5] and the lessons of other crises, supposedly helped guide his hand. The main 'lesson' Kennedy drew was not about appeasement per se – it was about preventing events from spinning out of political control (as they supposedly had in 1914).[6] In 1986, Richard Neustadt and Ernest May observed that 'the use of history appears to have contributed, demonstrably, to the high quality of analysis and management apparent during the missile crisis'.[7] But history had also been used to support very different options during the crisis. USAF Chief of Staff Curtis LeMay, for example, condemned the choice of a naval quarantine, rather than immediate airstrikes, as a sell-out. On Friday 19 October 1962 he stated: 'This blockade and political action I see leading into war. I don't see any other solution for it. It will lead right into war. This is almost as bad as the appeasement at Munich.'[8] One historian recently noted that, in this statement, LeMay had deployed 'their generation's ultimate metaphor for shortsightedness and cowardice, the 1938 appeasement of Hitler at Munich'.[9] When the crisis was over LeMay told a stunned Kennedy to his face: 'We have been had. It's the greatest defeat in our history. We should invade today.' For LeMay, the 'quarantine', as with Munich, had bought peace in the short term. Yet, as Chris Matthews argued in 2012, 'Kennedy's policy in the Cuban Missile Crisis may have involved appeasement, but the outcome would not ever be mistaken for Munich. Chamberlain's acquiescence to Hitler led to his grabbing the rest of Czechoslovakia. Kennedy's deal with Khrushchev would lead to the first treaty of the Cold War: the 1963 limited nuclear test ban treaty.'[10]

The historian and Kennedy adviser Arthur Schlesinger, Jr. described the Cuban Missile Crisis as 'the most dangerous moment in human history'.[11] That neither Berlin nor Cuba ended in nuclear war was more fortuitous accident than policy design.[12] The brinkmanship integral to traditional diplomacy had nearly led to war, being averted only because, in Secretary of State Dean Rusk's famous phrase of 24 October 1962: 'We were eyeball to eyeball and the other fellow just blinked.'[13] Dean Acheson was, perhaps, closer when he attributed the outcome to 'plain, dumb luck'[14] and around the world the nuclear near miss certainly gave pause for thought. As Macmillan had insisted, it was clear there were very real dangers in pursuing inflexible policies of brinkmanship that rejected compromise as tantamount to 'appeasement'.[15] The nuclear shadow undoubtedly caused Cold War statesmen to pause for thought when pursuing hard-line policies against nuclear-armed opponents. This was less of a consideration when the superpowers dealt with second-rank powers. President Lyndon Johnson, Kennedy's successor, cast the war in Vietnam in much the same way as Truman had done with Korea: 'The central lesson of our time is that the appetite of aggression is never satisfied. To withdraw from one battlefield means only to prepare for the next. We must say in Southeast Asia - as we did in Europe - in the words of the Bible: "Hitherto shalt thou come, but no further".'[16] Johnson was acutely aware that Chamberlain had gone down in history for having betrayed Czechoslovakia, and he did not want to be similarly condemned over South Vietnam. In vain, Hans J. Morgenthau sought to refute this variant of the 'Munich analogy': 'Mao Tse-tung is not Hitler. China's position in Asia is not similar to the position of Germany in Europe . . . and most importantly, you could stop Hitler with military force, but how are you going to stop 700 million Chinese?'[17] The Johnson administration was unmoved: there could be no appeasement in Vietnam.

While the war in Vietnam – and US involvement in it – escalated year-on-year, the Cold War in Europe thawed, albeit in uneven fashion as an era of détente dawned. In terms of the confrontation between the superpowers in Europe this culminated in the Conference on Security and Cooperation in Europe (CSCE). The Final Act of the CSCE, initialled in Helsinki by 35 signatories on 1 August 1975, addressed a number of outstanding issues in Europe (not least the question of frontiers). For one senior US official present at Helsinki this represented 'a substitute for a peace conference bringing the Second World War to a formal conclusion'.[18] The British attitude towards the CSCE was often ambiguous but, by the time the Final Act was concluded, the British had awkwardly embraced the process as inevitable.[19] Infused with a measure of Macmillan's enthusiasm for compromise with the Soviet bloc, the British governments of Harold Wilson

(1964–6, 1966–70 and 1974–6) and Edward Heath (1970–4) supported the innovative and conciliatory foreign policy (the *Neue Ostpolitik*) of the Federal Republic of Germany (FRG) towards the USSR and its satellites.[20] This supportive role had been adopted while the United Kingdom participated in the process that led to the Final Act of the CSCE, of which the *Neue Ostpolitik* was both a pre-requisite and a key component.[21] For critics in the FRG, Chancellor Willy Brandt's *Neue Ostpolitik* was an act of craven appeasement whereby Muscovite Imperialism was rewarded for its blatant disregard for international law since 1917. Such charges were mirrored at the international level by opponents of superpower détente such as Franz-Josef Strauß, the colourful German conservative politician, who denounced the Helsinki Final Act as a new Munich.[22] For such figures the Final Act, coming after the West's 'betrayal' of East Berlin (1953), Hungary (1956) and Czechoslovakia (1968), represented the institutionalization of the Soviet denial of freedom to its East Europe satellites.[23]

British governments had little time for an aggressive anti-appeasement stance towards the Soviets. The danger of nuclear war and the recognition that the Soviets were not going to leave Eastern Europe anytime soon led British policy makers to reject the moral absolutism in the rhetoric of Barry Goldwater (the defeated Republican candidate for president in 1964) and of Ronald Reagan (governor of California and a rising star in the Republican Party who was to challenge President Ford for the Republican nomination in 1976).[24] Typifying these tendencies, Goldwater had famously declared: 'I would remind you that extremism in the defense of liberty is no vice. And let me remind you also that moderation in the pursuit of justice is no virtue.'[25] This extremist rhetoric did not go down well in the United States and Lyndon Johnson crushed Goldwater in the 1964 presidential election.[26] The nuclear threat undoubtedly caused policy makers to pause before criticizing the Soviets. Following the Soviet invasion of Czechoslovakia in August 1968, although the leaders of both the Labour and Conservative parties made reference to 1938, the British Defence Secretary Denis Healey stated privately: 'the Russians used force to maintain the status quo, not to challenge it'. Publicly, Foreign and Commonwealth Secretary Michael Stewart told the Commons: 'In 1938 we all knew . . . that . . . Europe [was] . . . on the road to war; the only question was when the disaster would come, and it might be immediately upon us. That is not the situation we face now.'[27] The Soviet invasion of Czechoslovakia was acceptable as it did not pose a direct threat to neither British interests nor to European peace.[28] The invasion of Czechoslovakia, however distasteful, was not going to be allowed to become an obstacle to the major policy goal: détente.[29]

Although supportive of Brandt, and of détente generally, Prime Minister Heath, himself a staunch opponent of Chamberlainite appeasement in the 1930s,[30] advised the West German chancellor that 'in a climate of relaxation we shall have to be no less, and indeed more, on our guard'.[31] The British were acutely aware of general enthusiasm among Western publics for détente and they wished to avoid exclusion by means of any process that would consist primarily of bilateral American and West German negotiations with Moscow. Heath later stressed that, while Britain embraced preparations for the CSCE, '[w]e all knew that such a conference could result in strengthened Soviet hegemony in Europe, through the recognition of post-war divisions'.[32] In September 1972, a British Joint Intelligence Committee (JIC) report noted:

> In the conditions of détente fostered by the Soviet Union, Western Europe may be gradually deprived of credible United States support without providing a substitute of its own and may fail to attain the unity in the political and defence fields which will be necessary if Soviet influence and pressures on Western Europe are to be repelled.[33]

Many British policy makers were troubled by the notion that the acceptance of the status quo, and hence Soviet domination of Eastern Europe, had been made in the full knowledge of bad faith on the part of the Soviets. In January 1973 the British ambassador in Moscow lamented:

> The Russians use the expression 'détente' as a presentationally [sic] useful portmanteau term to embrace a series of objectives which in fact are not necessarily conducive to a genuine relaxation of tension at all: these objectives include the consolidation of the Soviet sphere of influence in Eastern Europe and Western acquiescence in it; the perpetuation of the division of Germany.[34]

Foreign and Commonwealth Secretary[35] Sir Alec Douglas-Home publicly announced that if security was a question of statesmen's good intentions (or past treaties they had concluded) then there would be little tension in Europe. Despite this 'a lack of trust and sincerity . . . will not be removed by any number of pious preambles'. In Douglas-Home's mind the 'security' dimension of the CSCE was intimately linked to the issue of human rights: 'Basket I will be empty unless there are plenty of eggs in Basket III.'[36] This was indicative of the fact that the British, fully conscious of their limited bargaining power, had decided to concentrate on ensuring that any agreement should include a pledge on respecting human rights.[37] A steering brief for the UK delegation to the CSCE highlighted that, of 'Specific British Considerations', the 'most important' was the securing of 'tangible benefits in the field of human [rights]' and a 'general recognition of the relevance of these subjects'.[38] Yet, for all the diplomatic gloss that the British government sought to apply to détente, the analogies with the era of Chamberlainite appeasement were easily made. In the November 1973 edition of *Encounter* magazine, Goronwy Rees wrote:

> There is perhaps an analogy between the policy of *détente* with the Soviet Union and the fatal policy of appeasement which, in the 1930s, Great Britain adopted towards National Socialist Germany. In Great Britain,

appeasement rested on the belief, stubbornly adhered to in spite of all appearances to the contrary, that it was possible to reach a dependable agreement with Hitler which would at the same time satisfy both his aspirations and our own aims; though Hitler had made it perfectly plain both by word and deed that they were irreconcilable. The belief was only abandoned when it was already too late to find any other reliable basis for British policy. One must hope that President Nixon and Dr Kissinger[39] are right in their calculations and have not made the same kind of error as Britain did with such fatal results.

Rees believed that détente, as with the appeasement of the 1930s, inspired opposition among those who believed that there were certain types of states with which it was not possible to compromise. Nazi Germany was such a state, as it 'had deliberately abandoned even the pretence of conforming to the normal rules and conventions which are the basis of civilised life'. For Rees the analogy was clear.

> In the same way, today, there are many people who cannot bring themselves to believe that any genuine basis of cooperation can be found with a state which, like the Soviet Union, systematically violates the constitutional rights of its own citizens, persecutes its writers, artists and intellectuals, uses terror and brutality as accepted instruments of state policy, condemns millions of people for trivial or non-existent offences to years of inhuman suffering and degradation, and recognises none of those fundamental liberties which belong inalienably to all human beings. One might as well believe that it was possible for a human being to negotiate a meaningful agreement with a gorilla.[40]

Sir William Hayter, when asked about the analogies between détente and appeasement, conceded that there were certainly parallels between the 1930s and the 1970s but, if one equated détente with appeasement in the latter's original pre-Munich sense – as 'an attempt to remove or diminish the dangers of war' – 'then appeasement is a perfectly desirable policy and one that we are entitled to pursue'. For Hayter, there was a difference between altering the status quo in favour of an aggressive dictator (as was done in 1938) and accepting a status quo you cannot alter (as in Hungary in 1956, Czechoslovakia in 1968 and with regard to détente in the 1970s). Thus the situation was not identical to 1938.

> [T]here the status quo was the independence of Czechoslovakia, and [over Munich] the British and French Governments put enormous pressure on Czechoslovakia to . . . surrender to Hitler. In 1968 the status quo was Czechoslovakia under Soviet hegemony from which the Czechoslovaks were trying to escape to some extent, and we could not intervene because by doing so we should most probably have caused a

world war. So although there is an analogy between the two situations, it is far from being a complete analogy.[41]

In the 1970s, once more faced with a continental dictatorship, British officialdom, as in the 1930s, sought to identify where they could best bring their 'pragmatic' vision to bear. In British eyes the stabilization of the frontiers of Europe was something that continentals would pay a price for.[42] As Lord Carrington later recalled: 'To the Nations of Continental Europe what matters most is the security of their land frontiers.'[43] While the goal of the recognition of frontiers had long stood at the forefront of Soviet demands for any East–West arrangement, the British now pursued their own aims as quid pro quo – in the field of human rights.[44]

Aware of the priority placed on the frontiers question by Moscow, the British sought to make acceptance of the territorial status quo conditional upon Soviet acceptance of the importance of the issue of human rights. Douglas-Home asserted: 'We may have to make it plain to the Russians that the Western negotiators operate within the framework of public opinion and that any further action against Soviet dissidents may seriously prejudice the atmosphere for the CSCE as a whole.'[45] Aware of Britain's marginal role in détente, the Labour government of Harold Wilson, which had come to power in February 1974, sought to smooth the path towards the Final Act. Foreign and Commonwealth Secretary James Callaghan saw matters in grand terms: 'We have the experience . . . to make a contribution out of all proportion to our . . . size and power . . . [in addressing] the problems facing the world. In these circumstances we may well have found the role for Britain which Dean Acheson asserted that we had lost with Empire. We are the bridge-builders.'[46] The new government therefore resolved to construct, in Callaghan's phrase, 'a safer and more productive relationship' with the USSR.[47] In this vein, Wilson sought to utilize his (rather self-imagined) special relationship with the Soviet Union.[48] The prime minister and his foreign secretary, acutely aware of Soviet sensibilities on the subject of frontiers historically, assured Soviet leader Leonid Brezhnev that the British would support the inviolability of European frontiers with all their power.[49] Wilson told the Cabinet that he and Callaghan now firmly believed that the Soviet Union had taken 'a political decision to improve their relations' with the West 'as part of their policy of detente'. Wilson also noted: 'An incidental but not unimportant benefit was that Mr Brezhnev had been led to redefine the expression "peaceful coexistence" which had hitherto formed part of the jargon of the international class struggle.'[50] The Cold War, it seemed, was thawing.

In the summer of 1975 the Wilson government watched approvingly as Moscow achieved a long-standing Soviet goal when the Final Act of the CSCE declared that the frontiers of Europe could only be changed peacefully and by mutual consent.[51] Despite Wilson's acquiescence, many in Britain denounced what they saw as another Yalta, another betrayal of the peoples of East and Central Europe. Winston Churchill MP, the grandson of the wartime leader, addressed the Commons on this issue. It was clear that he was seeking to emulate his namesake by his denunciation of appeasement.

> In the CSCE Agreement the Soviet Union is seeking to gain from the West formal acknowledgment of its conquests in the Second World War and, above all, its right to control indefinitely some 200 million people of Central and Eastern Europe who, before that war, were not under Soviet control. What, we may ask, are the feelings of those people? Unless the Soviet Union . . . is prepared to take fairly substantive . . . steps to liberalise and democratise its own society, unless it is, above all, prepared to give an undertaking that there will be no more Soviet invasions of Czechoslovakia and acknowledge that to have been a mistake, by going to this summit meeting and by putting their hands on behalf of the free people of the world to this document the leaders of the Western democracies could be in danger of signing a second Munich Agreement, signing away the rights of millions of people in far-away lands and, above all, duping their own people into believing that genuine détente and 'peace in our time' had been achieved.[52]

The Wilson government rejected such criticism out of hand. In a piece of rhetoric reminiscent of nothing so much as the Chamberlainite exaltation of pragmatism, the minister of state at the Foreign and Commonwealth Office (FCO), Roy Hattersley, had expressed the 'hope that as the years pass the hon. Member for Stretford (Mr. Churchill) will come to face the world as it is rather than as he would like it to be'.[53] Wilson commended his *Sowietpolitik* to the Commons just as, before him, Churchill had done after Yalta. 'This conference represented no more than a beginning, but I hope that the House will agree that it is a beginning in the right direction.'[54] Wilson was entitled to a degree of satisfaction as détente played well domestically.[55] This was not lost on the prime minister, a keen political animal, who imagined himself a nuclear age Castlereagh or Disraeli. Wilson, typically, went in for some diplomatic hyperbole when he declared that the signing of the Final Act of the CSCE made the 'legendary Congress of Vienna of 1814 and the Congress of Berlin of 1878 seem like well-dressed tea parties'.[56]

For their part, the Soviets were triumphant after Helsinki.[57] Having secured a pan-European agreement on frontiers, Moscow had deemed the accession to the human rights provisos a price worth paying. Following the signing of the agreement, Sir Terence Garvey, British ambassador in Moscow, took stock.

ILLUSTRATION 5.1 *Preparing for Helsinki: North Atlantic Council, Brussels, 29 May 1975. (from bottom) David K. E. Bruce (US ambassador to NATO), President Gerald R. Ford, Secretary of State Henry Kissinger, Foreign and Commonwealth Secretary James Callaghan and Prime Minister Harold Wilson.*

> [The CSCE] has been claimed by the Russians as a great diplomatic success and a major landmark in post-war history . . . 'Security in Europe' has meant for the Soviet Government the consolidation of the new territorial and political order established by Soviet arms, diplomacy and skulduggery in the years following 1944 . . . For them, the key importance of the Final Act of Helsinki lies in the multilateral acceptance of frontiers and of the political *status quo* . . . The main debit [for Moscow], is in Basket III. It was a major setback even to have to discuss . . . humanitarian subjects . . . [but] Basket III may nevertheless cause strain between Moscow and its allies . . . [as] the Russians cannot [now] easily bring the East Europeans back to the Soviet line.[58]

In actual fact the Soviet 'victory' on frontiers was not as complete as it had appeared at first sight, as Moscow had compromised in order to secure agreement. In December 1974, Brezhnev had visited Paris and, in talks with the French government (who were acting on behalf of the West), agreement had been reached over the question of Basket III. In order to achieve this breakthrough the French had given in to the Soviet demand that the CSCE should be finalized at an international summit.[59] For their part, the British now believed they had very good reasons for accepting the long-standing Soviet demands regarding frontiers. An unnamed British official recently testified that there were two reasons for British acquiescence on the frontier question.[60] First, the Final Act was not a registered treaty and the signatories were under no obligation under international law;[61] second, the fact that the West's demand that the principle of peaceful change was accepted ensured that the Soviet campaign to ensure that the frontiers of Europe be declared immutable was unsuccessful.[62]

Up until 1975, the claim to be the chief guarantor of existing frontiers (especially against the FRG) had been Moscow's strongest card in its justification of its presence in its East European satellites. This was severely undermined by the Final Act and the British believed that was at least part of the reason that the recognition of the frontiers was so strongly supported throughout the East European states.[63] The human rights provisions only added to British satisfaction on the frontier question. Sir David Hildyard, head of the British delegation in Geneva, phrased it thus: '[S]tarting from the premise that West had no practical alternative to the recognition of the *status quo* and that the *Ost-Verträge* had already taken a large step in this direction, I believe that we can conclude that a satisfactory price was exacted for this recognition.'[64]

Having acted in the role of facilitator (albeit in a rather limited fashion) the British sought subsequently to magnify both their role and the Western successes achieved by the Final Act.[65] The CSCE confirmed the two-bloc system as a known, if unloved, force for institutionalized stability in Europe. The British had accepted that détente was dependent upon embracing the territorial status quo in some form or another (this was something the

USSR had coveted since the 1940s). At the outset of the Cold War, British policy makers would have seen an acceptance of this state of affairs as reckless in the extreme. By the late 1940s, while an aggressive war to clear the Soviets out of Eastern Europe was rejected, so was the option of formally recognizing Soviet gains. Soviet domination of Eastern Europe endangered the security of Western Europe. Western Europe was therefore to be constructed as a bastion against Soviet expansionism by means of: first, the Marshall Plan; second, NATO; and third, the European Economic Community (EEC). These political and military arrangements meant that, long before 1975, British policy makers had accepted that recognition of Soviet control of Eastern Europe would not endanger a secure Western Europe (and would even act as a stabilizing force in the Cold War system). Risings such as those seen in the GDR in 1953 and Hungary in 1956 had no chance of success – and would only undermine everyone's security while leaving Soviet power intact.[66] The quid pro quo for human rights – the decision to recognize Soviet control of Eastern Europe – was thus an act of appeasement rooted firmly in *Realpolitik*. With appeasement left far behind, and the shadow of nuclear war cast by Cuba and Berlin at least as strong as Munich in the public imagination, by the 1970s the West was strong enough to negotiate, to make concessions, and to endure. Hitler's Germany had sought concessions precisely to overturn the territorial status quo in Europe. The détente of the 1970s, unlike the appeasement of the 1930s, had secured real concessions from an opponent that had sought *only* to institutionalize the territorial status quo in Europe.

By 1975, many British diplomats viewed the CSCE process a diplomatic prop for the EEC, allowing the West Europeans greater leverage in East-West relations. In March 1978, the British ambassador to Hungary reported of the Belgrade CSCE review conference as having its concluding document 'negotiated primarily by the . . . [EEC] Nine with the *other two* Superpowers, the US and the Soviet Union'.[67] Against this, the years after 1975 saw an increasing body of Western opinion that declared that the Final Act had allowed the USSR to greatly advance its cause. The view that the Soviet bloc had been the 'victors' in 1975 was, undoubtedly, initially shared by the Soviet bloc itself[68] and the whole Helsinki process was, in words of one author, 'a monument to the paradox of détente'.[69] As the so-called Second Cold War began in the late 1970s, a new generation of Cold Warriors denounced the CSCE, and détente generally, with increasing stridency. For Margaret Thatcher, leader of the British Conservative Party from February 1975, détente was a 'one of those soothing foreign terms which carries an ugly reality that plain English would expose'.[70] On the eve of the signing of the Final Act of the CSCE, she denounced the forthcoming agreement:

> Détente sounds a fine word. And, to the extent that there really has been a relaxation in international tension, it is a fine thing. But the fact remains that throughout this decade of détente, the armed forces of the Soviet

Union have increased, are increasing, and show no signs of diminishing. Mr. Brezhnev, in a speech in June 1972, made a statement on détente which is quoted in virtually every Soviet speech or article on the subject. He said that peaceful co-existence 'in no way implies the possibility of relaxing the ideological struggle. On the contrary we must be prepared for this struggle to be intensified and become an even sharper form of confrontation between the systems'.[71]

Thatcher's hostility to détente (and to the Final Act of the CSCE in particular) resonated strongly with the Conservative Party. After all, this was a party which had opposed Communism since 1917 and appeasement since 1939 (the intensity of both stances being due, in no small part, to the rhetoric of Winston S. Churchill). Against this, proponents of détente later argued that the Final Act meant that the frontier questions of the 'first' Cold War were displaced as a bone of East–West contention by human rights in the 'second' Cold War.

Following the arrival of Mikhail Gorbachev as Soviet leader in 1985, Callaghan pronounced the Final Act an 'important precursor of Perestroika'.[72] This was not Callaghan's view in the immediate aftermath of the Final Act: in March 1976 he gloomily predicted: 'We should not deceive ourselves that the Soviet Union will be willing, at least in our lifetime, to forgo or even relax its ultimate control of the Eastern European region.'[73] Given all of this we might usefully ask as to whether or not the British knew in 1975 that the Soviets were paying a sufficient price for the recognition of the frontiers of Europe?[74] Douglas Hurd (a prominent Conservative thinker on foreign policy and later Thatcher's foreign secretary) originally concurred with his leader, seeing the human rights provisions as 'empty phrases'. Yet, by his own account, he turned out to be mistaken. Contrary to all expectations, Helsinki *did* give the West 'a lever to prise open . . . the Soviet system'. Hurd enthused that Helsinki only gave the USSR 'what they already had in practice, namely the acceptance of the Yalta boundaries. In return they . . . recognised in treaty an obligation to respect human rights and thus gave the West a legal right to make representations when this obligation was neglected.'[75] But these words were written in 1997 – *after* the Cold War and the Soviet Union had passed into history.

In truth, the British never adhered to any single set of aims and objectives during the CSCE process.[76] The reality was that diplomats had only highlighted the Soviet record on human rights in the absence of any other potential area of vulnerability.[77] In February 1974 James Cable, head of the FCO Planning Staff, opined: 'We have no ambition to turn East European peoples against their governments, but we try to practice policies which make it easier rather than harder for governments to exercise whatever degree of independence from Moscow that they feel may be in their power.'[78] Yet whatever the private hopes of British officials with regard to the future of Eastern Europe, it was clear that the West had abandoned the rhetorical support of freedom in the Soviet bloc in return for a general settlement. Nevertheless, as with Munich, Western guilt over Helsinki was never far from the surface. One of the most effective critics of détente was the Soviet dissident and exile Aleksandr Solzhenitsyn. On 30 June 1975 he stated:

> I have tried to convey to your countrymen the constrained breathing of the inhabitants of Eastern Europe in these weeks when an amicable agreement of diplomatic shovels will inter in a common grave bodies that are still breathing. I have tried to explain to Americans that 1973, the tender dawn of détente, was precisely the year when the starvation rations in Soviet prisons and concentration camps were reduced even further. And in recent months, when more and more Western speechmakers have pointed to the beneficial consequences of détente, the Soviet Union has adopted a novel and important improvement in its system of punishment: to retain their glorious supremacy in the invention of forced-labor camps, Soviet prison specialists have now established a new form of solitary confinement – forced labor in solitary cells. That means cold, hunger, lack of fresh air, insufficient light, and impossible work norms; the failure to fulfill these norms is punished by confinement under even more brutal conditions.[79]

Many of those who had denounced the 'sell-outs' at Yalta and Potsdam now accepted the CSCE with equanimity (although even US Secretary of State Henry Kissinger fretted that the Final Act would be manipulated by the Soviets.[80]) How, asked Solzhenitsyn, could the West do this?

> [U]nder the cast-iron-shell of communism . . . there is occurring a liberation of the human spirit. New generations are growing up which are steadfast in their struggle with evil; which are not willing to accept unprincipled compromises; which prefer to lose everything – salary, conditions of existence and life itself – but are not willing to sacrifice conscience; not willing to make deals with evil.[81]

In a speech in Milwaukee on 16 July 1975, Kissinger made it clear that he had great respect for Solzhenitsyn as a writer (although he had advised President Ford not to see him).[82] Signally, the secretary of state also declared:

> If I understand the message of Solzhenitsyn, it is that the U.S. should pursue an aggressive policy to overthrow the Soviet system. But I believe that if his views became the national policy of the US, we would be confronted with considerable threat of military conflict . . . I believe that the consequences of his views would not be acceptable to the American people or to the world.[83]

In Britain, Solzhenitsyn's appeals also fell upon largely deaf ears. But Thatcher was listening.[84] She stated: 'when the Soviet leaders jail a writer, or a priest, or a doctor or a worker, for the crime of speaking freely . . . [they] reveal a regime that is afraid of truth and liberty; it dare not allow its people to enjoy the freedoms we take for granted, and a nation that denies those freedoms to its own people will have few scruples in denying them to others.' That being so, '[i]f détente is to progress then it ought to mean that the Soviet authorities relax their ruthless opposition to all forms and expressions of dissent. And as we talk of these things we naturally think of Alexander Solzhenitsyn and the other writers, thinkers and scientists who have fearlessly expressed their belief in freedom'.[85]

By the summer of 1975, the political reaction against détente/appeasement was gathering pace.[86] Détente attracted a 'transnational lobby of critics' that included Thatcher, Solzhenitsyn, Red China's Deng Xiaoping and Senator Henry Jackson (D-WA). All of these figures, to a greater or lesser degree, charged the West with appeasement. The general argument was that, because of the conceptual differences between the West's détente and the Soviet Union's 'peaceful co-existence', the latter was making significant gains.[87] Détente, in short, was a 'one-way street'.[88] Or, as the *New York Times* wrote: 'The thirty-five nations Conference on Security and Cooperation . . . should have never been convened. Never have so many people fought so long for so little.'[89] Early in 1976 Thatcher stated that 'we must . . . heed the warnings of those, like Alexander Solzhenitsyn, who remind us that we have been fighting a kind of 'Third World War' over the entire period since 1945 – and that we have been steadily losing ground . . . We must remember that there are no Queensbury rules in the contest that is now going on. And the Russians are playing to win.'[90] Such attacks moved an exasperated Kissinger to write:

> No policy will soon, if ever, eliminate the competition and irreconcilable ideological differences between the United States and the Soviet Union. Nor will it make all interests compatible. We are engaged in a protracted process with inevitable ups and downs. But there is no alternative to the policy of penalties for adventurism and incentives for restraint. What do those who speak so glibly about 'one-way streets' or 'preemptive concessions' propose concretely that this country do? What precisely has been given up? What level of confrontation do they seek? What threats would they make? What risks would they run? What precise changes in our defense posture, what level of expenditure over what period of time, do they advocate? How, concretely, do they suggest managing the U.S.–Soviet relationship in an era of strategic equality?[91]

Kissinger later conceded that he and Nixon had gone too far in stressing the 'geopolitical necessities' of the United States while their 'critics and successors tried to compensate by invoking absolute versions of American principles'.[92] For the latter, of course, Munich, Yalta and Helsinki fell on the wrong side of history. Opponents of Helsinki therefore continued to argue that the failure to aid 'freedom' in East Berlin in 1953, in Hungary in 1956 and in Czechoslovakia in 1968 echoed the failures of the Western powers during the era of appeasement prior to the Second World War. Opponents of détente with the Soviets invoked the spectre of appeasement with ease. In 1978, Walter Laqueur wrote:

> Underlying the appeasement of the 1930s was a trauma, that of World War I, the many hundreds of thousands of soldiers killed at Passchendaele and the Somme. Underlying the appeasement of the 1970s is the trauma of Vietnam. Democracies, with rare exceptions, always incline to pacifism, and they find it difficult to understand those who do not share this disposition: how can anyone be so unreasonable as to consider war an instrument for the solution of conflicts?[93]

In the United States, Reagan attacked President Ford's continued pursuit of détente, stating: 'Like an echo from the past, the voice of Winston Churchill's grandson . . . recently . . . [warned] that the spread of totalitarianism threatens the world once again [as] the democracies are "wandering without aim."'[94] Reagan later declared that: 'Negotiation with the Soviet Union must never become appeasement' as détente was 'a one-way street that the Soviet Union has used to pursue its own aims'.[95] Such rhetoric resonated strongly with Thatcher who, like Reagan, was an ideologue in matters of foreign policy, sharing the view that détente reinvigorated a system that would eventually collapse under the weight of its own contradictions.

> I always believed that our western system would ultimately triumph, if we did not throw our advantages away, because it rested on the unique, almost limitless, creativity and vitality of individuals. Even a system like that of the Soviets, which set out to crush the individual, could never totally succeed in doing so . . . This also implied that at some time the right individual could challenge even the system which he had used to attain power . . . That is why those who subsequently considered that I was led astray from my original approach to the Soviet Union because I was dazzled by Mr. Gorbachev were wrong. I spotted him because I was searching for someone like him. [96]

In a speech in 1976, Thatcher responded to Soviet jibes about her being an 'Iron Lady' by asserting: 'Yes I am an iron lady, after all it wasn't a bad thing to be an iron duke, yes if that's how they wish to interpret my defence of values and freedoms fundamental to our way of life.'[97] Small wonder that Thatcher was later to conclude: 'It is difficult to see any difference between appeasement and détente.'[98] When told by Soviet Premier Alexei Kosygin that the Soviet Union was a peace-loving state whose armaments were much overstated, Thatcher told him 'not to be so modest' – anyone who had seen a military parade in Red Square 'would underestimate the Soviet Union's [military] capacity'.[99] In June 1980, a suggestion by France's President Giscard d'Estaing to the effect that the Soviets were showing signs of moderation in their occupation of Afghanistan, was dismissed by Thatcher who opined that the French leader was 'half way to Neville Chamberlain'.[100] In her view, her accession to power in May 1979 marked the drawing of a line in the sand akin to the about-turn undertaken in British policy towards Hitler in March 1939. While lacking the dramatic turn of events of the post-March 1939 period, from May 1979 onwards Soviet Communism was to be opposed with a renewed vigour by a British government. In early 1980, Thatcher advised US President Jimmy Carter:

> For many years now, the West has sought to develop a sensible relationship with the Soviet Union which could minimise the risk of war, lower the level of armaments and develop mutually beneficial changes in the field of trade and human contacts. The Russians have chosen to interpret 'détente' much more narrowly, and have continued to pursue a policy of expansion and subversion wherever they felt they could get away with it. They may well have thought they could nibble away at our interests indefinitely. They need to be reminded in clear terms that this is not so.[101]

Henceforth, and for as long as Thatcher was at the helm, it was the rhetoric of resolution and defiance that would set the tone in the articulation of British foreign policy.

CHAPTER SIX

'We have ceased to be a nation in retreat': Margaret Thatcher, the Falklands War and the negation of Munich and Suez

[Britain is] attempting to appease simultaneously the Falkland Islanders on the one hand and the Argentines on the other, irrespective of the inconsistencies where this leads us.

UNNAMED BRITISH DIPLOMAT, Buenos Aires, 1970s[1]

I think that Maggie Thatcher sees herself as a Churchill

LIEUT. DAVID TINKER (RN), *HMS Glamorgan,* to Julian Salmon, 6 May 1982[2]

There is no such thing as a *little war* for a great Nation.

THE DUKE OF WELLINGTON[3]

The Falklands War began on Friday 2 April 1982, when Argentine forces invaded and occupied the British crown dependencies of the Falkland Islands and South Georgia. This unleashed what was, in the words of Britain's then-ambassador to the UN, a 'wholly unexpected and tempestuous crisis'.[4] The British retook the islands in a war that, by the time of the Argentine surrender on 14 June 1982, resulted in the deaths of 649 Argentine military personnel, 255 British military personnel and 3 Falkland Islanders.[5] This belies the fact that the war is sometimes characterized as an anachronistic colonial conflict that was entirely idiosyncratic, both in terms of the protagonists and the issues at stake. Jorge Luis Borges, the Argentine writer, famously said: 'The Falklands thing was a fight between two bald men over a comb.'[6] In actual fact, the Falklands War of 1982 was to prove of immense significance in the postwar history of appeasement as analogies with Munich and Suez abounded.[7] On hearing of the invasion, the Conservative MP Alan Clark lamented: 'It's all over. We're a Third World country, no good for anything.' Clark, a historian of some repute, wondered if 'it . . . felt like this in the Thirties . . . when the dictators, Hitler and Musso[lini], decided to help themselves to something – Durazzo, Memel, Prague – and all we could do was wring our hands and talk about 'bad faith'?[8] Such sentiments proved to be unduly pessimistic. Francis Pym, who became foreign and commonwealth secretary at the outset of the conflict, reassured his department: 'Self-determination of peoples has been a cornerstone of the international order at least since the foundation of the League of Nations. This is an important point of principle that must be upheld.'[9] One author spoke for the majority of the British population when he opined: 'It is a principle at stake – the same principle as was at stake when Hitler invaded the Sudetenland and Czechoslovakia. Our craven attitude then proved once and for all that appeasement is not only immoral, it does not pay.'[10] The mood of the political class reflected this. Defence Secretary John Nott later recalled: 'When a gun is pointed to your head, diplomacy has a tendency to veer towards appeasement. Yet appeasing the fascist junta in Argentina, once they had invaded British territory, was not on our agenda. There were only two choices: war or surrender. As circumstances later showed, there was never an honourable negotiated settlement in between.'[11] Labour's Lord Molloy stated that 'the ruling junta of Argentina are of the same ilk as those who trampled over Europe in the late Thirties and . . . therefore there can be no question of appeasement whatever.'[12] In the event, this proved to be the attitude of the majority of the British people.

The Falklands War proved to be one of the most intense arenas of debates about British collective memory, where appeasement had supposedly been expunged from the British psyche by two means: first, by a refusal to negotiate on the sovereignty of the islands after the Argentine invasion; and, second, by the expulsion of those invaders by means of Operation *Corporate*. Margaret Thatcher, a fervent admirer of Churchill,[13] had grown up with the 'Guilty Men' thesis and was a declared opponent of appeasement, who knew 'that by the Munich Agreement Britain had complicity in the great wrong that had been done to Czechoslovakia.'[14] Thatcher had famously been labelled the 'Iron Lady' for her uncompromising stance against the Soviet Union and her views on foreign policy were, to say the least, forthright.[15] Shortly after the Falklands were invaded Enoch Powell told the House of Commons:

The Prime Minister, shortly after she came into office, received a soubriquet as the 'Iron Lady'. It arose in the context of remarks which she made about defence against the Soviet Union and its allies; but there was no reason to suppose that the right hon. Lady did not welcome and, indeed, take pride in that description. In the next week or two this House, the nation and the right hon. Lady herself will learn of what metal she is made.[16]

As the British task force, assembled with impressive haste after the invasion, sailed south, American Secretary of State Alexander Haig urged her to reach a compromise with Argentina. Jim Rentschler, an aide to Haig, recalled Thatcher's staunch refusal to allow Argentina to gain *anything* from its invasion.

> I am pledged before the House of Commons, the Defense Minister is pledged, [and] the Foreign Secretary is pledged to restore British administration. I did not dispatch a fleet to install some nebulous arrangement which would have no authority whatsoever. Interim authority! [T]o do *what*? I beg you, I beg you to remember that in 1938 Neville Chamberlain sat at this same table discussing an arrangement which sounds very much like the one you are asking me to accept; and were I to do so, I would be censured in the House of Commons – and properly so! We in Britain simply refuse to reward aggression – that is the lesson we have learned from 1938.[17]

In his memoirs, Haig recalled that the prime minister had invoked Nelson and Wellington and 'rapped sharply on the table top and recalled that this was the table at which Neville Chamberlain sat in 1938 and spoke of the Czechs as a faraway people about whom we know so little'.[18] This version of history accorded with the heroic and Churchillian model, and the prime minister was clear what its lessons were. There were, however, many in her party who lacked her resolution. Indeed, some believed that the Falklands would do for Thatcher as Suez had done for Eden.[19] Ian Gilmour, Foreign and Commonwealth Office (FCO) spokesman in the Commons until September 1981, opined: 'We are making a big mistake. It will make Suez look like common sense'; Julian Critchley was '[w]orried that expectations are too high. He feels that the military difficulties may be unsurmountable'; and Eden's biographer, Robert Rhodes James, was meanwhile reported to be 'hopelessly defeatist, depressed and disloyal'.[20] For Thatcher such opinions represented nothing so much as the tradition of Chamberlainite appeasement. She wanted no part of it.

The 1982 conflict was the result of a protracted historical confrontation regarding the sovereignty of the Falkland Islands. Argentina had disputed British sovereignty over the Falklands since 1833[21] (a claim reiterated in the constitution of 1994).[22] The Argentine government saw the 1982 invasion as the re-occupation of sovereign territory and it remains unmoved in this attitude.[23] The British government, by contrast, viewed the 1982 invasion as an act of unprovoked aggression against a dependent territory and set its face against appeasement. The latter stance is maintained to this day – for two reasons. First, appeasement had contributed to the Argentine decision to invade in April 1982; second, a significant amount of blood was spilled to regain the islands. British Prime Minister David Cameron told the Falkland Islanders in December 2011: 'We will always maintain our commitment to you on any question of sovereignty. Your right to self-determination is the cornerstone of our policy. We will never negotiate on the sovereignty of the Falkland Islands unless you, the Falkland Islanders, so wish. No democracy could ever do otherwise.'[24] Thus, nearly 30 years after the successful liberation of the Falklands, a British prime minister was still framing his rhetoric with a decidedly Churchillian edge. In 2013 this stance was given diplomatic weight when the Falkland Islanders voted overwhelmingly to remain British.[25]

Ironically, given the manner in which the Falklands War came to encapsulate the postwar British rejection of appeasement, the attitude of the British Foreign Office towards the Falkland Islands before 1982 had long resembled a policy that would have appealed to the worst instincts of Chamberlain and R. A. Butler. Oddly, this attitude originated from a time when British Imperialism was at its very height. In 1910, Foreign Secretary Sir Edward Grey enquired as to why an Argentine map labelled the Falklands as belonging to Argentina. Sidney Spicer, of the FO's American Department, responded: '[I]t is difficult to avoid the conclusion that the Argentine government's attitude is not altogether unjustified and that our action has been somewhat high-handed.'[26] In 1911 Ronald Campbell, another FO official, concluded: 'We cannot easily make a good claim, and we have wisely done everything to avoid discussing the subject with Argentina.'[27] In 1936, the head of the American Department of the FO went so far as to concede that scrutiny of the British case over the Falklands could make His Majesty's government look like 'international bandits'! Such appeasing tendencies were only strengthened as the threat of Hitler focused the British official mind ever more intensely upon Europe. One unreleased FO file from 1940 is intriguingly titled 'Proposed offer by Her Majesty's Government to reunite Falkland Islands with Argentina and acceptance of lease'.[28] Although we can only speculate about this document's contents, the proposals contained therein may well represent the type of thinking that saw Britain, in its hour of greatest extremity, offering any potential ally a piece of British territory. This was the ultimate in pragmatic appeasement and was most notoriously employed when Churchill appeared prepared to countenance handing over Northern Ireland to Dublin in return for Éire's entry into the war against Germany.[29] When revealed, as with all such initiatives, it appeared unworkable and shameful in equal measure.

Hugh Bicheno, a staunch critic of the FCO's role in the lead up to the invasion of 1982, notes that the 'fuse for the Falklands War was lit' in December 1968 when Foreign Secretary Michael Stewart agreed a Memorandum of Understanding with Argentine Foreign Minister Nicanor Costa Méndez. This stated that when it could be shown to be in the 'best interests' of the Falkland Islanders 'the Government of the United Kingdom as part of a final settlement will recognize Argentina's sovereignty over the islands from a date to be agreed'.[30] From this date forward British policy pursued a curious dual track: it would negotiate with Buenos Aires but allow the islanders a right of veto.[31] The latter was guaranteed by the UK 'Falklands lobby' – which strongly opposed a 'sell-out' of the islanders. Lord Carrington, foreign and commonwealth secretary, 1979–82, later recalled that 'Parliament reckoned that negotiation was intended to lead to surrender'. This was unfortunate if, as Carrington later opined, negotiation was the only option if armed conflict was to be avoided in the long term.[32] The credibility gap in British policy over the Falklands grew over time: although, on occasion, London had even found it expedient to seek to square the circle by old-fashioned 'gunboat diplomacy'.

In 1952 and 1953, the British government had deployed Royal Navy units to the South Atlantic so as to demonstrate to Buenos Aires the seriousness of their intent.[33] In November 1977, when fifty Argentine 'scientists' landed on Southern Thule, fears of an Argentine invasion of the Falklands were very real. The then–Labour government of James Callaghan duly deployed a naval force in the South Atlantic under the codename Operation *Journeyman*.[34] On the eve of the Argentine invasion of the Falklands in 1982, Callaghan revealed the 1977 deployment to parliament: '[O]n a very recent occasion, of which I have full knowledge, Britain assembled ships which had been stationed in the Caribbean, Gibraltar and in the Mediterranean, and stood then about 400 miles off the Falklands in support of HMS "Endurance", and that when this fact became known, without fuss and publicity, a diplomatic solution followed.'[35] Understandably, Callaghan continued to try and make political capital out of this event. When, on 8 July, Thatcher asserted that had Labour been in power, it would not have fired a shot in the South Atlantic, Callaghan retorted: 'I tell the Rt. Hon. Lady, if we had been in power, we would not have needed to.'[36]

Callaghan's biographer, Ken Morgan, says that Maurice Oldfield's SIS (MI6) made sure that the Argentines were aware of the deployment of submarines before Ted Rowlands, a junior minister at the FCO, began negotiations with Buenos Aires on 13 December 1977.[37] Despite Morgan's claim, Callaghan is more circumspect in his memoirs, stating only: 'I informed the head of MI6 of our plan before the ships sailed and it is possible, as I hoped, some information reached the Argentinean Armed forces.'[38] Richard Deacon asserts that a former CIA man informed him that the Americans had been informed that, in November 1977, 'the Argentines had been told every detail of the British Fleet movements . . . through two other sources upon which the Argentines relied. It was very cleverly planted by an agent of MI6.'[39] Interviewed for a British Channel 4 documentary in 1992, Admiral Juan José Lombardo, commander of Argentina's submarine force in 1977, stated that Admiral Jorge Anaya, commander of the Argentine fleet, had asked if his conventional SSKs could deal with the

British SSNs. Lombardo's unambiguous 'No' scuttled plans for an invasion in November 1977.[40] David Owen, foreign and commonwealth secretary in 1977, later asserted that it was 'amazing' that the official inquiry into the origins of the war, the Franks Report, never 'rebuffed or corroborated' Callaghan's statement that he had told Oldfield 'to let his contacts in the Argentine Government know that our submarines were in the vicinity of the Falklands'.[41] Owen concludes that a 'tacit understanding' was reached within the Franks Committee to set aside what happened in 1977 'despite its importance' for assessing what happened in 1982. This arose because, the two Labour privy councillors (Harold Lever and Merlyn Rees) wanted to protect Callaghan's reputation, whilst the two Conservative privy councillors (Anthony Barber and Harold Watkinson) had no desire to investigate whether Carrington and Thatcher had allowed the invasion to happen by failing to act as the Labour government had done in 1977.[42]

In 2001, Peter Hennessy wrote that, while the Franks inquiry had concluded that there was no evidence of any communication ever having been received by the Argentines, he had been informed by a source within SIS that it very likely was.[43] In his official history Lawrence Freedman asserts that when he interviewed Callaghan the latter asserted that he had seen no harm in letting the Argentines knew about the general picture in 1977. In order to do this, he made a point of apprising Oldfield of the facts (in the expectation that the latter would tell the Americans who would, in turn, tell the Argentines). This, in Callaghan's words, was done by 'giving him a hint without actually telling him'. For his part, David Owen, told Freedman that he did not think that Oldfield had taken Callaghan's hint as Owen himself had expressly asked for secrecy in Cabinet.[44] Owen had also refused a Ministry of Defence (MoD) request to tell the US Navy about the deployment, 'for the very reason that I knew they had close links with the Argentine Navy and I did not want Argentina to know'.[45] Furthermore, Owen does not believe that Oldfield (who, as director of SIS, was nominally subordinate to the foreign secretary) would have disclosed the naval deployment without 'at least talking to me first'. In any case, '[n]o evidence has ever been found that he had been either instructed by [Callaghan] or acted on such instructions'.[46] Owen recently stated that, when Callaghan made these assertions in 1983, he was mistaken, possibly due to a memory lapse. Indeed, Owen stresses that there had never been any intention of letting Buenos Aires know (covertly or otherwise) about the deployment (which he stresses was 'preventative' *not* 'secretive').[47] Owen feared that any overt show of force would have been regarded as escalating matters.[48] 'Our naval policy was [therefore] an insurance policy, it did not of itself deter.'[49]

Hugh Bicheno, 'the deep cover officer at the 2-man SIS Buenos Aires station at the time',[50] writes in his history of the war that 'Prime Minister James Callaghan's government sent an attack submarine to the South Atlantic (under orders not to respond if attacked but to "surface or withdraw at high speed submerged"),[51] but since the Argentines did not know about it until after the 1982 invasion, the gesture served no deterrent purpose whatever.' And of Callaghan's later claim about the deterrent value of the 1977 deployment, Bicheno observes: 'In [March] 1982 Callaghan alleged he had used SIS channels to let the Argentines know about it in 1977. *He lied.*'[52] In 2013, Bicheno told this author: 'Not only can I confirm that [Callaghan's] was an outright lie because I was there [in Buenos Aires in 1977], but even [David] Owen admitted, years later, that there was no trace of any such action on file.' Furthermore: 'Nobody has contradicted this, and I saw a clip of Owen on TV laughing uneasily about it and saying that he had not been able to confirm the truth of Callaghan's allegation from the files in the FCO.'[53] Regardless, Freedman notes that, after the Argentine government engaged positively with Rowlands, the Royal Navy force was withdrawn on 20 December 1977, 'with no publicity about its mission'.

> It has remained something of a curiosity in the Falklands history as a precautionary deployment that turned out not to have been needed. Because it was precautionary Argentine awareness was never essential. Indeed, it was believed to be for the best that the ships returned home without anyone being any the wiser. Once their presence had become known, supposedly serving some deterrents purpose, then the risk was that they would be stuck there for an extended period.[54]

When Thatcher succeeded Callaghan as prime minister in May 1979, the talks between London and Buenos Aires were deadlocked. The British affirmed a willingness to continue with negotiations but there were very real constraints on what the Foreign and Commonwealth Office could, or would, offer. As Callaghan had advised his ambassador in Argentina in 1975: 'no British government, of whatever political complexion, would be able to reach any agreement [with Argentina] . . . over the sovereignty of the Falkland Islands'. Callaghan said that this would be the case until the islanders 'reassess[ed] where their interests lie'.[55] Concurring with Callaghan, both Lord Carrington and Ian Gilmour later asserted that the on-going dispute was bad for Argentina, the Falkland Islanders and the United Kingdom.[56] Thatcher, on the other hand, was quick to accuse the FCO, always suspect in any case,[57] of preparing to sell-out to foreign interests.[58] This suspicion was shared by many in the Conservative Party, especially on the Right. At a meeting of backbenchers to discuss the invasion of the Falklands, John Stokes MP spoke for many others when he asserted that there was a 'smell of appeasement' about the FCO.[59] Gilmour later defensively asserted: 'The traditional Foreign Office view of the Falklands, caricatured by its enemies as merely wanting to get rid of the Falkland Islands as soon as possible, was [in fact] based on a careful assessment of the situation.'[60] Nicholas Ridley, a minister at the FCO, had warned Carrington that negotiation with Argentina was 'the only valid option',[61] before infuriating the prime minister by proposing a leaseback solution over to the Falklands, following a visit to Buenos Aires in July 1979.[62] Although Ridley had warned the Falkland Islanders, in a manner resembling Chamberlain's treatment of the Czechoslovaks in the summer of 1938, that they could expect no help if they were invaded by Argentina,[63] Gilmour later asserted that these proposals were 'almost certainly the only way of avoiding a war'.[64] Ridley had told his Argentine opposite number: 'We had given up a third of the world's surface and found it beneficial to do so', believing the Falklands to be indefensible in any case. Thatcher responded coldly to the latter assertion by stating simply: 'We could bomb Buenos Aires if nothing else.'[65]

In September 1979, Carrington presented the prime minister with three policy options: first, a 'Fortress Falklands'; second, negotiations with Argentina about economic links with no discussion of sovereignty; and, third, negotiations about the substance of sovereignty. The foreign secretary favoured the latter option but, ominously, Thatcher scrawled on the file: 'I could not possibly agree to the line the Foreign Secretary is proposing'.[66] Carrington nevertheless repeatedly stressed that Argentina would, at some point, lose patience. In January 1980 the foreign secretary warned: 'There are pressures within Argentina, some of them resulting from inter-service rivalry, which carry with them the possibility of the Argentines taking measures against the Falkland Islands which could cause us serious difficulties.'[67] Carrington was, however, banging his head against a brick wall as his Cabinet colleagues had little appetite for leaseback. In a compromise that would – and could only – lead nowhere, Ridley was allowed to return to Buenos Aires.[68] The leaseback proposal thus limped forward hopelessly and, on 2 December 1980, Ridley put some (rather moderate) proposals before the House of Commons stressing that although the 'dispute is causing continuing uncertainty, emigration and economic stagnation in the islands . . . [although] we [are still] guided by the wishes of the islanders themselves'.[69] Having raised the hackles of the Falklands lobby, Ridley was, predictably, denounced in the Commons; and Carrington fared little better in the Lords (although the debate was characteristically genteel there). The attacks in the Commons,[70] and mirrored (albeit rather more politely) in the Lords,[71] were sustained by the prime minister's distaste for engaging in appeasement in negotiations with Argentina. The Liberal MP Russell Johnston spoke for all sides when he told Ridley that there was 'no support at all in the Falkland Islands or in this House for the shameful schemes for getting rid of these islands which have been festering in the Foreign Office for years'. Ridley should therefore disown 'those schemes' and, instead, work to improve the links between the United Kingdom and the Falklands.[72]

Carrington thought that the Ridley initiative had been 'right but rash',[73] and therefore required his personal intervention with the prime minister.

But when he broached the subject of leaseback with Thatcher, her response was described as 'thermo-nuclear'.[74] The FCO's insistence that meaningful negotiations on sovereignty should be pursued with Argentina ran against all of Thatcher's instincts. FCO diplomacy therefore had very little prospect of success as its 'pragmatism' was effectively obstructed by Thatcherite 'resolution' and populist anti-appeasement. Gilmour later described these attacks as constituting 'the silliest half hour that I ever heard in Parliament' as '[t]he blimps of all parties rushed in'. Gilmour recalls that when Carrington had tried to prevail upon Thatcher in this matter she had insisted on taking it to full Cabinet – unusually for a foreign policy matter. And, since Thatcher would oppose leaseback in Cabinet, it had no chance of being accepted as policy.[75] Max Hastings and Simon Jenkins commented: 'A compromise settlement was never achieved because the British Foreign Office proved more competent at negotiation with another government than its own.'[76] Stagnation now seemed the order of the day and Gilmour duly added a fourth option to Carrington's list of diplomatic options: 'do nothing and just hope for the best'.[77] In the event this was the option that was chosen by default. Henceforth, the Thatcher government's policy was thus one of general 'Micawberism', as the British ambassador in Buenos Aires commented in early 1982.[78]

Carrington, who resigned from the FCO (along with Richard Luce and Gilmour's successor, Humphrey Atkins) over the invasion, wrote on 6 April that 'the Argentinian invasion of the Falklands has been very deeply felt in this country – perhaps more deeply than any single event in our relations with the outside world for a generation. It has led to strong criticism of Government policy in Parliament and in the press. Most of this criticism has in my view been unfounded.'[79] Although he told Thatcher that he had been right to resign,[80] he added:

> On the question of wrong signals, I will add only this. The right signals, for us and for previous British governments, were to my mind to combine a clear readiness to negotiate with an equally clear determination to defend the islands if [the] need arose . . . I think that the fundamental difference between us and previous British Governments of either party was not in the signals we were sending, but in the fact that we were faced with a Government in Buenos Aires determined on action.[81]

The 'signals' given out by the British in the years before the invasion were certainly confusing. Bicheno opines: 'In the final analysis the most culpable accomplices were the British, because their policy of appeasement misled not only the Argentines but also the Americans into believing Britain would scuttle.'[82] There is a great deal of merit in this statement. Yet it must be understood that there was a great deal of uncertainty in British policy and in Britain's demonstration of its interests. If we see the FO/ FCO as an agent of appeasement in the years before 1982 we must, conversely, see the Falklands lobby and Parliament as an anti-appeasement counterweight. And, in the latter camp, Thatcher's presence was decisive.

In the United Kingdom, the political weight of the domestic Falklands Islands lobby meant that the political pressure against appeasing Argentina was intense. This meant that any number of MPs were always ready to publicly denounce any prospect of 'appeasing' Argentina over the Falklands (the attacks on Ridley in December 1980 being a case in point). Indeed, even Gilmour, a strong proponent of negotiation, told the Commons: 'We have many times made it clear that the interests of the Falkland Islanders are paramount, so there can be no question of a sell-out.'[83] Suspicious observers nevertheless continued to ask: exactly what were the British willing to negotiate with Buenos Aires? After all, the FCO's continued willingness to talk (and make concessions), along with certain other British government actions, looked like nothing so much as a prelude to appeasement. Callaghan was right when he later identified the decision to scrap HMS *Endurance*, made as part of John Nott's 1981 defence review, and the exclusion of the Falkland Islanders from full British citizenship under the 1981 Nationality Act as both sending the wrong message to Argentina (i.e. that Britain was disinterested in the Falklands).[84] For his part, Carrington resented those who opposed negotiations without advocating an effective British deterrence stance in the south Atlantic.[85] As late as 24 March 1982, Carrington had pleaded with Nott for a reprieve for HMS *Endurance* as a 'visible sign of our commitment' to the Falklands.[86] A month earlier, Nott had informed Carrington: 'I see no alternative than . . . sticking to our original decision and riding out the controversy'[87] and now the foreign secretary was told that the vessel's 'utility is marginal' and 'we cannot see our way to pay for her retention'.[88] At the same time, and despite the concerns about the fate of HMS *Endurance*, the FCO insisted to certain concerned MPs that the withdrawal of HMS *Endurance* 'in no way implies a diminution of our commitment to the Falkland Islands'. Ironically, it was noted that the same point should be made to the Argentine government if the matter was raised.[89]

In February 1982, Callaghan had protested publicly against the planned withdrawal of HMS *Endurance* in the Commons.[90] Having staved off the threat to the vessel as prime minister, Callaghan noted that Thatcher's statement to the effect that 'the defence capability of that ship is extremely limited',[91] 'showed that she did not grasp that the value of HMS *Endurance* was as a deterrent, a symbol that Britain would resist an armed attack, and a visible sign of British sovereignty'.[92] Similarly, the last under-secretary of state for defence for the Royal Navy, Keith Speed, thought that the decision to scrap HMS *Endurance* 'contribute[d] to the key events leading up to the South Atlantic conflict'.[93] In 1983, the Franks Report reached a similar conclusion.

In July 1981 the British Embassy in Buenos Aires reported . . . that several Argentine newspapers had carried prominently versions of a report of an article in *The Daily Telegraph* on the subject. The letter reported that all the newspaper articles highlighted the theme that Britain was 'abandoning the protection of the Falkland Islands'. An intelligence report in September 1981 quoted an Argentine diplomatic view that the withdrawal of HMS *Endurance* had been construed by the Argentines as a deliberate political gesture; they did not see it as an inevitable economy in Britain's defence budget since the implications for the Islands and for Britain's position in the South Atlantic were fundamental.[94]

By 1980, the Royal Navy had seriously diminished as a tool of British state policy, and the 1981 Defence Review[95] would only exacerbate matters further.[96] Speed had protested vehemently against the proposed cuts in the Royal Navy[97] – and was sacked for his pains in May 1981.[98] Thatcher's opponents point out that, for all her heroic posturing, her 'Finest Hour' in the summer of 1982 had been preceded by a deliberate weakening of Britain's defences. Gilmour, admittedly a staunch critic of the prime minister and all her works, said that Thatcher, '[u]nlike Chamberlain in 1937–39 . . . did not even try and prevent war taking place'.[99] The Royal Navy – the frontline against any threat from Argentina – was hit particularly hard by Thatcher's spending cuts and the first sea lord, Admiral Sir Henry Leach, asked the prime minister to pause 'before you and your Cabinet colleagues consider a proposition substantially to dismantle that Navy'. Leach warned: 'We are on the brink of a historic decision. War seldom takes the expected form and a strong maritime capability provides flexibility for the unforeseen. If you erode it to the extent envisaged I believe you will foreclose your future options and prejudice our national security.'[100] On 8 June 1981, Leach had an audience with the prime minister.

> The point he wished to emphasise most was the serious miscalculation which we would be making if we disregard the deterrent effect of major wartime capability on peacetime and even in the opening phases of hostilities. And, within this capability, it was the surface fleet which provided much of the deterrent effect, simply because it was visible . . . But if the surface fleet was cut in the way proposed, this would, in his view, unbalance our entire defence capability, and once the ships had gone, we should probably not be able to recover this century.[101]

On 29 March 1982, Speed had asked Nott: '[H]ow can we apparently afford [to spend] £8,000 million [on the Trident missile system] to meet a threat in 13 years' time . . . when we cannot afford £3 million to keep HMS "Endurance" on patrol to meet a threat that is facing us today?' Nott dismissively replied by simply asserting: 'I do not intend to get involved in a debate about the Falkland Islands now. These issues are too important to be diverted into a discussion on HMS "Endurance".'[102] The Falkland Islands, it seemed, were exempt from the principles of deterrence normally so beloved of the Thatcher government. In the emergency Commons debate on 3 April, Labour's Douglas Jay indicted the Thatcher government on two counts. First, appeasement and, second, weakening Britain's defences.

> [T]he Foreign Office is . . . saturated with the spirit of appeasement. I hope that, apart from anything else, the Foreign Office will now examine its conscience, if it has one . . . I trust that this event will put an end to the policy of unilateral disarmament of the Royal Navy, which the Government have been carrying on. Unilateral disarmament always invites aggression . . . The Secretary of State for Defence made an extraordinary statement on television last night. He said that if we took any military preparatory action it would spoil our efforts at diplomacy. Exactly the opposite is true. Diplomacy can succeed only if it is visibly supported by effective action . . . the whole history of this century has shown, if one gives way to this sort of desperate, illegal action, things will not get better, but will get worse.[103]

The Labour leader of the Opposition, Michael Foot, was outraged by the invasion and revisited his earlier incarnation as 'Cato'.[104]

> [The Falkland Islanders] have been betrayed . . . [and] the Government . . . [which] must now prove by deeds – they will never be able to do it by words – that they are not responsible for the betrayal and cannot be faced with that charge. That is the charge, I believe, that lies against them. Even though the position and the circumstances of the people who live in the Falkland Islands are uppermost in our minds – it would be outrageous if that were not the case – there is the longer-term interest to ensure that foul and brutal aggression does not succeed in our world. If it does, there will be a danger . . . but to people all over this dangerous planet.[105]

Foot later criticized those who attacked the war to liberate the Falklands for engaging in 'simple appeasement' and he, like Callaghan,[106] strongly backed the campaign – although many in the Labour Party did not.[107] Denis Healey, Foot's deputy, saw that the party was divided on the issue and tried – in vain – to moderate 'Michael's rhetoric' which was rooted in the fact that he saw the situation 'as a repetition of the Nazi challenge which Britain had failed to meet in the thirties'.[108] The divisions in the Labour Party provided a boon to the embattled government in the immediate aftermath of the invasion. Thatcher sought to build upon this by avoiding some of the more glaring mistakes in Britain's postwar history. Wholly aware of the lessons of the Suez debacle (the last occasion, incidentally, that the House of Commons had met on a Saturday), Thatcher resolved to attain two prerequisites that Anthony Eden had neglected. These were first, a mandate for physical force from the United Nations (UN); and, second, the support of the United States.[109] Thatcher also resolved, unlike Eden, to prepare for a military solution from the outset. After Lord Carrington had resigned the House of Commons seemed sated and the majority resolved to support the task force. Edward du Cann, a prominent Conservative backbencher, loftily declared:

> Every day now is crucial, for every day that the fait accompli is accepted, the harder it will be to remove it: ask the peoples of Afghanistan, Hungary or Poland about that. The world must face the fact that if one tolerates a single act of aggression, one connives at them all . . . Let us hear no more about logistics – how difficult it is to travel long distances. I do not remember the Duke of Wellington whining about Torres Vedras.[110]

Thatcher now pursued a triad strategy encompassing military, political and diplomatic elements. In the last category, Britain was least diminished in terms of national power,[111] and the perception that British diplomacy had managed to evade the precipitate decline suffered in the military and, more especially, the economic spheres was a widely held view. As one diplomat remarked at the UN in April 1982: 'Britain is a Morris Minor country, but with Rolls Royce diplomacy.'[112] On the evening of 3 April, Britain's UN ambassador, Sir Anthony Parsons, duly put a draft resolution to the Security Council. This demanded immediate Argentine withdrawal from the Islands and was adopted the following day as United Nations Security Council Resolution 502 (by ten votes to one against with four abstentions).[113] In addition, the United Kingdom received further political and diplomatic support from the Commonwealth, NATO and the European Economic Community (EEC).[114] This provided the essential political base for any military action. Suez had taught that one must negotiate and prepare for war simultaneously (and not consecutively). On 7 April, Carrington's successor, Francis Pym, stated:

> There will be time before the task force reaches the area to do everything possible to solve the problem without further fighting. We would much prefer a peaceful settlement. We will do all we can to get one, and we shall welcome and support all serious efforts to that end. The House and the country should be in no doubt about that. But if our efforts fail, the Argentine regime will know what to expect: Britain does not appease dictators.[115]

Although he had prudently attached himself firmly to the anti-appeasement camp, Pym was cast very much in the British diplomatic tradition that prized compromise above all.[116] David Owen reminded the Commons that faith in negotiation was, in fact, entirely in keeping with the Churchillian tradition. Owen thus hoped that Pym knew 'that he will carry the support of all hon. Members in giving a priority to peace? He has a well-established precedent. It was Sir Winston Churchill – no appeaser – who said: "Jaw-jaw is better than war-war".'[117] Pym agreed that, naturally, 'we want to achieve a peaceful solution'. But it was important to note that 'Sir Winston was also a great warrior, and on occasions it does happen – and it has happened – that in order to preserve principles of freedom and democracy, if it is not possible to achieve the result by peaceful means, other methods must be used. The House must face that.' That said, 'so long as there is any way in which I can . . . secure a peaceful solution, that is what my endeavour will be'.[118]

The mood in Britain in April and May 1982 was determinedly belligerent, and would-be appeasers had to tread carefully. Maurice Macmillan, Harold Macmillan's son, echoed his father's opposition to Munich when he warned the Commons: 'All democracies which negotiate with intransigent tyrants . . . at some stage have to ask the question: when does compromise become concession? At what stage does concession become appeasement? When does legitimate compromise over conflicting interests become the shameful surrender of vital principles?'[119] In this vein, the newly installed foreign and commonwealth secretary, Francis Pym, was viewed by many as having been cast in the appeasing tradition within British diplomacy. In his despatch of 9 April, Haig noted that, while Nott stood squarely behind the prime minister, the same could not be said for Pym. The latter, it was noted, did 'not share her position' and 'went surprisingly far in showing this in her presence'.[120] (Ironically, Haig was later to make common cause with Pym on the matter of negotiations.) Thatcher herself later recalled that 'Francis's appointment undoubtedly united the [Conservative] Party. But it heralded serious difficulties for the conduct of the campaign itself'.[121] This was due not least to the fact that Pym, a highly decorated veteran of the Second World War, was prepared to go that extra mile for peace. For Thatcher, that distance was eventually to cross the line marked 'appeasement'.

Although the securing of UNR 502 had been important, the Thatcher government knew that, in political, diplomatic and military terms, it was the attitude of the United States that counted.[122] Sir Frank Cooper, permanent secretary at the Ministry of Defence, later recalled that 'it was a clear case of aggression and fitted with all the American talk about democracy, so we would have been amazingly annoyed had the United States not supported [us]'. And, in order to get US support, the British government had no compunction at all about employing the analogy of Munich.[123] Despite this, the Reagan administration hesitated to side with Britain as significant elements within it were concerned by the prospect of Argentina turning to the Soviet Union for support.[124] The United States therefore initially sought to mediate an end to the conflict, although the majority of US politicians nevertheless harboured a strong desire to back Britain.[125] The White House was certainly under no illusions as to Thatcher's resolution. On 9 April 1982, Haig had warned Reagan:

[Thatcher] is clearly prepared to use force, owing to the politics of a unified nation and an angry parliament, as well as her own convictions about the principles at stake. Though she admits her preference for a diplomatic solution, she is rigid in her insistence on a return to the status quo ante, and indeed seemingly determined that any solution [will] involve some retribution.

In conclusion, Haig reported that 'we got no give in the basic British position, and only the glimmering of some possibilities . . . It is clear that they had not thought much about diplomatic possibilities. They will now, but whether they become more imaginative or instead recoil will depend on the political situation and what I hear in Argentina.'[126] That the *Junta* in Buenos Aires would be any more reasonable was the kind of wishful thinking that peace-seeking diplomats are prone to. The United States would soon have to pick a side – although this was not a straightforward task for a president who saw both protagonists as good allies against Soviet Communism. Fully aware of the importance of US support, Thatcher told Reagan that it was 'essential that America, our closest friend and ally, should share with us a common perception of the fundamental issues of democracy and freedom that are at stake'.[127] Fortunately, for the Thatcher government and the inhabitants of the Falkland Islands, the United States eventually gave staunch backing to the British. In his memoirs, Reagan states that he had no intention of letting the British down if push came to shove.[128] This hardly conveys an accurate picture, however. Richard Aldous has recently provided a more nuanced view, from which it is clear that Reagan hesitated long and hard before committing the United States to the British side.[129] Thatcher, a close friend of Reagan, had expected US support from the outset and took Washington's fence-sitting personally[130] (not least because it exacerbated British practical difficulties considerably). And, although the British government continued to use belligerent language, the weakness of the British military and naval position nevertheless caused her to be considerably less militant privately. Indeed, under pressure from Haig and the Americans, and less than two weeks after the Argentinian invasion, Thatcher viewed a 'diplomatic solution' as 'a considerable prize' while Pym asserted that '[i]t would be a remarkable achievement if this could be brought about, at a time when Britain's military position was still weak'.[131] This, naturally, encouraged Haig in his belief that he could persuade the British to come to terms.[132] In this, he was mistaken. For most British diplomats, Haig was respected but not rated. Robin Renwick, Britain's head of chancery in Washington, later said of Haig that his 'intentions were honourable but [he] had none of Kissinger's intellectual power, [and] had difficulty understanding that he was trying to bridge an unbridgeable gap'. When his staff reminded the British ambassador in Washington, Sir Nicholas Henderson, that Haig would quote Churchill to him ('In Victory: Magnanimity'), the unflappable Henderson replied that Churchill had been talking about magnanimity in the context of victory having been achieved.[133]

On 5 April, Reagan had caused consternation in London by asserting that the United States was friends with both sides[134] (a stance termed 'unhelpful' by Thatcher in Cabinet).[135] Part of the reason for this even-handedness lay in those figures in his administration that feared alienating Latin American opinion by siding against Argentina. Chief amongst these was Jeanne Kirkpatrick, the hard-line ambassador to the UN.[136] Parsons described one pro-Argentine outburst by Kirkpatrick as 'truly grotesque',[137] while Henderson had taken a 'public swipe' at her for attending an Argentine banquet in Washington on the night of the invasion.[138] The British naturally fretted about the influence of Kirkpatrick 'and the "hemisphere lobby"' in Washington,[139] although Henderson's exhausting charm offensive in Congress and on US television yielded immense benefits for the British.[140] In any case, Kirkpatrick's role was, fortunately, of very much less importance than was that of Secretary of Defense Caspar Weinberger, who provided essential matériel and intelligence support from the outset (while Reagan dithered).[141] Henderson later opined: 'It is impossible to exaggerate the contribution Weinberger made to our cause.'[142] This support even extended to the US the secretary of defense offering to lend the British an aircraft carrier.[143] Indeed, as soon as the task force sailed (and a full month before the administration formally declared its support for the United Kingdom) Weinberger had 'made it clear that we would supply them with everything they needed'.[144] This account, Henderson notes, 'flatly contradicts' Reagan's assertion that the United States provided no military assistance to the British during April 1982 (with the exception of the use of a military communications satellite).[145] Indeed, during the first meeting with Haig on 8 April, Thatcher 'expressed appreciation for U.S. cooperation in intelligence matters and in the use of [the U.S. military base at] Ascension Island'.[146] Given the inspiration for this assistance, when Thatcher thanked Reagan for the 'magnificent support' rendered by the US in the South Atlantic,[147] she might well have singled Weinberger out (although she later termed him 'magnificent').[148]

At this juncture there were still influential individuals working to avoid war. Foremost among these persons was the British foreign secretary, Francis Pym.[149] Nott later recalled that Thatcher and Pym

> approached the negotiations from opposite directions, and there was a frequent clash of wills . . . [a] fundamental conflict. Francis wanted to avoid an ugly and dangerous battle at all costs . . . He had seen war himself. Moreover, on his several visits to Washington he must have been increasingly influenced by Haig and other US military opinion to the effect that the whole exercise was beyond our capability.[150]

Pym thus agreed with Haig that they needed a way to avoid fighting and, between them, they drew up a number of draft proposals to end the crisis. Perhaps the most serious of these, in terms of its having any prospect of success, was submitted by the foreign secretary to the War Cabinet on 24 April 1982.[151] Pym asserted that these offered 'the best chance for a peaceful solution, [and] is clearly preferable to the military alternative and should be accepted'.[152] They were not welcomed by Thatcher. In her memoirs she termed the proposals 'conditional surrender',[153] and privately told Home Secretary William Whitelaw that they were unacceptable.[154] Thatcher believed that Pym had been influenced by Haig's play 'upon the imminence of hostilities and the risk that Britain would lose international support if fighting broke out. I told Francis that the terms were totally unacceptable. They would rob the Falklanders of their freedom and Britain of her honour and respect. Francis disagreed . . . We were at loggerheads.'[155] Thatcher understood only too well how diplomatic language, always justified by the maxim that any proposals under consideration were in the interests of 'peace', could have eroded the essentials of the British position in order to attain an agreement. Of the competing, and evolving 'peace' plans (of which, by April 24, there had been four), Thatcher noted: 'It is important to understand that what might appear at first glance to the untutored eye as minor variations in language between diplomatic texts can be of vital significance, as they were in this case.'[156] Such a sharp eye for detail arose out of her well-known aversion to 'consensus' (although she always insisted that she had no problem with 'agreement').[157]

Thatcher knew that Haig and Pym had updated the previous proposals (of 22 April) so as to make them acceptable to Buenos Aires. It was these modifications that 'went to the heart of why we were prepared to fight a war for the Falklands'.[158] Chief among her objections were: first, how far and how fast the British task force would have to withdraw; second, that sanctions against Argentina were to be abandoned as soon as the agreement was signed; third, proposals for a 'Special Interim Authority' would have allowed Argentina to manipulate matters in their favour with regard to which state would ultimately hold sovereignty over the islands; and, fourth, Pym effectively accepted the Argentine position that held that the situation could not revert to that which had existed before 2 April 1982. Thatcher later mused: 'Did Francis realise how much he had signed away?'[159] Thatcher's analysis was, largely correct, as Haig privately confessed: 'Our proposals, in fact, are a camouflaged transfer of sovereignty'.[160] Robin Renwick recently reflected:

> It was a huge act of folly on the part of the Argentine military to reject these various proposals, none of which offered a prospect of a return to the status quo, and under which they would have been able to gain a role in administering the islands. They did so because, having whipped up a political frenzy in Buenos Aires, they could not face having to withdraw from the islands with no certainty of a transfer of sovereignty.[161]

While Argentina blustered, Pym was out-manoeuvred by Thatcher and left isolated. Nott then proposed that the government give no reply to Haig's proposal but rather ask Haig to propose it to Buenos Aires first.[162] The Argentine *Junta*, with even less ability to compromise than the British government, would be unlikely to accept it, and if it did the whole question could be put before parliament. In the event, the Argentines proved agreeably intransigent. But, as Thatcher later conceded: 'I will never, ever, ever take a chance like that again. Those proposals were completely unacceptable to us and if the Argentineans had said yes we would have been in one hell of a mess.'[163] A relieved Thatcher sent a message Haig stating:

> This whole business started with an Argentine aggression. Since then our purpose together has been to ensure the early withdrawal by the Argentines in accordance with the Security Council Resolution. We think therefore that the next step should be for you to put your latest ideas to them. I hope that you will seek the Argentine government's view of them tomorrow and establish urgently whether they can accept them. Knowledge of their attitude will be important to the British Cabinet's consideration of your ideas.

Thatcher later recalled that 'a great crisis [had] passed'. Indeed, 'I could not have stayed as Prime Minister had the War Cabinet accepted Francis Pym's proposals. I would have resigned.'[164] Her suspicion of Pym's negotiations with the 'unreliable' Haig are explained by Brian Fall, Pym's private secretary, thus: 'She didn't want a Munich-like piece of paper to be produced.'[165] As Pym tried, in vain, to resurrect negotiations,[166] Thatcher concentrated on winning over Reagan. 'One stage in the effort to settle this crisis has now ended. It seems to me essential that, as we enter the next stage, the US and Britain should be seen to unequivocally on the same side, staunchly upholding these values on which the Western way of life depends.' Reagan replied that Argentina's intransigence 'had made it necessary to adopt a new posture towards Buenos Aires'.[167] Reagan now opined: 'I don't think Margaret Thatcher should be asked to concede anymore.' This stance was confirmed on 30 April by the National Security Council, where Haig warned: 'Unless Argentina softens on sovereignty, the British will go ahead and do some damage.'[168] Thatcher described that day as representing 'the end of the beginning of our . . . campaign to regain the Falklands'.[169] The Churchillian echo in this recollection is deliberate for,[170] although there were to be other peace initiatives,[171] the path to Thatcher's 'finest hour' was now clear.

Thatcher, like Reagan an unashamed Cold Warrior,[172] now played on the emotive nature of the 'Special Relationship': 'I cannot conceal from you how deeply let down [we] would feel if under these circumstances the U.S. were not now to give us its full support.'[173] After all, 'the friendship between the United States and Britain matters very much to the future of the free world'.[174] At home she was under strong pressure at home to resist appeasement. As Haig and Pym continued their efforts, Thatcher's press secretary warned her in May that some of the tabloid press 'feel there is smell of Munich in the air'.[175] When Pym was attacked for his flexibility in the Commons, this only spurred the prime minister on.[176] Reagan noted: 'The P.M. is adamant . . . She feels the loss of life so far can only be justified if they win. We'll see – she may be right.'[177]

On 26 May 1982, the prime minister laid bare the inexorable historical logic underlying the decision to resist Argentine aggression.

> The older generation in our country, and generations before them, have made sacrifices so that we could be a free society and belong to a community of nations [that] seeks to resolve disputes by civilised means. Today it falls to us to bear the same responsibility [and] we shall not shirk it. What has happened since that day, eight weeks ago, is a matter of history – the history of a nation which rose instinctively to the needs of the occasion . . . We worked tirelessly for a peaceful solution . . . [but] there comes a point when it is no longer possible to trust the good faith of those with whom one is negotiating. Playing for time is not working for a peaceful solution . . . It is simply leaving the aggressor with the fruits of his aggression. It would be a betrayal of our fighting men and of the Islanders if we had continued merely to talk, when talk alone was getting nowhere . . . If we, the British, were to shrug our shoulders at what had happened in the South Atlantic and to acquiesce in the illegal seizure of those far-away islands, it would be a clear signal to those with similar designs on the territory of others to follow in the footsteps of aggression. Surely we, of all people, have learned the lesson of history: that to appease an aggressor is to invite aggression elsewhere, and on an ever-increasing scale?[178]

Four days later, Thatcher stated: 'It used to be said by a great American politician, Dean Acheson, that Britain had lost an Empire but had not yet found a role. I believe Britain has now found a role. It is in upholding international law and teaching the nations of the world how to live.'[179] On 1 June, much to the satisfaction of the British, Reagan unequivocally identified Argentina as the aggressor.[180] Weinberger's assistance was now given a more public profile, although the United States was insistent that the degree of their commitment to Britain be downplayed so not to cause trouble for them in Latin America. Naturally, this secrecy disappointed Thatcher who wished to publicize US assistance so as to bolster Britain's international position.[181] Haig had not given up on his hopes of a negotiated settlement, however. A similarly minded Pym encouraged British ambassadors to put pressure on Thatcher to compromise on the Falklands, and persuaded the State Department to adopt a formula that would 'internationalize' the islands (which the vacillating Reagan espoused publicly on 3 June).[182] But Thatcher had long since rejected such fudges. Towards the war's end Thatcher brushed aside a suggestion from Foot that she might relent from demanding unconditional Argentine surrender (in order to enhance the prospects for future negotiations).

> Since our landings and the losses which we have incurred it would be unthinkable to negotiate about the future of the Islands as if everything were still as it had been before. That would be a betrayal of those whom we have called upon to make such great sacrifices, even to give up their lives, because of the important principles at stake. We cannot allow the Argentines to demonstrate that they have been able to achieve progress in their attempts to impose their sovereignty over the Islands as a result of their aggression.[183]

In truth, Thatcher was never going to accept Foot's plea, given that she had already refused to indulge Reagan on this score.[184] With victory at hand she had told the president: 'Britain had not lost precious lives in battle and sent an enormous Task Force to hand over The Queen's Islands.'[185] Argentina was to be humiliated; and its leaders were to be punished for their unprovoked act of aggression. After the war, the Conservative Right was keen to ensure that the FCO refrained from resorting to its appeasing ways once again. The Conservative MP Bernard Braine observed how 'the ambivalence in the conduct of [British] foreign policy had disheartened the Falkland Islanders and encouraged the Argentines'. For Braine: 'The tragedy is that we did not learn the lessons of our own history in time. We should have known that it is always fatal to appease the bully and shameful to let our own people down.'[186] For those commentators who were looking for echoes of the past, the Falklands War evoked memories of both Chamberlain and Churchill as British diplomats and politicians had, once again, sought to appease dictators. Thatcher was fortunate that her personal distance from such irresolute approaches allowed others (such as Carrington and his team) to 'carry the can' while she added substance to her moniker of 'Iron Lady'. The final element in the drama was provided by the suitably grisly nature of the opponents: a military dictatorship that had waged a 'dirty war' (ostensibly against left-wing terrorism) after seizing power in 1976.[187] The victory in the South Atlantic thus allowed admirers of Thatcher to point out that the Falklands War had resulted in the liberation of the people of Argentina, as the defeated *Junta* was forced to restore democracy in 1983.

Despite the euphoria, the feeling that the Falklands had been an unnecessary war that, moreover, was not in Britain's best interests continued to permeate sections of the FCO. Anthony Williams, the departing British ambassador in Buenos Aires, vented his frustration that Argentina had become an enemy of Britain when, he opined, there had been every chance of a 'special relationship' developing between the two states. Williams reflected that just as Sir Humphrey Trevelyan, ambassador in Cairo at the time of Suez (and exiled in London during the crisis), had sought – and failed – to resist unhelpful historical analogies so, too, had he been unsuccessful in this respect.

> In my own displaced embassy, which I now wind up, I have had to contest (*ab initio* and as though I had written nothing before) the portrayal of President Galtieri as a fascist dictator decreeing the invasion of the Falklands by an arbitrary act, much as Lord Trevelyan had then to contest the portrayal of Nasser's nationalization of the Canal on the whim of a tin pot Hitler. Let me echo him in urging that . . . there is more [now] to British relations with Argentina and Latin America than the crisis over the Falklands.

For Williams, the Falklands dispute was a tragedy: 'But for the bursting of this festering sore of the Islands, our relations with Argentina would have been exceptional.'[188] The question of whether or not relations with Argentina were ruined was, however, wholly secondary to the question of who, if anyone, was to blame for Argentina's invasion. In April 1982, a few days after the invasion, press reports began to appear that suggested the British government had known that an Argentine attack was imminent.[189] These reports, which were believed to have emanated from a British intelligence source in Argentina,[190] soon faded away for lack of substance. But once the war was over Franks was, of course, fully engaged with just such questions. Gilmour thought that it was nonsensical for the Franks Report to ask, as it did, whether or not the British government could have foreseen the invasion of 2 April 1982.[191] Instead, it should have asked: 'Did the government through its actions and its inaction run an unnecessarily large risk of war being started?' For Gilmour, 'the answer to that question . . . is undoubtedly yes'.[192] In the event, the question as to whether the British government could have known of the Argentine invasion beforehand was much reduced in the public mind by the drama and tragedy of war.

Victory greatly relieved the burdens imposed upon the government by the twin charges of neglecting the defence of the Falklands and of misreading the signals of war emanating from Buenos Aires in the spring of 1982. Carrington had carried the can for the 'appeasers' in the FCO. Yet, he had repeatedly warned Nott that the latter's plan to make defence cuts, and especially to axe HMS *Endurance*, would have serious repercussions. 'Any reduction [in UK defence presence in Falklands] would be interpreted by both the Islanders and the Argentines as a reduction in our commitment to the Islands and in our willingness to defend them.'[193] Despite Carrington's astute urgings, Nott would still later bemoan the fact that, in the FCO, very many 'good men had succumbed to the appeasement, and indignity, which goes under the name of "diplomacy"'.[194] In the wake of the Falklands War, Nott's ill-conceived defence cuts were half-forgotten and, mostly, abandoned. In December 1982, the government pledged that 'the Falklands Campaign [means that] we shall now be devoting substantially more resources to defence than had been previously planned'.[195] Such decisions were taken in an atmosphere that stressed the rejection of appeasement and the lesson that aggression 'must not pay' and, in the general election of 1983 the so-called 'Falklands Factor' yielded a handsome political dividend.[196] The Franks Report ensured that the triumph was completed by effectively absolving the Thatcher government of blame for the invasion. This was summed up in the infamous final paragraph of the report:

> There is no reasonable basis for any suggestion – which would be purely hypothetical – that the invasion would have been prevented if the Government had acted in the ways indicated in our report. Taking account of these considerations, and of all the evidence we have received, we conclude that we would not be justified in attaching any criticism or blame to the present Government for the Argentine Junta's decision to commit its act of unprovoked aggression in the invasion of the Falkland Islands.[197]

Callaghan famously mocked this ending, stating: '[F]or 338 paragraphs, the Franks Report painted a splendid picture, delineating the light and shade. The glowing colours came out. When Franks got to paragraph 339, he got fed up with the canvas that he was painting and chucked a bucket of whitewash over it.'[198] David Owen later observed that the Franks Committee had contained 'streetwise politicians and civil servants' who knew that the general public had little interest in apportioning blame. 'The mood of the country was "The war's over. We won, didn't we?".' For Owen, this was 'the best explanation for the total disjunction in the report. Its bland uncritical conclusions do not marry with the main text.'[199] In his memoirs, Callaghan summed matters up thus:

> Errors of omission and commission made by Ministers in administering routine matters can be shrugged off, but sterner standards apply when Ministers face great issues of public policy that result in war . . . Ministers who are confronted by evidence that is unclear, or officials who are uncertain, must be guided by their own judgement and act with foresight and dispatch. That is the ultimate test of leadership and on that count the Prime Minister and the Conservative Government is guilty.[200]

Early in 2013, new archival releases showed Thatcher testifying to Franks as to her total shock at the news of the invasion. This prompted Malcolm Allsop, a documentary filmmaker, to recall that, before the invasion, the British government had been trying to broker a compromise between the Falkland Islanders and Argentina as 'the Falklands were rather a post-colonial embarrassment for Britain'. (Talks with Buenos Aires apparently included 'a suggestion that Islanders might be paid to quit the Islands and go and live in New Zealand!) Nicholas Ridley had adopted an 'appeasing stance' and, when interviewed by Allsop, put up the usual noncommittal line about the Falklands. When Allsop asked Ridley what would happen when Argentina saw that the imminent elections for the ruling Falkland Islands Council would, inevitably, produce an overwhelming majority of 'hard-line "no compromise" members', Ridley replied chillingly: 'There will be a war', and left. Allsop thus concluded: 'Mrs Thatcher may well not have known that an Argentine invasion was likely, but to believe that her Foreign Office had no idea is palpable nonsense.'[201] In the wake of the Falklands victory, all accusations of any foreknowledge of Argentine intentions, as well as any suggestion of appeasement of Argentina, were, of course, denied. Foreign Secretary Francis Pym himself asserted:

> All Governments were aware of the costs and difficulties of defending and sustaining the islands if negotiations were to break down . . . [they] took the view that it was not only in the British interest, but in the long-term interest of the islanders themselves, that the problem should be solved and that the dangerous consequences of the dispute should be removed. It was the only way to avoid confrontation with Argentina, which would be difficult for Great Britain and tragic for the islanders. Suggestions of appeasement are nonsense. The Government and their predecessors were guided by one essential principle: that no settlement of the dispute could be contemplated that was not in accordance with the wishes of the Falkland Islanders and of this House. That has been and remains at the heart of our policy.

Much to Pym's relief the Franks Report either ignored or missed much that would have embarrassed the FCO.

> I am particularly grateful to Lord Franks and his colleagues for disposing in such categorical terms of the myth, to which the press, even some Members of this House and others have so often subscribed, that there was in some way a 'Foreign Office' policy on the Falklands, based on some alleged appeasement and on disregard for the islanders, which has over the years been foisted by officials on a succession of passive and pliant Ministers. In paragraph 284 of his report, Lord Franks concludes that "this damaging allegation" is totally without foundation.[202]

In 1984 Tam Dayell,[203] Labour's most troublesome MP on matters pertaining to the Falklands, asked when would the government 'make available to the public the Foreign Office file, entitled "Proposed offer by Her Majesty's Government to reunite Falkland Islands with Argentina and acceptance of lease" from 1940, which has been withdrawn from public scrutiny'. He was told that this document would be declassified after 50 years (i.e. in 1991).[204] The document was, however, later embargoed until 2015.[205] Quite why such a decision was taken was baffling, given the plethora of evidence available testifying to the (regularly demonstrated) willingness of British governments to barter over the rights of the Falkland Islanders throughout the twentieth century. Perhaps Whitehall prefers to continue to dismiss any such charges as idle speculation.

Whatever the debates on the rights and wrongs of the causes of the Falklands War, Thatcher had struck a blow against the paralyzing shame imbued by the memory of the appeasement of the 1930s.[206] The prime minister saw this as an essential part of the process of arresting British decline: 'We knew what we had to do and we went about it and did it.'[207] For Thatcher, the Falklands War, and not Munich, represented the dominant tradition in British history. When later challenged by Gorbachev on the legitimacy of the campaign, she proudly asserted: 'The Falklands are a British land populated by the British. It was invaded, and we removed the invaders.'[208] Britain, as John Nott later reflected, had recovered its 'pride after the shambles of Suez'.[209] Enoch Powell, returning to his question of 3 April 1982, duly pronounced Thatcher worthy of the sobriquet 'Iron Lady'.

> Is the right hon Lady aware that the report has now been received from the public analyst on a certain substance recently subjected to analysis and that I have obtained a copy of the report? It shows that the substance under test consisted of ferrous matter of the highest quality, that it is of exceptional tensile strength, is highly resistant to wear and tear and to stress, and may be used with advantage for all national purposes?[210]

Such hyperbole was hardly out of place in Britain in June 1982. Indeed, the outpouring of national pride that followed the victory in the Falklands War seemed to have created an atmosphere akin to the celebrations prompted by the relief of Mafeking in 1900.[211] The historian Thomas Pakenham observed:

> This has been a strange nostalgic experience, this old-fashioned Falkland Islands war which seems to have ended, bringing to the surface, as it did, all sorts of old-fashioned emotions like patriotism and pride. There was in Britain a sense of pulling together, of rediscovering an old cause. Most people seemed to feel, and to feel deeply, that it was a just war – quixotic but necessary, as had been such earlier conflicts as the Boer War, with which there are many striking analogies.[212]

Sir Nicholas Henderson, an outstanding diplomat not given to emotional outbursts, opined: 'There had been few international issues since 1945 about which the British felt so unanimously and so strongly. If it was asked why we bothered about a mere two thousand people at the other end of the world, it was worth remembering how bitterly the Americans had felt about their fifty-two hostages held in Iran.'[213] The author Frederick Forsyth was moved to write to 10 Downing Street offering to write a book

ILLUSTRATION 6.1 *The Iron Lady, Boudicca of the South Atlantic. Prime Minister Margaret Thatcher at the Conservative Party Conference, Brighton, 12 October 1984. Only hours before this picture was taken the Provisional IRA had killed five in an attempt to assassinate her by bombing the hotel in which she was staying.*

on the campaign, 'for those died down there, for those who survived, and for this country'.[214] Alexander Chancellor, writing in the pro-Conservative *Spectator*, reflected: 'Britain . . . looks set to be a more united and a more contented palace. This is the real cause for which so many people have died.'[215] On 3 July 1982, Thatcher herself declared:

> We have ceased to be a nation in retreat. We have instead a new-found confidence born in the economic battles at home and tested and found true 8,000 miles away. That confidence comes from the re-discovery of ourselves, and grows with the recovery of our self-respect. And so today, we can rejoice at our success in the Falklands and . . . that Britain has re-kindled that spirit which has fired her for generations past and which today has begun to burn as brightly as before. Britain found herself again in the South Atlantic and will not look back from the victory she has won.[216]

At the Falklands victory dinner in October 1982, Thatcher quoted the Duke of Wellington: 'There is no such thing as a little war for a great nation' and referred to 'the spirit of Britain which has never failed in difficulty days'.[217] Despite such highfalutin rhetoric, the shame of Munich and Suez had not been entirely exorcized; although they had entered into a new relationship with the nation's collective memory. More precisely, they had been transformed from the root cause of many *present* evils into shameful *past* actions. Part of this process was, undoubtedly, generational, but the shared experience of the Falklands War had played its part. Henceforth, although Munich and appeasement would continue to be invoked for political ends, for the great mass of the people such instances would now be allegorical in nature rather than evidencing the moral depravity of the British state.

CHAPTER SEVEN

In pursuit of a 'New World Order': liberating Kuwait, 1990–1

Got a call this morning at 7.30 from Margaret Thatcher. She is staunch
and strong and worries that there will be an erosion on force. She does
not want to go back to the U.N. on use of force, nor do I. She does
not want to compromise on the Kuwait government, nor do I.
In essence, she has not 'gone wobbly' as she cautioned me
a couple of weeks ago. I love that expression.

GEORGE H. W. BUSH, 7 SEPTEMBER 1990 [1]

I seem to smell the stench of appeasement in the air –
the rather nauseating stench of appeasement.

MARGARET THATCHER, 30 October 1990 [2]

After the Cold War passed into history in the late 1980s, the arrival of a
'New World Order' was supposedly heralded by a war against Iraq after the
latter had invaded Kuwait. After 1982 Thatcher, having added the Falklands
experience to her historical database on the dangers of appeasement, was
more convinced than ever of the rectitude of her wholehearted rejection
of appeasement. In the case of Kuwait, such feelings were strengthened
by the legacy of the British Empire. Indeed, given Britain's previous
hegemony in the region it is not too much to describe Britain's diplomats as
the midwives of Kuwaiti statehood. As US Secretary of State James Baker
observed: 'Kuwait had been carved out of Iraq by the British.'[3] Kuwait,
previously a protectorate within the British Empire, had long had great

strategic importance for Britain. As Harold Macmillan noted: 'Kuwait, with its massive oil production, is the key to the economic life of Britain – and of Europe.'[4] On 19 June 1961, Kuwait and Britain signed a friendship agreement that replaced the protection agreement of 1899 whilst securing the independence of Kuwait.[5] Only six days later Iraq declared its intention to annex Kuwait claiming that it had been an Iraqi territory (as part of the Ottoman territory of Basra) prior to the protection agreement of 1899.[6] On 27 June 1961, the Emir of Kuwait requested assistance from the Saudi and British governments. Macmillan's government then rapidly deployed troops, aircraft and ships to the area in Operation *Vantage*.[7] By that time the issue of oil had, if anything, increased in importance for London.

> Kuwait stands in the way of a consolidation of control of Middle East oil by one or more of the remaining major Middle East producers (Iraq, Saudi Arabia and Iran) or transit States (the United Arab Republic), and thus provides a valuable insurance that oil will continue to flow from the Middle East in adequate quantities and on reasonable terms (the Middle East supplies three-quarters of the oil used outside the Americas).[8]

Macmillan, so keen to engage in appeasement over Berlin, was resolution personified over Kuwait (although, of course, Iraq was no Soviet Union). In his diaries he revealed that, 'remembering Suez', he was careful to involve all of his senior ministers and, before deciding to commit forces, put matters before the entire Cabinet.[9] He also, in contrast to Eden during the Suez affair, carried his senior military figures with him. Nevertheless,

> [w]e worked through some long and anxious nights, esp [sic] when we thought [Iraqi Prime Minister] Kassem [Qasim] wd [sic] seize Kuwait City and territory virtually unopposed. Now our worry is the opposite. Since the Iraqi attack has *not* in fact developed, all the pressure is going to be turned on us. It is going to be expensive and difficult to stay; [and] hard to get out. The Opposition in Parlt [sic] have behaved pretty well – so far.[10]

Just as West Berlin represented an open-ended – and dangerous – commitment so, in confronting the Iraqi threat to Kuwait, the British government was faced with the economic cost of rejecting appeasement. This represented expenditure which economic limitations made unpalatable. This was especially so after the years 1955–6 (when, ironically, Macmillan had been chancellor of the exchequer) when, for the first time, the Treasury had achieved the ability to place a ceiling on defence expenditure.[11] Fortunately, HMG was relieved of the Kuwaiti commitment when, in the autumn of 1961, British forces were replaced by a force from the Arab League.[12] The British nevertheless remained alive to the dangers posed to their interests by any future threats to Kuwait's security. Ted Heath, the lord privy seal, thus advised the Cabinet: 'Our economic stake in Kuwait itself, and the central position of Kuwait to our oil operations in this whole area, are such that we should take all reasonable measures that we can to protect Kuwait.'[13]

The British defence secretary insisted that the United Kingdom retain a capability to assist Kuwait (although a request from the emir was deemed an essential prerequisite for any intervention).[14] On 4 October 1963, after Iraqi Prime Minister Abd al-Karim Qasim had been killed in a coup, Iraq reaffirmed its acceptance of Kuwaiti sovereignty and the boundary it had agreed to in 1913 and 1932 in the 'Agreed Minutes between the State of Kuwait and the Republic of Iraq Regarding the Restoration of Friendly Relations, Recognition, and Related Matters.'[15] Matters had been resolved – on the local level by regional actors, and in the global arena by the discipline imposed by the Cold War. This situation was transformed, however, in the wake of Iraq's exhausting war with Iran (1980–8) and with the end of the Cold War in 1989.

By 1990, Margaret Thatcher had grown in stature into one of the most eminent international politicians then in office. This was accompanied by an increasing tendency to concentrate policy making in her hands. She increasingly handled diplomacy herself as her annoyance with the 'appeasing' Foreign and Commonwealth Office (FCO) had grown progressively throughout her premiership (greeting any perceived lack of resolution with the refrain 'Typical Foreign Office').[16] Success in the Falklands War, and another election victory in June 1983, had afforded an increasingly strident Thatcher with the opportunity to wrest control of foreign policy from the FCO.[17] Henceforth, her 'personal diplomacy' dominated the rest of her tenure in Downing Street. Thatcher held the FCO 'type' responsible for many past sins and saw direct parallels between the era of appeasement in the 1930s and the era of détente. She saw it as her job to repudiate the past, as well as the present, appeasing tendency in her diplomats. To Thatcher's mind such people had betrayed Eastern Europe through appeasement at Munich, Yalta, East Berlin, Hungary, Czechoslovakia and Helsinki. In 1990, when it seemed likely that Soviet troops would crush the Lithuanian freedom movement, she was told by Soviet leader Mikhail Gorbachev that Lithuania was an internal Soviet problem and the 'Western leaders must not fall into [the] trap' of thinking it was an international problem. Unmoved, Thatcher replied:

> Western countries have a different view of Lithuania and Latvia, in the light of historic circumstances resulting in their occupation by Hitler and Stalin. We do not recognise their annexation by the Soviet Union *de jure*, although the Helsinki Final Act recognised it *de facto*. Therefore, the status of Lithuania is considered to be different from that of other Soviet republics.[18]

In 1987, when on a visit to Moscow, Thatcher told Gorbachev: 'We were once mistaken about your plans in Czechoslovakia. We thought you would not invade [in 1968] because that would damage your prestige in the world. Yet we were mistaken. We do not want to repeat that mistake.'[19] In September 1990 Thatcher visited Czechoslovakia itself (which had just divested itself of Communism in the 'Velvet Revolution'). She came with an apology: 'We failed you in 1938 when a disastrous policy of appeasement allowed Hitler to extinguish your independence. Churchill was quick to repudiate the Munich Agreement, but we still remember it with shame.'[20] For Thatcher, resolution in the face of contemporary threats, and atonement for the past sins of appeasement, were two sides of the same coin.

On 2 August 1990 Thatcher, who happened to be on her way to the United States, reacted to the news of Iraq's invasion of Kuwait in the same manner that she had responded to the Argentine invasion of the Falklands – by resolving to demonstrate that appeasement does not work. Recognizing the overwhelming importance of the US role, the prime minister immediately sought to stiffen the resolve of US President George H. W. Bush at a meeting in Aspen, Colorado.

> I told him my conclusions in the clearest and most straightforward terms. First, aggressors must never be appeased. We learned that to our cost in the 1930s. Second, if Saddam Hussein were to cross the border into Saudi Arabia he could go right down the Gulf in a matter of days. He would then control 65% of the world's oil reserves and could blackmail us all. Not only did we have to move to stop the aggression . . . we had to stop it quickly.[21]

Hitherto, the United States had undoubtedly pursued a policy that had sought to conciliate Iraq, despite Saddam's aggressive rhetoric against Kuwait. Many observers denounced this as appeasement once Kuwait had been invaded and US ambivalence was reflected in Bush's remarks of 2 August: 'We're not discussing intervention. I would not discuss any military options even if we'd agreed upon them. But one of the things I want to do at this meeting is hear from our Secretary of Defense, our Chairman, and others. But I'm not contemplating such action.' And, when asked if the United States was to send troops to the region, Bush replied: 'I'm not contemplating such action, and I again would not discuss it if I were.'[22] This has since been taken as indicating a lack of resolve (especially amongst Thatcher's acolytes). But this is hardly fair. In his diary the president reflected:

> I was careful in my remarks. I condemned the invasion and outlined the steps we had taken . . . I did not want my first public comments to threaten the use of American Military might, so I said I was not contemplating intervention, and, even if I knew we were going to use force, I would not announce it in a press conference. The truth is, at that moment, I had no idea what our options were. I did know for sure that aggression had to be stopped, and Kuwait's sovereignty restored. We had a big job ahead of

ILLUSTRATION 7.1 *President George H. W. Bush and Prime Minister Margaret Thatcher, Aspen, 2 August 1990. Thatcher told the assembled press: 'What has happened is a total violation of international law. You cannot have a situation where one country marches in and takes over another country which is a member of the United Nations.'*

us in shaping opinion at home and abroad and could ill afford bellicose mistakes at the start. What I hoped to convey was an open mind about how we might handle the situation until I learned all the facts.[23]

James Baker later seemed to apply the indelible mark of destiny on matters when he noted: 'On that very day [2 August 1990], the President of the United States was preparing to meet with the Prime Minister of Great Britain, an iron lady not known for counseling half measures in time of challenge.'[24] President Bush and National Security Advisor Brent Scowcroft were certainly under no illusions that Thatcher was unambiguous with regard to her belief in the dangers arising from Saddam's invasion.[25] Acutely aware of public opinion, and an anti-appeaser by conviction and experience,[26] Thatcher repeatedly invoked the 1930s analogy with regard to Iraqi invasion and occupation of Kuwait in 1990. She told Bush at Aspen on 2 August, in no uncertain terms: 'First [of all], aggressors must never be appeased. We learned that to our cost in the 1930s.'[27]

Thatcher did not, contrary to popular mythology,[28] tell the president that this was 'no time to go wobbly' (although she did give such advice a few weeks later).[29] Yet, as Dilip Hiro noted in 1992, after the Aspen meeting, the president returned to the White House 'reportedly at one with Thatcher's rhetoric'.[30] Despite this, Bush's reputation as a vacillator, allied to his initial moderation on 2 August – and reflected in his temperate language – had given the impression that the president suffered from Chamberlainite indolence. And Thatcher, like Churchill, had, by this stage, generated sufficient attendant mythology to be able to claim to be *the* chief mover in the West's response to Saddam's aggression. As had been the case during the Falklands crisis, the United Nations (UN) was the first port of diplomatic call. On 3 August 1990, the UN Security Council passed Resolution 660, condemning the invasion of Kuwait and demanding that Iraq unconditionally withdraw.[31] Thatcher later recalled:

> I was keenly aware that this would be the first post–Cold War test of the [UN] Security Council in crisis. I knew what happened in the 1930s when a weak and leaderless League of Nations had failed to stand up to Japanese, Italian and German aggression. The result was to encourage the ambitions of those regimes. The U.N. had been set up to correct the failings of the League, but the Cold War had created stalemate on the Security Council. Now, however, our improving relations with Moscow and our satisfactory ones with China offered the possibility that we could get their cooperation in forging international unity to oppose Iraq.[32]

These sentiments, as Gary Hess noted, were remarkably similar to those expressed on the Korean War by Truman in his memoirs.[33] The respective images of Bush (as Chamberlain) and of Thatcher (as Churchill) survived the testimony of figures such as Thatcher's press secretary, Sir Bernard

Ingham, who later recalled that 'George Bush had a backbone before he arrived in Aspen and did not acquire it from Mrs Thatcher . . . Her familiar distinctive contribution [was] a clear and simply expressed analysis of the situation.'[34] This is a fair summation as Thatcher's policy was, indeed, clear and free from any doubts. Keen to demonstrate his own resolution, Bush now adopted a Churchillian stance. On 5 August 1990, he stated:

> I view [Iraq's occupation of Kuwait] very seriously, not just that but any threat to any other countries, as well as I view very seriously our determination to reverse out this aggression. And please believe me, there are an awful lot of countries that are in total accord with what I've just said, and I salute them. They are staunch friends and allies, and we will be working with them all for collective action. This will not stand. This will not stand, this aggression against Kuwait.[35]

The leadership of the United States was the essential ingredient in any attempt to restore Kuwait's independence. If Saddam triumphed then any number of Gulf states would be at risk. Saddam, a new Nasser, would cast envious eyes across the region. Thatcher thus urged that 'we must do everything possible' to stop Saddam.[36] This included offering military assistance to King Fahd of Saudi Arabia. In fact, the US Secretary of Defense Dick Cheney rang Bush while the latter was in conference with Thatcher to tell her that Saudi Arabia had requested US troops (after some effective lobbying – on the subject of the Iraqi threat – by Cheney himself).[37] The Saudi monarch agreed immediately to accept 100,000 American troops in his country at once[38] (with the provisos that the United States keep the initial deployment secret; that there be no attack on Saddam without consultation; and that the troops leave after the threat from Saddam receded).[39] With 'Desert Shield' in place, Thatcher now urged Bush to prepare for war ('Desert Storm') in earnest. In doing this she drew upon her experiences in the Falklands War: 'As so often over these months [during Operation *Desert Shield*] I found myself reliving in an only slightly different form my experiences of the build-up to the battle for the Falklands.'[40] Signally, Thatcher told Bush how she had reversed the Argentine seizure of the Falkland Islands in 1982.[41]

On August 6, Thatcher met Bush once more. She urged him to invoke Article 51 of the UN Charter (the right of member states to self-defence). Thatcher's sense of rectitude far outweighed that of Bush, however (Baker later described Thatcher as 'a charter member of a school that may be described as do what you must now and worry about it later'.)[42] Bush was now firmly on board the anti-appeasement wagon, a fact that was reflected in the rhetoric of the president (himself a highly-decorated veteran of the Second World War). On 8 August, Bush told the American people that 'if history teaches us anything, it is that we must resist aggression or it will destroy our freedoms. Appeasement does not work. As was the case in the 1930's, we see in Saddam Hussein an aggressive dictator threatening his neighbors.'[43] At the Pentagon on 15 August Bush stated: 'A half century ago . . . the world paid dearly for appeasing an aggressor who should, and could, have been stopped. We are not going to make that mistake again.'[44] The massive build-up of allied forces in Saudi Arabia led the Conservative MP Alan Clark, a junior minister in the UK ministry of defence, to conclude that war was 'almost inevitable. It is the railway timetables of 1914, and the Guns of August.' In the spirit of 'war by timetable', Thatcher warned Bush on 17 October that any war would have to be won before the end of the campaigning season in March 1991.[45] In the meantime, Bush prepared the American people for war by denouncing appeasement in, of all places, Prague.

> A thousand miles to the south, this new commonwealth of freedom now faces a terrible test. Czechoslovakia was one of the first nations to condemn the outrage in the Persian Gulf . . . It is no coincidence that appeasement's lonely victim half a century ago should be among the first to understand that there is right and there is wrong, there is good and there is evil, and there are sacrifices worth making . . . There is no question that ours is a just cause and that good will prevail. The darkness in the desert sky cannot stand against the way of light. I salute your courageous President when he joins us in saying that Saddam Hussein's aggression must not be rewarded.[46]

On Thanksgiving Day, 22 November 1990, Bush declared: 'In World War II, the world paid dearly for appeasing an aggressor who could have been stopped early on. We're not going to make that mistake again. We will not appease this aggressor.'[47] The president had, decidedly, not gone 'wobbly'. Thatcher, the conviction politician, having successfully led the nation through a war in the Falklands, now saw herself in Churchillian terms. And, like Churchill, Thatcher sought to stiffen the nation's resolve through rhetoric. On 6 September 1990, Thatcher told the House of Commons:

> The issue [of the invasion of Kuwait] is one of importance to the whole world. It affects world security, world oil supplies and world economic stability. It affects the confidence of all small states, not only those in the Middle East. We have bitter memories of the consequences of failing to challenge annexation of small states in the 1930s. We have learned the lesson that the time to stop the aggressor is at once.[48]

Thatcher's instincts about the appeasing 'type' were confirmed in the run-up to the liberation of Kuwait by the US-led coalition in 1991. When Edward Heath, a former prime minister and a staunch opponent of appeasement in the 1930s, visited Iraq in the autumn of 1990 in order to persuade Saddam to release the British nationals he had seized, the charge of appeasement was widely made, not least by Thatcher herself[49] (whom Heath hated).

The headlines in British tabloids were predictably lurid, with examples including 'Heath: Appease Saddam' (the *Daily Express*); 'Traitor Ted' (the *Sun*) and 'Fury at Ted the Traitor' (the *Daily Star*).[50] Thatcher, who later compared 'Western weakness' towards Saddam with the appeasement of Hitler,[51] showed her contempt for those who sought to parley with Saddam by declaring in the Commons: 'I seem to smell the stench of appeasement in the air – the rather nauseating stench of appeasement.'[52] Of would-be 'appeasers', Thatcher later recalled: 'There is never any lack of people anxious to avoid the use of force. No matter how little chance there is of negotiations succeeding – no matter how many difficulties are created for the troops who are trying to prepare themselves for war – the case is always made for yet another piece of last-ditch diplomacy.' Thatcher told Mikhail Gorbachev's 'peace' envoy Yevgeny Primakov that Saddam 'must not be appeased.'[53] Against this, there remained those who questioned the manner in which *all* and *any* negotiations were denounced as appeasement. Labour's Tam Dayell asked Heath if he 'agree[d] that part of the difficulty is the confusion which equates dialogue with appeasement, when dialogue and appeasement are very different matters'? Heath replied:

> The hon. Gentleman is absolutely right, and I am afraid that 'appeasement' is used as a weapon against those who want to have what the hon. Gentleman calls dialogue, simply to whip up public feeling. Most of those who use it were not even alive in the 1930s, when it happened, and have never studied what the problems of appeasement were. Those of us who opposed it are aware of it very well . . . We reach the point at which the issues must be thrashed out, and I hope that when Mr. Baker goes to Baghdad and the silly arguments about dates are all settled, he will not simply say, 'Saddam, get out'. If he does, President Saddam will reply, 'Will you kindly leave Baghdad?' There must be discussion – if one does not like to use the word 'negotiation' – and he can discuss what are the outstanding problems with Kuwait.[54]

Despite such pleas, Saddam was continually, and successfully, depicted as 'another Hitler' in the West. It naturally followed that the appeasement of Saddam threatened a repeat performance of the Second World War. The success of this rhetorical strategy led two commentators to observe: 'It would not be a great exaggeration to say that the United States went to war [with Iraq in 1991] over an analogy.'[55] In addition to invoking the spectre of the 1930s, leading figures in the Bush administration repeatedly mentioned the Vietnam War as a framework for the invasion of Kuwait and the subsequent war.[56] Vietnam stood, of course, as the American equivalent of Britain's own national debacle, Suez. In 1990, patriotic Americans hoped that a war to liberate Kuwait would emulate the virtue of the Second World War and simultaneously re-cast Vietnam as a 'good war'. The references to the Second World War therefore had a dual role: to justify the coming war, and to 'rescue' the Vietnam War.

On 31 December 1990, in a private letter to his children, Bush wrote of the coming conflict in the Gulf and asked: 'How many lives might have been saved if appeasement had given way to force earlier on in the late 30s or early 40s? How many Jews might have been spared the gas chambers, or how many Polish patriots might be alive today? I look at today's crisis as "good" vs. "evil". Yes, it is that clear.'[57] Once the war of 1991 had liberated Kuwait, Bush continued to invoke the 1930s and 1940s in relation to Iraq and Kuwait. He wrote: 'I saw a direct analogy between what was occurring in Kuwait and what the Nazis had done, especially in Poland.' He also wrote that even though he had been criticized for comparing Hitler and Hussein, 'I still feel it was an appropriate one'.[58] Bush also seemed intent on exorcising the ghosts of Vietnam[59] by means of waging a war in the Persian Gulf that, in turn, was justified by a desire to atone for the sins of the 1930s. In 1992, one polemicist wrote:

> That no one saw the 'appeasement' theme for what it was – a conventional political ploy calculated principally to achieve an electoral victory for the president in 1992 – suggested the damage done to the American political process by an even more accomplished and brazen theatrical performer, that of George Bush's teacher and mentor, Ronald Reagan.[60]

Of course, such conclusions privileged the means of the morality of telling truth in politics over any ends of driving Saddam from Kuwait. For such critics Bush's wedding of national self-interest with morality in a new Jeffersonian paradigm[61] was a smokescreen for *Realpolitik*. Against this, Thatcher expressed fears that the international community risked repeating the errors of the 1930s by failing to match rhetoric with resolution.

> I felt that too much faith was being put in high-flown international declarations and too little attention paid to the means of enforcing them . . . The rhetoric of that time [1930s] struck me as uncannily like that which I was now hearing . . . when the League [of Nations] had failed to take action against the dictators and so prepared the way for the Second World War, struck me as equally damning of the kind of collective security upon which the future of post–Cold War stability and freedom was supposed to be based: 'What was everybody's business in the end proved to be nobody's business. Each one looked to the other to take the lead, and the aggressors got away with it.'[62]

In the event, Thatcher was forced to resign as prime minister in November 1990, before the liberation of Kuwait began. But she had played her role to the full. For her adherents, Thatcher's role in the formation of the coalition in 1990 set the seal upon her place as the arch British anti-appeaser of the postwar era. It coincided with the end of the Cold War that Nicholas Ridley, employing a certain level of hyperbole, asserted had been ended by the same coalition (of the United States, the Soviet Union and Britain) that had sought to perpetuate the wartime 'Grand Alliance' at Yalta in 1945. For Ridley, Thatcher's place in history was assured as '[t]he victories in the Falklands War and the Gulf War were largely due to her resolution.'[63] Thatcher had, it was true, acquired a formidable international reputation through her principled foreign policies. In her victorious 1987 election campaign she had also benefitted from her willingness to negotiate from strength[64] (famously declaring that Soviet leader Mikhail Gorbachev was a man she 'could do business with').[65] By 1990, however, her perceived intransigence and combative style was becoming increasingly unpopular with the electorate. This alarmed many MPs in Britain's ruling Conservative Party and internal opposition brought her down in November 1990.[66] By this stage Thatcher believed much of her own propaganda and in her memoirs she compared her fall with Churchill's ejection by the electorate in July 1945 ('democracy is no respecter of persons'). Typically, she viewed the advice of several of her senior Cabinet colleagues to resign (after failing to win the Conservative leadership on a first ballot) in Hobbesian terms. 'I was sick at heart . . . what grieved me was the desertion of those I had considered friends and allies into the weasel words whereby they had transmuted their betrayal into frank advice and concern for my fate.'[67] On the international stage, it seemed that Thatcher's confrontational approach to foreign affairs had been rendered obsolescent, as the Cold War had passed into history. Within a year events in the dying state of Yugoslavia would give her fall, and her rhetoric, added poignancy.

CHAPTER EIGHT

Appeasement and the politics of obstructionism: Britain and the dissolution of Bosnia

I see it as a puzzle . . . how experienced diplomats could fail to
understand the meaning of the aggressor's tactics. You think they
are only pretending to disbelieve the aggressor's statements and
under cover of negotiations for confirmation, they are groping
for a deal with the aggressor.

MAXIM LITVINOV, 1937 [1]

Peter Hain: 'The policy pursued by his Government and the whole of
the west has failed abysmally. The genocide, rape and ethnic cleansing
continue and, increasingly, the Government are speaking with the voice
of Joseph Chamberlain on this crisis.'
Douglas Hurd: 'I think that the hon. Gentleman has got
his Chamberlains mixed up.'
Peter Hain: 'Neville Chamberlain.'
Douglas Hurd: 'I am obliged.'

Exchange in the House of Commons, 1993 [2]

Douglas, Douglas, you would make Neville Chamberlain
look like a warmonger.

MARGARET THATCHER TO DOUGLAS HURD, 1993 [3]

Kuwait was liberated from Iraqi occupation after the coalition achieved
a crushing military victory in only eleven days in January and February
1991. Although military operations were halted before Saddam Hussein

was toppled, Prime Minister John Major celebrated nevertheless: 'although it may be unfashionable to think in such terms, it was morally the right thing to do: it gave a signal that the world expected certain standards in international behavior and would act to enforce them.'[4] This was, alas, an illusory marker as the resolution demonstrated by the British government over Kuwait gave way to a very different kind of foreign policy response to the wars in the former Yugoslavia where, as one British diplomat later noted: 'The dreaded word appeasement began to hang over the British government'.[5] Parallels with the failures of the 1930s were now drawn, and increasingly strident voices called for the international community to act against aggression – as it had done with Saddam Hussein.[6] This did not happen. For British Foreign Secretary Douglas Hurd the reason for this was clear: 'The aggression of Iraq against Kuwait was a simple act of aggression by one sovereign state against another. In Bosnia, we have a war in which the overwhelming majority of those fighting are Bosnians – Bosnian Serbs, Bosnian Croats and Bosnian Muslims . . . But the position is different from that which produced Desert Storm.'[7] In his memoirs, Hurd stated that while policy making was very straightforward over Kuwait in 1990–1, 'there was none of the intellectual and ethical questions which later beset our policy on Bosnia'.[8] All of this contributed to the fact that, as one US Department of Defense official pithily cracked of Western policy: 'We do deserts – we don't do mountains.'[9] Thus, while John Major's succession to the premiership made little difference to the resolution demonstrated by British policy towards occupied Kuwait,[10] this could not be said of the former Yugoslavia where its policy was widely viewed as being 'Chamberlainite'.[11]

A significant factor in the character of the British response to the former Yugoslavia undoubtedly lay in the personalities of the chief protagonists in London. John Major was a very different type of politician from his predecessor. Where she seemed to revel in conflict, he sought compromise; where she acted on principle, he engaged in practicalities. In terms of foreign policy, Major was far more in tune with the 'pragmatic' tradition of cautious policy making long favoured by the Foreign and Commonwealth Office (FCO). The straightforward identification of the guilty was rejected by the British government when shaping policy on the former Yugoslavia as the strident language of anti-appeasement, of right and wrong, was rejected in favour of muddying the waters at every possible turn. Hurd stressed the ethnic divisions and their historic nature in the former Yugoslavia. Unlike the Falklands, Kuwait or German unification the issues were very complex and confused in the former Yugoslavia – sufficiently so to ensure that there was never sufficient political pressure in Britain for the government to ever consider direct intervention.[12] The fact remains that, as the historian Kenneth Morgan noted in 2003, Hurd's 'recessive diplomatic stance in Bosnia, that "level killing field", brought him criticism as a latter-day appeaser.'[13]

The FCO (and its 'old boy', Douglas Hurd) set the agenda in the former Yugoslavia as Thatcher's bullish anti-appeasement was left behind.[14] Thatcher's irritation at the FCO had increased throughout her premiership and Hurd recalls that she greeted any deviation from her line as being: 'Typical Foreign Office'. As soon as Slovenia declared independence on 27 June 1991, Thatcher phoned Hurd and demanded intervention against the Serb 'aggressors'. In making this demand Thatcher was out-of-step with her party. Edward Heath spoke for many in the ruling Conservative Party when he later lamented: '[O]ur people seem to have forgotten that the Serbs supported us in the First World War, supported us in the Second . . . There's an ignorance of history which is lamentable.'[15] Hurd, a former private secretary to Heath, also disagreed with Thatcher's view of the Serbs and he therefore disregarded her strident (and unwanted) advice, confident that his was the majority view.[16] From this moment on, appeasement was back in the saddle for, as Hurd stated in 2001, '[t]here was no serious British national interest involved. No strategic. No commercial'.[17] A keen student of history, Hurd took a dispassionate view of Chamberlainite appeasement, and was indignant at charges of appeasement in Bosnia. Hurd argued that any British intervention would see initial public enthusiasm evaporate as the media asked: 'Haven't you forgotten Vietnam? Haven't you forgotten Northern Ireland? Are you really getting us involved in something to which there is no end?' Such logic failed to move US Senator Joseph Biden Jr. (D-DE), who noted: 'Two litmus tests can identify appeasers: frequent references to a "civil war involving age-old hatreds" and professed worry that lifting even an unfair embargo "would only fuel the fire." These excuses have been steady refrains from the West.'[18].

The international community's failure in the former Yugoslavia, and in Bosnia in particular, must be laid at the door of the West as a whole. Some commentators opined that the long history of the Great Powers' outside engagement with the Balkans had taught one overriding lesson: avoid all contact if at all possible.[19] The West's failure in the 1990s made nonsense of the 'New World Order' that the administration of George H. W. Bush was supposed to lead the international community into following the Cold War. Instead, too many Western statesmen and women fell back on simplistic explanations for the wars in the former Yugoslavia (on 30 September 1991, for instance, France's Roland Dumas told Hurd that the war in Croatia was a continuation of the Second World War).[20] Western inaction was undoubtedly encouraged by Washington's semi-detached attitude. This was not pre-ordained, however. Indeed, as soon as Warren Zimmermann arrived in Belgrade as US ambassador to Yugoslavia in March 1989 he had immediately criticized Serbia's president, Slobodan Milošević, for ignoring human rights (especially in Kosovo). This Zimmermann later asserted was a 'course correction' in US policy.[21] In the end, these good intentions counted for nothing and Milošević, like a latter-day mini-Hitler, proceeded to kill peace in Yugoslavia in piecemeal fashion.[22] The failure of the United

States to back up its warnings to Belgrade was a crucial consideration in Milošević's decision to proceed with its aggression. In the immediate wake of the First Gulf War, Robert J. McMahon's assessment of the international system was absolutely correct: 'Peace and order [globally] depend to a great extent on Washington's ability to convince adversaries and allies of its firmness, determination and dependability.'[23] The vacuum created by the subsequent low profile adopted by the United States in the former Yugoslavia was, thus, fatal to those in the international community who wanted to respond in a resolute manner.

Malcolm Rifkind, secretary of state for defence (1992–5) and foreign secretary (1995–7), was one of most effective proponents of appeasement during the war in Bosnia. In 1994 he lashed out at (what he saw as) naive critics asserting: 'This is a very messy, bloody war. This idea it can be sorted out in some neat clinical way is a nice aspiration, but totally unrealistic.'[24] Rifkind was not ashamed of his hard-headed attitude towards the wars in the former Yugoslavia. Indeed, in his first speech as foreign secretary he proudly attached himself to Lord Palmerston's famous maxim: 'The furtherance of British interests should be the only object of a British Foreign Secretary.'[25] And, as with Chamberlain's foreign policy at the time of Munich, the ruling Conservative Party's support of the Major–Hurd–Rifkind position gave very little reason for any modification of policy.[26] James Gow noted that 'London's position was one of pusillanimous realism, suffused initially with an interpretation of the conflict as ethnic and historical.'[27] Thus, as an essential part of the British strategy with regard to the former Yugoslavia, the British government was to substitute Thatcher's 'can do' mentality with an unbending insistence upon the intractable nature of the problem. Rifkind's predecessor, Douglas Hurd, told the Commons in April 1993:

> We are all conscious of the moral and public pressures on the international community to do more, to intervene more actively to stop the carnage. Those pressures are sincere and must be taken seriously. However, we also have to remember the nature of this problem. We are witnessing a civil war in Bosnia which is encouraged and overwhelmingly fuelled by Belgrade. We should not pretend that, from outside, we can ensure a solution. Even a prolonged military commitment by the international community could not guarantee that. It would convert Bosnia into a protectorate for an indefinite period without a certain outcome. In practice, no Government – I am not speaking about columnists – are seriously suggesting that.[28]

Once the war was over Hurd was far less strident: 'Humility is in order among those of us who handled policy toward Bosnia. We were groping for a way to end a savage war which went on far too long.'[29] But Hurd's claims during the war had already attracted widespread scepticism. John Nott, the former defence secretary, later denounced as 'British propaganda' the idea that Bosnia was a civil war and that all sides were equally culpable in terms of atrocities.[30] In assessing British priorities, John Major was accurate when he later asserted that, from the outset, 'our policy had to be dictated by two concerns: to save as many lives as we could, and to do all in our power to limit the conflict'.[31] In actual fact, British policy aimed at *slowing* the casualty rate and limiting the war *geographically* but not necessarily in terms of *duration*. The price for such a policy, seemingly deemed acceptable in London, often included the sacrifice of human rights and international law, but *never* British interests. The policy of obstructing attempts to intensify the international response to the wars in the former Yugoslavia became Britain's only consistent response and, paradoxically, was often disguised as an attempt to 'seek consensus' among the Western states. Here, the British found an ally in the United Nations, which repeatedly bent over backwards so as not to offend the Serbs.[32] The British government knew the UN's limitations and this was why it had been kept at arm's length, after having delivered an initial diplomatic mandate, in the 1982 Falklands War and over Iraq in 1990–1. The British carefully manipulated the West's desire to speak with one voice, knowing that no action would be taken as the lowest common denominator would dictate the international response. All too often Britain represented this lowest common denominator. It is, therefore, not too much to state that London bore a particular responsibility, over and above that of the West's collective responsibility, for the failures of the international community in the former Yugoslavia. As the *Economist* noted in 1992:

> No other country is well-placed as Britain to be statesmanlike over Bosnia . . . It faces none of the inhibitions distracting the other big Western players – the presidential campaign in the United States, the imminent referendum on the Maastricht treaty in France, Germany's constitutional qualms about sending forces abroad. John Major's government . . . is fresh from its election victory . . . [and] might reasonably be expected to be making the running on the Bosnian *imbroglio*.[33]

Hurd himself asserted that 'Britain plays a central role in world affairs. We owe this in part to our history, but we continue to earn it thorough active diplomacy and a willingness to shoulder our share of international responsibilities.' [34] Such factors were crucial in allotting Britain the central role in the former Yugoslavia after 1991.[35] This included the United Kingdom's unique position as a member of NATO, the European Community (EC), the Commonwealth, the Group of Seven and the UN Security Council. The leader of the Opposition, Neil Kinnock, was quite right when he observed: 'The basic question at issue is whether the United Kingdom is to be carried along in the wake of those changes [in Eastern Europe] or to be a driving force for change.'[36] British foreign policy had, in the words of Hurd, 'to be strenuous and energetic'[37] if the United Kingdom was to continue to 'punch above [its] weight',[38] and was to take a central role in the former Yugoslavia.[39] Britain's permanent seat on the Security Council of the UN, already challenged by Germany and Japan, was concomitant with playing an active role in UN peacekeeping operations[40] – a role Germany and Japan would then have a far more difficult time with fulfilling constitutionally. The British government therefore (superficially) acceded to the demands of what was disparagingly termed the 'something must be done' constituency[41] for three reasons. First, the domestic and international outcry was too great to ignore; second, it had little choice if she wished to remain a major player; and finally because it was recognized that it could be the slowest ship in that convoy (and hence slow the convoy to that speed) and thus prevent resolute action by the international community. In 1992, William Wallace asserted: 'We [the UK] have a common European agenda, on which there is a distinct British perspective.'[42] In the former Yugoslavia, however, that national 'perspective' often completely obscured the supranational 'agenda'. At times Hurd's contempt for the interventionists was blatant: 'The advice "Something must be done" is the least useful that can be given . . . Those who believe that it would be right to send our troops . . . to enforce a military solution should say so, not take refuge in the sort of rhetoric which is an obstacle to reality.'[43]

Many on the political Right in Britain supported Hurd's Bosnian policy because of the canonical belief in the 'national interest',[44] and the foreign secretary was careful to reassure his own party on this issue. In April 1993, Hurd stated:

> [I]t is the British national interest that justifies or does not justify our becoming involved in what amounts to a considerable number of tragedies and disasters. We have come to the view that it is a British national interest that we should do what we can to help bring peace to Bosnia and the former Yugoslavia, partly because the conflict is in Europe, whereas the other conflicts are not, and partly because we have been able to see a way in which we can do that . . . What we have done is entirely justified according . . . [to] the British national interest.[45]

From the inception of the wars in the former Yugoslavia the United States, by contrast, had as a declared aim the halting of Serb aggression – a goal that London only *professed* to share. In November 1995, Rifkind told the Commons: 'From the start, Britain has upheld the principles that internationally recognised borders must not be altered by force, and the legitimate rights of all ethnic groups must be properly protected by their governments.'[46] In truth, the aims of British policy were far more modest and based primarily on the principle of *Realpolitik*, the guiding principle of British foreign policy generally.[47] One might usefully note that, in such a worldview, 'the *role of legal and moral considerations in international politics is an ineffectual one*'.[48] This led the British government to dismiss calls for stronger action on humanitarian or moral grounds as irrelevant or impractical. The British government was therefore often cast as *the* chief obstruction to effective international action (small wonder that Bosnian President Alija Izetbegović asserted, as early as December 1992, that the British were 'the biggest brake on any progress').[49] One US official went so far as to observe: 'I learned to treat Britain as a hostile power . . . Britain was prepared to go to the wall against us on Bosnia – out to block anything, everything . . . I came to think of the British as like having the Russians around the state department . . . Your guys were usually so refined, but they were going crazy on this.'[50] Such views were confirmed by a senior British source within NATO who later conceded that many Americans were exasperated how, after the resolution demonstrated over Iraq, they 'really saw the Brits as Chamberlain-style appeasers'. Indeed, even within normally Anglophile elements in the State Department, the reaction against what was seen as the 'Chamberlain/appeasement/Munich' tendency among British officials was particularly strong.[51]

British policy towards the former Yugoslavia was, initially, formulated in an extremely ad hoc manner. This lay within the brand of diplomacy heralded as 'pragmatic' and historically beloved of British diplomats. This quintessentially British approach to foreign policy has been described as having come down from David Hume and Adam Smith, through Jeremy Bentham and John Stuart Mill, into 'an established scepticism about grand designs . . . a preference for practical detail over rhetoric and dogma'.[52] In the former Yugoslavia, this effectively meant acquiescence to 'ethnic cleansing' rather than support for human rights and international law. The British government instead preferred to emphasize the intractable nature of the problem, stressing 'historical experience' as the chief guide to policy formulation. Notions of a Balkan 'tinderbox', of June 1914[53] and of the 'Eastern Question' of the 1870s, were repeatedly invoked.[54] In May 1995 John Major stated:

> The Balkans have often enough been a tinderbox in history, and war memorials throughout the United Kingdom testify to the price paid in British blood for past Balkan turbulence. The Bosnian war by itself might not directly affect our interests, but a wider conflagration across the Balkans – leading to a wider Balkan war – most certainly would affect our strategic interests.

> If unchecked, the fighting in Bosnia could have ignited not only a Serb-Croat war in Croatia, but unrest in Kosovo and Macedonia. That could easily have dragged Albania, Bulgaria, Greece and Turkey into confrontation with one another. The Bosnian dispute has always contained within it the seeds of the nightmare of a wider Balkan war.[55]

Throughout the period 1991–5, British policy makers constantly stressed the supposed historic ethnic animosity in the former Yugoslavia. Typically,

Douglas Hogg, minister of state at the FCO, asserted: 'The dispute within Yugoslavia is largely ethnic and historic.'[56] Sir Peter Hall, the British ambassador in Belgrade, 1989–91, even informed Major at the outset of the war that 'the first thing you have to know about these people is that they like going around cutting each other's heads off.'[57] John Major bought into this rhetoric, if only to justify his government's policies, and later recalled: 'All sides exhumed memories from Yugoslavia's crypt of murder.'[58] The spectre of historical failure haunted the West and, at each stage of the conflict, historical analogies abounded on all sides. As one journalist noted: 'To use some badly devalued historical metaphors, the Americans see Munich, the betrayal of a small state by Great Powers bent on maintaining the status quo. The Europeans see Vietnam, a quagmire that will suck in their troops and destroy them.'[59] Shared national experience meant that the British public tended to be more wary than most of involvement in ethnic conflicts.[60] Public opinion in the United Kingdom was certainly receptive to arguments of the intractability of such conflicts after 25 years or so of strife in Northern Ireland (in similar fashion the 'Vietnam syndrome' can still be used to haunt the domestic American audience).[61] Major appreciated that Vietnam (and, more recently, Somalia) caused American opinion to oppose sending any troops to the former Yugoslavia but he was irritated by the hawkishness of many US politicians just the same.[62] FCO 'realism' was based on what they saw as Britain's experience of such 'ethnic feuds' in Palestine, India and Northern Ireland.[63] Thus, while the US administration condemned Serbian aggression, the British government preferred to focus on the 'inter-communal aspect of the war'.[64] The constant stress on the issue of ethnicity was part of an on-going effort to make the war seem intractable and, somehow, inevitable. Actively invoking one of the darker memories of Chamberlain's return from Munich, Major later asserted: 'We soon learned that an "agreement" made with states of the former Yugoslavia is one of history's less useful pieces of paper.'[65] In the Balkans there were, it seemed, Hitlers on all sides. And, although the public outcry in Britain was as loud as in virtually any other country, the UK government was largely successful in opposing resolute action – not least by portraying the conflict as an unending ethnic war.[66]

In 1991, Britain tended to look backwards rather than forwards, yearning for the relative certainties that Tito imposed upon Yugoslavia. After 1945 Britain's principal objective with regard to Tito's Yugoslavia was, in the parlance of the Foreign Office (FO), to establish a decent 'working relationship'.[67] In the immediate postwar era the United Kingdom had vital interests in the Middle East and the Mediterranean with Yugoslavia viewed as a vital 'link' power (between Italy and Greece) – essential for Western defence against Soviet encroachment.[68] Although in the minds of Soviet contemporaries, and many subsequent historians and policy makers in the West, the United States and the United Kingdom followed a co-ordinated policy over Yugoslavia at this time, this was hardly the case. Aware of

Tito's independence of mind, the British were early believers in his break from Moscow towards 'national communism'.[69] In 1945 the then–foreign secretary, Anthony Eden, had asserted: 'Our present policy towards Yugoslavia is . . . realistic and not over ambitious' and good relations with Tito represent 'one [of the] principal means of influencing Balkan affairs as a whole'.[70] Throughout the Cold War the United Kingdom maintained a more pragmatic approach to Communist Yugoslavia than the United States. Sir Orme Sargent, deputy permanent under-secretary at the FO, observed: 'Yugoslavia is strategically too important to our position in the Mediterranean and Greece and Italy for us to adopt a policy of sulking towards her.'[71] It was such pragmatism that had allowed the British to support Tito's Communist Partisans, rather than Draža Mihailović's Chetniks, during the Second World War. Such pragmatism was to remain the underlying rationale of British policy until the end of the Cold War and the undoing of the postwar division of Europe rudely interrupted the cosy predictability of south-eastern Europe in the eyes of British policy makers.

The West remained dogmatically wedded to the idea of a unitary Yugoslavia, long after it was obvious that no such entity existed.[72] Having played a major role in the establishment of the first Yugoslavia in 1919 (and the second in 1945) the British seemed especially reluctant to abandon the Yugoslav ideal. In his memoirs Hurd observed that 'Tito had built it into a substantial country . . . well respected because of his successful defiance of Stalin . . . The unravelling of the country after his death was not an inevitable disaster, but the result of shortsighted greed for power.'[73] In the Commons, Hurd similarly asserted:

> For 70 years the [ethnic] problem was not solved, but it was at least dormant – first under the monarchy, then under . . . Tito. People were not free, but at least during those 70 years – except during the Second World War – they were not killing each other. As the communist regime disintegrated, an effort – a worthwhile effort – was made to preserve Yugoslavia by consent. Sadly, that effort failed disastrously.[74]

When the leaders of the six republics of Yugoslavia met at the beginning of 1991, the West hoped for a successful resolution of the bitter disagreements in that country (thus ignoring crucial warning signs).[75] The British did, at least, warn Serbia (the biggest republic and that most wedded to unity) against the use of force.[76] Signally, however, John Major also made it clear that he would not 'encourage or support those who wish to change the relations in Yugoslavia either by individual disassociation or by imposing such internal relations that would eventually lead to the disintegration of Yugoslavia'.[77] For the Major government, secessionists such as President Franjo Tuđman of Croatia were identified as being the root cause of the problems in the former Yugoslavia.[78] Perhaps, as has been suggested by Sabrina Petra Ramet, secessionist movements in Scotland, Wales and

Northern Ireland have reinforced 'a more general antipathy towards fragmentation' amongst British policy makers.'[79] A more likely explanation lies, however, in the desire to discourage secessionism anywhere lest it encourage such movements in the increasingly fragile Soviet Union under Gorbachev.[80] On 30 June 1991 US Secretary of State James Baker, echoing a similar warning by Hurd, stated unequivocally that 'the US will not encourage or reward secession'.[81] Such statements gave the Serbs reason to believe that they had tacit support for keeping Yugoslavia together by forcible means.[82] Jonathan Eyal, director of studies at the Royal United Services Institute, termed this policy 'The Original Sin', as it gave a 'green light' to the Serbs to prevent Croatia and Slovenia from declaring independence from Yugoslavia.[83]

The upshot of the dichotomy in Western policy over Yugoslavia was a proposal by Hurd for a Yugoslav confederation (on the EC model) to balance the desire to avoid disintegration against the inadmissibility of the use of force. The lack of understanding about the extent to which the relations between Yugoslav republics had declined at this time led one FCO official to speculate that Croatia and Slovenia (the two republics keenest on independence) were 'ready to continue negotiations . . . about a new Yugoslavia'. Britain (and the EC for that matter) ignored the fact that a looser confederation was unacceptable to *any* of the protagonists and an EC delegation in Belgrade was reduced to expressing sadness that while the EC was growing together Yugoslavia was breaking apart.[84]

Following the declaration of independence by Croatia and Slovenia on 10 June 1991, war erupted in Slovenia. The war in Slovenia ended after only ten days with Yugoslav withdrawal. The fact that the war in Slovenia had been so short was due to the fact that Belgrade (capital of both Yugoslavia and Serbia) had decided to let that republic go as it contained very few non-Slovenes. This fact should not have been lost upon the West as it confirmed that Belgrade and the Yugoslav National Army (*Jugoslovenska Narodna Armija* – JNA) were not fighting to preserve Yugoslavia but rather to carve out a Greater Serbia.[85] In Croatia, the Serb minority asserted their independence via the *Republika Srpska Krajina* as war erupted there. Meanwhile, the West seemed to suffer a form of diplomatic paralysis. At a Western European Union (WEU) meeting on 19 August 1991 an attempt was made to frame an intervention in the former Yugoslavia. This failed because 'Douglas Hurd . . . killed the idea off'.[86] Hurd continued his obstructionism, under the guise of seeking international consensus, at a Council of Foreign Ministers meeting in September. For the time being the Bush administration was content to let the Europeans sort out the problem and would 'accept any resolution arrived at peacefully, democratically, and by negotiation'.[87] Unfortunately, following a pattern hardly deviated from since Suez, the British believed US participation in any peace deal to be indispensable.[88] Without such involvement, the British resolved to adopt a policy of appeasement towards the Serbs. In doing so the 'realist' policy of the British clashed repeatedly with more 'idealistic' impulses.[89]

Having failed to prevent armed conflict in Yugoslavia the EC was reduced to trying to manage it via cease-fires and a peace conference at The Hague.[90] On 2 September 1991, the EC brokered a cease-fire in Croatia and appointed Lord Carrington (British foreign secretary, 1979–82) as chair of a peace conference.[91] The president of the EC Council of Ministers, Hans Van den Broek, asked Carrington to solve the problem in less than two months; as he later remarked: 'We were all pretty ignorant of how difficult it was going to be.'[92] Carrington was pessimistic from the start as he, too, saw the war in ethnic terms and believed that compromise was well-nigh impossible.[93] From this time forward the British government now portrayed themselves as being in the forefront of the search for peace, although the reality was that they concentrated on frustrating calls for intervention, notably from France.[94] Nevertheless, the diplomats were busy as the subsequent international response to the wars in Croatia, and more particularly Bosnia-Herzegovina, revolved mainly around the extended discussion of various peace plans.[95] These peace plans were, as the *Economist* pointed out in 1992, flawed from the inception because they viewed 'Bosnia [as] a tragedy of revenge involving ancient feuds of churches and peoples, overlaid by score-settling for atrocities in the second world war'.[96] The widespread credence given to such pessimistic narratives, allied to the semi-detachment of the United States, meant that London was able to promote own its vision of Balkan diplomacy whilst often imposing its own agenda on matters.

Serbia was encouraged in its aggressive policies when, on 26 September 1991, a UN resolution (UNR 713) embargoed the export of arms to all of the states in the former Yugoslavia (incredibly, this had been passed at the request of Yugoslav Foreign Minister, Budimir Lončar). The embargo, seen by the British as essential in limiting the spread of violence, became a central pillar of British policy on the former Yugoslavia. Its effect was to simply freeze the imbalance in weaponry between the Serbs (who had dominated the JNA) and their opponents. Nevertheless, despite Article 51 of the UN charter (the right to self-defence), the embargo was maintained against *all* of the successor states of the former Yugoslavia.[97]

By late 1991, with nearly one-third of Croatia now controlled by the *Republika Srpska Krajina*, Germany was lobbying hard for the EC to recognize Slovenian and Croatian independence.[98] On 27 November 1991, in an address to the *Bundestag*, German Chancellor Kohl set 24 December 1991 as the date when Germany would recognize Slovenia and Croatia, whether or not anyone else would follow suit.[99] The British government was strongly opposed to any such policy, asserting that recognition would only strengthen Milošević in his nationalist agenda while fatally exposing Bosnia to Serb (and Croat) predatory ambitions.[100] One British official warned: 'Take one look at the map of Yugoslavia and you realise that, with the

sole exception of Slovenia, the nationalities and religions are so enmeshed
that there is no peaceful way of breaking Yugoslavia up . . . to support
independence for the republics is to sanction continuous civil war.'[101] In
truth, while fearing further fragmentation of the former Yugoslavia, the
British were also alarmed at the possible resurrection of the spectre of a
German-dominated *Mitteleuropa*.[102] On 13 December 1991, the British (and
the French) introduced an unsuccessful UN Security Council resolution –
aimed at Germany – warning against any country taking unilateral action
in Croatia.[103] Although the United Kingdom (and the United States) argued
that recognition would de-rail the peace process,[104] the German foreign
minister, Hans-Dietrich Genscher, asserted that recognition would halt
Belgrade's advance through Croatia while any further delay would only
encourage further Serb aggression.[105] Under intense German pressure,
Britain, and the rest of the EC, eventually acquiesced to recognizing Croatia
and Slovenia.[106] Hurd told the Commons:

> [I]f we wish to influence for the better what happens in Yugoslavia,
> the Government have concluded that it is best to do so by seeking and
> then implementing agreements among the Twelve. There is no sensible
> prospect of British influence for good in Yugoslavia if that influence is
> in rivalry or contradiction with the influence of other European powers.
> That is a national conclusion.[107]

Regardless of British motives, Lord Owen, the EC's peace envoy, found it
'surprising . . . that the French and the British, and their respective foreign
ministers, Dumas and Hurd, had argued so eloquently against recognition,
withdrew their opposition in favour of a deeply damaging EC consensus.'[108]
(Although John Major later dismissed the suggestion of quid pro quo on the
Maastricht Treaty as a 'preposterous notion'.[109]) Regardless, the recognition
of Croatia and Slovenia would now force Bosnia and Macedonia, left in a
Yugoslavia dominated by Serbia and Milošević, to seek independence and
completely destroy Yugoslavia. Observers murmured about an impending
period of 'Wreckognition'. Radovan Karadžić, the Bosnian Serb leader,
ominously observed that 'Bosnia does not exist anymore'.[110]

Izetbegović declared the independence of Bosnian-Herzegovina on 3
March 1992. The Bosnian Serbs immediately began erecting barricades
in Sarajevo and clashes soon began. On 6 April 1992, 51 years to the day
that Axis forces had invaded Yugoslavia, the Serbs launched an offensive in
eastern Bosnia. Only in August did a reluctant British government agree to
send 1,800 troops as peacekeepers[111] – although Major stressed the limited
nature of the British commitment, as he had not detected 'any support
in Parliament or in public opinion for operations which would tie down
large numbers of British forces in difficult and dangerous terrain for a long
period'.[112]

ILLUSTRATION 8.1 *Foreign Secretary Douglas Hurd and Bosnian President Alija Izetbegović on an inspection tour of Sarajevo, 17 July 1992. During the one-day visit by the foreign secretary a mortar shell landed outside the building in which he and Izetbegović were engaged in talks. Hurd emerged unscathed and unruffled. He then donned a flak jacket before telling reporters: 'If one were afraid of danger, one wouldn't have come.'*

As the then-holder of the EC presidency, Britain hosted a conference in London on the former Yugoslavia in August 1992. Here Major enunciated his so-called thirteen principles of civilised behaviour (dealing with human rights, refugees, diplomacy and possible sanctions). On the second day of the conference the EC, largely under Dutch pressure, drew up a resolution lambasting the Serbs. Major, fearing a Serb walkout, managed to avoid a vote on the resolution and compromised by reading out the resolution as a declaration instead. Despite this act of craven appeasement, Major, somewhat predictably, hailed the success of the Conference: 'We now know what needs to be done, how it needs to be done and by whom it needs to be done.' Such crowing rendered hollow the conference's final declaration in which the warring parties were advised: 'If they do not comply, the Security Council will be invited to apply stringent sanctions leading to total international isolation.'[113] Force was not mentioned; and only force would stop the Serbs.

British involvement in those forces the international community did send to the former Yugoslavia belied the non-interventionist bent of the Major government. Even when agreeing to participate in UN peacekeeping forces – UNPROFOR – in the former Yugoslavia, Defence Secretary

Malcolm Rifkind stressed that, in the event of any significant casualties, British forces would be immediately withdrawn.[114] It was nevertheless argued that the peacekeepers were doing little good and Thatcher stridently declared that the UN and Britain were 'feeding people but leaving them to be massacred'.[115] Prime Minister Major meanwhile rejected all American attempts at hardening Western attitudes towards Serb aggression and, instead, mouthed platitudes about a 'very messy and difficult problem, which is not capable of easy solution. That does not mean we can stand by and take no action whatsoever. It does mean we need to be very measured.'[116] Yet, despite the Serbian obstruction of humanitarian aid, there was very little stomach in London to invoke UN resolution 770 as a means of forcing aid through. The British government also worked to ensure that no one else took on the various militias. The reporter Martin Bell noted that the British insistence on using troops only 'to escort aid to the victims of the war rather than to prevent the aggression . . . was to pass food in the window while the murderer stood at the door'.[117] The British government contented itself with assurances that the mere presence of UNPROFOR itself acted as a check on the violence.[118] This assertion had the great advantage of being impossible to prove either way.

In early 1993, the so-called Vance -Owen Peace Plan (VOPP), named for the UN envoy Cyrus Vance and the EC representative Lord Owen, proposed the division of Bosnia into ethnic statelets.[119] The plan was hugely controversial and was deliberately vague so as to gain even a measure of acceptance by all sides.[120] Vance angrily dismissed talk of appeasement as 'hogwash'. 'If we refused to talk, on so-called moral grounds, to all parties to a conflict, how could we have ever settle any problem? [With] no viable alternative to a negotiated settlement . . . [it is] nonsense to say we are appeasers for talking to the people who can make a difference in our pursuit of a lasting settlement'.[121]

Despite assurances to the contrary, the VOPP effectively signalled that the international community now saw the idea of a multi-ethnic Bosnia as a dead duck. This did not prevent its being touted by Owen and the Europeans (the British in particular) as 'the only show in town'.[122] The British government seemed indecent in their haste to embrace partition (a solution which had 'solved' several problems in the past).[123] In sight of a Balkan Munich, the newly-installed Clinton administration's opposition to the VOPP angered the British.[124] In the event, the Bosnian Serbs rejected the plan and its death was confirmed by international opinion – a perfect instance of the widespread deployment of the word 'appeasement' sufficing to hole a diplomatic initiative below the waterline,[125] like a latter day Hoare–Laval Pact. This failure, combined with US criticism of the arms embargo, gave false hope to the Bosnian government.[126] For the British, the aggressive anti-appeasement rhetoric of the Clinton administration was thus significantly more harmful than the hapless inertia of the Bush administration.[127] While Major told a sceptical US government that escalation in Bosnia would bring down his government,[128] Clinton stormed to an aide: 'You just don't understand what bastards those Brits are!'[129]

Emotive rhetoric did not impress the British. Hurd justified his detachment by asserting that 'no side [in Bosnia] has the monopoly on evil',[130] while continuing to insist: 'It is a civil war in the sense that the huge majority – more than 90 per cent – of those fighting are Bosnian. They are Bosnian Serbs, Bosnian Croats and Bosnian Muslims.'[131] This cut little ice in Washington. Viewing the war in Bosnia as one of Serb aggression, the Clinton administration had opposed the VOPP[132] for rewarding ethnic cleansing and for setting a bad precedent.[133] One US official wisecracked: 'The only thing worse than the failure of Vance-Owen would be the success of Vance-Owen',[134] while Secretary of State Warren Christopher simply asserted: 'we do not like the maps'.[135] The Americans viewed London's position that there was no 'real British interest . . . at stake in Bosnia' with alarm. The British ambassador in Washington reported that the US administration believed that 'present policies would at best lead to a rump Muslim state in Bosnia, which would create a Palestinian problem in the middle of Europe . . . and [were] a recipe for major long-term problems'.[136] In truth, the Clinton administration was far more practised in its highfaultin anti-appeasement rhetoric than in actually halting Serbian aggression. As one: observer noted: 'The Clinton's administration's key failure in Bosnia and elsewhere has been to ignore the example of American history that rational calculation must precede rhetoric.'[137] Secretary of State Christopher arrived in Europe in April 1993 to lobby for the lifting of the arms embargo and for employing air strikes against the Serbs (the so-called 'lift and strike' option).[138] Major later noted with satisfaction (although rather misleadingly) that Christopher 'found no enthusiasm for [this] anywhere'.[139] And Christopher had, indeed, badly under-estimated Anglo-French hostility to the idea of lifting the embargo.[140] Hurd pointedly informed the Commons:

> We believe that we should be in the business of trying to stop the war and not equipping the parties to fight it out. The idea is understandably presented as giving the Muslims a chance to defend themselves against the more heavily armed and better-equipped Serbs. It is possible that in that way Muslims would get better access to weapons, but the impact on the military situation would be neither quick nor decisive. The Serbs, and possibly the Croats, might decide to attack before the Muslims became too strong.

Keen to encourage the notion of Bosnia as an intractable ethnic war, Hurd 'strongly opposed lifting the arms embargo as a counsel of despair'[141] that would only cause the war to spread.

Far from tilting the balance towards the Bosnian Muslims, lifting the embargo could lead to an increase in the supply of weapons to the

Serbs and the Croats. Violence could escalate and the humanitarian relief operations would become increasingly difficult and dangerous. If that were to happen, far from ending the suffering, that course would aggravate it. It could, more than any option seriously being considered, threaten an extension of the conflict into other parts of the former Yugoslavia or beyond. As arms flow into the area, the fighting could overflow out of it.[142]

Although able to frustrate the VOPP, the Clinton administration was unable to overcome European opposition to arming the Bosnian government. A halfway house was thus found in the creation of the so-called 'safe areas' in Bosnia (UN Resolution 824). This was a significant climb-down by the US government, which had long rejected such enclaves as they would consolidate Serb conquests while creating a permanent refugee problem.[143] The Clinton administration, having abandoned its attempts to lift the arms embargo, had effectively agreed to seal and contain the war in Bosnia. In effect, this was nothing less than a vindication of British policy.

The differences between Christopher and Hurd are not difficult to explain. As a retired USAF general later observed: 'The United States says that its objective is to end the war through a negotiated settlement, but in reality what it wants is to influence the outcome in favor of the Muslims.'[144] To the British such an outcome was a utopian irrelevance and Hurd was clear where his priorities lay: 'We must not allow the Atlantic alliance to fracture on this issue.'[145] In May 1993, the Europeans therefore agreed to effectively abandon the VOPP,[146] while the British secured the maintenance of the arms embargo as their price for acquiesence.[147] Although the VOPP could have been resurrected, Owen conceded that 'there was not the political or military will in Europe, without France and Britain, to do this'.[148]

In a rather cosmetic exercise, an agreement in Washington led to the so-called 'Joint Action Programme' (JAP) being undertaken by France, Russia, Spain, the UK and the US. This new initiative was a compromise of limited ambition designed only 'to contain and stabilise the situation and to put the brakes on the killing'.[149] This accepted containment as Western policy[150] and was seen as appeasement par excellence, akin to the policy of 'non-intervention' adopted during the Spanish Civil War. An outraged Michael Foot invoked the appeasement of the 1930s.

> [This is] a settlement to be compared with the combined triumphs of the aggressors and the appeasers when Mussolini seized Abyssinia or Hitler seized the Sudetenland or Stalin seized half of Poland . . . It looks as if the participants are much more interested in protecting themselves and in particular in attempting to conceal their past misjudgments, to use the mildest term to describe their past follies and crimes . . . [Douglas Hurd] is the western statesman who has been there all the

time and, maybe, he is the man to whom Slobodan Milosevic owes the most direct debt . . . Some great reporters in the 1930s described what was happening in Germany and Italy while our Foreign Office was content with its own lies. Who could ever have supposed that history would repeat itself with the same crime of aggression, and the same contemptible response?[151]

A German official bitterly remarked that the JAP had more to do with Western solidarity than achieving peace in Bosnia.[152] In the former Yugoslavia, the Western response was seen as 'the final "capitulation" of the international community before Serbian aggression'.[153] Western unity, it seemed, could 'only be forged on the basis of minimalist policies'.[154]

The British government remained confident that partition was the only solution and Hogg told the Commons: 'The principles contained within the Vance-Owen peace plan provide the framework for securing a political settlement to the conflict in Bosnia.'[155] Following London's lead, the EC promoted a 'Union of Three Republics', mediated by Owen and the UN envoy, Thorvald Stoltenberg. The US remained opposed to 'rewarding' ethnic cleansing and determined to frustrate the initiative,[156] but seemed content to accept the British position and did little except to emphasize 'containment'.[157] The ditching of the VOPP was disappointing for the British government who saw it as 'the best chance for a lasting peace in Bosnia'[158] but, in truth, it had given up little and gained much. Tiring of intransigence on all sides, Hurd warned that British troops would not stay in Bosnia 'indefinitely' if there were no prospect of peace.[159] The frustration of interventionist schemes, not least by British actions, meant that an internationally brokered partition deal now seemed inevitable.

On 5 February 1994, the Serb artillery shell that precipitated the so-called marketplace massacre had the unintended effect of upsetting British policy in Bosnia.[160] It did this in two ways. First it allowed the Bosnians to avoid the Owen–Stoltenberg fait accompli; and second, international opinion now demanded action. Owen himself feared that the international pressure to act against the Serbs would become irresistible when even the foreign secretary changed tack.[161] (Hurd later wrote: 'I was enough of a politician to know at once that the situation had fundamentally changed.')[162] At a NATO meeting in Brussels on 9 February 1994, and over British protests, a stiff ultimatum was issued to the Bosnian Serbs demanding the withdrawal of their artillery around Sarajevo.[163] The policy of appeasing the Serbs was, however, sustained when Russia (a traditional ally of the Serbs) was brought in by the British government.[164] London then covertly backed the Russian line – which was articulated thus: 'Our aim is to make sure that the ultimatum is never carried out, that the air strikes never take place.'[165] The British government could point to the fact that Russia was now on board: a fact that the Whitehall knew would make military action even more difficult to agree upon. Military action against the Bosnian Serbs therefore never materialized. That this was so came as a relief to Britain's General Michael Rose in Sarajevo, who asserted: 'You cannot fight war from white-painted vehicles.'[166] Such statements led the US commentator William Safire to dismiss Rose as 'the reincarnation of Neville Chamberlain'.[167] Despite this, Rose's stance confirmed nothing so much as the fact that UNPROFOR was now effectively shielding the Bosnian Serbs from Western military action by its own vulnerability to reprisals. The British government knew this and utilized it to fend off demands for meaningful military intervention to halt aggression in Bosnia.[168]

By June 1994 the so-called Contact Group (consisting of United States, United Kingdom, France, Russia and Germany) had formulated another plan for Bosnia. The plan was a largely American and Russian re-hash of the Owen–Stoltenberg plan although, nominally, it was possessed of far greater weight of 'carrot-and -stick'. [169] Aware that the United States would threaten coercive measures, the British (and the Russians) were willing to make secret concessions to the Serbs so as to thwart any US attempts to lift the arms embargo on the pretext of Serb intransigence. Its rejection of the Owen–Stoltenberg plan left the *Republika Srpska* totally isolated, but this was of little consequence as there seemed little prospect of coercive measures by the international community.[170] Prominent US politicians, such as Republican Majority Senate Leader Robert Dole (R-KS), nevertheless grew increasingly impatient with British policy, repeatedly advocated air strikes,[171] and called for the removal of Rose.[172] In late 1994, one journalist observed: 'Cynicism about US foreign policy is much in vogue in the chanceries of Europe, especially when it comes to Washington's plans for Bosnia. The ghost of Neville Chamberlain is hanging around the elegantly redecorated corridors of the Foreign Office these days, whispering that all you can expect from the Americans is words.'[173] Congressional agitation for an end to the arms embargo unnerved the British government as it demonstrated the way foreign policy formulation was shifting away from the White House and the bureaucracy, traditionally the places where Britain's interests were best understood. Yet the White House, too, was running out of patience with the British government and, in response to political pressure, the Clinton administration withdrew from the NATO/WEU enforcement of the arms embargo. This was a largely symbolic, but not insignificant, move indicating a new assertiveness that was to characterize subsequent US policy.[174]

The conclusion of the US-sponsored Muslim-Croat Federation in March 1994 heralded some progress from rhetoric to action by the United States.[175] However, it was the Serbian threat to the Bosnian town of Bihać in November 1994 that brought home to the United States their failures: 'The policy of pressure on the Serbs was in ruins and it was getting very nasty with the British, America was being called on its position, and NATO was falling apart.'[176] It was at this time too that Clinton's Democratic Party suffered significant reverses in mid-term Congressional elections and domestic political considerations now took a hand in US policy in the

Balkans.[177] As Lord Owen later wrote: 'The US position that it was immoral to put pressure on the Bosnian Muslims would, I felt, stand up only until President Clinton felt a real political need to rid himself of the electoral liability of Bosnia.'[178]

The fundamental British defence of its actions all along had been that the United States deployed no ground troops in Bosnia, whereas the British army was vulnerable as the backbone of UNPROFOR. The troops' presence meant that they were effectively being used by London to guard against the possibility of Western military action. The United States, therefore, came to desire the withdrawal of these troops in order to attain greater freedom of action. Madeline Albright, US envoy to the UN, instructed her staff 'to find out every day how many UN forces were still on Serb territory – until after Srebrenica in July 1995 (when the figure was zero)'.[179] In August 1995, Albright produced a memo which laid out a managed 'collapse of UNPROFOR', replaced by a two-pronged US 'diplomatic and military initiative'. Albright stated that the UNPROFOR presence is 'no longer in America's interest . . . This time, to muddle through is not enough.' Albright believed that since US troops were to be deployed anyway in the event of UNPROFOR's withdrawal, they should be deployed as the United States saw fit and with maximum military back-up. The United States conceded that territory trading and 'population transfer' might have to be tolerated and accepted the Contact Group plan as the basis for negotiations.[180] Western consensus was thus achieved only when the spectre of a bloody UN withdrawal under NATO (including the United States) protection began to loom large.[181]

In the summer of 1995, two Bosnian Serb offensives changed everything. One (which was successful) was launched against the eastern Bosnian 'safe' enclaves. This, paradoxically, allowed the UN to withdraw their potential 'hostage' forces to safety: thus removing the major obstacle to Western military action. [182] It also included the massacre of 8,000 Bosnian men and boys at Srebrenica. In the wake of this event, many observers, then and since, pointed an accusing finger at Hurd and the British government. French President Jacques Chirac said that the West's reaction to the fall of Srebrenica was 'a bit like the talks that Chamberlain and Daladier had held with Hitler at Munich'. Rifkind simply noted that Chirac's 'fine words' was not accompanied by any positive 'proposal'.[183] Such an attitude looks increasingly tired in hindsight. In 2012, one British academic wrote: 'It is time . . . to end the polite silence that has so far attended Hurd's conduct of this country's foreign affairs during the conflict. The Srebrenica massacre offers a dreadful warning of the dangers of a "realist" foreign policy that ignores the fundamental values holding liberal democracies together.'[184] But Srebrenica was a turning point: from this point on the continuation of the war in Bosnia was not to be tolerated by the West. The second Serb offensive of the summer of 1995 was an (unsuccessful) attempt to take Bihać in northwest Bosnia. The latter offensive caused the United States to look more favourably on Zagreb's desire to re-take the Serb Krajina – the key to saving Bihać. Thus, illicit arms supplies, much of which arrived with tacit, if not active, US connivance had been pouring into Tuđman's Croatia and, in consequence, Croatia quickly overran and 'cleansed' the Serbs from the Krajina region of Croatia.[185] This, in turn, substantially weakened the position of the Bosnian Serbs. The defeat of the Croatian Serbs, and their abandonment by Milošević was deemed by Clinton to have created a moment propitious for achieving a final peace.[186] And so it was.

By this juncture the credibility of the NATO alliance as at stake – and Washington knew it. Richard Holbrooke, the tough-talking assistant secretary of state, and now Clinton's peace envoy in the Balkans, stated unequivocally: 'How NATO does in Bosnia will define America's post–cold war role in European security.'[187] Repeated Serb provocations had thus been only part of the reason for pushing NATO into launching an intensive air campaign, although this allowed the Muslim-Croat federation to make substantial gains from the Bosnian Serbs, despite the British insistence that air power alone could not make a difference. This was the opportunity the United States had sought. By the autumn of 1995, a sort of military equilibrium had been established and the US administration began to apply real pressure for peace (not least due to vocal calls for action from Congress – which voted to raise the arms embargo on Bosnia).[188] Crucially, for once a Franco-American understanding isolated the British and London's obstructionism was circumnavigated.[189] This new vigour, personified by Holbrooke, culminated in the three weeks of all-party negotiations at Dayton, Ohio[190] which led to the conclusion of a formal agreement in Paris on 14 December 1995.[191] Clinton hailed ending the war with resolute action while pursuing negotiations at Dayton as symbolizing the continued effectiveness of US leadership of European security.[192] Keen to stress the moral imperative in US policy the president told the American public: 'We cannot stop all war for all time but we can stop some wars. We cannot save all women and all children but we can save many of them. We can't do everything but we must do what we can.'[193] In order to translate the agreement at Dayton into a settlement, a muscular interventionism supplanted the earlier insertion of 'peacekeepers' with limited mandates.[194] Ultimately, in the international order as constituted in 1995, only the United States could act as the arbiter of when, and when not, to appease.

Holbrooke was a long-standing critic of the British-led appeasement policy, viewing the situation in the former Yugoslavia as 'the greatest collective security failure of the West since the 1930s'.[195] The Americans, aware of the pitfalls of previous negotiations, had applied an uncompromising 'all-or-nothing' type formula, which eventually yielded an agreement.[196] Significantly, Tuđman and Milošević spoke for the Bosnian Croats and the Bosnian Serbs respectively, perhaps confirming Karadžić's earlier claim that 'Bosnia does not exist anymore'. The Dayton agreement was a hybrid solution to years of division within the West which bore more resemblance to the Congress of Berlin of 1878 than to any new European security architecture.[197] It was an external solution imposed upon unwilling and unhappy protagonists. In 1943, George Orwell had observed: 'The outcome of the Spanish war was settled in London, Paris, Rome, Berlin – at any rate not in Spain.'[198] With regard to the importance of the Great Powers, the same was true for the Bosnian War in 1995. The British representative at Dayton, Pauline Neville-Jones, political director in the FCO, states that her priority throughout the negotiations had been the maintenance of allied unity.[199] In truth, the previous four years had done terrible damage to relations between the United States and the United Kingdom.

The fact that Rifkind quoted Palmerston's famous dictum in his first speech as foreign secretary demonstrated the kind of thinking that caused the British government to behave as it did over the former Yugoslavia. The response to events in the former Yugoslavia demonstrated a vision in which all the major policy decisions were taken in terms of pure self-interest. Internationalism and notions of the 'New World Order' were completely overwhelmed in an exercise in *Realpolitik* that took little account of morality, international law and human rights. As the US diplomat Ivo H. Daalder observed: 'The appeasement of the Serbs has really hurt the image of Britain.'[200] This was certainly why some UK commentators asserted that it *was* in Britain's interests to adopt a less pessimistic attitude towards the former Yugoslavia. One of the fiercest critics of British government policy was Jeremy 'Paddy' Ashdown, the leader of the Liberal Democratic Party. In December 1992, he stated that British policy was 'spineless . . . redolent of the worst appeasement. The Government, with the Prime Minister in the lead, has . . . offered a green light to further Serb aggression and the destruction of Sarajevo.'[201] Five months later, Ashdown opined: 'The continent of Europe should have learnt 60 years ago that appeasement does not satisfy the appetite of aggressors; it increases it. We Europeans, of all people, should have learnt that lesson.'[202] Martin Bell, a journalist whose notoriety was greatly heightened by the war and who later became an MP, wrote: 'War is diplomacy's failure . . . [and] a foreign policy based only on considerations of national interest, and not at all of principle, is not only immoral but inefficient. It cannot cope with the challenges of the new world disorder. What we have is an interesting – and extremely British – discrepancy between what we do and what we say.'[203] In 1995 Lord Dubs, a onetime refugee from Nazi Germany, asked if

> British policy in former Yugoslavia should be dictated by what lies in the interests of this country? British interests are not enhanced by a policy of appeasement; a policy that allows ethnic killing to go on; a policy that has undermined the authority of the United Nations; and a policy that has put into danger in future years small countries which may fear nationalist aggression? Is it not time that our policy of appeasement, and

the West's policy of appeasement, stopped and that we played fair by the people of Bosnia and protected their lives and their interests?[204]

Echoing Cato, John Nott identified the guilty players in Bosnia: 'Major, Hurd, Rifkind, Owen, Carrington, Neville-Jones, General Rose and others . . . [are] the authors and the implementers of the old policy of negotiation and appeasement'.[205] In official circles, such criticism was rebuffed by pointing to the complexity of the situation and assurances that British foreign policy was formulated according to historical experience and meticulous calculation.[206] In the Commons, Douglas Hogg asserted:

> While there are clearly close parallels in moral terms between what has happened in Bosnia and what happened in Germany and as a result of Nazi policy, it is very wrong to regard Serbia as posing anything like the kind of strategic risk that Germany posed to Europe in the 1930s. Therefore, it is unwise to talk about appeasement in that sense. We are not embarking on a policy of war. By a range of policies, involving substantial pressure, we are seeking to get the Bosnian Serbs to withdraw from the territory that they have occupied.[207]

The FCO line was that: 'We should never have accepted the dismemberment of Yugoslavia, without having first settled the problems of minorities and frontiers.'[208] This smacked of a 'told-you-so' attitude, a feeling reinforced by Hurd's enquiry as to 'Who runs the place when the blue helmets have gone?'[209] This, naturally, implied that war was inevitable and would be again when the 'tribes' were left to their own devices once more. This was indicative of nothing so much as a belief in British moral superiority, and articulated by Rifkind thus:

> From the start, Britain has upheld the principles that internationally recognised borders must not be altered by force and that the legitimate rights of all ethnic groups must be properly protected by their Governments. We have therefore had three objectives – to save lives, to draw the parties away from the military option towards a negotiated settlement, and to prevent the spread of the conflict.[210]

In fact, Britain only came into peacekeeping reluctantly as a result of public opinion and the fact that other countries were ready to deploy troops. Once deployed the troops became an instrument of wider British policy: allowing the obstruction of attempts at military intervention by stressing their vulnerability. Drawing the parties away from the military option largely consisted of maintaining the arms embargo until events were decided militarily – and the losers accepted a fait accompli, disguised as a negotiated settlement. In time, this became largely indistinguishable from the aim of preventing the spread of the conflict. The Major government felt sure that the best way to stop direct Serbian intervention in neighbouring states of the former Yugoslavia was to ensure that the Serb minorities in those states achieved their aims themselves. In this way the wars in Croatia and Bosnia could be portrayed as 'civil' wars and difficult questions about 'external' aggression could be sidestepped.

The British government, always ready to refute calls for military intervention, summarized their arguments against military intervention in the former Yugoslavia, and Bosnia specifically, into a seemingly cogent doctrine.[211] The experience of the Second World War in Yugoslavia was repeatedly cited, relying on writers often overly sympathetic to Tito, such as Churchill's envoy to occupied Yugoslavia, Fitzroy Maclean.[212] Bosnia's mountainous terrain would, it was said, favour defenders. And it was widely asserted that the Germans maintained anything up to 36 divisions in Bosnia during the Second World War. The historian Norman Stone asked why Hurd, Carrington and FCO minister Lynda Chalker had been so badly briefed as to seemingly believe such figures.[213] Elsewhere, Stone dismissed the wild over-estimates of the number and quality of occupying German troops as a mere pretext for inaction and as '[a] bsolute cowardly twaddle'. In addition to manipulating history to refute calls for intervention, the British government ignored two salient facts. First, modern air power massively increased the prospects for success; and, second, any incursion would encounter at least some friendly local forces. General Sir Anthony Farrar-Hockley, former commander-in-chief of Allied Forces in Northern Europe, stated: 'If the Germans had had the sort of helicopters we've now got, Tito would never have lasted . . . you can't hide people and guns in woods any longer . . . Is it right to stand back and say, well this is another foreign country, another distant place? We despise Chamberlain for having said that, is that what we want to go back to?' The fact that any intervention was rejected because of the threat to the humanitarian relief effort was the most tenuous claim of all. Such thinking would have seemed ludicrous to many in Sarajevo as the shells fell about them; yet the maintenance of humanitarian aid seemed, to the British government, to be perfectly consistent with allowing the business of war to continue. Colonel Michael Dewar, deputy director of the International Institute for Strategic Studies, was perfectly right when he asserted: 'My view is that military intervention is perfectly feasible from a military point of view, and that Douglas Hurd and others, for entirely political reasons, are fighting shy of saying that it is viable. What they mean is that they do not think that it is politically desirable.'[214] Over-estimates of the forces that any intervention might encounter extended to the intelligence community. David Hannay, Britain's ambassador to the UN between 1990 and 1995, later recalled that he had asked Sir Rodric Braithwaite, chair of the Joint Intelligence Committee (JIC), why 'our [intelligence] assessments seemed . . . to contain a good deal of excessively alarmist group-think about the Serb capacity for retaliation'.[215]

All of the above is not to say intervention should have been entered into lightly, but its exclusion from the agenda by the Major government severely limited room for manoeuvre by the international community against the aggressors. Many British policy makers prided themselves on this approach to the former Yugoslavia claiming it allowed the West to successfully contain the war, to save lives and create an atmosphere conducive to achieving a workable peace. In this spirit, John Major hailed the Dayton agreement as a vindication of British policy.

> Many thousands have died in this conflict. Many thousands more have been saved by the actions of British troops and their allies . . . I am delighted that the political process that we set in train at the London Conference three years ago has finally borne fruit . . . This outcome would not have been achieved without the efforts over many months of the Contact Group countries – the US, European Union and the Russian Federation working together – and of the United Nations . . . The UK has played a leading role in the search for a peaceful settlement . . . We shall maintain our efforts in the new tasks which lie ahead, including at a Peace Implementation Conference which we plan to convene in London shortly.[216]

It is ironic in the extreme that it took General Ratko Mladić's Bosnian Serb offensives against the eastern 'safe havens' and the removal of UN troops from the most vulnerable areas, to free the Western air forces from their restrictions, thus allowing them to act against the Serbs. The success of the air offensive in 'levelling the playing field' also demonstrated the fact that the British government was incorrect in its belief that air power alone could not redress the balance (especially after taking into account the growing power of the Bosnian and, more especially, the Croatian military). Hurd, Major et al. nevertheless, had their defenders. Conor Cruise O'Brien, an Irish writer given to grand historical narrative, wrote in 1993:

> The ethical contours of these conflicts are not quite so simple as the public has been given to believe. We are being told, *ad nauseam*, that Slobodan Milosevic is Hitler *religious*. Milosevic is a Balkan warlord and, to that extent, has some points in common with Hitler. But he is not the only Balkan warlord who practises ethnic cleansing. The Croats, under their equally nasty Balkan warlord, Franco Tudjman, do the same sort of things, but nobody compares Tudjman to Hitler, even though he goes on in a similar vein about the Jews. The Croats get a better press than the Serbs, not because they deserve it, but because they have a powerful patron inside the Community and the Serbs do not.

Comparisons with Hitler are intoxicating, and should be avoided. It was by seeing Nasser as Hitler that Anthony Eden got Britain into Suez. John Major is in no danger of repeating that error.[217]

It was, of course, true that Serbia could not be compared directly to Nazi Germany; Belgrade did not really threaten any non-Balkan state; and 'ethnic cleansing' was not the Holocaust.[218] This ignored the point that the failure of British appeasement policy in the 1930's was not, at least not directly, one of failing to stop the Holocaust but rather one of failing to prevent the international situation to deteriorate to such a point where the Holocaust was possible. In the summer of 1995, the *Times Higher* asked a number of academics: 'Is the present attitude of western governments morally equivalent to the appeasement of Hitler in 1938/39?' Vernon Bogdanor argued: 'The situation is more like the attitude to Mussolini in Abyssinia, which was a failure to uphold collective security. The supine attitude towards Mussolini gave encouragement to other dictators. Morality does come into foreign policy; morality and self-interest are linked.' Celia Hawkesworth opined: 'To continue to negotiate with people whose policy is essentially fascist is akin to appeasement – I don't know how else to describe it.' Norman Stone raged that 'modern politicians' were worse than their predecessors.

> In the 1930s, it wasn't clear that the atrocities were going on. Today, it is all too clear that the atrocities are going on. In the 1930s, one of the big reasons for Munich was that the defences were not ready, whereas today the defences have been ready for several years. Also, in the 1930s there was an enemy worth taking seriously, whereas today the UN is facing a Balkan riff raff.

Brendan Simms stated that while it was the case that 'the Serbs have no plan for world domination' and 'that 'ethnic cleansing' is not – yet – equivalent to the . . . Holocaust', it nevertheless 'undoubtedly amounts to genocide as defined by the UN Convention on Genocide'. Given this, '[t]he racial state of Dr. [Radovan] Karadzic [*Republika Srpska*] is easily the nearest thing to the Third Reich that we have witnessed in Europe since 1945'. Steven Lukes believed that 'on the central question of appeasement . . . there is a moral equivalence. The issues at stake today are just as important as those in the 1930s. I am reminded of Edmund Burke's observation: "For evil to triumph requires only that good men do nothing". This is what we have been seeing in Bosnia.'[219] Such opinions were now widely expressed by British politicians. John Home Robertson, a Scottish Labour MP, told the Commons in May 1995: 'It is clear from today's speeches that some hon. Members regard Bosnia-Herzegovina as what might be described as a faraway place of which we know little, to borrow a phrase from another era of appeasement. We should be learning some lessons from history, perhaps especially in this anniversary year [of 1995].'[220] Such views were given weighty backing by Michael Foot, 'one-third' of Cato and a veteran of the 1930s struggle against Fascism, who opined caustically of British policy: 'A huge effort was made back here [in the UK] to get the story on the rails the Foreign Office wanted . . . a world war . . . was the only way of reversing the Hitler policy of a fascist conquest of Europe. If we don't have a reversal of policy here . . . we are going to be accepting the same thing.'[221] Tony Benn, Foot's old sparring partner on the Labour Left, disagreed: 'The suggestion – which that great peace monger Michael Foot seems to have overlooked – that the present position is a direct parallel with the position of Czechoslovakia in 1938 strikes me as wholly false.' [222] But to deny the comparison with the 1930s did not mean that wrongs had not been committed in the 1990s. As Bosnia descended into chaos, Jonathan Eyal had asserted:

> We [the West] sold Bosnia down the river . . . The truth is, however well people lived with each other before, too many crimes have gone by now for them to live together. That is the tragedy. So paradoxically, if you intervene to keep Bosnia together the only result will be that you divide it. They're all nationalists, they are not all as bad as each other, but they are all nationalists.[223]

The emotive, if coherent, nature of such statements cut little ice with the British government. One editorial in the *Economist* opined: 'It has become impossible to argue against intervening in the Balkans without sounding cowardly or callous.'[224] And even Hurd conceded that '[o]ne had to go back to the Spanish Civil War to find such a passionate, deep-seated distress about events in a foreign country, together with anger at the apparent passivity of the British Government.'[225] On one level, British policy during the Spanish Civil War bears comparison with Bosnia. In 1936 Stanley Baldwin's government was instrumental in implementing an arms embargo, enforced via the League of Nations 'Non-intervention Committee'. With 'containment' as British policy many British Conservatives were angered that outside support for the Republicans was prolonging the war and hindering what they saw as the chance for the peaceful resolution of existing grievances in Europe.[226] In the former Yugoslavia, the British government opposed lifting the arms embargo on the grounds that it would 'only prolong the fighting'.[227] The recognized governments of Croatia and Bosnia were, therefore, left at a permanent disadvantage in military terms.[228] No account was taken of the rights and wrongs of the situation when Hogg declared in 1993: 'The international community took the [embargo] decision at that time that we had to be committed to seeking a political solution instead of supplying arms and thereby making the situation worse.'[229] As in Spain in the 1930s, Whitehall's dispassionate diplomats prevailed in the former

Yugoslavia in the 1990s. Hurd could not crow openly, but he had succeeded in attaining most of his objectives.

In discussing the appeasement analogy of the 1930s, James Gow noted that there were 'striking parallels between Bosnia's situation and that of Czechoslovakia in the 1930s'. In this model the Bosnian Serbs, led by Radovan Karadžić, were the equivalents of the Sudeten Germans, under Konrad Henlein. An external aggressor was again pulling the strings, with Serbia's Slobodan Milošević taking on the role of Adolf Hitler. The British even played a similar role to Munich – through the EC – by their participation in international conferences on Bosnia, with one author opining 'it was . . . in 1992 that the real appeasement took place' as the EC conducted 'misguided negotiations . . . at which the weaker party was urged to make concessions to the bully, instead of being helped to stand up to intimidation'.[230] Hannay later recalled: 'I was continually critical to London of the fact that, whenever a crisis blew up, we seemed to devote more time and energy to frightening ourselves about the possible Serb reaction to a more robust policy response than we did to frightening the Serbs'.[231] A central pillar of British policy lay in the imposition and maintenance of the arms embargo, by almost any means and with any combination of allies they could muster.[232] The embargo mean that, when Douglas Hogg publicly urged the Bosnian Muslims that they 'have to acknowledge military defeat when it stares them in the face',[233] he was articulating the 'realist' belief that the recognition of the situation on the ground should be *the* basis for mediation. But, as Brankas Magaš noted: 'Here [in Bosnia] "realism" means not just recognising a *fait accompli*, but doing all you can to make it happen in the first place.'[234] Cyrus Vance shared Hogg's belief that stopping the fighting and the establishment of any kind of settlement, however unjust, was all. 'Frankly I'm getting fed up with this mindless criticism that doesn't face up to a central fact . . . In Bosnia there is no viable alternative to a negotiated settlement.' Yet, as Norman Cigar commented: 'what was uppermost was obtaining a settlement, with the provisions flowing from such a deal almost as an afterthought . . . such a settlement could not be easily achieved if the Bosnian government were in a better position to defend itself, since the Bosnians . . . might then be less likely' to accept partition, Serbian conquests and population displacement.[235]

During the Czechoslovakian Crisis of 1938, Ivan Maisky, the Soviet ambassador in London, remarked to Sir Alexander Cadogan that British policy seemed to be 'directed not at curbing the aggressor but at curbing the victim of aggression'.[236] Echoing this, President Clinton (admittedly not the most consistent voice on the former Yugoslavia) denounced the 'grave error' of the arms embargo against the Bosnian Muslims believing that 'the British and the French felt it was far more important to avoid lifting the arms embargo than to save the country'.[237] Such sentiments resonated with many politicians in Britain who invoked the 1930s and 1940s in support of their rhetorical denunciations of the government. Many Labour MPs were forthright in their attacks on the 'new' Chamberlainites. David Winnick told the Commons: 'The air of Munich pervades this place, which is very unfortunate when it comes to resisting aggression in other countries'; Nigel Griffiths similarly observed: 'The stench of Munich is in the air here and in Bosnia. Has not the Foreign Secretary learned any lessons from appeasing the Hitlers of this world?'; while Malcolm Wicks asserted that: 'In the face of genocide [and] more than 50 years after the Holocaust . . . British foreign policy has once again been one of appeasement.'[238] John Nott knew exactly where the blame lay for the appeasement in the Balkans.

> I am ashamed to say that the British Government, by a huge miscalculation, has been an unwitting accomplice to the destruction of these people. For every Bosnian saved from starvation by the outstanding humanitarian efforts of British troops, thousands have either died, been made homeless or become refugees through a policy of such incompetence and arrogance that it is akin to the appeasement of the Nazis.[239]

Paddy Ashdown, the international community's high representative to Bosnia Herzegovina between 2002 and 2005, later reflected: 'The generous way of putting it is that we were not ready for this. The less generous way is to say: "How was it possible to return to the politics of appeasement of the 1930s?"'[240] Charges of pursuing policies that one scholar opined were 'comparable with Neville Chamberlain's appeasement of Hitler in the late 1930's',[241] greatly angered British policy makers. Hurd has pointed out that Britain was by no means alone in her political reluctance to use force: 'The only thing which could have guaranteed peace with justice would have been an expeditionary force, creating if you like a new Northern Ireland, being there for how many years? And no government, no government has at any time proposed that.'[242] Hurd also took a swipe at those who failed to appreciate the 'realistic' appraisal of the situation made by the FCO: 'And that I think is a line which should run through any analysis because it cuts out so much of the rhetoric which has bedevilled this.'[243] Hurd, naturally angry at the repeated attacks on his person and his policies, regarded the 'comparison with Czechoslovakia and Munich [as being] way out of line', and the equation of the 1930s with the 1990s as 'a ludicrous analogy'. For Hurd and his adherents, the salient point was that the great majority of MPs were always hostile to the idea of intervening in Bosnia. Hurd insisted that, while the interventionist case was very much in the ascendancy after Dayton, during the Bosnian war there was no such international consensus. There is no arguing with such assertions. For many observers it is, however, far more difficult to accept Hurd's plea that, in Bosnia, the British government 'acted throughout in good conscience'.[244]

Throughout the debates on the dissolution of the former Yugoslavia, the British government sought to portray intervention as an 'all or nothing' issue. It is true that no government would have proposed a long-term expeditionary force, but if the West had effectively demonstrated that it would tolerate no forcible boundary changes (or mass expulsions of populations), that could well have been successful. The British saw the desired end as being one of shortening the violence regardless of the ramifications for human rights and international law. Consequently, the British often did not even pay lip service to the Western (admittedly, often empty) rhetoric of 'not rewarding aggression'. Hurd had himself stated: 'Military conquest in Bosnia cannot achieve gains which are accepted. It is not enough to fly flags over ruined towns and villages.' Paraphrasing Calgacus (from Tacitus's *Agricola*), Hurd continued: 'Worthwhile gains are not to be secured by making a desert and calling it peace.'[245] The reality of the effects of British policy was, however, quite different. A quick Serbian 'victory', however supposedly unpalatable, was preferable to a long drawn-out war with unpredictable consequences. The British government was unyielding in its belief that the shape of the final peace settlement would be essentially decided on the battlefield, resigning themselves to this end. By the adoption of a policy of obstructionism the United Kingdom consciously made this outcome more likely. To the British practitioners of *Realpolitik*, neither Milošević nor Tuđman (or anyone else of significance in the former Yugoslavia) was to be regarded as a 'war criminal' – at least not in the first instance. Instead, the leaders on all sides had to be treated as actors in the jungle of international politics with whom one, sooner or later, had to cut a deal. Hurd et al. would, of course, argue that they had pursued the interests of the British state and done what they could to alleviate a series of wars of staggering bitterness and complexity. Henry Kissinger once observed: 'A country that demands moral perfection of itself as a test of its foreign policy will achieve neither perfection nor security.'[246] This accorded perfectly with the worldview of the British government under John Major: a perspective that was demonstrated starkly during the wars of succession in the former Yugoslavia. Within a few short years, however, a new prime minister, Tony Blair, would place morality at the centre of international affairs. In this model, there was to be little room for appeasement.

CHAPTER NINE

'History will be my judge': Blair's wars and the moral case against appeasement

We have learnt by bitter experience not to appease dictators.
We tried it 60 years ago. It didn't work then and it
shouldn't be tried now.

TONY BLAIR, 1999[1]

The election of Tony Blair in 1997 heralded a new era of interventionism in British foreign policy with the new foreign and commonwealth secretary, Robin Cook, asserting a desire to make 'Britain a force for good in the world'.[2] By 2003 Blair had sent British forces to war five times – in Iraq (1998 and 2003); Kosovo (1999); Sierra Leone (2000) and Afghanistan (2001). The frequency of these campaigns was more reminiscent of one of Blair's nineteenth-century predecessors rather than of any recent holder of the office of prime minister. In seeking an explanation for this phenomenon, commentators inevitably focus on the person of Prime Minister Blair. As a politician Blair made no secret of his admiration for Thatcher's 'resolution',[3] while Jonathan Powell, Blair's former chief of staff, testifies that his boss realized that he could escape from the grind of domestic politics in the international arena. Thus, like so many of his predecessors, Blair became increasingly intoxicated with playing the role of foreign policy statesman.[4] In 2001, he told the Labour Party Conference: 'This is a moment to seize . . . let us re-order this world around us. Today, humankind has the science and technology to destroy itself or to provide prosperity to all. Yet science can't make that choice for us . . . the moral power of a world acting as a community, can.'[5] Blair matched Thatcher in his dismissal of appeasement and, in his own mind, he was no less an anti-appeaser, sharing her distaste for Milošević's treatment of a weak and divided West.[6] For Blair and his adherents, it was to their 'eternal shame' that the Major government, 'along with the rest of the global community, [had] stood by while Rwandan genocide and Bosnian ethnic cleansing took place'.[7] Increasingly convinced of the need to actively seek to right wrongs in international politics, Blair saw similarities between those who opposed the 2003 war in Iraq and the appeasers of the 1930s. This led him towards a Burkean vision of 'evil' triumphing when 'good men' do nothing. 'When people decided not to confront fascism, they were doing the popular thing, they were doing it for good reasons, and they were good people . . . but they made the wrong decision.'[8]

When the West decided to react to Milošević's suppression of the Kosovo Liberation Army (KLA) the British government became 'NATO's most strident hawk'.[9] The Kosovo intervention represented Blair's 'awakening',[10] and was lauded as such by Thatcher: 'coercive humanitarian intervention, which had been hitherto a novel doctrine of uncertain scope and fuzzy legality, now began to be declared the basis of a revived . . . New World Order.'[11] In contrast to Major and Hurd, Blair saw the former Yugoslavia, and the machinations of the Serbian President Slobodan Milošević, in moral terms. Serbian ambitions were thus frustrated by a NATO bombing campaign, which lasted from 24 March 1999 until 11 June 1999, before the deployment of the NATO-led peacekeeping force Kosovo Force (KFOR).[12] This success was to herald a new era of interventionism on the part of the Anglo-Americans.

As with every other policy initiative, the Blair government deployed its public relations machine to full effect over the intervention in Kosovo.[13] This slick operation easily outflanked those who had so successfully opposed intervention in Bosnia. Alan Clark, the maverick Conservative MP and arch proponent of *Realpolitik*, recorded in his diary: 'I am hugely depressed about Kosovo. These loathsome, verminous gypsies; and the poor brave Serbs. The whole crisis is media-driven . . . [as] an orthodoxy of public indignation is built up, stoked up . . . and the politicians have to respond.'[14] But, in truth, Blair was no knee-jerk politician on this matter. In a speech in Chicago in April 1999, Blair seized the moral high ground, asserting: 'We need to focus in a serious and sustained way on the principles of the doctrine of international community and on the institutions that deliver them.'[15] Backing words with action, Blair was a prime mover behind the war against Milošević which aimed at halting the ethnic cleansing of the Albanians in Kosovo in 1999. When air strikes had seemed insufficient for the task Blair pressurized US President Clinton to commence a ground war[16] – to which Blair was supposedly ready to commit nearly half of the

British army (some 50,000 soldiers).[17] Jonathan Powell later asserted that, in addition to the idealistic rationale for intervention in Kosovo, Blair saw that the failure to stand up to Milošević had created waves of refugees and an upsurge of crime in Europe.[18] Thatcher praised the Kosovo campaign as 'a just and necessary war' in which Blair 'showed real determination in conducting it'.[19] It was a new Falklands and 'a war that must be won . . . that the British people will want to see this through . . . [as] our cause is just'.[20] Such feelings were cordially reciprocated as Blair made it clear that he was on the side of the 'Iron Lady' rather than the 'Iron Chancellor'.

> Bismarck famously said the Balkans were not worth the bones of one Pomeranian Grenadier. Anyone who has seen the tear stained faces of the hundreds of thousands of refugees streaming across the border, heard their heart-rending tales of cruelty or contemplated the unknown fates of those left behind, knows that Bismarck was wrong.[21]

In line with his rather simplistic critique of Bismarckian *Realpolitik*, Blair asserted that: 'If you do act early, you have to do less, fewer people get hurt and you reduce the possibility that it spreads.'[22] In order to advance this line, Blair employed metaphor, morality and memory in a heady rhetorical cocktail which characterized his policy as integral to an 'epic battle' between 'good and evil'. In Chicago he had asserted: 'This is a just war, based not on any territorial ambitions but on values. We cannot let the evil of ethnic cleansing stand . . . We have learned twice before in this century that appeasement does not work. If we let an evil dictator range unchallenged, we will have to spill infinitely more blood and treasure to stop him later.'[23] In a speech in Sofia, Blair invoked the 'Eastern Question' of the 1870s.

> Today we face the same questions that confronted Gladstone . . . Does one nation or people have the right to impose its will on another? Is there ever a justification for a policy based on the supremacy of one ethnic group? Can the outside world simply stand by when a rogue state brutally abuses the basic rights of those it governs? Gladstone's answer in 1876 was clear. And so is mine today . . . it would have been easy to look the other way . . . [and] argue that bigger strategic issues were at stake than the fate of a few hundred thousand people in the Balkans . . . [that was wrong] wrong in 1876 over Bulgaria; and they are wrong in 1999 over Kosovo.[24]

The fact that Gladstone did not succeed in involving Britain in a direct intervention in the 1870s was skirted over. But intervention was surely, Blair hinted, what Gladstone would have embraced had he been alive at the end of the twentieth century. In 2000 a limited, but very successful, military intervention in Sierra Leone reinforced Blair's belief in the utility of force in a dangerous world.[25] The journalist Andrew Marr suggests that this experience and the success of British arms 'played to his sense of himself as a moral war leader'.[26] Blair himself later wrote that, in Sierra Leone, 'we had saved and then secured democracy'.[27] General Sir David Richards, British commander in Sierra Leone, later conceded that the success of the operations might well have given politicians a false sense of the utility of force as a panacea for future political problems.[28] Indeed, the historian Mark Mazower might have been thinking about Blair in particular, when he asserted: 'We hear a lot at present about the limits of diplomacy and the virtues of military force. True statecraft appreciates that force has its limits, too.'[29]

From the inception of the War on Terror in 2001, Blair favoured strong military action and utterly rejected appeasement.[30] The British government's decision to support regime change in Afghanistan and Iraq undoubtedly arose, at least in part, from charges of appeasement for having hesitated to act against Milošević for too long, and for then leaving him in power once the Kosovo War had ended.[31] Blair was determined that no such accusations would be made against him after the terrorist attacks of 11 September 2001. Prime Minister Blair therefore strongly supported President George W. Bush in his invasions of Afghanistan in 2001 and of Iraq two years later. Condoleezza Rice (national security advisor, 2001–5, secretary of state, 2005–9) observes that, even after their first meeting in February 2001, Bush and Blair saw 'that they shared something more than ideological kinship in the modern political sense. They shared values, and in time they would see that they shared a willingness to do difficult things . . . it would soon make them undertake, together, actions to radically change the status quo in world politics.'[32] Bush himself later recalled: 'As the years passed and the wartime decisions grew tougher, some of our allies wavered. Tony Blair never did.'[33] At home, such solidarity came at a price. The attack on Iraq in 2003 was particularly controversial in Blair's own party, causing a Commons rebellion of 139 Labour MPs,[34] with three ministers resigning (including the leader of the House, Robin Cook).[35] In his resignation speech Cook, a onetime enthusiast for the Kosovo intervention, stated:

> Only a year ago, we and the United States were part of a coalition against terrorism that was wider and more diverse than I would ever have imagined possible. History will be astonished at the diplomatic miscalculations that led so quickly to the disintegration of that powerful coalition . . . Our interests are best protected not by unilateral action but by multilateral agreement and a world order governed by rules.[36]

Elsewhere Cook wrote: 'If we believe in an international community based on binding rules and institutions, we cannot simply set them aside when they produce results that are inconvenient to us.'[37] Such sentiments cut little ice in Downing Street as limited measures, such as the 1998 bombing of

Iraq, were now viewed as half-hearted to the point of negligence. Indeed, Foreign Secretary Jack Straw later noted that the Iraqi ambassador to the UN expressed surprise at the ineffectual nature of the West's 1998 action.[38] Blair, determined that there would be no more half-measures, ignored Labour's multilateral tradition in foreign affairs[39] and refused to be hamstrung by convention. Critiques such as Cook's took too little account of the moral factors so dear to Blair's heart and, in order to combat old-fashioned multilateralism, the Blair government enlisted the help of history.

The lead up to the invasion of Iraq of 2003 saw the invocation of the 'lessons' of appeasement at a post–Cold War height in Britain. Blair constantly deployed 'Churchillian' rhetoric and later summed up his detestation of appeasement thus: 'If we had acted as we should have done in Bosnia or Rwanda, many lives would have been saved.'[40] After 2001, Blair was ideally positioned to impose his will upon parliament as he had won two general elections and been at the forefront of the NATO bombing campaign in Kosovo in 1999.[41] The invocation of the past – and of the 1930s in particular – was a key element in the PR campaign to justify the invasion of Iraq. In a similar vein, US Vice President Dick Cheney observed that in considering the question of Saddam Hussein's Iraq 'we should review . . . our own history' as speculation continues 'on how we might have prevented Pearl Harbor, and asking what actions might have averted the tragedies that rate among the worst in human history'.[42] For Blair, too, metaphorical allusions were key tools of manipulation.[43] As Paul Chilton has observed:

Metaphor is an element in the discourse of policymaking; it does not drive policy . . . It would be absurd to reduce [history] to the influence of metaphor. However, both cognitive analysts of policymaking and historians . . . have noted the part played by analogical reasoning and by metaphor. Whatever distinctions might be drawn between the two terms 'analogy' and 'metaphor', they can both be treated as manifestations of the cognitive process whereby one thing is seen in terms of another.[44]

From its inception Tony Blair's New Labour had ruthlessly exploited Conservative Party weaknesses which were, at least in part, rooted in rhetorical failure.[45] Blair's press secretary, Alastair Campbell, recognized the rhetorical mechanisms that were essential for success in modern politics: 'The problem was that New Labour was defined by our opponents as an electoral or political device. We had to show that [Blair] was New Labour out of conviction.'[46] In Opposition, Blair did not make one significant foreign policy speech as party leader[47] (after all, as he later observed, elections are won on domestic issues, and not on foreign policy).[48] Yet, once in office, Blair discovered, as had so many of his predecessors, that he could make a difference in international affairs. In foreign policy, Blair embraced the notion of Britain as a 'force for good' in the world and – after 9/11 – he embraced the War on Terror with hyperbolic verbiage.[49]

In Britain, opposition to the 2003 invasion of Iraq was widespread and even Blair's communications machine, the most formidable in British political history,[50] was hard-pushed to make the case for war. Peter Mandelson, a leading light in the creation of the New Labour brand and a staunch ally of Blair, recalled that he had aired doubts to Blair about the wisdom of attacking Iraq.[51] Blair nevertheless remained, as US Secretary of Defense Donald Rumsfeld noted, 'a persuasive advocate [and] the most eloquent public voice explaining the rationale and the sense of urgency for the coalition effort'.[52] In September 2002, a passionate Blair addressed a sceptical Trades Union Congress (TUC):

> So let me tell you why I say Saddam Hussein is a threat that has to be dealt with. He has twice before started wars of aggression. Over one million people died in them. When the weapons inspectors were evicted from Iraq in 1998 there were still enough chemical and biological weapons remaining to devastate the entire Gulf region. I sometimes think that there is a kind of word fatigue about chemical and biological weapons. We're not talking about some mild variants of everyday chemicals, but anthrax, sarin and mustard gas – weapons that can cause hurt and agony on a mass scale beyond the comprehension of most decent people.[53]

While Blair decried the manner in which the mantle of anti-appeasement had been solely the preserve of the Right in Britain, Jack Straw observed that there were many who, in the 1930s, had drawn the conclusion from the Great War that war had to be avoided at all costs. This list of pacifists included the 'weak-willed George Lansbury, Labour's leader from soon after the party's catastrophic defeat in 1931 until his brutal (and necessary) despatch by the great trade unionist Ernest Bevin in 1935'.[54] There was no place in New Labour for such utopianism abroad (as it had abandoned 'clause four' socialism at home). For Blair the naïveté of Lansbury in international affairs was not an option for a modern social democratic party.

> The key characteristic of today's world is interdependence. Your problem becomes my problem . . . Terrorism and weapons of mass destruction combine modern technology with political or religious fanaticism. If unchecked they will, as September 11 showed, explode into disorder and chaos. Internationalism is no longer a utopian cry of the Left; it is practical statesmanship.[55]

Trust in the unscrupulous was deemed a supreme danger in the international arena, and Blair and Bush decried the manner in which Iraq had misled the UN since the liberation of Kuwait in 1991.[56] Indeed, one could be forgiven for thinking that the leaders of the two states comprising the 'Special

Relationship' shared the same speechwriter. When Bush addressed the UN in September 2002, he stated that he had no wish to see that organization follow the League of Nations into oblivion.

> After generations of deceitful dictators and broken treaties and squandered lives, we dedicated ourselves to standards of human dignity shared by all, and to a system of security defended by all . . . We know that Saddam Hussein pursued weapons of mass murder even when inspectors were in his country. Are we to assume that he stopped when they left? The history, the logic, and the facts lead to one conclusion: Saddam Hussein's regime is a grave and gathering danger. To suggest otherwise is to hope against the evidence. To assume this regime's good faith is to bet the lives of millions and the peace of the world in a reckless gamble. And this is a risk we must not take.[57]

Blair similarly insisted that diplomacy must always be backed by military force. If this was not done then dictators would draw the same lesson as they had done in the past. The West therefore had to 'deal with the threat from this international outlaw and his barbaric regime' in order to forestall an inevitable recurrence of aggression. 'And I do not want it on my conscience that we knew the threat, saw it coming and did nothing.'[58] Blair would be no Chamberlain and history would remember him as an anti-appeaser. Resolution was all and Blair could even put a price on failure.

> I cannot say that this month or next, even this year or next, Saddam will use his weapons. But I can say that if the international community, having made the call for disarmament, now, at this moment, at the point of decision, shrugs its shoulders and walks away, he will draw the conclusion that dictators faced with a weakening will always draw: that the international community will talk but not act, will use diplomacy but not force. We know, again from our history, that diplomacy not backed by the threat of force has never worked with dictators and never will.[59]

Bush, too, rejected the role of appeaser, denounced the path of inaction and refused to allow the international situation to descend into a re-run of the 1930s, stating: 'This nation, in world war and in Cold War, has never permitted the brutal and lawless to set history's course. Now, as before, we will secure our nation, protect our freedom, and help others to find freedom of their own.'[60] Bush later recalled that, on 11 September 2001: 'My mind drifted back to history. I was looking at a modern-day Pearl Harbor. Just as Franklin Roosevelt had rallied the nation to defend freedom, it would be my responsibility to lead a new generation to protect America.'[61] For those proponents of war against Iraq, the 'lessons' of history all pointed policy in the same direction. In February 2003, Foreign Secretary Jack Straw stated:

The search for collective security has been the inspiration for some of diplomacy's most noble endeavours. It lay behind Woodrow Wilson's 14 points and the foundation of the League of Nations. After its collapse with the onslaught of dictatorship in the 1930s, the ideal found new expression in the great post-war institutions: the Bretton Woods System, the United Nations, NATO and the European Community. With the end of the cold war we finally had a chance to make the aspiration a reality. But the cruel irony is that as our continent has taken historic steps towards lasting peace and prosperity within its own neighbourhood, grave new threats have emerged.

This assertion, of course, ignored the logic and consequences of British policy during the wars in the former Yugoslavia. But Straw and the New Labour project would, naturally, have rejected any kinship with the grey regime of Major's 'Guilty Men'.

If we fail to back our words with deeds, we follow one of the most catastrophic precedents in history. The descent into war in the 1930s is a searing reminder of the dangers of turning a blind eye whilst international law is subverted by the law of the jungle. The League of Nations ultimately failed because its members lacked the courage and foresight to defend its founding principles with force. Good intentions were no match for aggression in Manchuria and Abyssinia.[62]

Although many commentators dismissed the historical analogies starkly drawn by Straw, such rhetoric was indicative of one thing: the government was bent on participating in the invasion of Iraq. In making his speech Straw *knew* that no government could equate any given situation with the 1930s and then do *nothing*. The manner in which the government attempted to use history led many to beat a path to the door of an assortment of historians so as to test the Blairite analogies.

Seeking to assess the veracity of the Blair government's use of history, the Left-leaning *Guardian* newspaper canvassed the opinions of many of the best historians of the modern and contemporary era. Sir Ian Kershaw dismissed the invocation of the 1930s as 'a spin on history. The parallels are as good as non-existent.' Mark Mazower was of the opinion that it was not 'a case either of 1939 or of 1956. I'm allergic to lazy historical analogies. History never repeats itself . . . The poet Joseph Brodsky, in his great essay *A Profile of Clio*, wrote that when history comes, it always takes you by surprise, and that's what I believe, too.' Eric Hobsbawm, a supporter of Soviet actions in Hungary and Czechoslovakia in 1956 and 1968 respectively, was succinct: 'The war which is likely to break out shortly is not like the Second World War. All comparisons with appeasement and Munich are so much hot air [that] merely justifies starting a war. No historian will believe them for a moment.' Richard Evans asserted: 'It is easy enough to brand the opponents of an invasion of Iraq as "appeasers", but this is [a] specious parallel with the past.' Avi Shlaim observed: 'Blair would do well to reflect on the lessons of Suez. Politicians, like everyone else, are free to repeat the mistakes of the past, but it is not mandatory to do so.' Paul Kennedy made the simple observation: 'It is also worth noting that, when Gladstone's government [of 1880–5] intervened in Egypt in 1882 – to uphold "order" against Muslim, anti-western radicals – it claimed it would leave that country soon. As it turned out, Britain didn't leave for another 73 years.' Norman Davies reflected on how many politicians were seeking to use the past, with Rumsfeld seeming 'to think that Churchill advocated a pre-emptive war against Germany. And no doubt some Iraqi professor, at this very minute, is polishing his thesis about Iraq being the "poor little Poland" waiting to be attacked by the new Hitler and Mussolini.'[63] In terms of policy making such arguments were, however, little more than parlour games for the chattering classes. Counterfactuals abounded as they had during the wars of succession in the former Yugoslavia and in the period before the liberation of Kuwait.

By late 2002, there was a definite moral edge to British policy towards Iraq. Ironically, in the name of Blair's 'internationalism', 'multilateralism' was an early victim. For the Blair government the UN, effectively beloved of the Major government for its ability to legitimatize inaction in Bosnia, was now seen as a tool, albeit an unwitting one, of appeasement. Straw opined that, under UN auspices, neither 'weapons inspections' nor a 'policy of containment' had worked.

> I told the Security Council on 5 February [2003], the UN's pre-war predecessor, the League of Nations, had the same fine ideals as the UN. Yet the League failed because it could not create actions from its words: it could not back diplomacy with a credible threat and, where necessary, the use of force. Small evils therefore went unchecked, tyrants became emboldened, then greater evils were unleashed. At each stage good men and women said, 'Not now, wait, the evil is not big enough to challenge'. Then before their eyes, the evil became too big to challenge. We had slipped slowly down a slope, never noticing how far we had gone until it was too late. We owe it to our history as well as to our future not to make the same mistake again.[64]

One commentator rightly noted that the message here was very obvious: 'Saddam Hussein equals Adolf Hitler.'[65] Although Blair had told Bush that he favoured a second UN resolution (as affording 'political and military protection'),[66] Jack Straw asserted that the existing UN resolutions[67] provided 'a sufficient basis in international law to justify military action.'[68] This contradicted the advice of the UK attorney general, who opined that UNR 1441 did 'not authorize the use of military force'.[69] But, advised by the JIC that Iraq had WMD capabilities and had ignored the UN resolutions, Blair found the insistence on a second resolution 'a bit odd in terms of . . . moral acceptability', as action had been taken in Kosovo without UN authority (which had been absent in Bosnia, Rwanda and Sierra Leone, too).[70] Such logic resonated in Washington as leading members of the Bush administration had taken 11 September as signalling the need, while simultaneously providing the justification, for a unilateral approach to foreign policy.[71] This should not be over-stated, however. Rumsfeld, for one, believed that 'it was not in America's interest to see the United Nations follow the path of its predecessor, the League of Nations, the organization that watched as Italy's Fascist forces invaded Abyssinia in 1935'.[72] Nevertheless, the unilateral tendencies displayed by Washington were not unprecedented.[73] Straw himself conceded that after 11 September 2001, the United States became far less willing 'to tolerate dangerous, rogue regimes'.[74] Such developments were reflected by the ascendancy of the so-called neoconservatives in Washington.[75] The growing influence of the latter was exemplified by Bush's 'Axis of Evil' speech – in which he denounced North Korea, Iran and Iraq.

> States like these, and their terrorist allies, constitute an axis of evil, arming to threaten the peace of the world. By seeking weapons of mass destruction, these regimes pose a grave and growing danger. They could provide these arms to terrorists, giving them the means to match their hatred. They could attack our allies or attempt to blackmail the United States. In any of these cases, the price of indifference would be catastrophic . . . [and] time is not on our side. I will not wait on events, while dangers gather. I will not stand by, as peril draws closer and closer. The United States of America will not permit the world's most dangerous regimes to threaten us with the world's most destructive weapons.[76]

Appeasement had perhaps never been further away from mainstream American thinking than at the moment of Bush's delivery of this speech. This was derived from what one recent book termed the 'obligation [on the US] to use its power to preserve and extend freedom's realm'.[77] For certain countries and regions such drives had been extended over many years and over different regimes (with China and Russia being notable examples here).[78] Seen thus, the notion that the United States is, at heart, isolationist and is, in fact, a 'reluctant Superpower', is illusory.[79] The contemporary rhetoric of Blair, Straw et al. must be understood as a set of responses to the US position. This meant that, in effect, the British government was buying into the traditional American sense of mission inherent in multiple overseas entanglements. Jonathan Powell asserts that the agenda of the US neocons and the UK liberal interventionists 'overlapped briefly' in Afghanistan and Iraq. For Powell the Blair government's 'liberal interventionists' opposed dictators because the international community 'had a duty to stop [them] but also because in the long run failure to stand up to their behaviour would

ILLUSTRATION 9.1 *President George W. Bush and Prime Minister Tony Blair, White House, Washington, DC, 7 June 2005. 'Our alliance with Great Britain is strong, and it's essential to peace and security. Together our two nations worked to liberate Europe from fascism; together we defended freedom during the Cold War. Today we're standing together again to fight the war on terror, to secure democracy and freedom in Iraq and Afghanistan and the broader Middle East, and to prevent the spread of weapons of mass destruction' (Bush, 7 June 2005).*

pose a threat at home'. The Bush administration's neocons, on the other hand, believed in 'the muscular defence of American interests and values'.[80] Whether Powell knew it or not, his description of the rationales behind the two (supposedly distinct), positions, mirrored almost exactly the coalition of disparate groups, which declared their motive to be either morality or self-interest (or both), that were ranged against Munich in 1938.

The Blair government's decision to sign up to the foreign policy project of the administration of George W. Bush was unprecedented, whatever the highs and lows of the British–American 'Special Relationship' since 1945.[81] Straw states that, although the US could easily have invaded Iraq alone, the Blair government rejected this as, ever since Suez, the British had always resolved to stay close to the Americans.[82] The British government's desire to ingratiate itself with the Bush administration was intense. Indeed, the ambassador to Washington, Sir Christopher Meyer, was apparently told by Jonathan Powell: 'We want you to get up the arse of the White House and stay there!'[83] Although Straw claims to have added a caveat to that imperative,[84] Mohamed ElBaradei, the Egyptian director general of the International Atomic Energy Agency (IAEA) between 1997 and 2009, recalls that Straw explained that the British wished to influence US policy privately by supporting Washington's line publicly. ElBaradei 'did not notice a whiff of British influence over U.S. policy during the Blair administration' believing the relationship to be a 'one-way street, with the British acting as spokespersons or apologists for U.S. behavior'.[85] ElBaradei's assertion is, of course, largely supposition. But some of his assessments resonate with the opinions of at least one influential 'insider': Michael Quinlan, a former permanent under-secretary of state at the British Ministry of Defence. Quinlan saw Blair's policy on Iraq as being motivated by three central considerations. First, Bush was intent on war; second, Britain could do nothing that would stop him; and, third, the British national interest dictated that it was best to follow the US lead. 'Put another way, the question may have been not so much whether the arguments were good enough to warrant the huge step of starting a war as whether they were bad enough to warrant the huge step of breaking with the United States.'[86] In addition, Jonathan Powell stressed: 'If you wanted to exercise . . . influence, you have to keep quiet about it.' Powell contrasted this with the French tendency to say 'things people want to hear' which results 'in our having less influence in Washington and less ability to change anything in the real world. It is for that reason that . . . Britain has always stuck to doing rather than saying.' In these terms, the Blair government rather outdid its predecessors, in both the scale and the intensity of its crusading zeal. This was never clearer than in Blair's speech preceding the Commons vote on the decision to go to war in Iraq on 18 March 2003.[87]

> There are glib and sometimes foolish comparisons with the 1930s. I am not suggesting for a moment that anyone here is an appeaser or does not share our revulsion at the regime of Saddam. However, there is one relevant point of analogy. It is that, with history, we know what happened. We can look back and say, 'There's the time; that was the moment; that's when we should have acted'. However, the point is that it was not clear at the time – not at that moment. In fact, at that time, many people thought such a fear fanciful or, worse, that it was put forward in bad faith by warmongers.

At this point in his speech, Blair read out a newspaper editorial that had been written in the wake of Munich. It had advised the population: 'Give thanks to your God. People of Britain, your children are safe. Your husbands and your sons will not march to war. Peace is a victory for all mankind . . . And now let us go back to our own affairs. We have had enough of those menaces, conjured up . . . to confuse us.' This aside set Blair up for invoking another swathe of the 'lessons' of history.

Now, of course, should Hitler again appear in the same form, we would know what to do. But the point is that history does not declare the future to us plainly. Each time is different and the present must be judged without the benefit of hindsight. So let me explain to the House why I believe that the threat that we face today is so serious and why we must tackle it. The threat today is not that of the 1930s. It is not big powers going to war with each other. The ravages that fundamentalist ideology inflicted on the 20th century are memories. The Cold War is over. Europe is at peace, if not always diplomatically. But the world is ever more interdependent. Stock markets and economies rise and fall together, confidence is the key to prosperity, and insecurity spreads like contagion. The key today is stability and order. The threat is chaos and disorder – and there are two begetters of chaos: tyrannical regimes with weapons of mass destruction and extreme terrorist groups who profess a perverted and false view of Islam.[88]

In his memoirs, Blair claims that he immediately regretted these references to the 1930s (and that he had very nearly omitted them). He claimed that he had not wished to conflate Saddam with Hitler but immediately contradicted himself by stating that he had wished to emphasize that people were happy in 1938 as, because of Munich, 'action had been averted'.[89] The inconsistency of Blair's sleek equation of multilateral international action with unilateral assertions of self-interest[90] had already made most historians antagonistic – but not all of them. Andrew Roberts, the right-wing British historian, saw close analogies with Chamberlainite appeasement and Churchill,[91] for whom 'apotheosis came in 1940'. Roberts believed that, for Blair, 'it will come when Iraq is successfully invaded and hundreds of weapons of mass destruction are unearthed from where they have been hidden by Saddam's henchmen'. Roberts opined that rarely 'in history are we allowed quite so exact a template as we have been given militarily by what happened in the Gulf in 1990–91, and politically by what happened in Europe in the 1930s. But this time, were the west not to act and Saddam [were] eventually to build nuclear bombs, he would have more destructive capacity even than did Hitler.'[92] The fact that Roberts was on the political Right made it evident to many on the Left that Blair had little need of their backing (although he would have liked it). For some observers the very fact that the Blair government had, in a virtually unprecedented move, submitted the decision to invade Iraq to the British parliament was a cause for celebration.[93] But the decision to do this (and the voting arithmetic of the House of Commons) had a fundamental influence on the propaganda machine of the government. As Blair told Jonathan Powell:

The persuasion job on this seems very tough. My own side are worried. Public opinion is fragile . . . Yet from a centre-left perspective, the case should be obvious. Saddam's regime is a brutal, oppressive military dictatorship . . . a political philosophy that does care about other nations – e.g. Kosovo, Afghanistan, Sierra Leone, and is proud to change regimes on the merits, should be gung-ho on Saddam. So why isn't it? Because people believe we are only doing it to support the US, and they are only doing it to settle an old score. And the immediate WMD problems don't seem obviously worse than three years ago. So we have to reorder our story and message.[94]

At the heart of the case for war on Iraq, at least in terms of its *presentation* to the public, lay the WMD programmes of Saddam Hussein. Although the evidence for these programmes was based on flawed intelligence,[95] both Blair and Bush have indicated that regime change was at the heart of the decision for war.[96] Blair later asserted that he would have supported the invasion even without any evidence for the presence of WMDs: 'When it comes to a decision like that, I think it is important that you take that decision as it were on the basis of what is right, because that is the only way to do it . . . The world is a better place with Saddam in prison not in power.'[97] Testifying before the Chilcot Inquiry,[98] Blair asserted that Saddam was a 'monster and I believe he threatened not just the region but the world'. At times, Blair was extraordinarily candid about the reasons for invading Iraq, conceding that British and American attitudes had 'changed dramatically' after the terrorist attacks of 11 September.[99] Straw asserted that while the threat from Iraq has not changed, the terrorist attacks had lowered the tolerance of the international community – and of the US in particular.[100] US National Security Advisor Condoleezza Rice opined in October 2004 that while 'Saddam Hussein had nothing to do with the actual attacks on America, Saddam Hussein's Iraq was a part of the Middle East that was festering and unstable, [and] was part of the circumstances that created the problem on September 11'.[101] Adopting a similar form of diplomatic and strategic 'linkage', Blair saw 'no real difference between wanting regime change and wanting Iraq to disarm: regime change was US policy because Iraq was in breach of its UN obligations'. In concluding his evidence to the Chilcot Inquiry, Blair asserted that morality, and not *Realpolitik*, was his guiding spirit.

> I know sometimes, because this happens out in the region, sometimes people will say to me, 'Well, Saddam was a brake on Iran'. Let's be clear, there is another view of foreign policy in this instance, which is the way, if we had left Saddam in place, he would have controlled Iran better. I really think it is time we learned, as a matter of sensible foreign policy, that the way to deal with one dictatorial threat is not to back another, that actually the best answer to what is happening in Iran is to allow the Iraqi people the freedom and democratic choice that we enjoy in countries like ours.[102]

Bush and Blair's insistence on doing what was deemed 'right' nevertheless led to some curious distortions of policy. The 'one per cent' doctrine of Vice President Dick Cheney, for example, held that *any* threat of harm – no matter how small – should lead to a disproportionately heavy response.[103] What makes for good rhetoric does not always make for good policy – especially when multiple threats dictate an inevitable process of prioritization in threat perception. In his memoirs Straw remained unrepentant: the British government's only error was the unprecedented decision to offer up 'nuggets of intelligence' to justify the war. According to Straw this was unnecessary as Saddam's violations of the various UN resolutions were sufficient cause for war.[104] That this war would be pre-emptive was nothing to be ashamed of. Indeed, as Condoleezza Rice, a leading advocate of such approaches within the Bush administration, later wrote:

> [T]he United States has long maintained the option of preemptive action to counter threats to our national security, and international law has for centuries recognized that nations need not suffer an attack before they can take actions against an imminent threat. Contrary to popular views, the only novel aspect of our articulation of the preemption strategy was the way in which we had to adapt the concept of 'imminent threat' to contemporary realities.[105]

Adopting the Israeli view that one defeat could be potentially catastrophic, Bush told the American people: 'Terrorists and terror states do not reveal these threats with fair notice, in formal declarations – and responding to such enemies only after they have struck first is not self-defense, it is suicide. The security of the world requires disarming Saddam Hussein now.'[106] At one with Bush in policy terms, Blair asserted that 'when dealing with dictators – and none in the world is worse than Saddam – diplomacy has to be backed by the certain knowledge in the dictator's mind that behind the diplomacy is the possibility of force being used'.[107] In the Commons on 24 September 2002, Blair declared:

> [I]f the international community, having made the call for disarmament, now . . . shrugs its shoulders and walks away, he will draw the conclusion that dictators faced with a weakening will always draw: that the international community will talk but not act, will use diplomacy but not force. We know, again from our history, that diplomacy not backed by the threat of force has never worked with dictators and never will.[108]

In truth, the 'straw man' of analogous comparison with the unacceptable spirit of the 1930s of appeasement had been raised by those self-same figures who sought to profit by their disassociation from it: namely Blair and Bush. The suggestion that inaction, often defined as anything short of war, would amount to 'appeasement' was often made by the advocates of a war against Iraq (who were also inordinately fond of invoking the past in support of their case).[109] Blair certainly saw a clear parallel between the 1930s and 2003: 'in both cases, our longing for peace blinds us to our enemies' determination to have their own way'. This, in turn, caused many in the West 'to excuse behaviour on the part of people and states that in other circumstances we would abhor.'[110] In private, Blair was apparently more willing to denounce his critics as 'appeasers'. Michael Portillo, a former minister of defence in Major's government, reacted sharply to the use of such a label: '"Appeasers" is how the Prime Minister describes critics who opposed the war in Iraq, we hear. It's an unattractive and not very exact comparison. Saddam and Hitler are both examples of criminal tyrants, but the threat to Britain from Iraq was less immediate.' This, Portillo believed, was a typical piece of self-aggrandizement: 'For the Prime Minister to use a simile from the 1930s may be another example of his lamentable hubris, because it implicitly casts him in the role of Winston Churchill.'[111]

The invasion of Iraq in 2003 completed Blair's personal journey towards moral crusader, exerting influence globally as a force for good. In doing this Blair emulated Thatcher, in terms of his radicalism at least.[112] Blair later

ILLUSTRATION 9.2 *President George W. Bush and Prime Minister Tony Blair, East Room, White House, Washington, DC, 25 May 2006. 'In his determination to do the right thing and not the easy thing, I see the spirit of Churchill in Prime Minister Tony Blair' (Bush, 4 February 2004).*

testified that his Chicago speech, by which much of his subsequent foreign policy can be understood, was based on 'a very simple notion': 'intervention to bring down a despotic dictatorial regime could be justified on grounds of the nature of that regime, not merely its immediate threat to our interests. It was an explicit rejection of the narrow view of national interest and set a policy of intervention in the context of the impact of globalization.'[113] With typically forthright insight, Thatcher asserted that Blair's Chicago speech was flawed and dangerous for equating intervention to alleviate suffering with the national interest: 'to pretend that the two objectives are always, or even usually, identical is humbug'.[114] On this point, Hurd agreed with his old boss – arguing that Blair had violated his own 'Chicago doctrine' by agreeing to invade Iraq. This was done by the false invocation of certain 'standards [as] universal' and a rhetorical position that 'disregards the facts' and corrupts policy.[115] Elsewhere Hurd observed that 'Saddam Hussein was a more hateful and murderous dictator than Nasser but neither was so formidable a threat to the Middle East, or to British interests, that all techniques of containment and deterrence were doomed. In each case the failure of appeasement in the 1930s was wheeled out to create a false justification of war.'[116] In his memoirs Hurd recorded:

> As . . . I grow older I become more suspicious of the straightforward, violent solution to international problems . . . the suggestion . . . that miseries and dangers are best remedied by actions whose immediate result would be the killing and maiming of individuals, many of whom will be innocent. It is argued on such occasions that the more distant effect of the use of force will be the sparing of lives and the curing of miseries and injustice. That may be so; it is foolish to be absolute in such a calculation. But a strict burden of proof, for example the Christian test of a just war, is required of those who send others to kill and be killed.[117]

The extreme caution inherent in Hurd's approach was fundamentally at odds with Blair's worldview. The foreign policy of minimal intervention, which had been pursued prior to Blair's arrival in Downing Street, had been the height of folly: 'If we had acted as we should have done in Bosnia or Rwanda, many lives would have been saved . . . In Iraq we forget the children that died under Saddam and would have continued to die had he remained in power.'[118] For Blair, there was a moral imperative to use whatever means were necessary – including military power – to ensure that the new interventionism became the global norm. In the long term, as he himself forecast, only history will judge him.

CONCLUSION

Appeasement, British foreign policy and history

I trust that a graduate student some day will write *a* doctoral essay on
the influence of the Munich analogy on the subsequent history of
the 20th century. Perhaps in the end he will conclude that
the multitude of errors committed in the name of 'Munich'
may exceed the original error of 1938.

ARTHUR SCHLESINGER, Jr[1]

The invocation of appeasement as an evil, designed to perform any number
of political tasks in the international and domestic arenas, has been an
enduring feature of foreign policy debates since 1945. And, if history shows
anything, it shows that this usually worked. This was due, in no small part,
to the association of Munich with humiliating shame and with abject failure.
This was felt keenly throughout the British nation as individuals, and not
always 'Great Men', recalled their own role in the tragedy of Chamberlainite
appeasement. James Callaghan, a man of moderate views who had become
prime minister in 1976, demonstrated this as well as anyone when he
wrote: 'I still recall the mingled relief and shame with which I heard the
news of the Munich settlement . . . I was ashamed of feeling such relief, and
ashamed too for the action of my country in unjustly sacrificing the Czechs
to an evil dictator.'[2] In 1990 Lord Annan identified the baleful effect that
appeasement had had upon the British national psyche.

The events that led to Munich left scars that never healed upon the minds of our generation. The 'lessons' of Munich misled politicians and the public for years to come. It led the Labour government to incur expenditure the country could not afford at the time of the Korean war – expenditure that was to split the party. It so obsessed Eden and Macmillan that over Suez they convinced themselves Nasser was Hitler. Munich was used to justify the Falklands war. It became a symbol of political misjudgement. Its history was distorted with verve by Michael Foot and Frank Owen when they wrote Guilty Men, as influential a pamphlet as the letters of Junius. The left captured those days and indicted Conservatives in the eyes of a generation.[3]

In a similar vein, and reflecting upon the distortions imposed on British postwar history by the legacy of the 1930s, Brian Harrison identified the 'appeasement story' as 'doubly harmful' as it had been repeatedly used 'as an emotive reach-me-down self-justificatory device in overseas or domestic situations which seemed to demand resolute action. The resolute action may have been needed, but the parallel was misleading – whether in Eden's handling of Nasser in 1956, Heath's handling of the miners in 1973–4, or of Thatcher's of Galtieri in 1982.'[4] This state of affairs was rooted in the failure of Idealism in the interwar period, which led to conciliatory diplomacy was castigated as being synonymous with appeasement (the consequence of which was the semi-hegemony of the Realist worldview in the formulation of British foreign policy after 1945).[5] Since the Second World War, statesmen and women have repeatedly invoked an abhorrence of appeasement as the ultimate justification for action in foreign policy. As Paul Kennedy wrote in 1976: 'Even today, while a foreign policy rooted in those traditional elements of morality, economy and prudence may be – indeed, is likely to be being – carried out, the last thing its executioners would desire would be to have the word "Appeasement" attached to it.'[6] We can certainly choose any number of decision-makers who have more or less asserted, as President Ronald Reagan did in 1986, that those 'who remember their history understand . . . that there is no security, no safety, in the appeasement of evil'.[7] In 2010, Paul Kennedy reflected on the unchanging nature of debates on what he termed 'the "A" word':

> 'Appeasement!' What a powerful term it has become, growing evermore in strength as the decades advance . . . talk of someone being an Appeaser brings us to a much darker meaning, that which involves cowardice, abandoning one's friends and allies, failing to recognize evil in the world – a fool, then – or recognizing evil but then trying to buy it off – a knave. Nothing so alarms a president or prime minister in the Western world than to be accused of pursuing policies of appeasement. Better to be accused of stealing from a nunnery, or beating one's family.[8]

Appeasement remains at the very centre of the 'history wars' in which competing political narratives seek to appropriate the past so as to achieve an intellectual ascendancy when debating wars and crises. When policy makers claim to have 'learned from history' they are immediately brought under media scrutiny, often by high-profile 'media dons' whose opinions are littered with allusions to events that were once common knowledge in British Grammar schools. Of course, such exercises have far more to do with modern mass democracy than with academic history. In the volume of his history of the Second World War that dealt with Chamberlainite appeasement, Winston Churchill, who so shaped the postwar debates on appeasement, assessed what exactly could be learned from what he termed the 'tragedy of Munich'.

> It may be well here to set down some principles of morals and action which may be a guide in the future. No case of this kind can be judged apart from its circumstances. The facts may be unknown at the time, and estimates of them must be largely guesswork, coloured by the general feeling and aims of whoever is trying to pronounce. Those who are prone, by temperament and character, to seek sharp and clear-cut solutions of difficult and obscure problems, who are ready to fight whenever some challenge comes from a foreign power, have not always been right. On the other hand, those whose inclination is to bow their heads, to seek patiently and faithfully for peaceful compromise, are not always wrong. On the contrary, in the majority of instances they may be right not only morally, but from a practical standpoint. How many wars have been averted by patience and persisting goodwill! Religion and virtue alike lend their sanctions to meekness and humility, not only between men but between nations. How many wars have been precipitated by firebrands! How many misunderstandings which led to wars could have been removed by temporising![9]

This nuanced view was, however, largely swept away by the simplicity of the 'Guilty Men' thesis, which Churchill himself did much to propagate. Donald Watt asserted in 1993 that Churchill's 'alternative to British policy [in the 1930s] lies . . . in the area of counterfactual history . . . The dismissal of all policy options save conflict as "appeasement", and the constant reiteration of the adage "appeasement never pays", are together one of the legacies of the Churchillian legend.'[10] The Churchillian rhetoric directed at Munich was crucial in damning the diplomacy of appeasement by means of phrases such as 'we have sustained a defeat without a war, the consequences of which will travel far with us along our road'.[11] That Chamberlain failed in his policy of appeasement is what most people recall first. That he failed while in pursuit of a policy now widely regarded as immoral is what damns him for all time. Hans J. Morgenthau noted that Chamberlain's appeasement was 'inspired by good motives; he was probably less motivated by considerations of personal power than were many other British prime ministers, and he sought to preserve peace and to assure the happiness of all concerned. Yet his policies helped to make the Second World War inevitable, and to bring untold miseries to millions.'[12] The damnation arising from failure had been clear to Jan Masaryk, Czechoslovak ambassador to London, when he told Chamberlain and Halifax: 'If you have sacrificed my nation to preserve the peace of the world, I shall be the first to applaud you. But, if not gentlemen, God help your souls.'[13] And, indeed the repudiation of the appeasement of Nazi Germany led to a rejection of appeasement per se. This was not only unhelpful, it was impossible – as if one suddenly announced that 'reason' or 'conciliation' had no place in the conduct of diplomacy. We can thus view the post-1945 continuities in British foreign policy through a prism where the 'A' word was studiously avoided (although, on occasion, the 'D' word (détente) was substituted for it).

The need to be seen to observe the 'lessons' of appeasement, not least by avoiding the use of the 'A' word, has been a constant consideration for policy makers – wherever they have figured within the history of British foreign relations. The primary instances of the impact of this on the conduct of British foreign policy include Attlee and Bevin's opposition to global Communism, Eden's stand against Nasser, Thatcher's refusal to yield to Argentine and Iraqi aggression, and Blair's moralizing interventionism. In those instances in which I have identified a British government as following at least some of the defining features of an appeasement policy – those of Macmillan over Berlin and of Major and Hurd over Bosnia – the same awareness of the 'rules' of postwar international relations applied. In these cases, the British government was careful to frame debates in terms of a desire to avoid escalation. And, so long as the label of appeaser was successfully fended off, there were good reasons for Macmillan and Hurd to pursue their policies. This is due not least to the fact that the proportion of the public that proved receptive to Chamberlain's rhetoric about avoiding war has, if anything, increased. Donald Watt notes that those post-1945 governments who have invoked the 'lessons of appeasement', have not always been successful. The United States 'in 1950, as in 1990, found, as did Britain in 1935, that taking the lead against an aggressor in the name of the world community risks many of its members seeing the resultant conflict as bilateral rather than collective in nature.' Furthermore, US references 'to the experience of the 1930s won . . . it little support in Britain in 1965–6 for its involvement in Vietnam.'[14] Such are the limits of historical analogy for policy ends.'[14]

Macmillan's policy of appeasement over Berlin entailed an emphasis on the danger of nuclear war over what were, in his view, essentially trifling issues. Robert Jervis notes that although the fear of being tarred as appeasers in the Munich tradition was strong, it was outweighed by the fear of nuclear war.[15] Here, Macmillan was right to have recognized the way in which nuclear weapons had undermined the rationale for putting strength before negotiation. As Aneurin Bevan observed in 1956:

> The advent of the hydrogen bomb has stalemated power among the Great Powers. The use of the threat of war, which formerly helped to solve many international difficulties . . . is no longer available to statesmen. The great powers are stalemated by their own power. This fact has created a vacuum in diplomatic thinking . . . [and] statesmen . . . have not adjusted themselves to that reality . . . The fact is that, there being no way of settling disputes between major nations by the resort to major war, the statesmen of the world have not got together to attempt to solve those problems which formerly were attempted to be solved by war.[16]

This is not to say that wars which did not involve the potential for nuclear war were easy to deal with. By the time of the Bosnian conflict in the 1990s, British policy dictated that the ethnic and intractable nature of the war required its isolation and containment. In both cases, the rights and wrongs of the matter were quite irrelevant. In Berlin and in Bosnia, although the British again chose the 'dishonourable' path, British policy was justified by references to what had happened in the summer of 1914 (while Macmillan's and Hurd's detractors preferred to make their analogies in reference to the autumn of 1938). At this juncture we might usefully recall debates on whether or not history instructs on an *applied* (or even a *theoretical*) plane. In answer to the question 'Does History repeat itself?' Sir Lewis Namier remarked:

> No two events or chains of events are identical any more than any two individuals or their lives. Yet the lives of all men can be summed up, as in Anatole France's story, in eight words: 'They were born, they suffered, and they died.' The elimination of individual variants, which tend to cancel out each other where large numbers are involved, is likely to disclose certain basic regularities. There may be cycles in history and a rhythm: but if there are, the range of our experience and knowledge is insufficient to establish them; and if there are not, the turn of our minds will still incline us to assume their existence and to invent them . . . Man is a repetitive, aping animal; and to basic regularities and individual variations he adds the element of imitation and expected repetition.[17]

In today's world, politicians remain keenly aware that an ability to identify their cause with that of the anti-appeasers or with the victims of Nazi aggression in the 1930s is an invaluable diplomatic asset. In December 2012, Israeli Prime Minister Binyamen Netanyahu articulated the historical lessons that he had drawn from the appeasement of Hitler. After Czechoslovakia had been sacrificed at Munich, the 'international community [had] applauded almost uniformly [and] without exception . . . [believing] that [this] would bring peace, peace in our time they said. But rather than bring peace, those forced concessions from Czechoslovakia paved the way to the worst war in history.'[18] A few days later, Israel's foreign minister, Avigdor Lieberman, expressed his government's anger over Palestinian diplomatic gains by comparing Israel's situation to that of Czechoslovakia in 1938 – before that state's betrayal by the West and destruction by the Nazis. Lieberman contrasted Western irresolution with Israel's determination to resist appeasement: 'When push comes to shove, many key leaders would be willing to sacrifice Israel without batting an eyelid in order to appease Islamic radicals and ensure quiet for themselves . . . We are not willing to become a second Czechoslovakia and sacrifice vital security interests.' Lieberman suggested that the reason for this appeasement was simple: Western self-interest derived from 'their need for Arab oil' and Muslim markets.[19] Lieberman's use of such rhetoric was perceptive for its understanding of his target audience. For, although Western publics care little for Israel's security, 'appeasement' and 'Munich' remain bywords for the failure of Western diplomacy, a diplomacy that betrayed peace and Czechoslovakia in 1938. By invoking such a view of history any statesman or stateswoman had long been able to assume the mantle of moral superiority. In such a worldview the security of the strong can only be assured by self-reliance, and of the weak by an ascendant morality in the conduct of international relations. In this vein of thought Lieberman asserted:

> All the expressions and promises of commitment to Israel's security from all around the world remind me of similar commitments made to Czechoslovakia in 1938 . . . We have already been through this with Europe at the end of the 1930s and in the 1940s. They already knew by the start of the 1940s exactly what was happening in the concentration camps, what was happening with the Jews and didn't exactly act. Today they admit that even in the 1930s they prevented Jews from coming to the land of Israel.[20]

After the Cuban Missile Crisis, the success of President Kennedy's propaganda machine pioneered the model of the informed leader learning from history. This still plays well with Western publics – although political opponents and the media are keen to disabuse audiences of the notion of the rational scholar-statesman. Nevertheless, the accepted narrative of the course of appeasement in the 1930s had provided British governments with an allegory that could be of considerable utility in justifying an *active* foreign policy. Ernest Bevin told the Labour Party Conference in 1950:

> Can you lay down your arms and be safe? China had no arms and Japan walked in, Abyssinia had no arms and Mussolini walked in . . . Czechoslovakia had no arms and a coup d'etat was carried out

one evening and their liberty was gone. Inside the iron curtain . . . there is no freedom. Do you want that to be extended? Would you sit down and let it be extended? I could not. I could not be a member of a party that decided that was their policy, and I do not believe you could either.[21]

In 1935, Bevin had denounced pacifism and appeasement in the Labour Party.[22] By 1950, Bevin's argument was in the ascendancy in British society. It was, indeed, something approaching orthodoxy. But appeasement did not disappear from British foreign policy formulation after 1945. Indeed, it was impossible for it to do so as its definition is, inevitably, elastic and entirely subjective. It was actually inevitable that, on occasion, diminishing British power had increased its (near-forbidden) utility. In actual fact, the appeasement 'tradition' continued throughout the postwar era (often under the banner of 'pragmatism') and its employment was seen by its Foreign Office proponents as something to be proud of. Richard Luce (minister of state at the FCO, 1981–2 and 1983–6) phrased matters thus:

I recall many allegations being made that the Foreign Office was rotten to the core with appeasement . . . British diplomacy, once praised, believe it or not, by General de Gaulle as the finest in the world, is designed to further British foreign policy and the national interest. We do not live in a cocoon in Britain. We have to live in the real world that surrounds us. We have to work with our friends. We have to talk and negotiate where necessary in order to reduce the risk of confrontation and war and to create stability.[23]

Such thinking was shared by Douglas Hurd, who saw impartiality as an essential part of the diplomat's world view. In practice, this was hugely controversial and Anthony Lewis opined that, over Bosnia, 'Hurd put one in mind of Chamberlain and Halifax.'[24] In assessing these powerful men, one might usefully recall the words of John Adams.

You ask how . . . all Europe has acted on the principle, 'that Power was Right' . . . Power always sincerely, conscientiously, *de tres bon foi*, believes itself right. Power always thinks it has a great soul and vast views beyond the comprehension of the weak; and that it is doing God service, when it is violating all his laws. Our passions, ambitions, avarice, love, resentment, &c., possess so much metaphysical subtlety, and so much overpowering eloquence, that they insinuate themselves into the understanding and the conscience, and convert both to their party; and I may be deceived as much as any of them, when I say, that Power must never be trusted without a check.[25]

Ed Vulliamy, a journalist who was among Hurd's fiercest critics over Bosnia, observed: 'To construct an argument for neutrality, one has to equate the perpetrator and the victim of violence, thus removing any ethical imperative.'[26] Yet, for Hurd, neutrality (or at least impartiality) was an essential precondition for British diplomatic engagement with the war in Bosnia. At the outset of the war, Hurd had identified the Serbs as the primary aggressors, yet a year later he stated: 'No side has a monopoly on evil . . . No one is blameless'.[27] For John Nott, this was a nonsense that was fundamentally deceitful. 'Another lie, often used in British propaganda, and stated by ministers in parliament, was that all sides were guilty of atrocities and 'were all as bad as one another'.'[28] The polar opposite of Hurd in terms of the neutrality question was Margaret Thatcher. It is certainly instructive to compare her rhetoric with that of Hurd.

> Appeasement has failed in the 1990s, as it failed in the 1930s. Then, there were always politicians to argue that the madness of Nazism could be contained and that a reckoning could somehow be avoided. In our own day too there has never been a lack of politicians and diplomats willing to collaborate with Milošević's Serbia. At each stage, both in the thirties and in the nineties, the tyrant carefully laid his snares, and naïve negotiators obligingly fell into them. [29]

Thatcher's formative years had caused her to regard the very concept of appeasement as an absolute abomination. Cultivated neutrality was neither desirable nor natural. For Hurd, such talk was too far removed from reality to be the basis for any foreign policy. Indeed, the crux of the debates about appeasement rests with this question as to whether or not neutrality is a desirable position for policy makers to adopt in international affairs. In 2009, Hurd observed: 'The policy of appeasement had powerful arguments in its favour. It had enjoyed a long and respectable history in the hands of Salisbury and, before him, of Castlereagh. Neville Chamberlain pursued the policy with integrity and determination.' But, too late, Chamberlain learned that Hitler would never keep his word and 'it is useless to appease rulers who [have] no intention of keeping their word'.[30] This, however, runs contrary to the fact that Milošević, the main target of Hurd's appeasement in the Bosnian War, rarely kept his word. What is more salient is the fact that Hurd had been successful *in* Bosnia. Kosovo could be dismissed as another matter altogether for two reasons: first, it occurred *after* Hurd and the Conservative Party had left office; and, second, Milošević had never signed any 'piece of paper' in which he had declared the Serb territories of Bosnia to be his 'last' territorial demand. Indeed, we might well ask if it is useful to seek to label Hurd an appeaser at all. Hugo Young perceptively identified the reasons why Hurd might conceivably escape the charge of appeasement by virtue of his being *successful* in attaining his policy ends.

Douglas Hurd is not Neville Chamberlain . . . [although] the comparison is tempting but inapt. Chamberlain is excoriated by history not because his appeasement of Hitler was immoral but because it was mistaken. He got Hitler's imperialist ambitions wrong and therefore helped precipitate a world war. Milosevic . . . whom Hurd and the rest of the world believe they have no alternative but to appease, has more limited ambitions. It is quite likely that he could be appeased indefinitely, as he devours only the territories he thinks he can defend.[31]

As a writer of history, Hurd has repeatedly articulated a defence of appeasement – in both empirical and theoretical terms. For Hurd: 'Peacemakers are invariably mocked until they succeed . . . [although] the peacemakers have their ration of praise; in phrases which have come down through twenty centuries and will be remembered when the arguments of today have been forgotten.'[32] One might well expect Hurd, as a fellow Conservative and practitioner of a cautious *Realpolitik*, to make positive (albeit highly qualified) noises about Neville Chamberlain. Perhaps more surprising on this score are the words of Tony Blair in his memoirs. Blair, after all, had secured his place in history by his espousal of a morally driven foreign policy wholly at odds with talk of 'a far-away country between people of whom we know nothing'. Blair, nevertheless, wrote: 'A comparison to Chamberlain is one of the worst British political insults. Yet what did he do? In a world still suffering from the trauma of the Great War, a war in which millions died, including many of his close family and friends, he had grieved; and in his grief pledged to prevent another such war.' This, for Blair, was '[n]ot a bad ambition; in fact, a noble one'.[33] Quite why this passage was included in his memoirs is not clear (although Blair could certainly identify with Chamberlain's self-righteous morality and his sense of mission). Most likely, Blair had simply come to appreciate the multitude of pressures, domestic and foreign, exerted on a serving prime minister.

History remembers Dwight D. Eisenhower more kindly than it does Neville Chamberlain. This is due not least to the fact that the soldier statesman is almost never regarded as an appeaser. Despite this, Eisenhower certainly understood that appeasement, in its proper definitional sense, had a place in international affairs. 'There is, in world affairs, a steady course to be followed between an assertion of strength that is truculent and a confession of helplessness that is cowardly.'[34] In this vein of reality, Eisenhower confessed to Macmillan: 'On Berlin we have no bargaining position.'[35] Macmillan himself, who took pride in being a staunch opponent of appeasement in the 1930s, had asserted in 1947 that 'if history, and especially recent history, teaches us anything, it is that a policy of weakness and appeasement is more dangerous than a policy of straightforwardness and firmness. In feebleness and uncertainty, and not in strength and resolution, lie the seeds of war.'[36] When he made that speech Macmillan was still an instinctive anti-appeaser. In 1947 this was a moral stance. Yet, the experience of office and the necessity of making policy meant that, by 1958, he adopted a very different attitude towards West Berlin. Part of the explanation here undoubtedly lies in the existence of nuclear weapons. For some the mere presence of such weapons encouraged appeasement by increasing the necessity of avoiding war.[37] Harold Macmillan, the onetime officer in the Grenadier Guards,[38] – was one such figure.

In today's world many of the debates on appeasement inevitably focus upon the foreign policy of the United States. The events of 9/11 completely discredited appeasement as a policy option in US political discourse (as Munich had once done in Britain). As the rhetoric about the 'axis of evil' swept all before it, neoconservative commentators ignored the fact that, during the late 1980s and early 1990s, US presidents George H. W. Bush and Bill Clinton had effectively pursued a policy of appeasement towards North Korea. This aimed at inducing Pyongyang to abandon its nuclear weapons programmes. In October 1994, North Korea agreed to freeze its nuclear programme and to grant access to International Atomic Energy Agency (IAEA) inspectors in return for certain concessions from Washington. The agreement was widely condemned in the United States by such figures as former Secretary of Defense Caspar Weinberger and Senator John McCain (R-AZ) as an act of appeasement whose substance was 'all carrot and no stick'.[39] Although there was, in fact, an implicit threat that if North Korea did not play ball the United States could still resort to force,[40] hardliners were able to make substantial political capital out of the very idea of the United States appeasing an upstart state such as North Korea. Those who had favoured a conciliatory approach despaired as, from 2001, Vice President Dick Cheney repeated assertions that '[w]e don't negotiate with evil, we defeat evil'. While the United States refused to engage with 'evil', the North Koreans duly developed a nuclear capability.[41]

After the terrorist attacks of 11 September 2001, President George W. Bush, while making war on terror, also effectively made war on appeasement. This meant that those states that failed to adopt a similar perspective to that adopted by the United States risked a serious rupture with Washington. The diminution in the willingness of many states to resort to force in the nuclear age has promoted suspicion among those with a more traditional view of the threat and use of force in international relations. And this is certainly a cause of tension in relations between the United States and Western Europe in recent years. In 2002, Walter Russell Mead, of the Council on Foreign Relations, argued: 'Americans just don't trust Europe's political judgment. Appeasement is its second nature. Europeans have never met a leader – Hitler, Mussolini, Stalin, Qaddafi, Khomeini, Saddam Hussein – they didn't think could be softened up by concessions.'[42] Those states that deviated from the post-9/11 US line on appeasement were infamously dubbed 'Old Europe' by Donald Rumsfeld. These states were distinguishable from the 'New Europe' of the former Soviet Empire who 'had a recent understanding of the nature of dictators, whether a Stalin, a

Ceauşescu, or a Saddam Hussein'.[43] Washington's worldview resonated in these states as it did in Israel, whose own extended war against terrorism had long since imbued that state with a fear of appeasement.[44]

After periodic bouts of enthusiasm for the logic of appeasement stretching from Yalta to Bosnia, the 'War on Terror' saw Britain in the vanguard of loyal adherents to the morally absolute model of anti-appeasement. The morality underlying this conception was, however, no mere abstract concept. If the existence of nuclear weapons had provided a rationale for moderation in Cold War confrontations with Soviet Union – in order, of course, to pursue détente *not* appeasement[45] – then matters were seen to have changed after 11 September 2001. Bush and Blair's 'War on Terror' necessitated what we might term a 'war on appeasement', which involved the (mis)appropriation of history at every turn.[46] Chamberlainite appeasement and Munich lay at the very centre of these processes, although the analogies were often flawed. As Gerhard L. Weinberg noted in 2002:

> For those intent on waging war against Iraq, the word 'Munich' is shorthand for 'appeasement'. It has been brandished against those – be they European governments, leading congressional Democrats, or cautious Republicans and State Department officials – who are not fervently committed to a U.S.-led battle to overthrow the regime of Saddam Hussein.
>
> Yet those who talk of Munich . . . in the context of today do little justice either to the dilemma of those who negotiated with Adolf Hitler then or to those who must weigh the need for military action today. Rather than adding depth to our debate, this historical analogy has been deployed in a shallow way to intimidate political foes as much as the enemies who mean us actual harm.[47]

In a similar vein, Keith Robbins advised that, with regard to the past of appeasement, the only 'lesson of Munich [is] that there should be no lessons'.[48] Such aphorisms do not, however, deter policy makers from seeking the legitimacy afforded by being known to have taken the 'lessons' of history on board. As part of the rhetorical strategy deployed after 9/11, the US administration let it be known that the president regarded Churchill as his model.[49] Echoing Kennedy's 1962 learning process from *The Guns of August*, the fact that Bush had read Lynne Olson's *Troublesome Young Men* was publicized.[50] This was a wholly rational and logical strategy for, as Jeffery Record recently noted: 'No historical event has exerted more influence on post–World War II U.S. presidential use-of-force decisions than the Anglo-French appeasement of Nazi Germany that led to the outbreak of World War II.'[51] When the fact that *Troublesome Young Men* had influenced Bush became public knowledge Olson, naturally keen to further heighten the profile of her book, wrote that a comparison of Bush and

Churchill was historically improbable. In Churchill's place she proposed Neville Chamberlain as a model for Bush (referring to the latter's lack of experience of international diplomacy and tendency to unilateralism).

> People see in Churchill and Chamberlain what they want to see . . . according to their own political philosophy. I've received congratulatory letters and e-mails from people who see similarities between the current U.S. woes in Iraq and Chamberlain's disastrous conduct of the so-called phony war in 1939–40. But I've also gotten fan mail from readers who favorably compare the Tory rebels' courageous fight against Chamberlain to the Bush administration's campaign against those opposing the Iraq war.[52]

Olson, no doubt, pleased Liberal opponents of Bush by mocking his attempts to strike a Churchillian pose. His legitimacy, and that of his wars, would be, by extension, undermined. And she was probably right. Alas, being right (while valued by scholars and intellectuals) has little to do with modern mass politics. The mere act of disclosing Bush's interest in history (and thus allowing him to draw the proper conclusions from its 'lessons') had already done their work. Highlighting the inconsistencies in, and the misuses of, history by Bush and Blair will only convince a certain (limited) proportion of the population of the rectitude of any given point of view. Hurd was right when he asserted that wars and crises usually elicit two polar reactions in Britain: first, do nothing unless Britain's national interests are involved; second, do something as it is the nation's *duty* to alleviate suffering. Of the need to reconcile these two positions, Hurd noted:

> I recall what Gladstone said in 1879 at Dalkeith: remember that the sanctity of life in the hill villages of Afghanistan among the winter snows is as inviolate in the eye of Almighty God as can be your own . . . Somewhere between those two extreme answers, as I am afraid I must term them – somewhere between the saloon bar and Gladstone – lies the policy that any British Government would in practice seek to follow.[53]

In assessments of the perpetual questions facing the makers of British foreign policy Gladstone's worldview is always contrasted with that of Disraeli. In 1876, while Gladstone headed widespread protests over Turkish atrocities against civilians in Bosnia-Herzegovina and Bulgaria, Prime Minister Disraeli strongly resisted calls for intervention. Disraeli dismissed Gladstone's bestselling pamphlet *The Bulgarian Horrors and the Question of the East*, stating: 'of all Bulgarian horrors [it is] perhaps the greatest'.[54] For Disraeli, Gladstone's moral impulses were a dangerous distraction. Disraeli was insistent that no British government should lose sight of the national interest: 'What our duty is at this critical moment is to maintain the Empire of England. Nor will we ever agree to any step, though it may obtain for a moment comparative quiet and a false prosperity, that hazards the existence of that Empire.'[55]

NEUTRALITY UNDER DIFFICULTIES.

DIZZY. "BULGARIAN ATROCITIES! I CAN'T FIND THEM IN THE 'OFFICIAL REPORTS'!!!"

ILLUSTRATION C.1 Punch, 5 August 1876. The bitter dispute that arose between William E. Gladstone and Prime Minister Benjamin Disraeli regarding the latter's refusal to act against the Turkish atrocities in Bulgaria effectively defined the parameters of debates on appeasement and intervention for generations of British policy makers.

For Hurd, the policy choice represented by the respective positions of Gladstone and Disraeli was neither new nor likely to disappear anytime soon. The two traditions in British foreign policy were exemplified by Lord Castlereagh's pragmatic, conciliatory foreign policy and George Canning's more muscular, interventionist one.[56] The necessity of retaining *both* traditions as a policy option continues, not least as they are rendered *timeless* by their utility at given *times* and *places*. One might usefully recall that, when Alexander I of Russia complained of 'those who have betrayed the cause of Europe', Talleyrand asserted: 'that, Sire, is a question of dates'.[57] In this vein, conciliatory approach to the Soviets, deemed unacceptable in the late 1940s, was tolerated in the mid-1970s precisely as 'a question of dates'. After 1945, in order to rehabilitate diplomacy, while repudiating the mindset that had led to Munich, the West had embraced the policy of 'Containment'.[58] By its ability to introduce restraint into foreign policy, without signalling weakness to a watchful international community, this term was surely one of most useful euphemisms in diplomatic history.[59] Today, any number of commentators remain willing to denounce the malign influence of appeasement upon the foreign policies of the West.[60] In Britain, the 2013 debate on whether or not to intervene in the Syrian civil war once more saw the invocation of the era of appeasement.[61] The perceived irresolution of the West over Syria led Israel's economics and trade minister, Naftali Bennett, to observe: 'The international stuttering and hesitancy on Syria just proves once more that Israel cannot count on anyone but itself. From Munich 1938 to Damascus 2013 nothing has changed. This is the lesson we ought to learn from the events in Syria.'[62] The shadow of Munich thus remains a long one, continuing to influence the foreign policy of any number of states. Unsurprisingly, this is especially so in the country that is the most famous past victim of appeasement (the Czech Republic),[63] and in the state that fears it most in the present (Israel). During a 2012 debate between presidential candidates in the Czech Republic, Miloš Zeman asserted that:

If, in 1936, when Hitler occupied the Rhineland, France and England had attacked Germany, there would have been neither World War II, nor the Holocaust. Pacifists said that Hitler was a peacemaker. And because of that there was a war and the Holocaust . . . This gets me to the idea of the preventive attack, which is today current thinking with regard to the Iranian missile installations. Words are a nice thing, but sometimes actions are far more important. The European Union repeats the mistake of appeasement, the appeasing tactic, used back then against Hitler, and today against the fundamentalist, Islamic terrorists. Appeasement, and this relates to the preventive attack, never pays off in the long run.

Zeman, the Social Democrat leader and eventual winner of the presidential election, asserted that for these reasons he would support an Israeli pre-emptive attack on Iran. This would require courage and the Czech Republic would alienate Israel's enemies, but it would be the *right* thing to do.[64] Such moral absolutism, naturally, rests on what is *right* while too often neglecting to consider what the *best* course of action is. In his memoirs, Edward Heath, a staunch opponent of the appeasement of Hitler who was later denounced as an appeaser for his insistence upon the necessity of keeping a diplomatic channel open to Saddam Hussein in 1990, despaired as to the estrangement of the basic tenets of diplomacy from their real meaning.

> Above all, negotiation is not appeasement. Appeasement involves a sacrifice of a moral principle in order to avert aggression. Negotiation requires some change on the status quo in order to make progress, without giving up any basic point of principle. This is the very stuff of diplomacy and, throughout history, negotiation has been the only peaceful way of resolving serious differences between nations.[65]

This is nothing less than a recognition that foreign policy has, on occasion, to be used in order to seek to address grievances and not just for the purpose of defending the status quo. In 1961, Walter Lippmann simply, but correctly, observed that 'you can't decide . . . questions of life and death for the world by epithets like appeasement.'[66] Years earlier, E. H. Carr had written that 'peaceful change can only be achieved through a compromise between the utopian conception of a common feeling of right and the realist conception of a mechanical adjustment to a changed equilibrium of forces. That is why a successful foreign policy must oscillate between the apparently opposite poles of force and appeasement.'[67] In rejecting such an elementary truth, the rhetoric of postwar anti-appeasement often caused policy makers to embrace morally-driven absolutist positions in international affairs. The employment of such a policy-making formula always renders a number of policy options permanently unavailable. In a dangerous world such an approach will, sooner or later, have tragic consequences.

NOTES

Introduction

1 Alfred Duff Cooper, *Talleyrand* (London: Jonathan Cape, 1932), p. 252.

2 Robert Self, *Neville Chamberlain: A Biography* (Farnham: Ashgate, 2006), p. 435.

3 David Lloyd George, 1917. R.H.S. Crossman, *The Charm of Politics: And Other Essays in Political Criticism* (London: Hamish Hamilton, 1958), p. 44

4 Georg Wilhelm Friedrich Hegel, *The Philosophy of History* (New York: Dover Publications, 1956 [1837]), p. 6. On the problematic nature of deriving 'lessons' from history and of historical analogy generally, see Arno J. Mayer, 'Vietnam Analogy: Greece, Not Munich', *Annals of International Studies*, 1 (1970), pp. 224–32; Hans Morgenthau, 'Remarks on the Validity of Historical Analogies', *Social Research*, 39.2 (1972), pp. 360–4; Alejandro Portes, 'Hazards of Historical Analogy', *Social Problems*, 28.5 (1981), pp. 517–9; Luciano Canfora, 'Analogie et Histoire', *History and Theory*, 22.1 (1983), pp. 22–42; and Yaacov Y. I. Vertzberger, 'Foreign Policy Decisionmakers as Practical-intuitive Historians: Applied History and Its Shortcomings', *International Studies Quarterly*, 30.2 (1986), pp. 223–47.

5 Paul M. Kennedy, 'The Tradition of Appeasement in British Foreign Policy, 1865–1939', *British Journal of International Studies*, 2.3 (1976), pp. 195–215. For a similar argument regarding Munich, see Paul W. Schroeder, 'Munich and the British Tradition', *Historical Journal,* 19.1 (1976), pp. 223–43. See also Geoffrey Hicks, '"Appeasement" or Consistent Conservatism? British Foreign Policy, Party Politics and the Guarantees of 1867 and 1939', *Historical Research*, 84.225 (2011), pp. 513–34.

6 On the significance of the language employed with regard to historical terminology, see David Reynolds, *From World War to Cold War: Churchill, Roosevelt, and the International History of the 1940s* (Oxford: Oxford University Press, 2006), pp. 331–51 (see esp. pp. 337–9 on 'appeasement').

7 Kennedy, 'The Tradition of Appeasement in British Foreign Policy, 1865–1939', p. 195. Italics in the original. See also Paul M. Kennedy, 'The Logic of Appeasement', *Times Literary Supplement*, 28 May 1982.

8 *Hansard*, HC Deb, 5th Series, v. 188, c. 420–1, 18 November 1925.

9 Anthony Eden had described his foreign policy as aiming at 'the appeasement of Europe as a whole'. *Hansard*, HC Deb, 5th Series, v. 310, c. 1446, 26 March 1935.

10 Robert Rhodes James, *Anthony Eden* (London: Papermac, 1987), p. 164.

11 *Hansard*, HL Deb, 5th Series, v. 559, c. 121, 17 November 1994. Max Beloff was Gladstone Professor of Government and Public Administration at Oxford University, 1957–74

12 Beloff had actually said: 'The Foreign Office has been taken over by the advocates of appeasement to a much greater extent than in the 1930s. By "appeasement" I refer to the view that Britain has no possibility of exerting an independent role in the world; that its role will be confined to being a good little boy in Europe.' *Hansard*, HL Deb, 5th Series, v. 559, c. 121, 17 November 1994.

13 Beatrice, Baroness Seear, Liberal Democrat. *Hansard*, HL Deb, 5th Series, v. 559, c. 121, 17 November 1994. To this Beloff replied: 'My Lords, that may well be true, but I do not believe that that affects my argument.' *Hansard*, HL Deb, 5th Series, v. 559, c. 121, 17 November 1994.

14 Stella Rudman, *Lloyd George and the Appeasement of Germany, 1919–1945* (Newcastle upon Tyne: Cambridge Scholars Publishing, 2011), p. 5.

15 Donald Cameron Watt, 'Churchill and Appeasement' in Robert Blake and Wm. Roger Louis (eds), *Churchill* (Oxford: Oxford University Press, 1993), p. 213.

16 Keith Robbins, *Appeasement* (Oxford: Wiley-Blackwell, 2nd edn 1997), p. 6.

17 Paul Schroeder, 'Napoleon's Foreign Policy: A Criminal Enterprise', *The Journal of Military History*, 54.2 (1990), pp. 152–3. The Treaty of Amiens was signed between Great Britain and France on 25 March 1802. The resulting 'Peace of Amiens' lasted until 18 May 1803. On this, see John Grainger, *The Amiens Truce: Britain and Bonaparte, 1801–1803* (Woodbridge, NJ: Boydell Press, 2004). For a discussion of Peace of Amiens as an act of British appeasement, see Ernst L. Presseisen, *Amiens and Munich: Comparisons in Appeasement* (The Hague: Martinus Nijhoff, 1978).

18 John Charmley, 'Traditions of Conservative Foreign Policy' in Geoffrey Hicks (ed.), *Conservatism and British Foreign Policy: The Derbys and Their World* (Farnham: Ashgate, 2011), pp. 215–28. Three examples that we might cite here are British policy towards the United States, Prussia-Germany and Russia in the nineteenth and early twentieth centuries. On these, see Duncan Andrew Campbell, *Unlikely Allies: America, Britain and the Victorian Beginnings of the Special Relationship* (London: Continuum, 2007); Iestyn Adams, *Brothers across the Ocean: British Foreign Policy and the Origins of the Anglo-American 'Special Relationship' 1900–1905* (London: I.B. Tauris, rev. edn 2012); D. N. Raymond, *British Policy and Opinion during the Franco-Prussian War* (New York: Columbia University Press, 1921); Paul M. Kennedy, *The Rise of the Anglo-German Antagonism, 1860–1914* (London: Allen & Unwin, 1980); Beryl J. Williams, 'The Strategic Background to the Anglo-Russian Entente of August 1907', *Historical Journal*, 9.3 (1966), pp. 360–73; and Ira Klein, 'The Anglo-Russian Convention and the Problem of Central Asia, 1907–1914', *Journal of British Studies*, 11.1 (1971), pp. 126–47.

19 On Aberdeen's policies, see Muriel Evelyn Chamberlain, *The Character of the Foreign Policy of the Earl of Aberdeen, 1841–6* (Oxford: Oxford University Press, 1961).

20 T. G. Otte, *The Foreign Office Mind: The Making of British Foreign Policy, 1865–1914* (Cambridge: Cambridge University Press, 2011). For an insightful

assessment of the roots of, and the rationale for, appeasement in the 1930s, see Zara Steiner, *The Lights that Failed: European International History, 1919–1933* (Oxford: Oxford University Press, 2005), pp. 635–816.

21 Paul Kennedy, 'A Time to Appease', *The National Interest*, 108 (2010), pp. 8–9.

22 *Hansard*, HC Deb, 3rd series, v. 97, c. 122, 1 March 1848. Thatcher, in conversation with Mikhail Gorbachev in 1984, asserted (after Palmerston): 'Nations have no permanent friends or allies, they only have permanent interests.' Richard Aldous, *Reagan and Thatcher: The Difficult Relationship* (London: Hutchinson, 2012), p. 277.

23 Diary entry for 11 May 1940. Friedrich Kellner, '*Vernebelt, verdunkelt sind alle Hirne': Tagebücher 1939–1945*, volume 1, ed. Sascha Feuchert, Robert Martin Scott Kellner, Erwin Leibfried, Jörg Riecke and Markus Roth (Göttingen: Wallstein Verlag, 2011), p. 71. After the demise of the Third Reich, Friedrich Kellner, a veteran of the First World War, helped resurrect the Social Democratic Party of Germany (*Sozialdemokratische Partei Deutschlands*, SPD) in Laubach, Hessen.

24 On this, see John H. Herz, 'The Relevancy and Irrelevancy of Appeasement', *Social Research*, 31.3 (1964), pp. 296–320.

25 Cato, *Guilty Men* (London: Victor Gollancz, 1940). Cato's 15 'guilty men' were Neville Chamberlain, Sir John Simon, Sir Samuel Hoare, Ramsay MacDonald, Stanley Baldwin, Lord Halifax, Sir Kingsley Wood, Ernest Brown, David Margesson, Sir Horace Wilson, Sir Thomas Inskip (Lord Caldecote), Leslie Burgin, James Richard Stanhope, the seventh Earl Stanhope, William Shepherd Morrison and Sir Reginald Dorman-Smith. Cato, *Guilty Men*, p. 6.

26 Diary entry for 14 June 1940. Kellner, '*Vernebelt, verdunkelt sind alle Hirne*', v. 1, p. 75.

27 Richard Toye, 'The Churchill Syndrome: Reputational Entrepreneurship and the Rhetoric of Foreign Policy since 1945', *British Journal of Politics and International Relations*, 10.3 (2008), p. 365. On Churchill's rhetoric and his use of metaphor, see Jonathan Charteris-Black, *Politicians and Rhetoric: the Persuasive Power of Metaphor* (Basingstoke: Palgrave Macmillan, 2nd edn, 2011), pp. 52–78.

28 Robert Self, 'Neville Chamberlain and the Long Shadow of the "Guilty Men"', *Conservative History Journal*, 7 (2008), p. 19.

29 Winston S. Churchill, *The Second World War, Volume I, The Gathering Storm* (London: Cassell, 8th edn, 1966 [1948]), pp. 199–200. Quotes at p. 199.

30 Diary entry for 12 November 1940. Kellner, '*Vernebelt, verdunkelt sind alle Hirne*', v. 1, p. 105.

31 Self, 'Neville Chamberlain and the Long Shadow of the "Guilty Men"', p. 21.

32 Watt, 'Churchill and Appeasement', pp. 214, 200.

33 Donald Cameron Watt, 'Appeasement: The Rise of a Revisionist School?', *Political Quarterly*, 36.2 (1965), p. 197. The ascendancy achieved by the 'Guilty Men' thesis, and the public opprobrium attached to the makers of interwar British foreign policy, contributed to Foreign Office support for the publication of the *Documents on British Foreign Policy 1919–1939* series from 1947 onwards.

Many of the documents in this published series, perhaps unsurprisingly, lent weight to the case of those who stressed the anti-appeasement element within the interwar Foreign Office. Uri Bialer, 'Telling the Truth to the People: Britain's Decision to Publish the Diplomatic Papers of the interwar Period' in Keith Wilson (ed.), *Forging the Collective Memory: Government and International Historians Through Two World Wars* (Oxford: Berghahn, 1996), p. 283. With regard to the latter point, a 1951 volume on British policy after Munich seemed to demonstrate a greater degree of foresight and calculation on the part of the British government than many observers had hitherto given it credit for. For the relevant volume, see *Documents on British Foreign Policy, 1919–1939*, Third Series, volume iv, 1939, *The Aftermath of Munich, October 1938-March 1939* (London: HMSO, 1951).

34 See, for example, Keith Robbins, *Munich 1938* (London: Cassell, 1968); W. N. Medlicott, *Britain and Germany: The Search for Agreement 1930– 1937* (London: Athlone, 1969); and Neville Thompson, *The Anti-Appeasers: Conservative Opposition to Appeasement in the 1930's* (Oxford: Clarendon Press, 1971).

35 See, for example, R. A. C. Parker, *Chamberlain and Appeasement: British Policy and the Coming of the Second World War* (London: Macmillan, 1993) and Frank McDonough, *Neville Chamberlain, Appeasement, and the British Road to War* (Manchester: Manchester University Press, 1998).

36 On the historiography of appeasement, see Charles Webster, 'Munich Reconsidered: A Survey of British Policy', *International Affairs*, 37.1 (1961), pp. 137–54; Robert Skidelsky, 'Going to War with Germany: Between Revisionism & Orthodoxy', *Encounter*, 39.1 (1972), pp. 56–65; D. C. Watt, 'The Historiography of Appeasement' in Alan Sked and Chris Cook (eds), *Crisis and Controversy: Essays in Honour of A.J.P. Taylor* (London: Macmillan, 1976), 110–29; Paul M. Kennedy, 'Appeasement and British Defence Policy', *British Journal of International Studies*, 4.2 (1978), pp. 161–77; Stephen G. Walker, 'Solving the Appeasement Puzzle: Contending Historical Interpretations of British Diplomacy during the 1930s', *Review of International Studies*, 6.3 (1980), pp. 219–46; J. L. Richardson, 'New Perspectives on Appeasement: Some Implications for International Relations', *World Politics*, 40.3 (1988), pp. 289–316; Talbot Imlay and Paul Kennedy, 'Appeasement' in Gordon Martel (ed.), *The Origins of the Second World War Reconsidered* (London: Unwin Hyman, 2nd edn, 1999), pp. 116–34; Sidney Aster, 'Appeasement: Before and after Revisionism', *Diplomacy & Statecraft*, 19.3 (2008), pp. 443–80; Daniel Hucker, 'The Unending Debate: Appeasement, Chamberlain and the Origins of the Second World War', *Intelligence and National Security*, 23.4 (2008), pp. 536–51. In McDonough's edited volume, see David Dutton, 'Guilty Men? Three British Foreign Secretaries of the 1930s'; Frank McDonough, 'When Instinct Clouds Judgement: Neville Chamberlain and the Pursuit of Appeasement with Nazi Germany, 1937– 39'; Jeffrey Record, 'Appeasement: A Critical Evaluation Seventy Years On'; Robert J. Young, 'A Very English Channel: Britain and French Appeasement'; and Talbot Imlay, 'Politics, Strategy and Economics: A Comparative Analysis of British and French "Appeasement"' in Frank McDonough (ed.), *Origins of the Second World War: An International Perspective* (London: Continuum, 2011), pp. 144–67, 186– 204, 223–37, 238–61, 262–77.

37 Aster, 'Appeasement: Before and after Revisionism', p. 463.

38 Skidelsky, 'Going to War with Germany', p. 58.

39   Charmley, 'Traditions of Conservative Foreign Policy', p. 227.

40   Diary entry for 12 November 1940. Kellner, *'Vernebelt, verdunkelt sind alle Hirne'*, v.1, p. 105. Kellner was specifically referring to a newspaper piece that opined: 'With Neville Chamberlain's death, one of the first warmongers [*Kriegsbrandstifter*] steps off the stage of world politics.' *Hessische Landeszeitung*, 11 November 1940.

41   Churchill, *The Gathering Storm*, p. x.

42   Paul Addison, 'The Three Careers of Winston Churchill', *Transactions of the Royal Historical Society*, 6th series, 11 (2001), pp. 183–200.

43   The Nobel Prize in Literature for 1953 was awarded to Winston S. Churchill 'for his mastery of historical and biographical description as well as for brilliant oratory in defending exalted human values'. Eugene L. Rasor, *Winston S. Churchill, 1874–1965: A Comprehensive Historiography and Annotated Bibliography* (Westport, CT: Greenwood Press, 2000), p. 30. Churchill accepted the prize thus: 'Since Alfred Nobel died in 1896 we have entered an age of storm and tragedy. The power of man has grown in every sphere except over himself. Never in the field of action have events seemed so harshly to dwarf personalities. Rarely in history have brutal facts so dominated thought or has such a widespread, individual virtue found so dim a collective focus.' Lady Churchill read out this Banquet Speech, as the Laureate was unable to attend the Nobel Banquet at the City Hall in Stockholm, 10 December 1953. Horst Frenz (ed.), *Nobel Lectures: Literature 1901–1967* (Amsterdam: Elsevier Publishing Company for the Nobel Foundation, 1969), p. 493.

44   Peter Clarke, *Mr Churchill's Profession: Statesman, Orator, Writer* (London: Bloomsbury, 2012), p. 198.

45   Devin O. Pendas, 'Testimony' in Miriam Dobson and Benjamin Ziemann (eds), *Reading Primary Sources: The Interpretation of Texts from Nineteenth- and Twentieth-Century History* (London: Routledge, 2009), p. 227. Robert Self quotes Churchill thus: 'Poor Neville will come badly out of history. I know, I will write that history'. Self, 'Neville Chamberlain and the Long Shadow of the "Guilty Men"', p. 19.

46   Richard Toye, *Lloyd George & Churchill: Rivals for Greatness* (London: Macmillan, 2007), p. 5.

47   Clarke, *Mr Churchill's Profession*, p. 198.

48   Watt, 'Churchill and Appeasement', p. 214.

49   R. A. C. Parker, *Churchill and Appeasement* (London: Macmillan, 2000), p. ix. For an examination of the alternatives to appeasement, see Andrew David Steadman, *Alternatives to Appeasement: Neville Chamberlain and Hitler's Germany* (London: I.B. Tauris, 2011).

50   On counterfactual history, see H.R. Trevor-Roper, 'The Lost Moments of History', *New York Review of Books*, 35.16 (27 October 1988), pp. 61–7; and Niall Ferguson, 'Virtual History: Towards a "chaotic" Theory of the Past', in *Virtual History: Alternatives and Counter Alternatives and Counterfactuals* (London: Papermac, 1997), pp. 1–90.

51   Angus Hawkins, 'Derby Redivivus: Reflections on the Political Achievement of the 14th Earl of Derby', in Geoffrey Hicks (ed.), *Conservatism and British Foreign Policy*, pp. 28–9.

52 Samuel Eliot Morrison, 'Sir Winston Churchill: Nobel Prize Winner', *Saturday Review*, 36.44, 31 October 1953, pp. 22–3.

53 David Reynolds, *In Command of History: Churchill Fighting and Writing the Second World War* (London: Allen Lane, 2004). See also David Reynolds, 'Churchill's Writing of History: Appeasement, Autobiography and *The Gathering Storm*', *Transactions of the Royal Historical Society* (Sixth Series), 11 (2001), pp. 221–47.

54 David Reynolds, review of Clarke, *Mr Churchill's Profession, The Guardian*, 21 July 2012.

55 On this, see Klaus Larres, *Churchill's Cold War: The Politics of Diplomacy* (New Haven, CY: Yale University Press, 2002), pp. 174–355; and Uri Bar-Noi, *The Cold War and Soviet Mistrust of Détente, 1951–1955* (Brighton: Sussex Academic Press, 2007).

56 Wesley K. Wark, 'Appeasement Revisited', *International History Review*, 17.3 (1995), p. 546.

57 Paul M. Kennedy 'The Tradition of "Appeasement" in British Foreign Policy, 1865–1939' in *Strategy and Diplomacy 1870–1945: Eight Studies* (London: Fontana, 1983), p. 13.

58 See, for example, Ed Vulliamy, 'Bosnia: The Crime of Appeasement', *International Affairs*, 74.1 (1998), pp. 73–92; and Nader Mousavizadeh (ed.), *The Black Book of Bosnia: The Consequences of 'Appeasement'* (New York: Basic Books, 1996).

59 *Hansard*, HC Deb, 6th Series, v. 221, c. 983, 24 March 1993.

60 Robert J. Beck, 'Munich's Lessons Reconsidered', *International Security*, 14.2 (1989), p. 162.

61 *Hansard*, HC Deb, 5th Series, v. 382, c. 1004–5, 5 August 1942; Cmd. 6739, *Policy of His Majesty's Government in the United Kingdom in Regard to Czechoslovakia*, HMSO, 1942. On British policy and the history of the Munich Agreement during the Cold War, see R. Gerald Hughes, 'The Ghosts of Appeasement: Britain and the legacy of the Munich Agreement', *Journal of Contemporary History*, 48.4 (2013) pp. 688–716.

62 Edgar A. Mowrer, 'Preface' to C.J. George, *They Betrayed Czechoslovakia* (Harmondsworth: Penguin, 1938), p. v.

63 See, for example, Andrei Mertsalov, *Munich: Mistake or Cynical Calculation? Contemporary Non-Marxist Historians on the Munich Agreement of 1938* (Moscow: Novosti Press Agency, 1988). For a vigorous refutation of Marxist-Leninist readings of Munich, see Donald N. Lammers, *Explaining Munich: The Search for Motive in British Policy* (Stanford, CA: Hoover Institution/ Stanford University, 1966).

64 Margaret Thatcher, *The Path to Power* (London: HarperCollins, 1995), p. 27.

65 Alfred Duff Cooper, *Old Men Forget: the Autobiography of Duff Cooper* (London: Rupert Hart-Davis, 1954), p. 246. For the evolution of Duff Cooper's thinking, see John Julius Norwich (ed.), *The Duff Cooper Diaries 1915–1951* (London: Phoenix, 2006), pp. 255–72 (30 August–30 September 1938).

66 Christopher Meyer, *Getting Our Way: 500 Years of Adventures and Intrigue: The Inside Story of British Diplomacy* (London: Phoenix, 2010), p. 230.

67 Ian Colvin, *None So Blind: A British Diplomatic View of the Origins of World War II* (New York: Harcourt, Brace & World, 1965), p. 103; Jörg Später, *Vansittart: Britische Debatten über Deutsche und Nazis 1902–1945* (Göttingen: Wallstein Verlag, 2003), p. 66.

68 Diary entry for 31 December 1938. John Barnes and David Nicolson (eds), *The Empire at Bay: The Leo Amery Diaries 1929–1945* (London: Hutchinson, 1988), p. 541; Patrick Cosgrave, *R.A. Butler: An English Life* (London: Quartet Books, 1981), pp. 41–63; Anthony Howard, *RAB: The Life of R.A. Butler* (London: Jonathan Cape, 1987), pp. 70–87. For a forensic demolition of Butler's memoirs, see Paul Stafford, 'Political Autobiography and the Art of the Plausible: R.A. Butler at the Foreign Office, 1938–1939', *Historical Journal*, 28.4 (1985), pp. 901–22. In May 1940, it was Leo Amery who, addressing Chamberlain, famously quoted Oliver Cromwell's dismissal of 'The Rump' in 1653: 'You have sat too long here for any good you have been doing. Depart, I say, and let us have done with you. In the name of God, go.' *Hansard*, HC Deb, 5th Series, v. 360, c. 1150, 7 May 1940. Lloyd George told Amery afterwards that he could not remember a parliamentary speech having 'so dramatic a climax'. Diary entry for 7 May 1940. *The Empire at Bay*, p. 592.

69 Diary entry for 9 May 1939 (Channon was Butler's parliamentary private secretary). Robert Rhodes James (ed.), *'Chips': The Diaries of Sir Henry Channon* (London: Phoenix, 1996), p. 197. On Butler's intimate association with appeasement and Munich, see John Campbell, *Pistols at Dawn: Two Hundred Years of Political Rivalry from Pitt & Fox to Blair & Brown* (London: Jonathan Cape, 2009), pp. 251–2. Harold Macmillan later termed Butler 'the most cringing of Munichites'. Alastair Horne, *Macmillan 1984–1957* (London: Macmillan, 1988), p. 297.

70 Lord Home, *The Way the Wind Blows* (London: Collins, 1976), pp. 67–8.

71 Beatrice Heuser, 'Modern Man's Myths: The Influence of Historical Memory on Policy-Making' in Fritz Taubert (ed.), *Mythos München* (Munich: Oldenbourg, 2002), p. 370.

72 Telford Taylor, *Munich: The Price of Peace* (Garden City, NY: Doubleday, 1979), p. 978.

73 Hugh Trevor-Roper to Bernard Berenson, 25 November 1956. Richard Davenport-Hines (ed.), *Letters from Oxford: Hugh Trevor-Roper to Bernard Berenson* (London: Phoenix, 2007), p. 209.

74 Noel Annan, *Our Age: The Generation that Made Post-War Britain* (London: Fontana, 1991), p. 265. Noel Gilroy Annan, Lord Annan (1916–2000), was a British military intelligence officer, author and academic. After 1945 he served as a senior officer in the political division of the British Control Commission for Germany. On this, see Noel Annan, *How Dr. Adenauer Rose Resilient from the Ruins of Germany* (London: Institute of Germanic Studies, University of London, 1983) and Noel Annan, *Changing Enemies: The Defeat and Regeneration of Germany* (London: HarperCollins, 1995).

75 Daniel Hucker, *Public Opinion and the End of Appeasement in Britain and France* (Farnham: Ashgate, 2011), p. 255.

76 George Orwell, 'In Defence of P. G. Wodehouse' (*Windmill*, July 1945), *The Collected Essays, Journalism and Letters of George Orwell: volume 3: As I Please*, ed. Sonia Orwell and Ian Angus (London: Penguin, 1970), pp. 402–3.

77 David Chuter, 'Munich, or the Blood of Others' in Cyril Buffet and Beatrice Heuser (eds), *Haunted by History: Myths in International Relations* (Oxford: Berghahn, 1998), p. 65.

78 Andrei S. Markovits and Simon Reich, 'The Contemporary Power of Memory: The Dilemmas for German Foreign Policy' in John S. Brady, Beverly Crawford and Sarah Elise Williarty (eds), *The Postwar Transformation of Germany: Democracy, Prosperity, and Nationhood* (Ann Arbor, MI: University of Michigan, 1999), p. 445.

79 Geoffrey Cubitt, *History and Memory* (Manchester: Manchester University Press, 2007), p. 2 (quote), pp. 58–62.

80 Luca Ratti, *Britain, Ost- and Deutschlandpolitik, and the CSCE (1955–1975)* (Bern: Peter Lang, 2008), p. 190.

81 J. V. Polišenský, *Britain and Czechoslovakia: A Study in Contacts*, 2nd rev. ed. (Prague: Orbis, 1968). This book stresses, for example, the links between Sudeten German landowners and the British aristocracy (p. 77). For similar, see R. W. Seton-Watson, *A History of the Czechs and Slovaks* (London: Hutchinson, 1943).

82 Patrick Finney, '"And I will tell you who you are": Historiographies of Munich and the Negotiation of National Identity' in Taubert (ed.), *Mythos München*, esp. pp. 324–32.

83 Enoch Powell, BBC Radio 4, 10 February 1991.

84 Peter Hennessy, *Never Again: Britain, 1945–51* (London: Jonathan Cape, 1992), p. 2.

85 Maurice Halbwachs, *On Collective Memory*, trans. and ed. Lewis A. Coser (Chicago, IL: University of Chicago Press, 1992), p. 38.

86 Alon Confino, 'Collective Memory and Cultural History: Problems of Method', *American Historical Review*, 102.5 (1997), p. 1388.

87 Zara Steiner, 'The Historian and the Foreign Office' in Pamela Beshoff and Christopher Hill (eds), *Two Worlds of International Relations: Academics, Practitioners and the Trade in Ideas* (London: Routledge, 1994), pp. 44–5.

88 Markovits and Reich, 'The Contemporary Power of Memory', p. 445; Aleida Assmann, 'Transformations between History and Memory', *Social Research*, 75.1 (2008), pp. 49–72; Fredrik Logevall and Kenneth Osgood, 'The Ghost of Munich: America's Appeasement Complex', *World Affairs*, 173.2 (2010), p. 26.

89 Jan-Werner Müller, 'Introduction: the Power of Memory, the Memory of Power and the Power over Memory' in Jan-Werner Müller (ed.), *Memory and Power in Post-War Europe* (Cambridge: Cambridge University Press, 2002), pp. 22–3.

90 Schroeder, 'Napoleon's Foreign Policy', p. 152.

91 Peter J. Beck, *Using History, Making British Policy: The Treasury and the Foreign Office, 1950–76* (London: Palgrave Macmillan, 2006), p. 15.

92 There are a number of recent works dealing with British attitudes towards Munich in the period between 1938 and 1945. The best yet published is Vít Smetana's *In the Shadow of Munich: British Policy towards Czechoslovakia from the Endorsement to the Renunciation of the Munich Agreement (1938–1942)* (Prague: Karolinum, 2008). See also Martin D. Brown, *Dealing with Democrats:*

The British Foreign Office's Relations with the Czechoslovak Émigrés in Great Britain, 1939–1945 (Frankfurt am Main: Peter Lang, 2006); Martin D. Brown, 'A Munich Winter or a Prague Spring? The Evolution of British Policy towards the Sudeten Germans from October 1938 to September 1939' in H. H. Hahn (ed.), *Hundert Jahre sudetendeutsche Geschichte: Eine völkische Bewegung in drei Staaten* (Frankfurt am Main: Peter Lang, 2007), pp. 257–73.

93 See, for example, Hugh Trevor-Roper's review of John Wheeler-Bennett's *Munich: Prologue to Tragedy* (New York: Duell, Sloan and Pearce, 1948) in *New York Times*, 8 August 1948. In March 1938 Harold Macmillan, then a young Conservative MP, had told a meeting of the women's branch of the Conservative Party in Stockton: 'Many people have felt and many historians have felt that if [Foreign Secretary] Sir Edward Grey and the Liberal Government of 1914 had made it perfectly clear in July of that year that this country would support Belgium if attacked, there might never have been a war.' *Northern Echo*, 18 March 1938. Quoted in Harold Macmillan, *Winds of Change 1914–1939* (London: Macmillan, 1966), p. 543.

94 Andrew Roberts, *'The Holy Fox': The Life of Lord Halifax* (London: Phoenix, 1997), pp. 123–75.

95 Norman Rose, 'The Resignation of Anthony Eden', *Historical Journal*, 25.4 (1982), pp. 911-31. For an earlier critique of Eden on this score, see R. H. S. Crossman, 'After the Resignation' (1938) in *The Charm of Politics*, pp. 49–53.

96 David Dutton, 'Power Brokers or just Glamour Boys: The Eden Group, September 1939–May 1940', *English Historical Review*, 476.118 (2003), pp. 412–24; Keith Middlemas, *The Strategy of Appeasement: The British Government and Germany, 1937–39* (Chicago, IL: Quadrangle Books, 1972), pp. 71, 296, 452; and Lynne Olson, *Troublesome Young Men: The Rebels Who brought Churchill to Power in 1940 and Helped Save Britain* (London: Bloomsbury, 2007), pp. 177–9.

97 Maurice Cowling, *The Impact of Labour 1920–1924: The Beginning of Modern British Politics* (Cambridge: Cambridge University Press, 1971), pp. 3–4. On Cowling and rhetoric, see Philip Williamson, 'Maurice Cowling and modern British political history' in Robert Crowcroft, S. J. D. Green and Richard Whiting (eds), *Philosophy, Politics and Religion in British Democracy: Maurice Cowling and Conservatism* (London: I.B. Tauris, 2010), pp. 136, 138–40.

98 Richard Toye, 'The Rhetorical Premiership: A New Perspective on Prime Ministerial Power Since 1945', *Parliamentary History*, 30.2 (2011), pp. 175–92.

99 The time frame of this book inevitably means that the evidential base of the book requires adjustment, depending upon which era is under consideration. The constraints of UK archival release legislation (in short, the so-called Thirty-year rule) mean that the latter chapters are derived of a documentary basis that is distinct from (chronologically) earlier ones. There is, of course, a qualitative difference between the nature of the sources used, for example, about Churchill in the 1950s (where we have personal papers, public records, diaries and the like) and about, for instance, the Blair years (1997–2007), where (in general) we do not. Such factors naturally affect the way in which one sees the policy-making process. In the latter case (Blair) that process is viewed primarily through the prism of rhetoric for public consumption, and has rather less archival material with which to gain insights into the inner workings of government. All of this

does not affect the basic argument of this book, which examines the manner in which the history (and nature) of appeasement has been used (and misused) for political ends in postwar Britain. For further discussion of the problems that confront the contemporary historian, see Peter Catterall, 'What (if anything) Is Distinctive about Contemporary History?', *Journal of Contemporary History*, 32.4 (1997), pp. 441–52; Marc Trachtenberg, *The Craft of International History: A Guide to Method* (Princeton, NJ: Princeton University Press, 2006), pp. 146–62; Martin Johnes, 'On Writing Contemporary History', *North American Journal of Welsh Studies*, 6.1 (2011), pp. 20–31; and Peter Hennessy, *Distilling the Frenzy: Writing the History of One's Own Times* (London: Biteback, 2012), pp. 16–22.

100   Terrance L. Lewis, *Prisms of British Appeasement: Revisionist Reputations of John Simon, Samuel Hoare, Anthony Eden, Lord Halifax and Alfred Duff Cooper* (Brighton: Sussex Academic Press, 2009).

101   Macmillan, *Winds of Change 1914–1939*, p. 582.

102   Lewis Namier, *Diplomatic Prelude, 1938–1939* (London: Macmillan, 1948) and *Europe in Decay: A Study in Disintegration, 1936–40* (London: Macmillan, 1950); John Wheeler-Bennett, *Munich: Prologue to Tragedy* (London: Macmillan, 1948); A. L. Rowse, *All Souls and Appeasement: A Contribution to Contemporary History* (London: Macmillan, 1961) and *Appeasement: A Study in Political Decline 1933–1939* (New York: W.W. Norton, 1961) and Margaret George, *The Warped Vision: British Foreign Policy, 1933–1939* (Pittsburgh, PA: University of Pittsburgh Press, 1965).

103   Schroeder, 'Munich and the British Tradition', p. 242. It was no coincidence that, in chronological terms, such developments in the historiography in appeasement was accompanied by a wave of historians who sought to shift the blame for the Cold War onto the West. On this, see Robert H. Ferrell, *Harry S. Truman and the Cold War Revisionists* (Columbia, MO and London: University of Missouri Press, 2006). For a stimulating discussion of the Cold War revisionist school, see J.L. Richardson, 'Cold-War Revisionism: A Critique', *World Politics*, 24.4 (1972), pp. 579–612. This was a review article of the following works: Gabriel Kolko, *The Politics of War: Allied Diplomacy and the World Crisis of 1943–1945* (New York: Random House, 1968); Gar Alperovitz, *Atomic Diplomacy: Hiroshima and Potsdam* (New York: Simon and Schuster, 1965) and *Cold War Essays* (New York: Doubleday Anchor, 1970); and David Horowitz, *From Yalta to Vietnam: American Foreign Policy in the Cold War* (Harmondsworth: Penguin, 1967).

104   Roy Douglas, 'Chamberlain and Eden, 1937–38', *Journal of Contemporary History*, 13.1 (1978), pp. 97–116; Roy Douglas, 'Chamberlain and Appeasement' in Wolfgang J. Mommsen and Lothar Kettenacker (eds), *The Fascist Challenge and the Policy of Appeasement* (London: Allen and Unwin, 1983), pp. 79–88; David Dilks, '"We must hope for the best and prepare for the Worst": The Prime Minister, the Cabinet and Hitler's Germany 1937–1939', *Proceedings of the British Academy*, LXXIII (1987), pp. 309–52; Philip M. Taylor, 'Appeasement: Guilty Men or Guilty Conscience?', *Modern History Review*, 19.2 (1989) pp. 34–7.

105   Skidelsky, 'Going to War with Germany', p. 58. By way of example, one might note how archival revelations supplemented A. L. Rowse's *All Souls*

and Appeasement. On this, see Sidney Aster (ed.), *Appeasement and All Souls: A Portrait with Documents, 1937–1939* (Cambridge: Cambridge University Press for the Royal Historical Society, 2004). In 1993, Rowse had said that the title of his book had perpetuated 'the idea that the college as such was associated with that fatally mistaken policy. This was not so.' 'Diary: Hotbed of cold feet?', *The Times*, 23 September 1993.

106   John Charmley, *Chamberlain and the Lost Peace* (London: Curtis, 1989), p. 212. For a similar line of argument, see Patrick J. Buchanan, *Churchill, Hitler and the Unnecessary War: How Britain Lost Its Empire and the West Lost the World* (New York: Crown, 2008).

107   A. J. P. Taylor, *The Origins of the Second World War* (London: Hamish Hamilton, 1961).

108   Martin Gilbert and Richard Gott, *The Appeasers* (London: Weidenfeld and Nicolson, 1963).

109   Isaac Deutscher, 'Review of A.J.P. Taylor, *The Origins of the Second World War*', *The Wiener Library Review*, 15.3 (1961), p. 41.

110   Taylor, *The Origins of the Second World War*, p. 71.

111   On the responses to Taylor over a generation, see Esmonde M. Robertson (ed.), *The Origins of the Second World War* (London: Macmillan, 1971); Wm. Roger Louis (ed.), *The Origins of the Second World War: A.J.P. Taylor and His Critics* (New York: Wiley, 1972); Gordon Martel (ed.), The *Origins of the Second World War Reconsidered: The A.J.P. Taylor Debate after Twenty-Five Years* (London: Allen & Unwin, 1986) and, in an expanded second edition, as Gordon Martel (ed.), *The Origins of the Second World War Reconsidered: A.J.P. Taylor and the Historians* (London: Routledge, 1999).

112   Taylor, *The Origins of the Second World War*, p. 7.

113   H. R. Trevor-Roper, 'A.J.P. Taylor, Hitler, and the War', *Encounter*, 17.1 (1961), p. 88.

114   Taylor, *The Origins of the Second World War*, p. 7.

115   Watt, 'Appeasement: The Rise of a Revisionist School?', p. 191.

116   Martin Gilbert, *The Roots of Appeasement* (London: Weidenfeld and Nicolson, 1966).

117   Maitland exhorted the historian to remember that what is now in the past was once in the future. R. Gerald Hughes, 'Of Revelatory Histories and Hatchet Jobs: Propaganda and Method in Intelligence History', *Intelligence and National Security*, 23.6 (2008), p. 849.

118   David Dilks, 'Appeasement Revisited', *University of Leeds Review*, 15 (1972), p. 53.

119   Maurice Cowling, *The Impact of Hitler: British Politics and British Policy 1933–1940* (Cambridge: Cambridge University Press, 1975), pp. 5, 5, 9, 12.

120   During the Falklands War one US official later noted that '[Admiral Sir Terence] Lewin concurs with a view that Dick Walters claims he heard from some Brit *[sic]* military colleagues, namely, that Chamberlain's appeasement policy at Munich was dictated by the Imperial Chiefs of Staff, who told the King's First Minister that they needed at least a year to rearm sufficiently and that Chamberlain had to buy that time at any price'. Diary entry: London, 12

April 1982. Thatcher Archive (Churchill Archive Centre): 'James Rentschler's Falklands diary 1 April–25 June 1982', p. 10.

121   The Treasury's role in appeasement was first systematically examined in B. J. Wendt, *Economic Appeasement: Handel und Finanz in der britischen Deutschlandpolitik 1933–1939* (Düsseldorf: Bertlesmann Universitätsverlag, 1971). Gladwyn Jebb later noted that the use of the term 'economic appeasement' in the 1930s marked the 'first time that the famous word gained any currency and it certainly did not then connote a policy of giving the Nazis everything they wanted; merely a possible means of achieving a 'peaceful solution''. Lord Gladwyn, *The Memoirs of Gladwyn Jebb* (London: Weidenfeld and Nicolson, 1972), p. 65. The findings of Wendt's book were developed by a number of authors: Robert P. Shay, *British Rearmament in the Thirties: Politics and Profits* (Princeton, NJ: Princeton University Press, 1977); G. C. Peden, 'A Matter of Timing: The Economic Background to British Foreign Policy, 1937–1939', *History*, 69.225 (1984), pp. 15–28; G. C. Peden, *British Rearmament and the Treasury, 1932–1939* (Edinburgh: Scottish Academic Press, 1979); G. C. Peden, *Treasury and British Public Policy, 1906–1959* (Oxford: Oxford University Press, 2000); and Keith Neilson, 'The Defence Requirements Sub-Committee, British Strategic Foreign Policy, Neville Chamberlain and the Path to Appeasement', *English Historical Review*, 118.477 (2003), pp. 651–84.

122   See, for example, Norman H. Gibbs, *Grand Strategy*, Volume I, *Rearmament Policy* (London: Her Majesty's Stationery Office, 1976); T. C. G. James, *Air Defence of Great Britain*, Volume I, *The Growth of Fighter Command, 1936–1940* (London: Frank Cass, 2001).

123   For example, S. W. Roskill, *Naval Policy between the Wars*, 2 vols (London: Collins, 1968 and 1976); H. Montgomery Hyde, *British Air Policy between the Wars* (London: Heinemann, 1976); and Brian Bond, *British Military Policy between the Wars* (Oxford: Oxford University Press, 1980).

124   Wm. Roger Louis, *British Strategy in the Far East 1919–1939* (Oxford: Clarendon Press, 1971); Lawrence R. Pratt, *East of Malta, West of Suez* (Cambridge: Cambridge University Press, 1975); Stephen L. Endicott, *Diplomacy and Enterprise: British China Policy 1933–1937* (Manchester: Manchester University Press, 1975); Ann Trotter, *Britain and East Asia 1933–1937* (Cambridge: Cambridge University Press, 1975); James Neidpath, *Singapore Naval Base and the Defence of Britain's Eastern Empire, 1919–1941* (Oxford: Clarendon Press, 1981); and Arthur J. Marder, *Old Friends, New Enemies: The Royal Navy and the Imperial Japanese Navy*, Volume 1, *Strategic Illusions, 1936–1941* (Oxford: Oxford University Press, 1981).

125   Ritchie Ovendale, *Appeasement and the English Speaking World* (Cardiff: University of Wales Press, 1975); and Robert F. Holland, *Britain and the Commonwealth Alliance 1918–39* (London: Macmillan, 1981).

126   Callum A. MacDonald, *The United States, Britain and Appeasement 1936–1939* (London: Macmillan, 1981); and David Reynolds, *The Creation of the Anglo-American Alliance 1937–41* (London: Europa Publications, 1981).

127   On this, see Peden, *British Rearmament and the Treasury, 1932–1939*.

128   G. C. Peden, 'Economic Aspects of British Perceptions of Power on the Eve of the Cold War' in J. Becker and F. Knipping (eds), *Power in Europe? Great*

Britain, France, Italy and Germany in a Postwar World, 1945–1950 (Berlin and New York: Walter de Gruyter, 1986), pp. 237–61; G. C. Peden, 'Economic Aspects of British Perceptions of Power' in Ennio Di Nolfo (ed.), *Power in Europe? II: Great Britain, France, Germany and Italy and the Origins of the EEC, 1952–1957* (Berlin and New York: Walter de Gruyter, 1992), pp. 139–59.

129   See G. C. Peden, *Arms, Economics and British Strategy: From Dreadnoughts to Hydrogen Bombs* (Cambridge: Cambridge University Press, 2007).

130   On this, see: W. R. Rock, *Appeasement on Trial: British Foreign Policy and its Critics: 1938–1939* (North Haven, CT: Archon Press, 1966); Franklin Reid Gannon, *The British Press and Germany 1936–1939* (Oxford: Oxford University Press, 1971); M. Ceadel, *Pacifism in Britain 1914–45* (Oxford: Clarendon Press, 1980); Richard Griffiths, *Fellow Travellers of the Right: British Enthusiasts for Nazi Germany, 1933–39* (London: Constable, 1980); and Hucker, *Public Opinion and the End of Appeasement in Britain and France.*

131   Gannon, *The British Press and Germany 1936–1939,* p. 288.

132   Michael C. Williams, 'The Politics of Theory: Waltz, Realism and Democracy' in Ken Booth (ed.), *Realism and World Politics* (London: Routledge, 2011), p. 57. When discussing his and Nixon's approach to Vietnam, Kissinger noted the distorting effect that public opinion has on foreign policy formulation. In order to illustrate his point he argued that, while Munich had been a terrible mistake, in the short-term it had made Chamberlain very popular while isolating Churchill in the country and the Conservative Party. If the Nixon administration similarly courted popularity by acceding to the wishes of the vocal domestic lobby that wanted to get out of Vietnam, this would only 'usher in a period of disintegrating American credibility that would only accelerate the world's instability.' Henry Kissinger, *The White House Years* (London: Weidenfeld and Nicolson and Michael Joseph, 1979), p. 292. Harold Wilson's mediation efforts over Vietnam were denounced as 'appeasement' by opponents. Sir Ian Orr-Ewing MP opined: 'Any appeasement, we learned – we learnt the hard way – does not pay against Communist or other dictatorships. Why should we try to coerce the Americans into appeasing Communist expansion in [Vietnam]? To my mind . . . the Americans are trying to contain Communism east of Suez as we sought to do very successfully with our confrontation to Indonesia.' *Hansard,* HC Deb, 5th Series, v. 745, c. 958, 21 April 1967. President Johnson did not share Wilson's stated belief that a 'solution could be reached'. Lyndon Baines Johnson, *The Vantage Point: Perspectives of the Presidency 1963–1969* (London: Weidenfeld and Nicolson, 1972), p. 255.

133   Robbins, *Appeasement,* p. 8.

134   Marvin Swartz, *The Politics of British Foreign Policy in the Era of Disraeli and Gladstone* (Basingstoke: Macmillan, 1985), p. 1.

135   David Dutton, *Neville Chamberlain* (London: Arnold, 2001), p. 2.

136   Interview with Margaret Thatcher. Charles Moore, *Margaret Thatcher: The Authorized Biography: Volume One: Not for Turning* (London: Allen Lane, 2013), p. 19.

137   Pieter Geyl, *Napoleon: For and Against,* trans. Olive Renier (New Haven, CT: Yale University Press, 1967 [1948]), p. 18.

138   Sidney Aster, 'Guilty Men: The Case of Neville Chamberlain' in Patrick Finney
       (ed.), *The Origins of the Second World War* (London: Bloomsbury Academic,
       1997), p. 66.

139   Parker, *Chamberlain and Appeasement*, p. 347.

140   Aster, 'Guilty Men: The Case of Neville Chamberlain', p. 75. It is often argued
       that Chamberlain's anti-Communism blinded him, and his supporters, to the
       dangers from Hitler. For an extreme exposition of this case, see Alvin Finkel
       and Clement Leibovitz, *The Chamberlain-Hitler Collusion* (Rendlesham, UK/
       Halifax, NS: Merlin Press/James Lorimer, 1997). The book makes reference
       (eight times!) to Chamberlain's letter of 13 September 1938 to George VI,
       which stated that Nazi Germany and Great Britain were 'the two pillars of
       European peace and buttresses against communism' (first quoted, p. 13).

141   Viscount Templewood (Sir Samuel Hoare), *Nine Troubled Years* (London:
       Collins, 1954), p. 375.

142   Vansittart's replacement, Sir Alexander Cadogan (permanent under-secretary
       at the Foreign Office, 1938–46) was possessed of a vision of *Realpolitik* that
       survived both Munich and the war unscathed. In 1972, David Dilks noted
       that Cadogan 'looked on Yalta much as he had looked at Munich. Both
       agreements entailed serious injury to the rights of states which could not
       defend themselves against large and predatory neighbours; both reflected the
       military and geographical facts; neither was a matter for pride or for fierce self-
       reproach, since it hardly lay in British power at the material time to do other;
       both looked better on signature than in the hard after-light.' David Dilks (ed.),
       The Diaries of Sir Alexander Cadogan, 1938–194 (London: Cassell, 1971),
       p. 633.

143   Taylor, *The Origins of the Second World War*, p. 235. Many supporters of
       appeasement continued to defend Munich as a wholly justifiable last attempt
       at avoiding war. Sir Nevile Henderson, the British ambassador to Germany
       between 1937 and 1939, opined: 'Had Hitler stopped after Munich, co-
       operation with him would still have been possible, and the world might have
       ended by acclaiming his genius and by condoning some of the means by
       which he achieved his German ends.' Nevile Henderson, *Failure of a Mission:
       Berlin 1937–1939* (London: Hodder and Stoughton, 1940), pp. 294-5. Even
       after the war had broken out, Henderson had acclaimed many of Hitler's
       'social reforms' for being on 'highly advanced democratic lines' whilst noting
       that 'the unity of Great Germany was a reality that had to be faced'. In the
       long-term, Henderson believed: 'History alone will determine whether Herr
       Hitler could have diverted Nazism into normal channels, whether he was the
       victim of the movement which he had initiated, or whether it was his own
       megalomania which had driven it beyond the limits which civilisation was
       prepared to tolerate.' Cmd. 6115, Germany No. 1 (1939), *Final Report by the
       Right Honourable Nevile Henderson G.C.M.G. on the circumstances leading
       to the termination of his mission to Berlin, September 20, 1939* (London:
       HMSO, 1939), pp. 2, 3.

144   The so-called Cliveden Set (a term apparently coined by the Communist
       journalist Claud Cockburn) was but the most high profile of the Establishment
       proponents of appeasement. This group consisted of an aristocratic

Germanophile social network. Cockburn later referred to Lords Astor, Halifax, Londonderry and Lothian as leading members of the group. He noted that, after the *Cagoulards*, people had taken to referring to them as 'Cagoulords'. Cockburn later termed anyone who sought to advance the career or goals of Hitler as a 'Clivedenite'. Claud Cockburn, *The Devil's Decade* (London: Sidgwick & Jackson, 1973), p. 229. See also, Norman Rose, *The Cliveden Set: Portrait of an Exclusive Fraternity* (London: Pimlico, 2011). Noel Annan dismissed the notion of the Cliveden Set as a conspiracy of appeasers as typical Cockburn rumour-mongering. Annan, *Our Age*, p. 197. Note: The *Cagoulards* were members of a 1930s French fascist organization (the *Comité secret d'action révolutionnaire*). They received the name Cagoulards from the word *cagoule*, a hood worn by members of the organization at secret meetings.

145 E. H. Carr, *The Twenty Years' Crisis: An Introduction to the Study of International Relations* (London: Macmillan, 1940), p. 186.

146 John Bright, Birmingham, 29 October 1858, J. E. Thorold Rogers (ed.), *Speeches on Questions of Public Policy by John Bright, M.P.* (London: Macmillan, 2nd edn, 1869), p. 399.

147 Churchill, *The Gathering Storm*, p. 38.

148 Watt, 'Churchill and Appeasement', pp. 199, 211, 214.

149 Carr quoted in Walter Laqueur, *The Fate of the Revolution: Interpretations of Soviet History from 1917 to the Present* (New York: Scribner's, 1987), p. 114.

150 *Hansard*, 5th Series, HC Deb, v. 482, c. 1367, 14 December 1950.

151 Harold Macmillan, *The Blast of War 1939–1945* (London: Macmillan, 1967), p. 3.

152 Ian Hall argues that the appeasement of the 1930s caused the political ideology of 'realism' to fall into disrepute in the United Kingdom (which he contrasts with the concept's postwar ascendancy in the United States). Ian Hall, 'Power Politics and Appeasement: Political Realism in British International Thought, c. 1935–1955', *British Journal of Politics and International Relations*, 8.2 (2006), pp. 174–92. See also Lucian M. Ashworth, 'Did the Idealist-Realist Debate Really Happen? A Revisionist History of International Relations' in Brian C. Schmidt (ed.), *International Relations and the First Great Debate* (Abingdon: Routledge, 2012), pp. 67–70.

153 W. N. Medlicott, *British Foreign Policy since Versailles: 1919–1963* (London: Methuen, 1968), p. xix.

Chapter 1

1 David Carlton, 'Churchill and the Two Evil Empires' in David Cannadine and Roland Quinault (eds), *Winston Churchill in the Twenty First Century* (Cambridge: Cambridge University Press, 2004), p. 176.

2 Note by Cabinet Secretary, Sir Norman Brook. Gill Bennett, *Six Moments of Crisis: Inside British Foreign Policy* (Oxford: Oxford University Press, 2013), p. 11.

3   Diary entry for 21 June 1941. John Colville, *The Fringes of Power: Downing Street Diaries: Volume One: 1939-October 1941* (London: Sceptre, 1986), p. 480.

4   Of such processes, Arnold Wolfers later noted: 'Some weak countries seek safety by getting on the bandwagon of an ascending power, hoping somehow to escape complete subjugation once their powerful "friend" has gained supremacy.' Arnold Wolfers, 'The Balance of Power in Theory and Practice' in his *Discord and Collaboration: Essays on International Politics* (Baltimore, MD: Johns Hopkins University Press, 1962), p. 124.

5   Lothar Kettenacker, 'The Anglo-Soviet Alliance and the Problem of Germany, 1941–1945', *Journal of Contemporary History*, 17.3 (1982), p. 435. Following the invasion of the USSR in 1941, an editorial in *The Times* laid out the brutal realities of the international situation and the prospects for a lasting peace. 'Those who made the Vienna settlement of 1815 were less affected by sentiment and took less account of abstract ideals than [did] the peace-makers of Versailles. But the settlement proved more enduring because it was based on a shrewder estimate of the relative strength of the principal European powers. No peace settlement can last which is not rooted in the realities of power.' The piece concluded that: 'the direct community of interest created by Hitler's invasion [of the USSR] can be projected onto the future and becomes applicable to the future settlement of Europe. Leadership in Eastern Europe is essential if the disorganization of the past twenty years is to be avoided [and this] leadership can fall to only Germany or to Russia.' Editorial: 'Peace and Power', *The Times*, 1 August 1941. Following such logic, Churchill informed Roosevelt that, with regard to the territorial acquisitions made by Stalin since 1 September 1939, it was necessary to exempt the Soviet Union from the provisions of the Atlantic Charter. Churchill to Roosevelt, 7 March 1942. Francis L. Loewenheim, Harold D. Langley and Manfred Jonas (eds), *Roosevelt and Churchill: Their Secret Wartime Correspondence* (London: Barrie and Jenkins, 1975), p. 186. This proposed appeasement of Stalin effectively invalidated Churchill and Roosevelt's express 'desire to see no territorial changes that do not accord with the freely expressed wishes of the peoples concerned'. Atlantic Charter, joint declaration by Churchill and Roosevelt, 14 August 1941. Ellis Wasson (ed.), *Sources and Debates in Modern British History: 1714 to the Present* (Oxford: Wiley-Blackwell, 2012), p. 218.

6   Curtis Keeble, *Britain, the Soviet Union and Russia* (New York: St. Martin's Press, 2000), p. xii. On wartime relations, see Graham Ross (ed.), *The Foreign Office and the Kremlin: British Documents on Anglo-Soviet Relations 1941–45* (Cambridge: Cambridge University Press, 1984).

7   Josef Foschepoth, 'British Interest in the Division of Germany after the Second World War', *Journal of Contemporary History*, 21.3 (1986), pp. 391–2. The British were careful not to provoke the Soviet Union in any way. In 1943 Peter Loxley, private secretary to the FO permanent secretary, informed Valentine Vivian, deputy head of SIS, that it was important that SIS must not operate in the Soviet Union, 'despite Soviet espionage in this country'. Loxley to Vivian, 20 October 1943. Keith Jeffery, *MI6: The History of the Secret intelligence Service 1909–1949* (London: Bloomsbury, 2010), p. 566.

8 As foreseen by Josef Goebbels, Nazi minister of propaganda. See Josef Goebbels, 'Das politische Bürgertum vor der Entscheidung', *Das Reich*, 4 February 1945.

9 On the postwar history of Britain and Munich, see R. Gerald Hughes, 'The Ghosts of Appeasement: Britain and the legacy of the Munich Agreement', *Journal of Contemporary History*, 48.4 (2013), pp. 688–716.

10 TNA: PRO: FCO 33/ 2165, Western Department brief for Douglas-Home for NATO Council, 11 June 1973.

11 Andrei Mertsalov, *Munich: Mistake or Cynical Calculation? Contemporary Non-Marxist Historians on the Munich Agreement of 1938* (Moscow: Novosti Press Agency, 1988), p. 69. Mertsalov was a member of the Institute of History of the Academy of Sciences of the USSR.

12 On this, see Benjamin B. Fischer, 'The Katyn Controversy: Stalin's Killing Field', *Studies in Intelligence*, 43.3 (1999/2000), pp. 61–70; George Sanford, *Katyń and the Soviet Massacre of 1940: Truth, Justice and Memory* (London: Routledge, 2005); and Anna M. Cienciala, Natalia S. Lebedeva and Wojciech Materski (eds), *Katyn: A Crime Without Punishment* (New Haven, CT: Yale University Press, 2007); Allen Paul, *Katyń: Stalin's Massacre and the Triumph of Truth* (DeKalb, IL: Northern Illinois University Press, 2010); and Alexander Etkind, Rory Finnin et al., *Remembering Katyń* (Cambridge: Polity Press, 2012).

13 Diary entry for 14 April 1943, *The Goebbels Diaries*, trans. and ed. Louis P. Lochner (London: Hamish Hamilton, 1948), p. 253.

14 Janusz K. Zawodny, *Death in the Forest: The Story of the Katyn Forest Massacre* (Notre Dame, IN: University of Notre Dame Press, 1962), p. 15.

15 Eden-Sikorski meeting, 24 April 1943. Halik Kochanski, *The Eagle Unbowed: Poland and the Poles in the Second World War* (London: Penguin, 2013), pp. 339–40. Churchill also warned Sikorski against protesting directly to Stalin. Martin Gilbert, *Road to Victory: Winston S. Churchill 1941–1945* (London: Heinemann, 1986), p. 385. On Polish despair over British reactions to Katyń, see the interview with Edward Raczyński, Polish minister of foreign affairs in London between 1941 and 1943: Michael Charlton, *The Eagle and the Small Birds: Crisis in the Soviet Empire: From Yalta to Solidarity* (London: BBC, 1984), pp. 16–9, 27–9.

16 TNA: PRO: FO 371/ 34568 [C 4230/258/G55] memorandum of conversation between the prime minister and General Sikorski, 15 April 1943.

17 Edward Raczyński, *In Allied London: The Wartime Diaries of the Polish Ambassador* (London: Weidenfeld and Nicolson, 1962), p. 140.

18 TNA: PRO: PREM 3/ 353 [C6160/258/55] and TNA: PRO: FO 371/ 34577 [C1660/258/5] O'Malley to Eden, Tel. No. 51, 24 May 1943.

19 George Orwell: 'Who Are the War Criminals?' (*Tribune*, 22 October 1943), *The Collected Essays, Journalism and Letters of George Orwell: volume 2: My Country Right or Wrong*, ed. Sonia Orwell and Ian Angus (London: Penguin, 1970), p. 367. Italics in the original.

20 Robert Rhodes James, *Anthony Eden* (London: Papermac, 1987), p. 281.

21 Romania (USSR: 90%), Bulgaria (USSR: 75%, later changed to 80%), Greece (Britain: 90%). Hungary and Yugoslavia (50% each, although Hungary later

changed to USSR: 80%). Winston S. Churchill, *The Second World War, Volume 6, Triumph and Tragedy* (London: Cassell, 1954), p. 198. See also Albert Resis, 'The Churchill-Stalin Secret "Percentages" Agreement on the Balkans, Moscow, October 1944', *American Historical Review*, 83.2 (1978), pp. 368–87; Panos Tsakaloyannis, 'The Moscow Puzzle', *Journal of Contemporary History*, 21.1 (1986), pp. 37–55; P. G. H. Holdich, 'A Policy of Percentages? British Policy in the Balkans after the Moscow Conference of October 1944', *International History Review*, 9.1 (1987), pp. 28–47; K. G. M. Ross, 'The Moscow Conference of October 1944 (Tolstoy)' in William Deakin, Elisabeth Barker and Jonathan Chadwick (eds), *British Political and Military Strategy in Central, Eastern and Southern Europe in 1944* (London: Macmillan, 1988), pp. 67–77.

22 Henry Kissinger, *Diplomacy* (New York: Simon and Schuster, 1994), p. 414. Sir Ian Jacob, assistant secretary to the war cabinet, later noted that there was nothing that could stop Soviet domination of central and eastern Europe, 'other than starting a war'. Charlton, *The Eagle and the Small Birds*, p. 42. For a superior recent account of the ruthless creation of the Soviet empire in Europe, see Anne Applebaum, *Iron Curtain: the Crushing of Eastern Europe, 1944–56* (London: Allen Lane, 2012). On Communist repression in central and eastern Europe, see Mark Kramer (ed.), *The Black Book of Communism: Crimes, Terror, Repression* (Cambridge, MA: Harvard University Press, 1999), pp. 363–456.

23 Cato, *Guilty Men* (London: Victor Gollancz, 1940), p. 60.

24 David Reynolds, *Summits: Six Meetings that Shaped the Twentieth Century* (New York: Basic Books, 2007), p. 145.

25 Frank Roberts, *Dealing with Dictators* (London: Weidenfeld and Nicolson, 1991), p. 76; John Charmley, 'Neville Chamberlain and the Consequences of the Churchillian Hegemony' in Frank McDonough (ed.), *Origins of the Second World War: An International Perspective* (London: Continuum, 2011), p. 183; Nikolai Tolstoy, *Victims of Yalta* (London: Corgi, rev. edn 1979), p. 96–7.

26 TNA: PRO: FO 954/20A, McCallum to Eden, 31 January 1944; Walter Lippmann, 'Today and Tomorrow', *Herald Tribune*, 5 April 1955. Ronald Steel, *Walter Lippmann and the American Century* (Boston, MA: Little, Brown & Co., 1980), p. 416.

27 A. J. P. Taylor, *'Diary', London Review of Books*, 1–14 April 1982, *An Old Man's Diary* (London: Hamish Hamilton, 1984), p. 72; A. J. P. Taylor, *English History 1914–1945* (Oxford: Oxford University Press, 2nd edn, 1975), p. 475; on the Polish protest against Yalta, see Kochanski, *The Eagle Unbowed*, p. 506. Gladwyn Jebb later indicted President Franklin Roosevelt and Harry Hopkins, FDR's unofficial emissary to Churchill, as the chief appeasers of Stalin – before, during and after Yalta. Charlton, *The Eagle and the Small Birds*, p. 44.

28 *Hansard*, HC Deb, 5th Series, v. 408, c. 1303, 1304–5, 1307, 27 February 1945. Dunglass, no friend of Churchill, had been Chamberlain's parliamentary private secretary at the time of Munich. Despite the fact that Dunglass had been at Munich, and remained loyal to Chamberlain, his past was never really a handicap to his future career. D. R. Thorpe, *Supermac: The Life of Harold MacMillan* (London: Chatto and Windus, 2010), p. 135.

29 Diary entry for 27 February 1945. Nigel Nicolson (ed.), *The Harold Nicolson Diaries 1907–1964* (London: Phoenix, 2005), p. 345. Against this, 'Chips'

Channon noted: 'I am horrified by the inconsistency of some Members of Parliament, members of society, who went about abusing Mr Chamberlain about appeasement in 1938 and 1939 and now meekly accept this surrender to Soviet Russia.' Diary entry for 28 February 1945. Robert Rhodes James (ed.), *'Chips': The Diaries of Sir Henry Channon* (London: Phoenix, 1996), pp. 398–9.

30 Taylor, *English History 1914–1945*, p. 716. On opposition to Yalta in Britain, see Fraser J. Harbutt, *Yalta 1945: Europe and America at the Crossroads* (Cambridge: Cambridge University Press, 2010), pp. 334–5.

31 A. L. Rowse, 'The summing up – Churchill's place in history' in Charles Eade (ed.), *Churchill by his Contemporaries* (London: Hutchinson, 1953), p. 504; Charlton, *The Eagle and the Small Birds*, p. 44. Basil Liddell Hart warned Eden: 'the situation into which we are getting is even more crazy than that of 1938–39'. Richard Carr, *Veteran MPs and Conservative Politics in the aftermath of the Great War: The Memory of All That* (Farnham: Ashgate, 2013), p. 168.

32 Diplomaticus (Konni Zilliacus), *Can the Tories Win the Peace? And How They Lost the Last One* (London: Victor Gollancz, 1945), pp. 19–20.

33 On this, see R. B. McCallum and Alison Readman, *The British General Election of 1945* (London: Oxford University Press, 1947); and Scott Kelly, 'The Ghost of Neville Chamberlain': Guilty Men and the 1945 Election', *Conservative History Journal*, 4 (2005), pp. 18–24.

34 R. M. Douglas, *The Labour Party, Nationalism and Internationalism, 1939–1951* (London: Routledge, 2004), pp. 141–2.

35 Kelly, 'The Ghost of Neville Chamberlain', pp. 22, 23. Quote at p. 23.

36 Quintin Hogg, *The Left Was Never Right* (London: Faber & Faber, 1945), pp. 183–4.

37 Harold Macmillan, *Tides of Fortune 1945–1955* (London: Macmillan, 1969), pp. 31–2.

38 Peter Hennessy, *Never Again: Britain, 1945–51* (London: Jonathan Cape, 1992), p. 67. Hennessy, it should be noted, is far less convinced on this score (pp. 56–86).

39 Anne Deighton, 'Britain and the Cold War, 1945–1955' in Melvyn P. Leffler and Odd Arne Westad (eds), *The Cambridge History of the Cold War, Volume I: Origins* (Cambridge: Cambridge University Press, 2010), pp. 118–22.

40 John H. Herz, 'The Relevancy and Irrelevancy of Appeasement', *Social Research*, 31.3 (1964), p. 296.

41 Paul Ward, *Red Flag and Union Jack: Englishness, Patriotism and the British Left, 1881–1924* (Woodbridge: RHS/Boydell Press, 1998), p. 202.

42 Ernest R. May, *'Lessons' of the Past: The Use and Misuse of History in American Foreign Policy* (New York: Oxford University Press, 1973), p. 33. Such sentiments were driven by the 'shame' of Yalta. On this, see Athan G. Theoharis, *The Yalta Myths: An Issue in U.S. Politics, 1945–1955* (Columbia, MO: University of Missouri Press, 1970).

43 David Reynolds, *From World War to Cold War: Churchill, Roosevelt, and the International History of the 1940s* (Oxford: Oxford University Press, 2006), p. 280.

44 On this, see Wolfram Kaiser, 'Against Napoleon and Hitler: Background Influences on British Diplomacy' in Wolfram Kaiser and Gillian Staerck (eds), *British Foreign Policy 1955–64: Contracting Options* (Basingstoke: Macmillan, 2000), pp. 110–31. With regard to Philip II, Louis XIV, Napoleon and Wilhelm II, Churchill made just this point to the Conservative Committee on Foreign Affairs in March 1936. On this, see John Charmley, 'Traditions of Conservative Foreign Policy' in Geoffrey Hicks (ed.), *Conservatism and British Foreign Policy: The Derbys and Their World* (Farnham: Ashgate, 2011), p. 215.

45 On this, see F. H. Hinsley, *Power and the Pursuit of Peace: Theory and Practice in the History of Relations between States* (Cambridge: Cambridge University Press, 1963), esp. pp. 153–85.

46 *Hansard*, HC Deb, 5th Series, v. 437, c. 1965, 16 May 1947.

47 Mark Phythian, *The Labour Party, War and International Relations, 1945–2006* (London: Routledge, 2007), p. 29

48 Remarks at Cabinet Committee GEN75, 25 October 1946. Peter Hennessy, *Cabinets and the Bomb* (Oxford: Oxford University Press 2007), p. 48; Kenneth O. Morgan, *Britain Since 1945: The People's Peace* (Oxford: Oxford University Press, 2001), p. 54; Alex Danchev, 'In the Back Room: Anglo-American Defence Cooperation, 1945–1951' in Richard J. Aldrich (ed.), *British Intelligence, Strategy and the Cold War, 1945–51* (London: Routledge, 1992), p. 221; Robert H. Paterson, *Britain's Strategic Nuclear Deterrent: From before the V-Bomber to Beyond Trident* (London: Frank Cass, 1997), p. 117.

49 Meeting with General Lucius Clay, US Military Governor, and General Pierre Koenig, French Military Governor, 31 March 1948. *Foreign Relations of the United States (FRUS)*, 1948, Vol. II: *Germany and Austria* (Washington DC: US Government Printing Office, 1973), p. 159.

50 On Britain's role here, see Avi Shlaim, 'Britain, the Berlin Blockade and the Cold War', *International Affairs*, 60.1 (1983–4), pp. 1–14.

51 On Britain and the creation of NATO, see TNA: PRO: CAB/129/30, CP. (48) 249, 'North Atlantic Treaty and Western Union', memorandum by Bevin, 2 November 1948; and John Baylis, *The Diplomacy of Pragmatism: Britain and the Formation of NATO, 1942–1949* (Basingstoke: Macmillan, 1993).

52 Robert Skidelsky, 'Going to War with Germany: Between Revisionism & Orthodoxy', *Encounter*, 39.1 (1972), p. 58.

53 On this, see TNA: PRO: CAB/128/15, CM. (49) 19th Conclusions, 10 March 1949; and Alan Bullock, *Ernest Bevin: Foreign Secretary 1945–1951* (New York: W.W. Norton, 1983), pp. 513–682.

54 Alan Bullock, 'Ernest Bevin, Foreign Secretary', *The Listener*, 14 October 1982. See also Bullock, *Ernest Bevin*, pp. 571–80, 588–94.

55 Shlaim, 'Britain, the Berlin Blockade and the Cold War', p. 3.

56 *Hansard*, HC Deb, 5th Series, v. 446, c. 384, 22 January 1948.

57 *Hansard*, HC Deb, 5th Series, v. 452, c. 2233, 30 June 1948.

58 *Hansard*, HC Deb, 5th Series, v. 452, c. 2218, 30 June 1948.

59 TNA: PRO: CAB/128/13, CM. (48) 54th Conclusions, 26 July 1948.

60 TNA: PRO: CAB/128/17, CM. (50) 39th Conclusions, 27 June 1950.

61 Winston S. Churchill, *The Second World War, Volume I, The Gathering Storm* (London: Cassell, 8th edn, 1966 [1948]), p. 16.

62 Melvyn P. Leffler, *A Preponderance of Power: National Security, the Truman Administration, and the Cold War* (Stanford, CA: Stanford University Press, 1992), p. 21.

63 Jeremi Suri, *Henry Kissinger and the American Century* (Cambridge, MA: Harvard University Press, 2007), p. 19.

64 Richard E. Neustadt and Ernest R. May, *Thinking in Time: The Uses of History for Decision Makers* (New York: The Free Press, 1986), pp. 41, 89.

65 Harry S. Truman, *Memoirs, Volume Two, Years of Trial and Hope* (New York: Doubleday, 1956), pp. 332–3.

66 On 12 January 1950, in a speech entitled 'Crisis in China – An Examination of United States Policy', Secretary of State Dean Acheson said of the Communist victory of October 1949: 'Many [people], . . . bewildered by events in China, failed to understand the [situation and] looked for esoteric causes, and charged American bungling. No one in his right mind could believe that the Nationalist regime had been overthrown by superior military force.' Dean Acheson, *Present at the Creation: My Years at the State Department* (New York: W.W. Norton 1969), p. 355.

67 Quoted in Robert J. Donovan, *The Tumultuous Years: The Presidency of Harry S. Truman, 1949–53* (New York: W.W. Norton, 1982), p. 256.

68 Kenneth Harris, *Attlee* (London: Weidenfeld & Nicolson, 1995), pp. 156–7; Nicklaus Thomas-Symonds, *Attlee: A Life in Politics* (London: I.B. Tauris, 2012), p. 86.

69 C. R. Attlee, *As It Happened* (London: William Heinemann, 1954), pp. 91–2. By the end of the Second World War, Attlee and Bevin 'were . . . acutely aware of the combination of Russian old-time and Communist modern Imperialism which threatened the peace of Europe'. Attlee, *As It Happened*, pp. 146–7.

70 Bullock, *Ernest Bevin*, p. 813; Thomas-Symonds, *Attlee*, pp. 196–7.

71 TNA: PRO: FO 371/ 84091, Kenneth Younger, minister of state at the FO, to Ernest Bevin, 11 July 1950.

72 Martin Gilbert, *Winston S. Churchill: Never Despair, 1945–1965* (London: William Heinemann, 1987), pp. 535–59.

73 'Yardstick from Tokyo', *Life*, 4 December 1950. On 6 January 1950 the Attlee government recognized Mao Zedong's People's Republic of China. TNA: PRO: CAB/128/16, CM. (49) 72nd Conclusions, 15 December 1949. This had been agreed in Cabinet on the recommendation of Ernest Bevin. On this, see TNA: PRO: CAB/129/37, CP. (39) 214, 'Recognition of the Chinese Communist Government', memorandum by Ernest Bevin, 24 October 1949; and TNA: PRO: CAB/129/37, CP. (49) 248, 'Recognition of the Chinese Communist Government', memorandum by Ernest Bevin, 12 December 1949.

74 TNA: PRO: CAB/129/37, CP. (39) 214, 'Recognition of the Chinese Communist Government', memorandum by Ernest Bevin, 24 October 1949.

75 Zhong-ping Feng, *The British Government's China Policy, 1945–1950* (Keele: Ryburn, 1994), p. 9.

76 For a comparative study of Anglo-American attitudes towards China between 1949 and 1972, see Victor S. Kaufman, *Confronting Communism: U.S. and British Policies toward China* (Columbia, MO: University of Missouri Press, 2001).

77 On this, see Herbert W. Briggs, '*Relations Officieuses* and Intent to Recognize: British Recognition of Franco', *The American Journal of International Law*, 34.1 (1940), pp. 47–57.

78 Ritchie Ovendale, 'Britain and the Cold War in Asia' in Ritchie Ovendale (ed.), *The Foreign Policy of the British Labour Government, 1945–1951* (Leicester: Leicester University Press, 1984), p. 130.

79 M. L. Dockrill, 'The Foreign Office, Anglo-American Relations and the Korean War, June 1950–June 1951', *International Affairs*, 62.3 (1986), p. 466.

80 Callum Macdonald, *Korea: The War before Vietnam* (London: Macmillan, 1986), p. 75; Bullock, *Ernest Bevin*, pp. 820–2, 825.

81 TNA: PRO: FO 800/ 517, Strachey to Bevin, 2 January 1951.

82 Peter Lowe, 'The Significance of the Korean War in Anglo-American Relations, 1950–53' in Michael Dockrill and John Young (eds), *British Foreign Policy: 1945–56* (Basingstoke: Macmillan, 1989), p. 126.

83 TNA: PRO: CAB/128/17, CM. (50) 39th Conclusions, 27 June 1950.

84 *Life's* Tokyo correspondent wrote the editorial piece.

85 *Postwar Foreign Policy Preparation, 1939–45* (Washington, DC: Department of State, Publication No. 3580, 1950), p. 14.

86 Editorial: 'Yardstick from Tokyo', *Life*, 4 December 1950.

87 Leffler, *A Preponderance of Power*, p. 405.

88 Kenneth O. Morgan, 'Labour and the Special Relationship' in *Ages of Reform: Dawns and Downfalls of the British Left* (London: I.B. Tauris, 2011), p. 186. Churchill had seemingly advocated the threat of the use of nuclear weapons to force a withdrawal of the Soviets from Berlin in 1948. Shlaim, 'Britain, the Berlin Blockade and the Cold War', p. 4.

89 Roger Dingman, 'Atomic Diplomacy during the Korean War', *International Security*, 13.3 (1988–9), p. 67.

90 TNA: PRO: PREM 8/ 1560, 'Top Secret – Record of Washington Talks – Atomic Weapons', 4 December 1950.

91 In late 1949 Bevin had accepted that the US government would not approve of British recognition of the PRC: 'The United States Government felt strongly that as long as there was any opposition to the Communist régime it would be a stab in the back if recognition were to be accorded.' TNA: PRO: CAB/129/37 CP. (49) 248, 'Recognition of the Chinese Communist Government', 12 December 1949.

92 'No Appeasement in Korean War, Attlee Avers', *Prescott Evening Courier*, 6 December 1950.

93 On this, see R. Ovendale, 'Britain, the United States, and the Recognition of Communist China', *Historical Journal*, 26.1 (1983), pp. 139–58.

94 Harry S. Truman Library, Independence, MO (HSTL): 'Selected Records Relating to the Korean War', statement by Truman, 27 June 1950.

95 TNA: PRO: PREM 8/ 1357, COS (50) 357, 'Soviet Interceptor Fighter Aircraft Development', note by the Chief of Air Staff, Marshal of the Royal Air Force John Slessor, 17 November 1950. 25 Nene and 30 Derwent engines were exported to the USSR.

96 Adam B. Ulam, *Stalin: The Man and His Era* (London: Tauris Parke, 2007 [1989]), p. 709.

97 Stanley Sandler, *The Korean War: No Victors, No Vanquished* (Lexington, KY: University of Kentucky Press, 1999), p. 175.

98 In 1950, the Coordinating Committee for Multilateral Export Controls (CoCom) was established. Its member states were Australia, Belgium, Canada, Denmark, France, West Germany, Greece, Italy, Japan, Luxembourg, Netherlands, Norway, Portugal, Spain, Turkey, the United Kingdom and the United States. On this, see Yoko Yasuhara, 'The Myth of Free Trade: The Origins of COCOM 1945–1950', *The Japanese Journal of American Studies*, 4 (1991), pp. 127–48; and Michael Mastanduno, *Economic Containment: CoCom and the Politics of East-West Trade* (Ithaca, NY: Cornell University Press, 1992).

99 Under Secretary of State George Ball told President Johnson in 1964 that British government export credits to Cuba had been granted despite the fact that Cuba was not regard as being credit worthy. Given that the export was not in the British national interest either, he was confident that he could prevail upon the British to desist from such exports to Cuba in the future. US National Archives College Park (NACP), College Park, MD: White House meeting between President Johnson, Under Secretary of State Ball, Secretary of State Rusk, Secretary of Defense McNamara, DCI McCone (CIA), Colonel King (CIA) and Desmond Fitzgerald (CIA), 1 April 1964.

100 NACP: SNIE 3–11/12–82, 'The Soviet Gas Pipeline in Perspective', CIA SNIE, 21 September 1982.

101 Campbell Craig, *Glimmer of a New Leviathan: Total War in the Realism of Niebuhr, Morgenthau, and Waltz* (New York: Columbia University Press, 2003), p. ix.

102 The phrase most notably associated with the American strategist Herman Kahn; see especially his *Thinking about the Unthinkable* (London: Weidenfeld & Nicolson, 1962).

103 'Mr Baldwin on Aerial Warfare – A Fear for the Future', *The Times*, 11 November 1932. Baldwin stated: 'I think it is well also for the man in the street to realise that there is no power on earth that can protect him from being bombed. Whatever people may tell him, the bomber will always get through, and it is very easy to understand that, if you realise the area of space.' *Hansard*, HC Deb, 5th Series, v. 270, c. 632, 10 November 1932. Ironically, a 1963 study concluded that the recent advances in defensive countermeasures meant that 'the [British 'V'] bomber will not always get through', and thus advocated that Britain prioritize the Polaris SSBN force. Robert E. Hunter, *The World Today*, 19.3 (1963), pp. 98–107.

104 On this, see Uri Bialer, *The Shadow of the Bomber: The Fear of Air Attack and British Politics, 1932–39* (London: Royal Historical Society, 1980).

105 Norman Maclean, *How Shall We Escape? Learn or Perish* (London: Hodder and Stoughton, 1934), pp. 174–5. Quoted in Richard Overy, 'Saving Civilization: British Opinion and the Coming of War in 1939' in David Welch and Jo Fox (eds), *Justifying War: Propaganda, Politics and War in the Modern Age* (Basingstoke: Palgrave Macmillan, 2012), p. 185.

106 Kirk Willis, 'The Origins of British Nuclear Culture, 1895–1939', *Journal of British Studies*, 34.1 (1995), pp. 59–89. Quotes at pp. 82, 83.

107 Thomas Schelling, *The Strategy of Conflict* (Cambridge, MA: Harvard University Press, 1960), pp. 188, 194. Bertrand Russell denounced this as madness. In 1959 he wrote: 'Since the nuclear stalemate became apparent, the governments of East and West have adopted the policy which Mr. Dulles calls "brinkmanship". This is a policy adapted from a sport which, I am told, is practiced by some youthful degenerates. This sport is called "Chicken"!' Bertrand W. Russell, *Common Sense and Nuclear Warfare* (London: George Allen & Unwin, 1959), p. 30.

108 Chamberlain radio broadcast: 27 September 1938. 'How horrible, fantastic, incredible it is that we should be digging trenches and trying on gas masks here because of a quarrel in a far-away country between people of whom we know nothing. It seems still more impossible that a quarrel which has already been settled in principle should be the subject of war.' Neville Chamberlain, *In Search of Peace* (New York: G.P. Putnam's, 1939), p. 393.

109 A. J. P. Taylor, *A Personal History* (London: Coronet, 1984), p. 174.

110 On this era, see Cecelia Lynch, *Beyond Appeasement: Interpreting Interwar Peace Movements in World Politics* (Ithaca, NY: Cornell University Press, 1999).

111 Quoted in Beatrice Heuser, *The Evolution of Strategy: Thinking War from Antiquity to the Present* (Cambridge: Cambridge University Press, 2010), p. 358.

112 Ken Booth, 'Bernard Brodie' in John Baylis and John Garnett (eds), *Makers of Nuclear Strategy* (London: Pinter, 1991), pp. 19–56.

113 Bernard Brodie, *The Absolute Weapon: Atomic Power and World Order* (New York: Harcourt, 1946), p. 76.

114 James, *Anthony Eden*, p. 339. The Labour-supporting *Daily Mirror* newspaper coined the phrase, for which Churchill later won a libel case against it. On this episode, see Gilbert, *Never Despair*, p. 648.

115 D. R. Thorpe, *Eden: The Life and Times of Anthony Eden First Earl of Avon, 1897–1977* (London: Chatto and Windus, 2003), p. 360. Eden later said the Opposition charges over Suez were 'unworthy . . . a cruel and unjust charge. It echoes the 1951 accusations of warmongering'. *Hansard*, HC Deb, 5th Series, v. 558, c. 298, 13 September 1956.

116 James, *Anthony Eden*, pp. 338–9. On the 1937 National Defence Contribution, see Robert P. Shay, Jr., 'Chamberlain's Folly: The National Defence Contribution of 1937', *Albion*, 7.4 (1975), pp. 317–27.

117 Churchill speech in Plymouth (Devonport), 23 October 1951. Robert Rhodes James (ed.), *Winston S. Churchill: His Complete Speeches, 1897–1963: Volume VIII: 1950–1963* (London: Chelsea House Publishers, 1974), p. 8282.

118　Sir Robert Vansittart was a senior diplomat in the period before and during the Second World War (principal private secretary to the prime minister, 1928–30; permanent under-secretary at the FO, 1930–8) and a staunch enemy of Chamberlainite appeasement and, indeed, of the German people.

119　*Hansard*, HL Deb, 5th Series, v. 171, c. 619, 2 May 1951.

120　*Hansard*, HL Deb, 5th Series, v. 171, c. 683, 2 May 1951.

121　Gilbert, *Never Despair*, pp. 704–6.

122　TNA: PRO: CAB/128/26 (C.C. (53)), 46th Conclusions, 28 July 1953.

123　Alex Danchev, *On Specialness: Essays in Anglo-American Relations* (London: Macmillan, 1998), p. 126. Bevin told Nehru on 5 January 1951 that 'the United States is still a young country and the Administration was too apt to take unreflecting plunges. We had made it our business to try to restrain them.' Bevin minute, 5 January 1951, TNA: PRO: FO 371/ 92776.

124　Callum MacDonald, *Britain and the Korean War* (Oxford: Basil Blackwell, 1990), p. 95.

125　Nancy Bernkopf Tucker, *The China Threat: Memories, Myths, and Realities in the 1950s* (New York: Columbia University Press, 2012), p. 145.

126　Gilbert, *Never Despair*, pp. 917–18; Roy Jenkins, *Churchill* (London: Pan, 2002), p. 873.

127　Michael Lumbers, *Piercing the Bamboo Curtain: Tentative Bridge-Building to China during the Johnson Years* (Manchester: Manchester University Press, 2008), p. 56. Emphasis in the original.

Chapter 2

1　Henry A. Kissinger, *A World Restored: Metternich, Castlereagh and the Problems of Peace, 1812–1822* (Boston, MA: Houghton Mifflin, 1973 [1957]), p. 3.

2　General Omar Bradley, Armistice Day, 1948. Quoted in E. U. Condon, 'Scientists and the Federal Government', *Bulletin of Atomic Scientists*, 8.6 (1952), p. 180.

3　Quoted in James Cable, 'The Geneva Conference: After a Decent Interval' in Elizabeth Jane Errington and B. J. C. McKercher (eds), *The Vietnam War as History* (New York: Praeger, 1990), p. 43.

4　TNA: PRO: CAB/129/53 C (52) 202, 'British Overseas Obligations', memorandum by Sir Anthony Eden to Cabinet, 18 June 1952.

5　Ibid.

6　Klaus Larres, *Churchill's Cold War: The Politics of Personal Diplomacy* (New Haven, CT: Yale University Press, 2002), pp. 190–2.

7　*Hansard*, HC Deb, 5th Series, v. 515, c. 895, 897, 896, 11 May 1953.

8　*Hansard*, HC Deb, 5th Series, v. 515, c. 896, 11 May 1953. See also Gilbert, *Never Despair*, pp. 831–2; Heinrich Bodensieck (ed.), *Die Deutsche Frage seit dem Zweiten Weltkrieg* (Stuttgart: Klett, 1985), p. 57.

9 Yvonne Kipp, *Eden, Adenauer und die deutsche Frage: Britische Deutschlandpolitik im internationalen Spannungsfeld 1951–1957* (Paderborn u.a: Ferdinand Schöningh Verlag, 2002), p. 394.

10 See TNA: PRO: PREM 11/ 428; TNA: PRO: PREM 11/ 449; TNA: PRO: PREM 11/ 905. For discussion of the Federal Republic of Germany and Churchill's initiative, see Anthony Glees, 'Churchill's Last Gambit: What the "Secret Documents" Reveal about the Prime Minister's Adventurous Initiative in 1953 on the Reunification (and "Neutralisation"?) of Germany . . . and Why Dr. Adenauer Prevailed', *Encounter*, 64.4 (1985), pp. 27–35.

11 Dairy entry for 12 May 1953. *The Macmillan Diaries: The Cabinet Years 1950–1957*, ed. Peter Catterall (London: Pan, 2004), p. 232.

12 TNA: PRO: CAB/129/53 C (52) 202, 'British Overseas Obligations', memorandum by Sir Anthony Eden to Cabinet, 18 June 1952. Eden stressed only that it *might* be possible to reduce British forces in Germany in subsequent years. 'A further substantial alleviation might be possible in 1954 and subsequent years if the build-up of German contingents enables us to reduce British forces in Germany without endangering the common Western defence effort.' This, alas, ignored the alarm that a reduction in British forces might induce in the Federal Republic's erstwhile *Western* allies.

13 Ibid.

14 *FRUS 1952–1954*, volume VI, *Western Europe and Canada* (Washington, DC: United States Government Printing Office, 1986), pp. 964–75.

15 President Dwight D. Eisenhower letter and draft resolution to Vice President Richard M. Nixon and the speaker of the House, Representative Joseph W. Martin Jr. (R-MA), 20 February 1953. Zygmunt C. Szkopiak (ed.), *The Yalta Agreements: Documents prior to, during and after the Crimea Conference 1945* (London: The Polish Government in Exile, 1986), p. 152.

16 In 1987, the conservative policy analyst and writer Michael Johns opined: 'Ever since the Bolshevik Revolution, the negotiating process with the Soviets and their surrogates has proven an unmitigated disaster for the United States and its allies. From Yalta, where Roosevelt sold out Poland and the rest of Eastern Europe to Stalin, to the Paris peace talks, where North Vietnam signed an agreement it had no intention of following, the Soviets have used negotiations as a means of expanding their empire.' Michael Johns, 'Peace in Our Time: The Spirit of Munich Lives On', *Policy Review*, 41 (June 1987), p. 71.

17 On this, see Jeff Broadwater, *Eisenhower and the Anti-Communist Crusade* (Chapel Hill, NC: University of North Carolina Press), pp. 26–53.

18 Brian White, *Britain, Détente and Changing East–West Relations* (London: Routledge, 1992), p. 50. On this visit, see Thomas W. Maulucci, Jr., 'Konrad Adenauer's April 1953 Visit to the United States and the Limits of the German-American Relationship in the Early 1950s', *German Studies Review*, 26.3 (2003), pp. 577–96.

19 TNA: PRO: FO 800/ 794 [C 1074/ 14], Churchill-Adenauer meeting, 10 Downing Street, 15 May 1953; TNA: PRO: FO 371/ 103705 [C 1074/ 7] Adenauer press conference, London, 16 May 1953.

20 Klaus Larres, *Politik der Illusionen: Churchill, Eisenhower und die deutsche Frage, 1945–1955* (Göttingen: Vandenhoeck und Ruprecht, 1995), pp. 194–6.

21 Churchill to Eisenhower, 8 August 1953, Peter G. Boyle (ed.), *The Churchill-Eisenhower Correspondence, 1953–1955* (Chapel Hill, NC: University of North Carolina Press, 1990), p. 166.

22 Despite its failure, Coral Bell later heralded this moment as the birth of détente as a 'Western aspiration'. Coral Bell, *The Diplomacy of Détente* (London: Martin Robertson, 1977), pp. 6 ff. In 1977, Foreign Secretary David Owen highlighted how the Final Act of the Helsinki process (in 1975) had stabilized the international system, specifically tracing the roots of détente back to 1953 (David Owen speech, London, 3 March 1977). Cmnd. 6932, *Selected Documents Relating to Problems of Security and Cooperation in Europe 1954–77* (London: HMSO 1977), p. 334.

23 Sir William Hayter, *The Kremlin and the Embassy* (London: Hodder & Stoughton, 1966), p. 107. Gladwyn Jebb, ambassador to the United Nations between 1950 and 1954, disliked the moderate stance of Malenkov, suspecting the hand of the traitors Guy Burgess and Donald Maclean. Jebb thus informed Hayter that he was happy when Khrushchev and Bulganin initiated a tougher Soviet foreign policy. See Lord Gladwyn, *The Memoirs of Lord Gladwyn* (London: Weidenfeld and Nicolson, 1972), p. 277.

24 Lord Gladwyn, *The Memoirs of Lord Gladwyn*, pp. 277–8.

25 Michael Foot, *Aneurin Bevan 1897–1960*, ed. Brian Brivati (London: Indigo, 1997), pp. 457–8. Quote at p. 458.

26 Harold Macmillan, *Tides of Fortune 1945–1955* (London: Macmillan, 1969), p. 512.

27 Larres, *Churchill's Cold War*, pp. 251–2.

28 At this point in the speech, Labour MP Emrys Hughes called out 'Realism'. *Hansard*, HC Deb, 5th Series, v. 531, c. 799, 29 July 1954.

29 *Hansard*, HC Deb, 5th Series, v. 531, c. 799–800, 29 July 1954.

30 Larres, *Churchill's Cold War*, p. 252; Glees, 'Churchill's Last Gambit', p. 34.

31 Kipp, *Eden, Adenauer und die deutsche Frage*, pp. 155, 197.

32 On 11 July 1953 Adenauer told the *Bundestag*: 'I am very happy about the unanimity among the parties in the Bundestag that the content of the Potsdam agreement must be sharply rejected.' Quoted in GDR (ed.), *The Wall and Humanity* (East Berlin: GDR Information Office, 1962), p. 9.

33 Adenauer later recalled: 'It was my conviction that the Soviet Union aimed at a period of détente in order to solve the [inner] problems the Soviet leadership found itself confronted with. Yet, there was no indication the USSR had changed its inner goal . . . to conquer the world through communism.' Quoted in Klaus Larres 'Germany and the West: The "Rapallo factor" in German Foreign Policy from the 1950s to the 1990s' in Klaus Larres and Panikos Panayi (eds), *The Federal Republic of Germany since 1949: Politics, Society and Economy before and since Reunification* (London: Longman, 1996), p. 290(n).

34 Konrad Adenauer, *World Indivisible* (London: George Allen & Unwin, 1956), p. 36. Dean Rusk later recalled that Adenauer was the ultimate 'Cold Warrior', someone who was forever giving him books on the expansionist tendencies of the Slavs. John F. Kennedy Library, Boston, MA (hereafter JFKL), Oral History Project, Dean Rusk: interview number four by Denis O' Brien, Washington,

13 March 1970, p. 177. In 1961, Adenauer advised President John F.: 'In the centuries of Czars, at least since Peter the Great, Russia was already aggressive and intent upon constantly increasing its territory, especially towards the West . . . Communism has not weakened Russian nationalism; on the contrary, it has strengthened it. Mr. Khrushchev, too, in my opinion is primarily a Russian nationalist and only secondarily a Communist.' JFKL: POF Box 117, Adenauer to Kennedy, 4 October 1961.

35 F. S. Northedge and Audrey Wells, *Britain and Soviet Communism: The Impact of a Revolution* (London: Macmillan, 1982), p. 124.

36 Diary entry for 20 July 1954. *The Macmillan Diaries: The Cabinet Years 1950–1957*, p. 335.

37 D. R. Thorpe, *Eden: The Life and Times of Anthony Eden, First Earl of Avon 1897–1977* (London: Chatto, 2003), pp. 400–5. Sir Frank Roberts later recalled that Eden 'had one great year in 1954 – he got the Garter.' When making a list of Eden's achievements for 1954, Churchill nevertheless told Roberts: 'I know what you are going to say; you are going say that I haven't put Suez in. I don't think that it was an achievement.' Churchill College, Cambridge: British Diplomatic Oral History Programme (BDOHP): Sir Frank Roberts, interviewed by John Hutson, 3 July 1996, p. 17.

38 Sir Anthony Eden, *Full Circle: The Memoirs of Sir Anthony Eden* (London: Cassell, 1960), p. 188. The best account of the Trieste dispute is still Jean Baptiste Duroselle, *Le conflit de Trieste, 1943–1954* (Brussels: Éditions de L'Institut de sociologie de L'Université libre de Bruxelles, 1966).

39 TNA: PRO: CAB/128/28, C.C. 55, 23rd Conclusions, Cabinet meeting, 14 March 1955.

40 Larres, *Churchill's Cold War*, pp. 367–70; Eden, *Full Circle*, pp. 265–6.

41 Winston Churchill to Jock Colville, 4 April 1955. John Colville, *The Fringes of Power: Downing Street Diaries: Volume Two: 1941–April 1955* (London: Sceptre, 1987), p. 379. One might usefully compare Churchill's rhetoric here with that of Louis XV, who famously observed: 'Après moi, le deluge.'

42 Comment recorded in Richard Crossman's dairy, 7 April 1955. Janet Morgan (ed.), *The Backbench Diaries of Richard Crossman* (London: Hamish Hamilton and Jonathan Cape, 1981), p. 416. Walter Elliot (1888–1958) – a close friend of Eden – was a prominent Scottish Unionist Party (Conservative) MP who came close to resigning over the Munich Agreement.

Chapter 3

1 Sir Anthony Eden, *The Memoirs of Sir Anthony Eden: The Reckoning* (London: Cassell, 1965), p. 19.

2 On this, see Ian Pendlington, 'Waiting for Winston', *Conservative History Journal*, 6 (2007), pp. 13–14.

3 In 1929 Churchill had written of Lord Curzon: 'The morning had been golden; the noontide was bronze; and the evening lead. But all were solid, and

each was polished till it shone after its fashion.' Winston S. Churchill, *Great Contemporaries* (London: Odhams Press, 1947), p. 226.

4 D. R. Thorpe, 'What We Failed to Learn from Suez', *Daily Telegraph*, 1 November 2006.

5 The best single-volume history of Suez is Keith Kyle, *Suez: Britain's End of Empire in the Middle East* (London: I.B. Tauris, 2011 edn). See also David Carlton, *Britain and the Suez Crisis* (Oxford: Basil Blackwell, 1988); Wm. Roger Louis and Roger Owen (ed.), *Suez 1956: The Crisis and Its Consequences* (Oxford: Clarendon Press, 1989); W. Scott Lucas, *Divided We Stand: Britain, the United States and the Suez Crisis* (London: Hodder & Stoughton, 1991); Cole C. Kingseed, *Eisenhower and the Suez Crisis of 1956* (Baton Rouge, LA: Louisiana State University Press, 1995); Louise Richardson, *When Allies Differ: Anglo-American Relations during the Suez and Falklands Conflicts* (London: Macmillan, 1996); Diane B. Kunz, *The Economic Diplomacy of the Suez Crisis* (Chapel Hill, NC: University of North Carolina Press, 1991, 2009); Saul Kelly and Anthony Gorst (eds), *Whitehall and the Suez Crisis* (London: Frank Cass, 2000); Simon C. Smith (ed.), *Reassessing Suez 1956: New Perspectives on the Crisis and Its Aftermath* (Farnham: Ashgate, 2008).

6 Sue Onslow, *Backbench debate within the Conservative Party and its influence on British Foreign Policy, 1948–57* (Basingstoke: Macmillan, 1997), p. 122; David Dutton, *Anthony Eden: A Life and Reputation* (London: Arnold, 1997), p. 57; Hansard, HC Deb, 5th Series, v. 276, c. 617, 23 March 1933; Cadogan diary entry for 1 December 1941, David Dilks (ed.), *The Diaries of Sir Alexander Cadogan, 1938–1945* (London: Cassell, 1971), p. 415.

7 Patrick Cosgrave, *R.A. Butler: An English Life* (London: Quartet, 1981), p. 12.

8 TNA: PRO: CAB 129/54 C (52) 267, 'Suez Canal', memorandum by Sir Anthony Eden for the Cabinet, 28 July 1952.

9 Nicholas Bethell, *The Palestine Triangle: The Struggle between the British, the Jews and the Arabs, 1935–48* (London: Deutsch, 1979); Roza I. M. El-Eini, *Mandated Landscape: British Imperial Rule in Palestine, 1929–1948* (London: Routledge, 2006); Calder Walton, 'British Intelligence and the Mandate of Palestine: Threats to British National Security Immediately after the Second World War', *Intelligence and National Security*, 23.4 (2008), pp. 435–62. On British difficulties in Palestine, see TNA: PRO: FO/800/484 [T.93/45], Attlee to Truman, 16 September 1945.

10 For the relationship between Abadan and Suez within the Conservative Party, see Sue Onslow, 'Battlelines for Suez: the Conservatives and the Abadan crisis 1950–1951', *Contemporary British History*, 17.2 (2003), pp.1–28. The Abadan Crisis arose when Iran nationalized the Iranian assets of the Anglo-Iranian Oil Company (AIOC) and expelled Western companies from oil refineries in Abadan. In doing so, the Iranians abrogated an agreement that would have expired in 1993. Nikki R. Keddie, *Modern Iran: Roots and Results of Revolution* (New Haven, CT and London: Yale University Press, 2003), p. 101.

11 TNA: PRO: CAB 129/ 46, C.P. (51) 172, 'Persia: Seizure of Abadan Island', memorandum by the Chiefs of Staff, 29 June 1951.

12 See, for example, the Cabinet discussions at TNA: PRO: CAB 128/20, CM (51) 58th Conclusions, 4 September 1951.

13 C. R. Attlee, *As It Happened* (London: William Heinemann, 1954), pp. 175–6.

14 On this, see Wm. Roger Louis, 'Britain and the Overthrow of the Mosaddeq Government' and Mark J. Gasiorowski, 'The 1953 Coup d'État Against Mosaddeq' in Mark J. Gasiorowski and Malcolm Byrne (eds), *Mohammad Mosaddeq and the 1953 Coup in Iran* (New York: Syracuse University Press, 2004), pp. 126–77, 227–60; Fariborz Mokhtari, 'Iran's 1953 Coup Revisited: Internal Dynamics versus External Intrigue', *Middle East Journal*, 62.3 (2008), pp. 457–88.

15 The ailing Bevin was moved to the post of Lord Privy Seal in March 1951. He died a month later. Upon his demotion, he supposedly observed: 'I am neither a Lord, nor a Privy, nor a Seal.' Francis Beckett, *Clem Attlee* (London: Richard Cohen Books, 1997), p. 285.

16 TNA: PRO: CAB 128/20, CM (51) 58th Conclusions, 4 September 1951.

17 TNA: PRO: FO 371/ 98694, 'Anglo-US Joint Action Concerning Persian Oil', FO Minute, Sir James Bowker, Assistant Under-Secretary supervising Middle Eastern affairs, 23 August 1952.

18 Harry S. Truman Library, Independence, MO (HSTL): Oral History Interview with George C. McGhee by Richard D. McKinzie, Washington, DC, 11 June 1975. McGhee recalled that Mosaddeq was 'a delightful fellow' and 'very anti-British. He didn't trust the British at all.' Unfortunately, '[h]e [also] had an unreal attitude towards the importance of Iranian oil. He thought we would offer any price to keep Iran in the western community. We made it very clear we wanted Iran to stay in the western community, but then we couldn't upset the world oil industry. The result of this was that the Iranian oil fields were closed down for three years, during which they didn't ship any oil.'

19 TNA: PRO: FO 371/ 104613, 'Anglo-US Efforts to Settle the Oil Dispute with Persia', FO Minute, Sir Pierson Dixon (deputy under-secretary of state, FO), 19 February 1953.

20 Thorpe, *Eden*, p. 474.

21 Clifton Daniel, 'U.S. and Britain Confronted by Dilemma on Help to Iran', *New York Times*, 11 August 1952.

22 HSTL/ USNA: 'Prospects for Survival of Mosaddeq Regime in Iran', CIA Special Estimate, SE-33, 14 October 1952.

23 Diary entry for 29 January 1953. Evelyn Shuckburgh, *Descent to Suez: Diaries 1951–56*, ed. John Charmley (London: Weidenfeld, 1986), p. 75; Michael T. Thornhill, 'Eden, Churchill and the Battle of the Canal Zone, 1951–54' in Smith (ed.), *Reassessing Suez 1956*, p. 37. Appeasement was not unprecedented in its employment as a tactic to bolster British interests in the Middle East. See, for example, Michael J. Cohen, 'Appeasement in the Middle East: The British White Paper on Palestine, May 1939', *Historical Journal*, 16.3 (1973), pp. 37–58.

24 D. R. Thorpe, *Selwyn Lloyd* (London: Jonathan Cape, 1989), p. 211.

25 Eden assured Churchill that the British retained great freedom of action in the Canal Zone. TNA: PRO: FO 800/ 775 (PM/54/112), Eden to Churchill, 26 July 1954. The Chiefs of Staff convinced the British government that it was nuclear and thermonuclear weapons, rather than the 80,000 troops in the Suez Canal Zone, that were the key to halting any possible Soviet thrust into the Middle

East. Peter Hennessy, *Having It so Good: Britain in the Fifties* (London: Penguin, 2007), p. 308.

26 Robert Rhodes James, *Anthony Eden* (London: Papermac, 1987), p. 383. For the Suez Group's arguments against withdrawal from Suez, see Onslow, *Backbench debate within the Conservative Party and its influence on British Foreign Policy, 1948–57*, pp. 167–72. For a list of Suez Group MPs and the Anti-Suez Group MPs within the Conservative Party, see Onslow, pp. 296–7 and 298 respectively.

27 *Hansard*, HC Deb, 5th Series, v. 531, c. 816, 29 July 1954.

28 *Hansard*, HC Deb, 5th Series, v. 531, c. 785, 29 July 1954.

29 L. J. Butler, *Britain and Empire: Adjusting to a Post-Imperial World* (London: I.B. Tauris, 2002), p. 112. The Suez Canal Company would only become Egyptian government property in November 1968 under the terms of the treaty.

30 TNA: PRO: CAB 128/29, CM (55) 34th Conclusions, 4 October 1955.

31 Selwyn Lloyd, *Suez 1956: A Personal Account* (London: Jonathan Cape, 1978), p. 21.

32 Diary entry for 12 March 1956. Shuckburgh, *Descent to Suez*, p. 346. Tony Shaw, *Eden, Suez and the Mass Media: Propaganda and Persuasion during the Suez Crisis* (London: I.B. Tauris, 2009), pp. 7–8.

33 Kyle, *Suez*, p. 115. Guy Mollet was acutely aware of history, and was especially mindful of the French 'betrayals' of the republic in the Spanish Civil War and of Czechoslovakia at Munich. Alistair Horne, *A Savage War of Peace: Algeria 1954–1962* (London: Papermac, 3rd edn 1996), p. 162.

34 Henry Kissinger, *Diplomacy* (New York: Simon and Schuster, 1994), p. 529.

35 John Lewis Gaddis, *We Know Now: Rethinking Cold War History* (Oxford: Oxford University Press, 1998), p. 172.

36 Julian Amery, 'The Suez Group: A Retrospective on Suez' in S. I. Troen and M. Shemesh (eds), *The Suez-Sinai Crisis 1956* (London: Frank Cass, 1990), pp. 117, 123.

37 Sir Anthony Eden, *Full Circle: The Memoirs of Sir Anthony Eden* (London: Cassell, 1960), p. 579.

38 Birmingham University Library: Neville Chamberlain Papers, NC 18/1/1032, Neville Chamberlain to Hilda Chamberlain, 17 December 1937.

39 USNA: 'The Likelihood of a British-French Resort to Military Action against Egypt in the Suez Crisis', CIA Special National Intelligence Estimate, SNIE 30–5–56, 19 September 1956 (my emphasis); Nigel Nicolson MP, letter of 21 September 1956. Quoted in Onslow, *Backbench debate within the Conservative Party and its influence on British Foreign Policy, 1948–57*, p. 212. Nigel was the son of Harold Nicolson.

40 *Hansard*, HC Deb, 5th Series, v. 558, c. 65, 12 September 1956.

41 Douglas Hurd, *Choose Your Weapons: The British Foreign Secretary – 200 Years of Argument, Success and Failure*, (London: Phoenix, 2011) p. 359.

42 Polls showed that while a huge majority of the population believed that Nasser's action was illegal (68% to 14%), only a minority favoured military action (33% against 47%). Philip Towle, *Going to War: British Debates from Wilberforce to Blair* (Basingstoke: Palgrave Macmillan, 2009), p. 137.

43 On 2 November 1956 the *News Chronicle* published a poll where 40% agreed
    with Eden's policies (with 46% against). By 14 November – that is, after the
    military intervention – the figures were 53% for Eden and 32% against. On
    11 November the *Observer* reported that its letters were overwhelmingly against
    its anti-Eden editorial policy. Thorpe, *Eden*, p. 573(n).

44 Robert Skidelsky, 'Suez' (1970) in *Interests and Obsessions: Historical Essays*
    (London: Papermac, 1994), p. 318.

45 *Hansard*, HC Deb, 5th Series, v. 557, c. 1613, 2 August 1956.

46 *Hansard*, HC Deb, 5th Series, v. 558, c. 9, 12 September 1956.

47 Skidelsky, 'Suez', pp. 325–7.

48 *Hansard*, HC Deb, 5th Series, v. 558, c. 176, 13 September 1956. On 2 August,
    Gaitskell had told the Commons: 'If Colonel Nasser's prestige is put up
    sufficiently and ours is put down sufficiently, the effects of that in that part of
    the world will be that our friends desert us because they think we are lost, and
    go over to Egypt.' *Hansard*, HC Deb, 5th Series, v. 557, c. 1620–1, 2 August
    1956. Eden quoted this in the Commons on 12 September. *Hansard*, HC Deb,
    5th Series, v. 558, c. 14–15, 12 September 1956.

49 *Hansard*, HC Deb, 5th Series, v. 558, c. 176, 13 September 1956.

50 Kyle, *Suez*, pp. 272–90.

51 Skidelsky, 'Suez', pp. 320–1.

52 TNA: PRO: CAB 128/30, CM (56) 62nd Conclusions, 28 August 1956.

53 *Hansard*, HC Deb, 5th Series, v. 558, c. 15, 12 September 1956.

54 *Hansard*, HC Deb, 5th Series, v. 558, c. 15, 12 September 1956. Quoted in TNA:
    PRO: ZPER 34/ 208, *The Illustrated London News*, 22 September 1956.

55 *Hansard*, HC Deb, 5th Series, v. 332, c. 49–50, 21 February 1938.

56 *Hansard*, HC Deb, 5th Series, v. 558, c. 299–300, 13 September 1956.

57 Diary entry for 13 September 1956, *The Macmillan Diaries: The Cabinet Years
    1950–1957*, ed. Peter Catterall (London: Pan, 2004), p. 598. At a speech at
    the UN in September 1956, Macmillan compared the contemporary situation
    to Hitler's re-occupation of the Rhineland in 1936. Richardson, *When Allies
    Differ*, pp. 191–2.

58 Diary entry for 20 September 1956, *The Macmillan Diaries: The Cabinet Years
    1950–1957*, p. 601.

59 Summed up in Harold Macmillan's wartime quip: 'These Americans represent
    the new Roman Empire and we Britons, like the Greeks of old, must teach them
    how to make it go.' Quoted in Jonathan Colman, *A 'Special Relationship'?
    Harold Wilson, Lyndon B. Johnson and Anglo-American Relations 'at the
    Summit', 1964–8* (Manchester: Manchester University Press, 2004), p. 4

60 TNA: PRO: CAB/129/53 C (52) 202, 'British Overseas Obligations', memorandum
    by Sir Anthony Eden to Cabinet, 18 June 1952.

61 Eden, *Full Circle*, p. 427.

62 TNA: PRO: PREM 11/ 1098, Eden to Eisenhower, 5 August 1956. Peter G.
    Boyle (ed.), *The Eden-Eisenhower Correspondence, 1955–1957* (Chapel Hill,
    NC: University of North Carolina Press, 2005), p. 158. On Eden's references to

Nasser as Mussolini see the Shuckburgh diary entries for 29 January 1956 and 3 March 1956. Shuckburgh, *Descent to Suez*, pp. 327, 341.

63 Kissinger, *Diplomacy*, p. 531.

64 Eden to Eisenhower, 27 August 1956. Boyle (ed.), *The Eden-Eisenhower Correspondence, 1955–1957*, p. 161.

65 TNA: PRO: PREM 11/ 1102, (T 423/ 56), Eden to Eisenhower, 1 October 1956. Anthony Eden, *The Suez Crisis of 1956* (Boston, MA: Beacon Press, 1968), p. 135; Boyle (ed.), *The Eden-Eisenhower Correspondence, 1955–1957*, p. 172; Eden, *Full Circle*, p. 498.

66 In a perceptive review from 1938, Crossman opined: '[T]he Eden myth, which neglects his real qualities and eulogizes virtues which he never possessed, is a dangerous illusion.' R. H. S. Crossman, 'After the Resignation' in *The Charm of Politics: and Other Essays in Political Criticism* (London: Hamish Hamilton, 1958), p. 53. This piece was a review of Alan Campbell Johnson, *Anthony Eden: A Biography* (London: Hale, 1938).

67 *Hansard*, HC Deb, 5th Series, v. 558, c. 84–5, 12 September 1956.

68 This was agreed in the Protocol of Sèvres agreed reached between the governments of Israel, France and the United Kingdom between 22 and 24 October 1956 at Sèvres, a suburb of Paris. On this, see Avi Shlaim, 'The Protocol of Sèvres, 1956: Anatomy of a War Plot', *International Affairs*, 73.3 (1997), pp. 509–30.

69 'Eden's War', front-page editorial, *Daily Mirror*, 1 November 1956.

70 *Hansard*, HC Deb, 5th Series, v. 558, c. 1448, 5 November 1956.

71 Laszlo Borhi, *Hungary in the Cold War, 1945–1956: Between the United States and the Soviet Union* (Budapest: Central European University Press, 2004), p. 251.

72 Janos M. Rainer, 'The Road to Budapest, 1956: New Documentation on the Kremlin's Decision to Intervene', *The Hungarian Quarterly*, 36 (1996), pp. 24–41 and 37 (1996), pp. 16–31; Johanna Granville, 'In the Line of Fire: The Soviet Crackdown on Hungary, 1956–57', *Journal of Communist Studies and Transition Politics*, 13.2 (1997), pp. 1–63; Mark Kramer, 'New Evidence on Soviet Decision-Making and the 1956 Polish and Hungarian Crises', *Cold War International History Project Bulletin*, 8.9 (1997), pp. 358–84; Mark Kramer, 'The Soviet Union and the 1956 Crises in Hungary and Poland: Reassessments and New Findings', *Journal of Contemporary History*, 3.2 (1998), pp. 163–214.

73 Dwight D. Eisenhower, *The White House Years: Waging Peace, 1956–61* (London: Heinemann, 1966), pp. 74–99.

74 D. R. Thorpe, *Supermac: The Life of Harold Macmillan* (London: Chatto and Windus, 2010), p. 366.

75 Boyle (ed.), *The Eden-Eisenhower Correspondence, 1955–1957*, p. 183.

76 R. H. S. Crossman, 'History and Legend' (1952) in *The Charm of Politics*, p. 239.

77 D. C. Watt, 'Introduction' to J. T. Emmerson, *The Rhineland Crisis 7 March 1936: A Study in Multilateral Diplomacy* (London: Maurice Temple Smith/ London School of Economics, 1977), p. 13. Despite their own 'appeasement complex',

US policymakers rejected Eden's comparison of the Middle East in 1956 with the European situation in the 1930s. Yuen Foong Khong, *Analogies at War: Korea, Munich, Dien Bien Phu, and the Vietnam Decisions of 1965* (Princeton, NJ: Princeton University Press, 1992), p. 5. On the invocation of the past by US policy makers during the Cold War, see Ernest R. May, *'Lessons' of the Past: The Use and Misuse of History in American Foreign Policy* (New York: Oxford University Press, 1973). On its specific application to Munich and the 1930s, see Göran Rystad, *Prisoners of the Past? The Munich Syndrome and Makers of American Foreign Policy in the Cold War* (Lund, Sweden: CWK Gleerup, 1982); and Khong, *Analogies at War*, esp. pp. 174–205.

78 Skidelsky, 'Suez', p. 314.

79 *Hansard*, HC Deb, 5th Series, v. 560, c. 688, 12 November 1956.

80 Eden to Caccia, ambassador to the United States, 31 January 1960. Thorpe, *Eden*, p. 478.

81 *Hansard*, HC Deb, 5th Series, v. 560, c. 689, 12 November 1956.

82 Edward Heath, *The Course of My Life: My Autobiography* (London: Hodder & Stoughton, 1998), p. 169.

83 Simon Heffer, *Like the Roman: The Life of Enoch Powell* (London: Phoenix, 1999), pp. 122–3. In the Commons, Julian Amery MP stated: 'whatever differences there may be on Middle Eastern policy on this side of the House, all of us wholeheartedly condemn the part played by the United States, by the party opposite and by a small handful of hon. Members on this side of the House in bringing us to the humiliating withdrawal [from Suez].' *Hansard*, HC Deb, 5th Series, v. 561, c. 889–90, 3 December 1956. Julian was the son of Leo Amery.

84 TNA: PRO: AIR 8/ 1940, General Sir Charles Keightley, C-in-C UK Middle East Land Forces/C-in-C Operation *Musketeer*. Report on Suez operations in the Eastern Mediterranean, November-December 1956, 11 October 1957.

85 Diary entry for 10 November 1956. Harold Nicolson, ed. Nigel Nicolson, *The Harold Nicolson Diaries 1907–1964* (London: Phoenix, 2005), p. 453.

86 Taylor writing in 1965. Quoted in Kyle, *Suez*, p. xvii.

87 Hans J. Morgenthau, *Politics among Nations: The Struggle for Power and Peace*, ed. Kenneth W. Thompson (New York: Alfred A. Knopf, 5th edn 1985), p. 6.

88 Kenneth O. Morgan, 'Failure in a League of Its Own: Review of *Anthony Eden* by Robert Rhodes James', *Guardian*, 17 October 1986.

89 Michael Foot and Mervyn Jones, *Guilty Men, 1957* (London: Victor Gollancz, 1957).

90 Kenneth O. Morgan, *Michael Foot: A Life* (London: Harper Perennial, 2008), p. 173.

91 Frank Verity, *Guilty Men of Suez* (London: Truth Publishers, 1957), pp. 2, 46.

92 Paul Johnson, *The Suez War*, introduction by Aneurin Bevan (London: MacGibbon and Kee, 1957), pp. 25–6. On the Conservative Party and the roots of its 'Munich psychosis', see Richard Carr, *Veteran MPs and Conservative Politics in the aftermath of the Great War: The Memory of All That* (Farnham: Ashgate, 2013), pp. 160–9.

Chapter 4

1 Macmillan, dep, C. 21/1, BOD, HMD: 5 August 1961.

2 On this, and Macmillan's subsequent political career, see Simon Ball, *The Guardsmen: Harold Macmillan, Three Friends and the World They Made* (London: HarperCollins, 2004).

3 Macmillan supported A.D. Lindsay against Quintin Hogg, the government candidate, in the 1938 Oxford by-election, declaring: '[T]he issue is too vital for progressive Conservative opinion to allow itself to be influenced by party loyalties, or to tolerate the present uncertainty regarding the principles governing our foreign policy.' 'The By-Election at Oxford', *The Times*, 24 October 1938.

4 Harold Macmillan, *Winds of Change 1914–1939* (London: Macmillan, 1966), pp. 513–607.

5 Lord Avon, 'Man of Munich', review of Iain Macleod's *Neville Chamberlain*, *Times Literary Supplement*, 1 December 1961, p. 857

6 For assessments of the Berlin Crisis, see William R. Smyser, *From Yalta to Berlin: The Cold War Struggle over Europe* (New York: St Martin's Griffen, 1999); Michael Beschloss, *Kennedy v Khrushchev: The Crisis Years 1960–1963* (New York: Faber and Faber, 1991); Ann Tusa *The Last Division: Berlin and the Wall* (London: Hodder & Stoughton, 1996); John Gearson and Kori Schake (eds), *The Berlin Wall Crisis* (Basingstoke: Macmillan, 2002). On Macmillan and Berlin, see John Gearson, *Harold Macmillan and the Berlin Wall Crisis, 1958–62* (London: Macmillan, 1998); Anthony J. Nicholls, '"Appeasement" or "Common Sense"? The British Response to the Building of the Berlin Wall, 1961' in Ursula Lehmkuhl, Clemens A. Wurm and Hubert Zimmermann (eds), *Deutschland Großbritannien, Amerika: Politik, Gesellschaft, und Internationale Geschichte im 20. Jahrhundert: Festschrift fur Gustav Schimdt zum 65. Geburtstag* (Wiesbaden/ Stuttgart: Steiner, 2003), pp. 45–60.

7 D. R. Thorpe, *Supermac: The Life of Harold Macmillan* (London: Chatto and Windus, 2010), pp. 387–8.

8 Following a visit to the USA, Macmillan reported that the 'prevailing mood in Washington [was] . . . favourable to . . . closer Anglo-American co-operation'. TNA: PRO: CAB/128/31 (C.C. 57), 76th Conclusions, 28 October 1957.

9 Arthur Schlesinger Jr., *A Thousand Days: John F. Kennedy in the White House* (London: Deutsch, 1965), p. 376; Sean Greenwood, *Britain and the Cold War 1945–91* (Basingstoke: Macmillan, 2000), p. 158.

10 Brian White, *Britain, Détente and Changing East–West Relations* (London: Routledge, 1992), p. 59. Of Geneva, Gladwyn Jebb recalled: 'The so-called science of "Summitry" was now being pursued with zeal and intelligence by the Foreign Office under the high direction of that convinced Summiteer Harold Macmillan, whose favourite subject it was.' Lord Gladwyn, *The Memoirs of Lord Gladwyn* (London: Weidenfeld and Nicolson, 1972), p. 276.

11 Alastair Horne, *Macmillan 1957–1986* (London: Macmillan, 1989), p. 311.

12 R. A. Butler, *The Art of the Possible* (London: Hamish Hamilton, 1971), pp. 257–8.

13 *Hansard*, HC Deb, 5th Series, v. 419, c. 1167, 20 February 1946; Harold Macmillan, *Tides of Fortune 1945–55* (London: Macmillan, 1969), pp. 120–1. On the origins of the *Politik der Stärke*, see Joost Kleuters, *Reunification in West German Party Politics from Westbindung to Ostpolitik* (Basingstoke: Palgrave Macmillan, 2012), pp. 39–45.

14 William Taubman, *Khrushchev: The Man and His Era* (New York: W.W. Norton, 2003), p. 407.

15 Steven L. Rearden, *Council of War: A History of the Joint Chiefs of Staff, 1942–1991*(Washington, DC: NDU Press, 2012), p. 199.

16 Henry A. Kissinger, *Diplomacy* (New York: Simon & Schuster, 1994), p. 570. Khrushchev always maintained that he sought only international recognition of the GDR. Nikita Khrushchev, *Khrushchev Remembers*, trans. Strobe Talbott (London: Andre Deutsch, 1971), p. 453.

17 Alastair Horne, *Macmillan 1957–1986* (London: Macmillan, 1989), p. 311.

18 TNA: PRO: PREM 11/ 2992, de Zulueta to Macmillan, 6 May 1960.

19 Memcon, Camp David, 20 March 1959, *FRUS 1958–1960*, volume VIII, pp. 520–1.

20 Harold Macmillan, *Pointing the Way 1959–1961* (London: Macmillan, 1972), p. 389; TNA: PRO: FO 371/ 145818 [WG 1071/ 67G] 'Berlin and Germany', memo by Sir Gladwyn Jebb, 18 January 1959.

21 National Intelligence Estimate (NIE), 12 November 1957 'Main Threats in Soviet Capabilities and Policies, 1957–1962', *FRUS 1955–1957*, volume XIX, *National Security Policy* (Washington, DC: United States Government Printing Office, 1990), p. 667; National Security Council Report: 'Statement of Policy on US policy towards East Germany', Washington, DC, 7 February 1958, *FRUS 1958–1960*, volume IX, p. 707; discussion of the 354th meeting of the National Security Council, Washington, DC, 6 February 1959, *FRUS 1958–1960*, volume IX, p. 628; Eisenhower-Macmillan Memorandum of Conversation, Camp David, 28 March 1960, *FRUS 1958–1960*, volume IX, p. 259.

22 For Eisenhower's account of his rebuttal of Secretary of War Henry L. Stimson's arguments for using the atomic bombs against Japan, see Dwight D. Eisenhower, *The White House Years: Mandate for Change 1953–1956* (London: Heinemann, 1963), pp. 312–3.

23 Memorandum of Conversation Macmillan-Eisenhower, Sussex, 29 August 1959, *FRUS 1958–1960*, volume IX, p. 27; TNA: PRO: PREM 11/ 3345, Macmillan-Adenauer meeting, Admiralty House, 22 February 1961.

24 Kennedy-Macmillan summary of discussion, Washington, DC, 28 April 1962. *FRUS 1961–1963*, volume XV, *Berlin Crisis, 1962–1963* (Washington, DC: United States Government Printing Office, 1994), p. 123.

25 David K. E. Bruce, US ambassador to Bonn, to Department of State, 10 August 1959. *FRUS 1958–1960*, volume IX, *The Berlin Crisis, 1959–1960; Germany; Austria* (Washington, DC: United States Government Printing Office, 1993), p. 2.

26 Konrad Adenauer, *Erinnerungen 1955–1959* (Stuttgart: DVA, 1967), pp. 468–71; Henning Köhler, *Adenauer: Eine Politische Biographie* (Frankfurt aM:

Propyläen, 1994), pp. 1015, 1022; Daniel Gossel, *Briten, Deutsche und Europa: die Deutsche Frage in der britischen Außenpolitik, 1945–1962* (Stuttgart: Steiner, 1999), pp. 189–202.

27 Macmillan, *Pointing the Way*, p. 317–18; Bruce to Department of State, 10 August 1959, *FRUS 1958–1960*, volume IX, pp. 1–2; Bruce to Department of State, 26 April 1959, *FRUS 1958–1960*, volume VIII, *The Berlin Crisis, 1958–1959; Foreign Ministers Meeting, 1959* (Washington, DC: United States Government Printing Office, 1993), p. 645.

28 Diary entry for 27 May 1959. Robert H. Ferrell (ed.), *The Eisenhower Diaries* (London: Norton, 1981), p. 363. Adenauer believed that Macmillan 'had absolutely no notion what a dangerous situation we were in'. Konrad Adenauer, *Erinnerungen 1959–1963* (Stuttgart: DVA, 1968), p. 27.

29 Dulles to Bruce, 17 November 1958, *FRUS 1958–1960*, volume VIII, p. 83; Department of State–Joint Chiefs of Staff Meeting, Washington, DC, 21 November 1958, *FRUS 1958–1960*, volume VIII, p. 102.

30 US embassy, London, to Department of State, 25 April 1959, *FRUS 1958–1960*, volume VIII, p. 641.

31 Macmillan, dep, C. 21/1, BOD, HMD: 4 March 1959.

32 Nicholls, '"Appeasement" or "Common Sense"?', p. 59.

33 Klaus Wiegrefe, 'Mauerbau: "Sehr ernste Risiken"', *Der Spiegel*, 15 August 2011.

34 TNA: PRO: CAB 133/293, trip to Moscow (top secret annex), 21 February 1959–3 March 1959.

35 *Hansard*, HC Deb, 5th Series, v. 601, c. 450, 4 March 1959.

36 Mark Bonham Carter, Liberal MP. *Hansard*, HC Deb, 5th Series, v. 608, c. 1418–19, 8 July 1959.

37 Dwight D. Eisenhower, *The White House Years: Waging Peace 1956–61* (London: Heinemann, 1966), pp. 553–9. The collapse of the Four-Power summit at Paris in May 1960, following the shooting down of the U2 spy plane piloted by Gary Powers, demonstrated the limits of Macmillan's influence with the Superpowers. Thorpe, *Supermac*, pp. 470–3.

38 Lord Gladwyn, *The Memoirs of Lord Gladwyn*, p. 321.

39 Macmillan, dep, C. 21/1, BOD, HMD: 10 August 1960.

40 Macmillan *Pointing the Way*, p. 389.

41 Macmillan, *Tides of Fortune*, p. 586; Harold Macmillan, *Riding the Storm 1956–1959* (London: Macmillan, 1971), p. 298; Kennedy-Macmillan Memorandum of Conversation, 6 April 1961, *FRUS 1961–1963*, volume XIV, p. 43.

42 Robert Blake, *The Decline of Power 1915–1964* (London: Paladin Books, 1986), pp. 390–1.

43 Nicholls, '"Appeasement" or "Common Sense"?', p. 52.

44 TNA: PRO: PREM 11/ 2876, Macmillan to Dulles, Downing Street, 5 February 1959.

45 Macmillan, dep, C. 21/1, BOD, HMD: 4 March 1959.

46 Macmillan's hopes for Kennedy's administration were high. Macmillan, dep, C. 21/1, BOD, HMD: 2 November 1960; TNA: PRO: PREM 11/3325,

memorandum by the Prime Minister for the Cabinet, 29 December 1960. On Kennedy's policies and Berlin, see Schlesinger Jr., *A Thousand Days*, pp. 343–64; and Kleuters, *Reunification in West German Party Politics from* Westbindung *to* Ostpolitik, pp. 92–5.

47 Memorandum of Conversation, Kennedy and Macmillan, 6 April 1961, *FRUS 1961–1963*, volume XIV, p. 42.

48 Memorandum of Conversation, Kennedy-Macmillan, Washington, DC, 5 April 1961, *FRUS 1961–1963*, volume XIV, p. 37.

49 Douglas Brinkley, *Dean Acheson: The Cold War Years 1953–71* (New Haven, CT: Yale University Press, 1992), p. 117.

50 Brinkley, *Dean Acheson*, p. 141.

51 TNA: PRO: FO 371/ 160536, Sir Evelyn Shuckburgh, FO submission, 22 June 1961. Soon afterwards, Macmillan gleefully noted: 'Dean Acheson's eclipse is likely to be a good thing for us.' TNA: PRO: PREM 11/3616, Macmillan to Home, 11 July 1961.

52 Arthur Schlesinger recalls a particularly high level of agreement between Macmillan and Kennedy on the threat of nuclear war at their meeting in 10 Downing Street on 5 June 1961. Schlesinger Jr., *A Thousand Days*, pp. 340–1. See also the memorandum from General Maxwell Taylor, the president's military representative, to Kennedy, 12 July 1961, *FRUS 1961–1963*, volume XIV, p. 186.

53 TNA: PRO: PREM 11/ 3348, FO Memo for Macmillan, 28 July 1961.

54 Richard Lamb, *The Macmillan Years 1957–1963: The Emerging Truth* (London: John Murray, 1995), p. 343.

55 TNA: PRO: FO 371/ 160535, Evelyn Shuckburgh, Aide Mémoire for Macmillan, 5 June 1961.

56 Those who subscribe to such a view often invoke Wilhelm II's note of 28 July 1914, stating that 'every cause for war has vanished'. Wilhelm II to State Secretary von Jagow, 28 July 1914. Immanuel Geiss (ed.), *Julikrise und Kriegsausbruch 1914*, volume II (Hanover: Verlag für Literatur und Zeitgeschehen, 1964), pp. 184–5. On the debates on the origins of the First World War, see Annika Mombauer, *The Origins of the First World War: Controversies and Consensus* (London: Longman, 2002).

57 Derived from A. J. P. Taylor's infamous book *The Course of German History* (London: Hamish Hamilton, 1945). On this, see R. J. Granieri, 'A.J.P. Taylor on the "Greater" German problem', *The International History Review*, 23.1 (2001), pp. 28–50; and N. J. W. Goda, 'A.J.P. Taylor, Adolf Hitler, and the Origins of the Second World War', *International History Review*, 23.1 (2001), pp. 97–124.

58 TNA: PRO: PREM11/ 3358, Macmillan to Foreign Secretary Selwyn Lloyd, 16 December 1959.

59 Taylor himself opined: 'In my opinion we learn nothing from history except the infinite variety of men's behaviour. We study it, as we listen to music or read poetry, for pleasure, not for instruction.' A. J. P. Taylor, 'The Radical Tradition: Fox, Paine and Cobbett' in *The Trouble Makers: Dissent over Foreign Policy, 1792–1939* (London: Panther, 1969), p. 22.

60 On this, see R. Gerald Hughes, *Britain, Germany and the Cold War: The Search for a European Détente, 1949–1967* (London: Routledge, 2007), pp. 59, 61–3; and R. Gerald Hughes, 'A Coalition of "Compromise and Barter": Britain and West Germany in the Cold War, 1945–1975' in Matthew Grant (ed.), *The British Way in Cold Warfare: Intelligence, Diplomacy and the Bomb, 1945–75* (London: Continuum, 2009), pp. 72–5.

61 TNA: PRO: PREM 11/ 3358, Home to Macmillan, 19 January 1961.

62 'We see Germany – free of debt, and making little contribution to defence, seizing the trade of the world from under our noses.' Diary entry for 21 July 1956. Peter Catterall (ed.), *The Macmillan Diaries: The Cabinet Years 1950–57* (London: Pan, 2004), p. 576.

63 Memorandum of discussion at the 445th Meeting of the National Security Council, Washington, DC, 24 May 1960, *FRUS 1958–1960*, volume IX, p. 510.

64 TNA: PRO: PREM 11/ 3348, draft minute from Macmillan to Home, 24 June 1961.

65 Chiefs of State/Heads of Government meeting, Paris, 15 May 1960, *FRUS 1958–1960*, volume IX, pp. 434–5.

66 Macmillan-Eisenhower Memorandum of Conversation, 20 March 1959, *FRUS 1958–1960*, volume III, *National Security Policy* (Washington, DC: United States Government Printing Office, 1996), p. 838.

67 See, for example, TNA: PRO: DEFE 13/ 342, GOC, Berlin, to Harold Watkinson, Secretary of State for Defence, 10 July 1961; TNA: PRO: FO 371/ 160542 [CG 1071/ 145], 'Report of the Four Power Working Group on Germany and Berlin', Paris, 28 July–4 August 1961.

68 TNA: PRO: FO 371/ 160542 [CG 1071/ 151], Roberts to FO, 8 August 1961. See also Frank Roberts, *Dealing with Dictators* (London: Weidenfeld and Nicolson, 1991), p. 210.

69 TNA: PRO: PREM 11/3603, Roberts to FO, 3 July 1961. Evidencing this, see Khrushchev's comments to the effect that a divided Germany must continue. Llewellyn Thompson-Khrushchev Memorandum of Conversation, Moscow, 23 February 1961, *FRUS 1961–1963*, volume XIV, p. 15.

70 TNA: PRO: PREM 11/ 3348, Roberts to FO, 2 August 1961.

71 Jacqueline Tratt, *The Macmillan Government and Europe* (Basingstoke: Macmillan, 1996), p. 56.

72 Macmillan, dep. C. 21/1, BOD, 2 November 1960.

73 Macmillan, *Riding the Storm*, p. 242.

74 CAB 130/153, GEN 624/10, 9 June 1958. *British Documents on the End of Empire, Volume IV: II, The Conservative Government and the end of Empire 1957–1964* (London: HMSO, 2000), p. 43.

75 TNA: PRO: PREM 11/ 3325, Memorandum for the Cabinet, 29 December 1960. Khrushchev claimed that Macmillan conceded that only the US and USSR mattered in international affairs. Nikita Khrushchev, *Khrushchev Remembers*, introduction, commentary and notes by Edward Crankshaw; trans. and ed. Strobe Talbott (London: Andre Deutsch, 1971), p. 506.

76 Macmillan, *Pointing the Way*, pp. 306, 392.

77 TNA: PRO: PREM 11/ 2986, de Zulueta to Macmillan, 8 March 1960; Macmillan, dep, C. 21/1, BOD, HMD: 19 December 1960.

78 Robert S. McNamara, *In Retrospect: The Tragedy and Lessons of Vietnam* (New York: Vintage, 1996), p. 96; Robert F. Kennedy, *Thirteen Days: A Memoir of the Cuban Missile Crisis* (New York: W.W. Norton, 1969), p. 127.

79 Maxwell D. Taylor, *Swords and Plowshares: A Memoir* (New York: De Capo, 1990), p. 205. Taylor was Chairman of the Joint Chiefs of Staff, 1962–4.

80 Summary of President Kennedy's Remarks to the 496th Meeting of the National Security Council, Washington, DC, 18 January 1962, *FRUS 1961–1963*, volume VIII, *National Security Policy* (Washington, DC: United States Government Printing Office, 1996), p. 242.

81 Fred Kaplan *The Wizards of Armageddon* (New York: Simon and Schuster, 1983), p. 328; Philip Nash 'Bear Any Burden? John F. Kennedy and Nuclear Weapons' in John Lewis Gaddis, Philip H. Gordon, Ernest R. May and Jonathan Rosenberg (eds), *Cold War Statesmen Confront the Bomb: Nuclear Diplomacy since 1945* (Oxford: Oxford University Press, 1999), p. 121. For a summary of the origins and evolution of the doctrine of 'Massive Retaliation', see Marc Trachtenberg, *A Constructed Peace: The Making of a European Settlement* (Princeton, NJ: Princeton University Press, 1999), pp. 158–69.

82 On nuclear strategy in this era, see Lawrence Freedman, *The Evolution of Nuclear Strategy* (London: Palgrave Macmillan, 3rd edn 2003), pp. 72–85.

83 McGeorge Bundy, *Danger and Survival: Choices about the Bomb in the First Fifty Years* (New York: Random House, 1988), p. 488.

84 Theodore C. Sorensen, *Kennedy* (London: Pan, 1965), p. 588.

85 Robert Ehrlich, *Waging Nuclear Peace: the Technology and Politics of Nuclear Weapons* (Albany, NY: State University of New York Press, 1985), p. 143; Elizabeth Pond, *Beyond the Wall: Germany's Road to Unification* (Washington, DC: Brookings Institute, 1993), p. 36.

86 Although the United States would not necessarily face the catastrophe that the United Kingdom would, General Maxwell Taylor informed Kennedy that the '[o]utcome of SIOP-62 execution will produce U.S. casualties of about 16 million at a minimum.' Memorandum from Taylor to Kennedy, 19 September 1961, *FRUS 1961–1963*, volume VIII, p. 128. Note: the Single Integrated Operational Plan (SIOP) was the United States' general plan for nuclear war from 1961 to 2003.

87 On 30 July 1914, Russian Foreign Minister Sazonov informed Tsar Nicholas II that Russia had only two alternatives – full mobilization or none. Full mobilization would mean a general war but military necessity dictated matters. On this, see R. S. Alexander, *Europe's Uncertain Path 1814–1914: State Formation and Civil Society* (Oxford: Wiley-Blackwell, 2012), pp. 300–1.

88 CIA National Intelligence Estimate (NIE), 17 January 1961, *FRUS 1961–1963*, volume VIII, p. 7.

89 Paul H. Nitze, *From Hiroshima to Glasnost: At the Centre of Decision – A Memoir* (London: Weidenfeld and Nicolson, 1990), p. 247.

90   Trachtenberg, *A Constructed Peace*, p. 294.

91   Christopher Andrew and Vasili Mitrokhin, *The Mitrokhin Archive: The KGB in Europe and the West* (London: Allen Lane, 1999), p. 721.

92   TNA: PRO: CAB 133/240, Eisenhower–Macmillan Record of Meeting, Camp David, 21 March 1959.

93   Eisenhower-Macmillan Memorandum of Conversation, 20 March 1959, *FRUS 1958–1960*, volume VIII, p. 521; Eisenhower, *The White House Years: Waging Peace 1956–1961*, p. 354; Campbell Craig, *Destroying the Village: Eisenhower and Thermonuclear War* (New York: Columbia University Press, 1998), pp. 100–2; Tusa, *The Last Division*, p. 160.

94   Richard K. Betts, *Nuclear Blackmail and Nuclear Balance* (Washington, DC: Brookings Institute, 1987), p. 107.

95   Richard J. Aldrich, *The Hidden Hand: Britain, America and Cold War Secret Intelligence* (London: John Murray, 2001), p. 556.

96   Charles de Gaulle, *Memoirs of Hope*, trans. Terence Kilmartin (London: Weidenfeld & Nicolson, 1971), pp. 217 (quote), 249, 260. See also Jean Lacoutre, *De Gaulle: The Ruler 1945–1970*, trans. Alan Sheridan (London: Harvill, 1993), p. 338.

97   Macmillan, dep, C. 21/1, BOD, HMD: 1 December 1960.

98   TNA: PRO: PREM 11/3325, memorandum by the Prime Minister, 29 December 1960. This echoed Churchill's thinking: 'You have heard the old doctrine of the balance of power. I don't accept it. Anything like a balance of power in Europe will lead to war. Great wars usually come only when both States think they have good hopes of victory.' Speech by Winston Churchill broadcast on BBC Radio, 15 November 1934, House of Lords Library: LG/G/4/5/7.

99   Jeremy Stocker, *Britain and Ballistic Missile Defence 1942–2002* (London: Frank Cass, 2004), p. 239.

100 In 1961 the British defence secretary was informed that the Gagarin mission 'shows the world that the Soviets could if necessary carry the arms race into space'. TNA: PRO: DEFE 13/ 342, Strong to Watkinson, 17 April 1961.

101 TNA: PRO: PREM 11/ 3348, Macmillan to Kennedy, 28 July 1961,

102 John F. Kennedy, *Why England Slept* (London: Hutchinson, 1940), p. 234.

103 Sorenson, *Kennedy*, p. 602.

104 In 1961, John F. Kennedy told Walt Rostow that his father's reputation as an appeaser caused him to fear being similarly tarred. Andrew L. Johns, *Vietnam's Second Front: Domestic Politics, the Republican Party, and the War* (Lexington, KY: University Press of Kentucky, 2012), p. 21. On Joe Kennedy's paranoid delusions about the 'Jewish Question', see Laurence Leamer, *The Kennedy Men: 1961–1963* (New York: Harper, 2002), p. 134.

105 *Hansard*, HC Deb, 5th Series, v. 643, c. 199, 27 June 1961.

106 Gearson, *Harold Macmillan and the Berlin Wall Crisis*, p. 171. Geoffrey McDermott, deputy commandant in Berlin, saw Home as 'a great one for appeasement'. R. Gerald Hughes, *Britain, Germany and the Cold War: The Search for a European Détente, 1949–1967* (London: Routledge, 2007), p.

196(n). The Labour Party was naturally keen to publicize Home's past. Gordon Schaffer, *Do You Want War over Berlin?* (London: Gladiator, 1961), pp. 6–7. On Home, Chamberlain and appeasement, see D. R. Thorpe, *Alec Douglas-Home* (London: Sinclair-Stevenson, 1996), pp. 63–107. Home's appeasing tendencies persisted and, in 1972, escalating violence caused him to advise Heath to seek a united Ireland. Edward Heath, *The Course of My Life: My Autobiography* (London: Hodder & Stoughton, 1998), p. 436.

107   TNA: PRO: CAB 129/106, C (61) 116, 'Berlin', memorandum by Lord Home, 26 July 1961. With an eye to the 1930s, Home had opined of the British position on Berlin: 'If we can get [President] Kennedy to adopt this sort of line as his own it will be very good and will enable us to avoid appearing to be the ones who advocate compromise.' Home to Macmillan, 27 May 1961. *Documents on British Policy Overseas* (DBPO), s.III, v.VI, *Berlin in the Cold War, 1948–1990* (London: Whitehall Publishing/Routledge, 2009), document 224 (CD-ROM). Home's ideas resonated with certain figures in the US administration. Paul Nitze, US assistant secretary of defense for international security affairs (ISA) between 1961 and 1963, recalls that, after the Cuban Missile Crisis, he was asked by President Kennedy to think about a long-term solution to the problem of Berlin. Nitze 'realized that this would call for radical steps.' He proposed that the West recognize the GDR in return for a widening of the land access routes to West Berlin. Kennedy did not pursue the idea. Nitze, *From Hiroshima to Glasnost*, pp. 207–8 (quote at p. 207).

108   TNA: PRO: CAB 128/35 (C.C. 30), 30th Conclusions, 6 June 1961. Home was reporting on his (and the prime minister's) conversation with President Kennedy in London on 5 June 1961. For Schlesinger's account of the Kennedy visit to London, see Schlesinger, Jr., *A Thousand Days*, pp. 339–41.

109   Gearson, *Harold Macmillan and the Berlin Wall Crisis*, p. 171.

110   TNA: PRO: FO 371/ 160536 [Tel. 1454], Sir Harold Caccia, ambassador to the United States, to Home, 16 June 1961.

111   Macmillan, *Pointing the Way*, p. 391.

112   TNA: PRO: FO 371/ 160541 [CG 1072/ 11], Rusk to Home, 5 August 1961.

113   TNA: PRO: FO 371/ 160541 [CG 1072/ 12], Home to Macmillan, August 6, 1961.

114   TNA: PRO: FO 371/ 160540 [CG 1072/ 17], Mr. Creswell minute, Washington, DC, to FO, 3 August 1961.

115   Paul Maddrell, *Spying on Science: Western Intelligence in Divided Germany 1945–1961* (Oxford: Oxford University Press, 2006), pp. 236–70.

116   Kennedy-Macmillan conversation, 6 April 1961, *FRUS 1961–1963*, volume XIV, p. 44.

117   Vladislav Zubok and Constantine Pleshakov, *Inside the Kremlin's Cold War: From Stalin to Khrushchev* (Cambridge, MA: Harvard University Press, 1996), p. 249.

118   Dean Rusk, *As I Saw It* (London: Penguin Books, 1990), p. 190.

119   TNA: PRO: FO 371/ 160502 [CG 1071/ 92], Bernard Ledwidge, political adviser to Major General Sir Rohan Delacombe, General Officer Commanding

(GOC) Berlin, to John Killick, Head of Western Department FO, 19 June 1961.

120 Rusk-Home, Record of Conversation, 5 June 1961, *FRUS 1961–1963*, volume XIV, p. 102.

121 TNA: PRO: FO 371/ 160535 [CG 1071/ 45], GOC, Berlin, to FO, 1 June 1961.

122 TNA: PRO: FO 371/ 160542 [CG 1071/ 145], A. Rumbold, record of quadripartite meeting at the Quai d'Orsay, Paris, 5 August 1961.

123 Stephen Dorril, *MI6: Fifty Years of Special Operations* (London: Fourth Estate, 2000), p. 707.

124 BOD, M259/61, Macmillan to Home, 12 August 1961.

125 Lawrence Freedman, *Kennedy's Wars: Berlin, Cuba, Laos and Vietnam* (Oxford: Oxford University Press, 2000), p. 73.

126 Smyser, *From Yalta to Berlin*, p. 163.

127 Horne, *Macmillan 1957–1986*, p. 312.

128 TNA: PRO: FO 371/ 160547 [WG 1053/ 11], Macmillan to Kennedy, 27 August 1961.

129 Tusa, *The Last Division*, p. 305.

130 TNA: PRO: FO 371/ 160509 [WG 1052/ 1], Steel to FO, 14 August 1961.

131 TNA: PRO: FO 371/ 160509 [WG 1052/ 2], Caccia to FO, 13 August, 1961; Walter C. Dowling, Bonn Embassy, to Department of State, 14 August 1961, *FRUS 1961–1963*, volume XIV, p. 328; TNA: PRO: FO 371/ 160544 [WG 1054/ 2], Record of Conversation with Kennedy, Sir Evelyn Shuckburgh to FO, 15 August 1961.

132 TNA: PRO: FO 371/ 160544 [WG 1054/ 8], Caccia to FO, 16 August 1961; TNA: PRO: FO 371/ 160547 [WG 1054/ 12], Caccia to FO, 30 August 1961; TNA: PRO: FO 371/160551 [WG 1054/ 32], E. E. Tomkins to FO, 12 September 1961.

133 TNA: PRO: FO 371/ 160547 [WG 1054/ 14], E. E. Tomkins Minute, Western Department FO, 18 August 1961.

134 Macmillan, dep, C. 21/1, BOD, HMD: 28 August 1961; Harold Macmillan, *At the End of the Day 1961–1963* (London: Macmillan, 1973), p. 483. TNA: PRO: CAB/128/35 (C.C. 61), 49th Conclusions, 5 September 1961

135 TNA: PRO: FO 371/ 160549 [WG 1054/ 23], Mr. Dalton, Warsaw, to FO, 8 September 1961.

136 John Lewis Gaddis, *George F. Kennan: An American Life* (London: Penguin, 2011), pp. 557–8.

137 Taylor to Kennedy, 4 September 1961, *FRUS 1961–1963*, volume XIV, p. 392.

138 Minutes of the Berlin Steering Group, 15 August 1961, *FRUS 1961–1963*, volume XIV, p. 334.

139 The President's News Conference, 30 August 1961, *Public Papers of the Presidents of the United States, John F. Kennedy, 1961* (Washington, DC: United States Government Printing Office, 1962), p. 574.

140 Telegram from the Department of State to US Embassy, Bonn, 4 September 1961, *FRUS 1961–1963*, volume XIV, p. 391.

141 Bundy, *Danger and Survival*, p. 367; Rusk, *As I Saw It*, p. 195; Nitze, *From Hiroshima to Glasnost*, pp. 199–200. This exposed Kennedy's earlier, belligerent, rhetoric as essentially hollow. See, for example, John F. Kennedy, 'A Democrat looks at Foreign Policy', *Foreign Affairs*, 36.1 (1957), pp. 46, 49.

142 Smyser, *From Yalta to Berlin*, p. 157, Beschloss, *Kennedy V Khrushchev*, p. 278.

143 TNA: PRO: CAB 128/35 (C.C. 30), discussion between Kennedy and Macmillan, Admiralty House, 5 June 1961.

144 Kennedy to Brandt, 18 August 1961; Kennedy to Rusk, 14 August 1961, *FRUS 1961–1963*, volume XIV, pp. 352, 332.

145 Rusk stated: 'It would be particularly unfortunate if an explosion in East Germany were based on expectation of immediate Western military assistance.' Rusk to US Embassy, Bonn, 12 August 1961, *FRUS 1961–1963*, volume XIV, p. 324.

146 Delacombe ordered British troops to keep away from the border during the construction of the Berlin Wall so to avoid any sort of incident. TNA: PRO: FO 371/ 160510, Delacombe (GOC), Berlin, to FO, 17 August 1961.

147 Lord Avon,'Man of Munich', *TLS*, 1 December 1961.

148 TNA: PRO: FO 371/ 160546, Caccia to FO, 22 August 1961; TNA: PRO: FO 371/ 160549 , de Zulueta to the House of the Resident Clerk, 7 September 1961.

149 Department of State to US Embassy, Bonn, 4 September 1961, *FRUS 1961–1963*, volume XIV, p. 390.

150 Zubok and Pleshakov, *Inside the Kremlin's Cold War*, p. 256.

151 On Rusk's opinions, see TNA: PRO: FO 371/ 160553 [CG 1017/ 6], Sir Patrick Dean to FO, 25 September 1961; TNA: PRO: CAB/129/106, C. (61) 149, 'Berlin', memorandum by Lord Home, 3 October 1961.

152 *Hansard*, HC Deb, 5th Series, v. 646, c. 316, 317, 18 October 1961.

153 TNA: PRO: FO 371/ 160562 [CG 1070/ 1], Kennedy-Macmillan telephone conversation, 27 October 1961; TNA: PRO: CAB/129/107, C (61) 194, 'Berlin', note by Harold Macmillan, 28 November 1961. Home told the Cabinet: 'If General de Gaulle or Dr. Adenauer agree to negotiations, our aim must be to finalise the Western negotiating position without delay.' TNA: PRO: CAB/129/106, C. (61) 184, 'Berlin', memorandum by Lord Home, 21 November 1961.

154 Thorpe, *Alec Douglas-Home*, p. 228.

155 Kennedy-Macmillan, Memorandum of Conversation, Bermuda, 21 December 1961, *FRUS 1961–1963*, volume XIV, pp. 699, 697–8, 702. See also: TNA: PRO: PREM 11/3782 and JFKL: POF Box 117, Bermuda Conference, 20–3 December 1961.

156 *Hansard*, HC Deb, 5th Series, v. 416 c. 786, 23 November 1945.

157 TNA: PRO: CAB/129/106, C. (61) 149, 'Berlin', memorandum by Lord
     Home, 3 October 1961 and TNA: PRO: CAB/129/106, C. (61) 184, 'Berlin',
     memorandum by Lord Home, 21 November 1961; Nikita Khrushchev,
     Khrushchev Remembers: The Glasnost Tapes, trans. and ed. Jerrold L. Schecter
     with Vyacheslav V. Luchkov, foreword by Strobe Talbott (Boston, MA: Little,
     Brown & Co., 1990), p. 170; CIA National Intelligence Estimate (NIE), 17
     January 1961. *FRUS 1961–1963*, volume VIII, p. 5. A visit to West Berlin in
     early 1962 only confirmed Home in his belief that the Wall had stabilized the
     GDR and that securing the access routes to West Berlin had to be the priority
     in negotiations. TNA: PRO: CAB/129/108, C. (62) 15, 'Visit to West Berlin',
     memorandum by Lord Home, 15 January 1962.

Chapter 5

1 *Hansard*, HC Deb, 5th Series, v. 715, c. 1817, 8 July 1965.

2 'A Time for Choosing', Los Angeles, 27 October 1964. Ronald Reagan Library,
   Simi Valley, CA: pre-presidential papers (series I), Box 44, 27 October 1964.

3 Margaret Thatcher, *The Path to Power* (London: HarperCollins, 1995), p. 348.

4 Foreign and Commonwealth Office planning paper on détente and the
   future management of East-West relations [RS 081/ 1], 23 November 1976,
   Documents on British Policy Overseas (DBPO), s.III, v.III, *Détente in Europe,
   1972–1976* (London: Whitehall Publishing/ Routledge, 2001), p. 461. US
   National Archives College Park (NACP), Maryland: Llewellyn Thompson,
   Moscow, to Secretary of State Dean Rusk, 27 May 1961 (762.00/5–2761).

5 Barbara Tuchman, *The Guns of August* (New York: Macmillan, 1962). For
   Tuchman's own opinions on the lessons of history, see Barbara Tuchman,
   'Is History a Guide to the Future' in Stephen Vaughn (ed.), *The Vital Past:
   Writings on the Uses of History* (Athens, GA: The University of Georgia Press,
   1985), pp. 296–301.

6 Robert F. Kennedy, *Thirteen Days: A Memoir of the Cuban Missile Crisis*
   (New York: W.W. Norton, 1969), p. 62.

7 Richard E. Neustadt and Ernest R. May, *Thinking in Time: The Uses of History
   for Decision Makers* (New York: The Free Press, 1986), p. 16.

8 Sheldon Stern, *The Cuban Missile Crisis in American Memory: Myths versus
   Reality* (Stanford, CA: Stanford University Press, 2012), p. 163; Ernest R. May
   and Philip Zelikow, *The Kennedy Tapes: Inside the White House during the
   Cuban Missile Crisis* (Cambridge, MA: The Belknap Press/Harvard University
   Press, 1997), p. 178; Theodore C. Sorensen, 'The Leader Who Led', *New York
   Times*, 18 October 1997.

9 Stern, *The Cuban Missile Crisis in American Memory*, p. 163.

10 Michael Beschloss, *The Crisis Years: Kennedy and Khrushchev, 1960–1963*
    (New York: Harper Collins, 1991), pp. 543–4; Chris Matthews, 'How John
    F. Kennedy's Appeasement Strategy Averted a Nuclear Holocaust', *New
    Republic*, 14 October 2012.

11 Arthur Schlesinger, Jr., *A Thousand Days: John F. Kennedy in the White House* (New York: First Mariner, 2002), p. xiv. Paul Nitze disagreed on this point: 'To my mind, the Berlin Crisis of 1961 was a time of greater danger of nuclear confrontation with the Soviet Union than the Cuban missile crisis of 1962.' Paul H. Nitze, *From Hiroshima to Glasnost: At the Center of Decision – A Memoir* (London: Weidenfeld and Nicolson, 1990), p. 205.

12 B. Gregory Marfleet, 'The Operational Code of John F. Kennedy during the Cuban Missile Crisis: A Comparison of Public and Private Rhetoric', *Political Psychology*, 21.3 (2002), p. 545. See also: Rolf Steininger, *Der Mauerbau: die Westmächte und Adenauer in der Berlinkrise 1958–1963* (Munich: Olzog, 2001); and Michael Dobbs, *One Minute to Midnight: Kennedy, Khrushchev and Castro on the Brink of Nuclear War* (New York: Knopf, 2008).

13 Dean Rusk, *As I Saw It* (New York: W.W. Norton, 1990), p. 237.

14 Dean Acheson, 'Homage to Plain Dumb Luck' in Robert A. Devine (ed.), *The Cuban Missile Crisis* (Chicago, IL: Quadrangle. Books, 1971), pp. 197–8.

15 The Berlin Wall Crisis demonstrated to the West German government the impossibility of persisting with the 'Policy of Strength'. On this, see Hanns Jürgen Küsters, 'Konrad Adenauer und Willy Brandt in der Berlin-Krise 1958–1963', *Vierteljahrshefte für Zeitgeschichte*, 40.4 (1992), pp. 483–542. For the evolution of US views, see Georg Schild, 'Die Kennedy-Administration und die Berlin-Krise von 1961', *Zeitschrift für Geschichtswissenschaft*, 42.8 (1994), pp. 703–11.

16 President Lyndon B. Johnson, 'Peace without Conquest', address at Johns Hopkins University, 7 April 1965. *Public Papers of the Presidents of the United States: Lyndon B. Johnson, 1965*, Volume I (Washington, DC: Government Printing Office, 1966), p. 395.

17 Melvin Small, 'Some Lessons of Munich' in Melvin Small (ed.), *Appeasing Fascism: Articles from the Wayne State University Conference on Munich after Fifty Years* (New York: University Press of America, 1991), p. 94; Morgenthau on NBC's *Meet the Press*, 16 May 1965: quoted in Louis B. Zimmer, *The Vietnam War Debate: Hans J. Morgenthau and the Attempt to Halt the Drift into Disaster* (Lanham, MD: Lexington Books: 2011), p. 100. On the significance of the 'Munich analogy' in US domestic politics, see Andrew L. Johns, *Vietnam's Second Front: Domestic Politics, the Republican Party, and the War* (Lexington, KY: University Press of Kentucky, 2012), pp. 17–18, 327. The North Vietnamese also suffered from their own 'Munich syndrome', and feared being pushed into accepting a compromise peace. In April 1965, Prime Minister Pham Van Dong confessed to the French general delegate in Hanoi: 'We don't want a Munich which will spare us from war now but bring dishonor upon us.' Pierre Asselin, '"We Don't Want a Munich": Hanoi's Diplomatic Strategy, 1965-1968', *Diplomatic History*, 36.3 (2012), p. 548. Given such attitudes – on both sides – it is small wonder that the war in Vietnam escalated sharply from 1965 onwards.

18 John J. Maresca, *To Helsinki: The Conference on Co-operation on Security and Cooperation in Europe, 1973–1975*, foreword by William E. Griffith, (London: Duke University Press, 1987, 2nd edn), p. 3.

19 R. Gerald Hughes, 'Britain, East-West Détente and the CSCE' in Vladimir Bilandžić, Dittmar Dahlmann and Milan Kosanović (eds), *From Helsinki*

to Belgrade: The First CSCE Follow-up Meeting and the Crisis of Détente (Göttingen, Germany: Vandenhoeck and Ruprecht/Bonn University Press, 2012), pp. 119–42.

20 On this, see Gottfried Niedhart, 'Zustimmung und Irritationen: Die Westmächte und die deutsche *Ostpolitik* 1969/ 70' in Ursula Lehmkuhl, Clemens A. Wurm and Hubert Zimmermann (eds), *Deutschland, Großbritannien, Amerika: Politik, Gesellschaft und Internationale Geschichte im 20. Jahrhundert* (Wiesbaden/ Stuttgart: Steiner, 2003), pp. 227–46.

21 Disputes about whether or not the Helsinki Final Act was an exercise in appeasement or détente mirrored the internal disputes over the *Ostpolitik* in the FRG. For a summary of the debates between those arguing that *Ostpolitik* stabilized the Soviet system, against those who held that it undermined it, see Noel Cary, 'Reassessing Germany's Ostpolitik', *Central European History* ('Part 1: From Détente to Refreeze', 33.2 (2000), pp. 235–62; 'Part 2: From Refreeze to Reunification', 33.3 (2000), pp. 369–90).

22 Kenneth Dyson 'The Conference on Security and Cooperation in Europe: Europe Before and After the Helsinki Final Act' in Kenneth Dyson (ed.), *European Détente: Case Studies of the Politics of East-West Relations* (London: Frances Pinter, 1986), p. 92.

23 In the *Bundestag* on 25 July 1975, the German conservative opposition cited this as one of the reasons for voting against the FRG signing the Final Act (thus becoming the only major West European political grouping to do so). On the debates in West Germany over the CSCE, see Petri Hakkarainen, *A State of Peace in Europe: West Germany and the CSCE, 1966–1975* (New York: Berghahn, 2011).

24 In one of his most famous speeches Reagan had stated: 'Every lesson in history tells us that the greater risk lies in appeasement, and this is the specter our well-meaning liberal friends refuse to face – that their policy of accommodation is appeasement, and it gives no choice between peace and war, only between fight and surrender.' Ronald Reagan, 'A Time for Choosing', address on behalf of Senator Barry Goldwater (R-AZ). Ronald Reagan Library, Simi Valley, CA: pre-presidential papers (series I), Box 44, 27 October 1964.

25 Republican National Convention, 16 October 1964. Jonathan M. Schoenwald, *The Rise of Modern American Conservatism* (New York: Oxford University Press, 2001), p. 144. Goldwater denounced Truman's foreign policy as appeasement as soon as he was elected to the Senate in 1952. Johns, *Vietnam's Second Front*, p. 46. From then on, Goldwater's unstinting anti-communism was evident. On the divergence between the Democratic and Republican platforms on foreign policy in 1964 and after, see Rick Perlstein, *Before the Storm: Barry Goldwater and the Unmaking of the American Consensus* (New York: Hill and Wang, 2001).

26 On this, see Jeffrey J. Matthews, 'To Defeat a Maverick: The Goldwater Candidacy Revisited, 1963–1964', *Presidential Studies Quarterly*, 27.4 (1997), pp. 662–78.

27 Prime Minister Harold Wilson stated: 'For just as this people had thrilled at the stirrings of freedom in Czechoslovakia over these past months . . . so equally our people, all of us, were chilled by the feeling that we had been here before, that

the tragedy of those months of August and September, 1938, just 30 years ago, was being enacted once again before our eyes.' Edward Heath observed that: 'It is right that Parliament at this time should be the expression of this country's conscience, for Czechoslovakia has deep and poignant memories for most of us in this House. On three occasions, in 1938, 1948 and 1968, Czechoslovakia has been the victim of aggression. In 1938, it was my generation and that of the Prime Minister and many of our colleagues on both sides of the House who felt sick in the pit of the stomach when we heard of what was happening to that small country, and we knew then that war within the immediate future was unavoidable.' Healey: TNA: PRO: CAB 148/ 25, OPD (68) 17, 25 September 1968; Wilson, Heath, Stewart: *Hansard*, HC Deb, 5th Series, v. 769, cc. 1274, 1285, 1417, 26 August 1968.

28 In 1948, by contrast, the Communist take-over in Czechoslovakia was deemed to constitute a potential threat to Western Europe and actually increased the anti-Soviet thrust of British policy. Geraint Hughes, 'British Policy towards Eastern Europe and the Impact of the "Prague Spring", 1964–68' in *Cold War History*, 4.2 (2003/4), p. 117.

29 Marc Trachtenberg argues that US President Lyndon Johnson took essentially the same line. Marc Trachtenberg, 'The Structure of Great Power Politics, 1963–1975' in Melvyn P. Leffler and Odd Arne Westad (eds), *The Cambridge History of the Cold War, volume 2, Crises and Détente* (Cambridge: Cambridge University Press, 2010), pp. 482–502.

30 Edward Heath, *The Course of My Life: My Autobiography* (London: Hodder and Stoughton, 1998), pp. 46–71.

31 Heath to Brandt, 27 September 1971. Quoted in Gottfried Niedhart, 'The British Reaction towards *Ostpolitik*: Anglo-West German Relations in the Era of Détente 1967–1971' in Christian Haase (ed.), *Debating Foreign Affairs: The Public and British Foreign Policy since 1867* (Berlin: Philo, 2003), p. 136

32 Heath, *The Course of My Life*, pp. 486–7.

33 DBPO, s.III, v.I, *Britain and the Soviet Union, 1968–1972* (London: HMSO, 1998), pp. 515–16.

34 Sir John Killick, ambassador in Moscow, to Sir Alec-Douglas-Home, 4 January 1973 [WRG 3/303/1], DBPO, s.III, v.III, p. 191(n). The draft statement on the 1973 defence estimates noted: '[T]he steady increase in the military capability of the Soviet Union underlines the importance for the West of clearly identifying and keeping in view its own policy objectives.' TNA: PRO: CAB/129/167/3 (CP (73)), memorandum by Lord Carrington, 16 January 1973.

35 The Foreign Office and the Commonwealth Office merged in 1968.

36 Douglas-Home speech, 5 July 1973. Cmnd. 6932, *Selected Documents Relating to Problems of Security and Co-operation in Europe 1954–77* (London: HMSO, 1977), pp. 159, 160.

37 One senior FCO official noted in April 1973: 'Basket three is becoming the focal point of our tactics.' George Walden, First Secretary, East European and Soviet Division FCO to Crispin Tickell, Head of Western Department FCO [EN 2/4], 16 April 1973, DBPO, s.III, v.II, *Conference on Security and Co-operation in Europe, 1972–1975* (London: HMSO, 1998), p. 120. In fact, human rights

eventually appeared in Basket I not Basket III (although many eminent scholars continue to make this mistake). On this, see Richard Davy, 'Helsinki Myths: Setting the Record Straight on the Final Act of the CSCE, 1975', *Cold War History*, 9.1 (2009), pp. 5–6. The misunderstanding perhaps arises from the fact that while Basket I includes Principle VII ('Respect for human rights and fundamental freedoms, including the freedom of thought, conscience, religion or belief'), Basket III is concerned with cooperation in humanitarian and other fields (including movement of people and human contacts). Principle VII and Basket III together have thus come to be known as 'The Human Dimension' of the Final Act. Commission of Security and Cooperation in Europe: US Helsinki Commission, www.csce.gov/index.cfm?FuseAction=AboutHelsinkiProcess.OSCE.

38 FCO Steering Brief for the UK Delegation to Stage II of CSCE [WDW 1/18], 13 September 1973, DBPO, s.III, v.II, p. 185.

39 For Kissinger's account, and defence, of détente, see Henry Kissinger, *Diplomacy* (New York: Simon and Schuster, 1994), pp. 733–61; and Henry Kissinger, *Years of Renewal* (New York: Simon and Schuster, 1999), pp. 92–120.

40 R, 'Column', *Encounter*, 41.5 (1973), pp. 35–6. Goronwy Rees ('R'), 1909-1979, was a Welsh journalist, academic and writer. After working for the *Guardian* and the *Spectator*, Rees became principal of the University College of Wales Aberystwyth between 1953 and 1957. He resigned after revelations about his friendship with the traitor Guy Burgess. In 1999, Rees was named as a spy by the KGB defector Vasili Mitrokhin. Christopher Andrew and Vasili Mitrokhin, *The Sword and the Shield: The Mitrokhin Archive and the Secret History of the KGB* (New York: Basic, 1999), pp. 79–80. On Rees and his career, see Goronwy Rees, *Sketches in Autobiography*, ed. and intro. John Harris (Cardiff: University of Wales Press, 2001).

41 G. R. Urban, interview with Sir William Hayter, 'Sovereignty, Appeasement and Détente' in G. R. Urban (ed.), *Détente* (London: Temple Smith, 1976), pp. 38–40 (quotes at p. 39 and p. 40). Hayter had been UK ambassador to the USSR, 1953–7.

42 On the British exercise of *Realpolitik* on European frontier questions, see R. Gerald Hughes, 'Unfinished Business from Potsdam: Britain, West Germany, and the Oder-Neiße line, 1945–1962', *International History Review*, 27.2 (2005), pp. 259–94; and R. Gerald Hughes, "Possession Is Nine Tenths of the Law': Britain and the Boundaries of Eastern Europe since 1945', *Diplomacy and Statecraft*, 16.4 (2005), pp. 723–47.

43 Lord Carrington, *Reflect on Things Past: The Memoirs of Lord Carrington* (London: Collins, 1988), pp. 228–9. While not untypical, one might usefully reflect that such 'island-centric' views rather neglected the sensitivity of the question of the land border that Britain itself had shared with the Irish state since 1922.

44 By the mid-1980s, the British were stressing their long-standing goals with regard to human rights and the CSCE process. See, for example, TNA: PRO: FO 973/476, FCO Background Brief, 'Vienna CSCE Follow-Up Meeting: Background and Chronology', October 1986.

45 Douglas-Home to Killick, Moscow, 14 September 1973, DBPO, s.III, v.II, p. 179(n).

46 Sir Michael Palliser, *Britain and British Diplomacy in a World of Change*, The Annual David Davies Memorial Lecture, 11 December 1975 (London: The David Davies Memorial Institute of International Studies, 1975), p. 8. Antonio Varsori has demonstrated how the British had already failed in this role in the 1950s. Antonio Varsori, 'Britain as a Bridge between East and West' in Wilfried Loth (ed.), *Europe, Cold War and Coexistence, 1953–1965* (London: Frank Cass, 2004), pp. 7–22.

47 Keith Hamilton, 'Cold War by Other Means' in Wilfried Loth and Georges-Henri Soutou (eds), *The Making of Détente: Eastern and Western Europe in the Cold War, 1965–75* (London: Routledge, 2008), p. 177. On Callaghan's belief that the British could smooth the path for Western negotiation with the USSR, see Kenneth O. Morgan, *Callaghan: A Life* (Oxford: Oxford University Press, 1997), pp. 451–3.

48 Sir Michael Palliser (private secretary to Wilson, 1966–9; permanent under-secretary of state, and head of diplomatic service, FCO, 1975–1982): interview with author, London, 25 July 2000. The Soviets were well aware of Wilson's illusions on this score and Brezhnev flattered Wilson by talking up the influence of the United Kingdom internationally. TNA: PRO: FCO 41/ 1781, meeting between Wilson and Brezhnev at the Kremlin, 13 February 1975.

49 Meeting between Wilson and Brezhnev at the Kremlin, 13 February 1975, DBPO, s.III, v.III, p. 365; TNA: PRO: FCO 41/ 1781, meeting between Wilson, Callaghan, Gromyko and Brezhnev at the Kremlin, 14 February 1975.

50 TNA: PRO: CAB 128/56/9, CC (75) 9th Conclusions of the Cabinet, 20 February 1975. The prime minister also noted the 'enhanced' prospects for UK exports to the USSR.

51 The Helsinki Final Act stated: 'The participating States regard as inviolable all one another's frontiers as well as the frontiers of all States in Europe and therefore they will refrain now and in the future from assaulting these frontiers . . . they will also refrain from any demand for, or act of, seizure and usurpation of part or all of the territory of any participating State.' Conference on Security and Co-Operation in Europe, Final Act, Helsinki, 1 August 1975: Robert V. Daniels (ed.), *Documentary History of Communism*, Volume 2: *Communism and the World* (London: I.B. Tauris, 1986), p. 367.

52 *Hansard*, HC Deb, 5th Series, v. 895, c. 1309, 15 July 1975.

53 *Hansard*, HC Deb, 5th Series, v. 895, c. 1286, 15 July 1975.

54 *Hansard*, HC Deb, 5th Series, v. 897, c. 231, 5 August 1975.

55 Ben Pimlott, *Harold Wilson* (London: HarperCollins, 1992), p. 703.

56 Speech by Wilson, Helsinki, 30 July 1975. *Selected Documents Relating to Problems of Security and Co-operation in Europe 1954–77*, p. 216. In private Wilson was more restrained. He later concluded: '[I]t is disappointingly true that [the provisions of the CSCE] have been more a statement of principle than anything approaching a reality.' Harold Wilson, *Final Term: The Labour Government 1974–76* (London: Weidenfeld & Nicolson/Michael Joseph, 1979), p. 175.

57 This had been a Soviet goal since Potsdam and Moscow had pressed for a pan-European conference to enshrine this since the 1950s. TNA: PRO: FO 973/ 476, FCO Background Brief, 'Vienna CSCE Follow-Up Meeting: Background and Chronology', October 1986. Arkady Shevchenko, a Soviet diplomat at Helsinki, stated that the USSR's paramount goal on frontiers was derived of the fact that '[t]hey had no doubts that it was their Empire [in eastern Europe] and they wanted the West to recognise their presence there.' Michael Charlton, *The Eagle and the Small Birds: Crisis in the Soviet Empire: From Yalta to Solidarity* (London: BBC, 1984), p. 137.

58 Sir Terence Garvey to Foreign Secretary James Callaghan, 9 September 1975 [ENZ 3/303/1], DBPO, s.III, v.II, pp. 475–8.

59 Angela Romano, *From Détente in Europe to European Détente: How the West Shaped the Helsinki CSCE* (Brussels: Peter Lang, 2009), pp. 199–200.

60 Davy, 'Helsinki myths', p. 8.

61 On this, see: 'Vienna Convention on the Law of Treaties' (initialled on 23 May 1969), http://untreaty.un.org/ilc/texts/instruments/english/conventions/1_1_1969. pdf.

62 Davy, 'Helsinki myths', p. 8. On FRG policy here, see Gottfried Niedhart, 'Peaceful Change of Frontiers as a Crucial Element in the West German Strategy of Transformation' in Oliver Bange and Gottfried Niedhart (eds), *Helsinki 1975 and the Transformation of Europe* (Oxford: Berghahn, 2008), pp. 39–52.

63 See, for instance, the FCO paper 'East European Attitudes to the CSCE' [EN 2/5], DBPO, s.III, v.II, pp. 24–33. On 30 July 1975, Callaghan told Kissinger: 'No Soviet government can ever justify invasion again.' To this, the secretary of state replied: 'CSCE will not prevent it, but it can never be explained again.' On the hollow nature of the Soviet 'victory' on frontiers, Kissinger himself later wrote: '[T]he "inviolability of frontiers" provisions did no more than reaffirm clauses already contained in the postwar allied peace treaties between 1946 and 1949 . . . and in Willy Brandt's . . . *Ostpolitik* treaties.' Kissinger, *Years of Renewal*, pp. 644, 648.

64 Sir David Hildyard, UKMIS Geneva to Callaghan, 25 July 1975 [WDW 1/22], DBPO, s.III, v.II, p. 451.

65 In 1977, Foreign Secretary David Owen highlighted how the Final Act had stabilized the international system, specifically tracing the roots of détente back to 1953. David Owen speech, London, 3 March 1977, *Selected Documents Relating to Problems of Security and Co-operation in Europe 1954–77*, p. 334. In terms of the significance of 1953, it is not clear if Owen is referring to Stalin's death, Churchill's 'eastern Locarno' speech (which had called for the recognition of the postwar frontiers of Eastern Europe) – or both.

66 For example, TNA: PRO: FCO 28/ 90, Goronwy Roberts MP, Minister of State at the FCO to Michael Stewart, 13 June 1968.

67 Richard Parsons, Budapest, 23 March 1978. DBPO, s.III, v.II, p. 487; my emphasis. (Despite this the FCO simply noted that the 'Belgrade meeting did nothing more than agree that further CSCE meetings should be convened'.) TNA: PRO: FO 973/ 476, FCO Background Brief, 'Vienna CSCE Follow-Up Meeting: Background and Chronology', October 1986. Elsewhere Belgrade

has been termed 'The Abortive Meeting'. See, Alexis Heraclides, *Security and Co-Operation in Europe: The Human Dimension, 1972–1992* (London: Frank Cass, 1993), pp. 51–5.

68 See, for example, 'Evaluation of the Helsinki Final Act by the Czechoslovak Party Presidium, April 28, 1976', document 78 in Vojtech Mastny and Malcolm Byrne (eds), *A Cardboard Castle? An Inside History of the Warsaw Pact 1955–1991* (Budapest: CEU Press, 2005), pp. 397–401. Signally, the editors of this volume comment: 'The document does not reveal any concerns as yet over the Basket III human rights issue, but those would very soon materialize' (p. 397).

69 Dyson 'The Conference on Security and Cooperation in Europe', p. 104.

70 Thatcher, *The Path to Power*, p. 348.

71 Margaręt Thatcher, 'Speech to Chelsea Conservative Association', 26 July 1975. Margaret Thatcher Foundation, www.margaretthatcher.org/speeches.

72 Morgan, *Callaghan*, p. 453.

73 Hamilton, 'Cold War by Other Means' in Loth and Soutou (eds), *The Making of Détente*, p. 179. Installed as prime minister in April 1976, James Callaghan informed the Soviet news agency (TASS) in July that 'the Final Act was the beginning rather than the end of the process'. 'Introduction' to *Selected Documents Relating to Problems of Security and Co-operation in Europe 1954–77*, p. 28.

74 For an answer in the affirmative, see D. C. Thomas, *The Helsinki Effect: International Norms, Human Rights, and the Demise of Communism* (Princeton, NJ: Princeton University, 2001).

75 Douglas Hurd, *The Search for Peace: A Century of Peace Diplomacy* (London: Warner Books, 1997), p. 79. For confirmation of Hurd's view see the opinion of David Owen (foreign secretary, 1977–9). David Owen, *Time to Declare* (London: Michael Joseph, 1991), pp. 337–8. An FCO brief from 1986 correctly noted that the West's insistence on adherence to the human rights' provisos of Helsinki was bearing fruit. TNA: PRO: FO 973/ 476, FCO Background Brief, 'Vienna CSCE Follow-Up Meeting: Background and Chronology', October 1986.

76 See, for example, K. J. Holsti, 'Bargaining Theory and Diplomatic Reality: The CSCE Negotiations', *Review of International Studies*, 8.3 (1982), pp. 159–70.

77 As argued by, for example, Keith Hamilton, *The Last Cold Warriors: Britain, Détente and the CSCE, 1972–1975* (Oxford: European Interdependence Research Unit, St. Antony's College, 1998).

78 Hamilton, 'Cold War by Other Means' in Loth and Soutou (eds), *The Making of Détente*, pp. 175–6.

79 Speech at an American Federation of Labor and Congress of Industrial Organizations (AFL-CIO) dinner in Washington. Paul Kengor, *The Crusader: Ronald Reagan and the Fall of Communism* (New York: Harper Perennial, 2007), p. 50.

80 Stephen Kieninger, 'Transformation or Status Quo: The Conflict of Stratagems in Washington over the Meaning and Purpose of CSCE and MBFR, 1969–1973' in Bange and Niedhart (eds), *Helsinki 1975 and the Transformation of Europe*, p. 78. Years later, after the Cold War and the Soviet Union had passed into history,

Kissinger wrote: 'Turning points often pass unrecognized by contemporaries . . . [but] with the passage of time [Helsinki] came to be appreciated as a political and moral landmark that contributed to the progressive decline and eventual collapse of the Soviet system over the next decade and a half.' Kissinger, *Years of Renewal*, p. 635.

81 Aleksandr Solzhenitsyn, *Détente, Democracy, and Dictatorship*, Daniel J. Mahoney (Preface), Irving Louis Horowitz (Contributor) and Arthur Schlesinger, Jr. (Contributor) (New York: Transaction Publishers, 3rd edn 2009), p. 53

82 Kissinger, indeed, regarded *The Gulag Archipelago* as a 'moral event' – which he showed the president. But, following Kissinger's advice, on 2 July 1975 President Ford announced that he would not see Solzhenitsyn. Robert G. Kaufman, *In Defense of the Bush Doctrine* (Lexington, KY: The University Press of Kentucky, 2007), p. 62.

83 'The Nation: Confronting the Critics', *Time*, 28 July 1975. See also Jussi Hanhimäki, *The Flawed Architect: Henry Kissinger and American Foreign Policy* (New York: Oxford University Press, 2004), p. 436. Kissinger later conceded that, in 1975, he had no idea that the human rights provisions of the CSCE would undermine the Soviet bloc (Hanhimäki, *The Flawed Architect*, p. 437).

84 Charles Moore, *Margaret Thatcher: The Authorized Biography: Volume One: Not for Turning* (London: Allen Lane, 2013), pp. 310–12.

85 Margaret Thatcher, 'Speech to Chelsea Conservative Association', 26 July 1975. Margaret Thatcher Foundation, www.margaretthatcher.org/speeches.

86 See, for example, George Ball, 'Capitulation at Helsinki', *The Atlantic Community Quarterly*, 3.3 (1975), pp. 286–8; Alexander Solzhenitsyn, 'The Big Losers in World War III', *The Atlantic Community Quarterly*, 13.3 (1975), pp. 293–5.

87 Brian White, *Britain, Détente and Changing East–West Relations* (London: Routledge, 1992), p. 21.

88 As argued by Richard Pipes: 'Détente and Reciprocity', interview with G. R. Urban, in Urban (ed.), *Détente*, pp. 174–97; Richard Pipes, *US–Soviet Relations in the Era of Détente* (Boulder, CO: Westview Press, 1981).

89 Editorial, 'European "Security" and . . . Real Détente', *New York Times*, 21 July 1975.

90 Margaret Thatcher, 'Speech at Kensington Town Hall ("Britain Awake")' (The Iron Lady)', 19 January 1976. Margaret Thatcher Foundation, www.margaretthatcher.org/speeches. Thatcher's admiration for Solzhenitsyn was reinforced when the two met in 1983. TNA: PRO: PREM 19/ 1103, Thatcher-Solzhenitsyn meeting, 10 Downing Street, 11 May 1983. At this meeting Solzhenitsyn warned the prime minister that Britain was in as dangerous a position as it had been in 1940.

91 Henry Kissinger, 'America's Permanent Interests', speech to the Boston World Affairs Conference, Boston, MA, 11 March 1976. 'Secretary of State Henry Kissinger's Public Addresses during the Ford Administration', Gerald R. Ford Library and Museum, www.ford.utexas.edu/library/document/dosb/addresses.pdf. That same month, Goronwy Rees observed: 'What is Dr Kissinger's foreign policy but a public, and voluntary, declaration that for the United States the day for great enterprises is over and that henceforward she must limit herself, in her foreign policy, to such

modest objectives as are compatible with appeasement of the Soviet Union? One should not be mistaken about Dr. Kissinger. His object is to contain the Soviet Union, not to surrender to it; just as it was the object of Mr Neville Chamberlain to contain National Socialist Germany. Appeasement is the form which containment takes if one believes one is negotiating from a position, not of strength, but of weakness. But Henry Kissinger should not be surprised if many people, including his own countrymen, are bewildered by the complexity of his manoeuvres.' R, 'Column', *Encounter*, 46.3 (1976), p. 41.

92 Kissinger, *Diplomacy*, p. 761.

93 Walter Laqueur, 'The Psychology of Appeasement' in *The Political Psychology of Appeasement: Finlandization and Other Unpopular Essays* (New Brunswick, NJ: Transaction Books, 1980), p. 135.

94 'To Restore America', Ronald Reagan campaign address, 31 March 1976. Jussi M. Hanhimäki, *The Rise and Fall of Détente: American Foreign Policy and the Transformation of the Cold War* (Washington, DC: Potomac, 2013), p. 199. Reagan's successes in early presidential primaries caused Ford to ban the word 'détente' from his campaign altogether. Raymond L. Gartoff, *A Journey Through the Cold War: A Memoir of Containment and Coexistence* (Washington, DC: Brookings Institution, 2001), p. 327.

95 Official announcement of intent to run for president, New York Hilton, 13 November 1979. The National Review (ed.), *Tear Down This Wall: The Reagan Revolution: A National Review History* (New York: Continuum, 2004), p. 14; News conference, 29 January 1981. Scott Ritter, *Dangerous Ground: America's Failed Arms Control Policy, from FDR to Obama* (New York: Nation), p. 252.

96 Margaret Thatcher, *The Downing Street Years* (London: HarperCollins, 1993), p. 452.

97 Moore, *Margaret Thatcher*, p. 333.

98 Thatcher, *The Path to Power*, p. 348.

99 TNA: PRO: PREM 19/ 124, prime minister's stop-over in Moscow, talks with Kosygin, 26 June 1979. Bryan Cartledge, private secretary (Overseas Affairs) to the prime minister, Moscow, to R. L. Wade-Grey, deputy secretary (Foreign Affairs) Cabinet Office, London, 26 June 1979.

100 Moore, *Margaret Thatcher*, p. 564.

101 TNA: PRO: PREM 19/ 136, Thatcher to Carter, 26 January 1980. For similar, see TNA: PRO: PREM 19/ 137, Thatcher to Carter, 3 March 1980. DBPO, s.III, v.VIII, *The Invasion of Afghanistan and UK–Soviet Relations, 1979–1982* (London: Whitehall Publishing/Routledge, 2012), pp. 131–3. Zbigniew Brzezinski, US national security advisor, had warned Carter that there was a perception that his administration was weak in its dealings with the Soviets: 'I believe that both for international reasons as well as for domestic political reasons you ought to *deliberately toughen both the tone and substance of our foreign policy*.' Jimmy Carter Library, Atlanta, GA: Brzezinski Files, box 24, NSC weekly report #109, 13 September 1979. Emphasis in the original.

Chapter 6

1 Lawrence Freedman, *The Official History of the Falklands Campaign, Volume 1: The Origins of the Falklands War* (London: Routledge, rev. edn 2007), p. 17.

2 Hugh Tinker (ed.), *A Message from the Falklands: The Life and Gallant Death of David Tinker, Lieut. R.N., From His Letters and Poems* (London: Penguin, 1983), p. 180. Tinker was killed when an *Exocet* missile struck HMS *Glamorgan* on 12 June 1982. Two days later the Argentines surrendered.

3 Wellington to Fitzroy Somerset, 1838. Hew Strachan, *Wellington's Legacy: The Reform of the British Army 1830–1854* (Manchester: Manchester University Press, 1984), p. 271. Italics in the original.

4 TNA: PRO: FCO 58/ 2750, Sir Anthony Parsons to Francis Pym MP, Valedictory Despatch, 'Britain at the United Nations', New York, 22 June 1982.

5 Charles Moore, *Margaret Thatcher: The Authorized Biography: Volume One: Not for Turning* (London: Allen Lane, 2013), p. 749. Moore notes that the exact Argentine figure is disputed (p. 749(n)).

6 Editorial: 'Falkland Islands: Imperial Pride', *The Guardian*, 19 February 2010. In Cabinet, James Callaghan once asked if the Falkland Islands were of any value to Britain at all. Diary entry for 28 March 1968. Barbara Castle, *The Castle Diaries, 1964–1976* (London: Papermac, 1990), p. 207. On the dispute over the Falklands, see Castle's entries for 24 September and 5, 11 December 1968 (pp. 258, 284, 285).

7 Paul Latawski, 'Invoking Munich, Expiating Suez: British Leadership, Historical Analogy and the Falklands Crisis' in Stephen Badsey, Rob Havers and Mark Grove (eds), *The Falklands Conflict Twenty Years On* (London: Frank Cass, 2005), pp. 226–36.

8 Diary entry for 2 April 1982. Alan Clark, *Diaries: Into Politics 1972–1982*, ed. Ion Trewin (London: Phoenix, 2001), pp. 310, 311.

9 TNA: PRO: FCO 7/ 4490, Pym, 'Falklands: Credibility of Our policy', guidance telegram no. 63, 19 April 1982.

10 Bevis Hillier, 7 June 1982. Cecil Woolf and Jean Moorcroft Wilson (eds), *Authors Take Sides on the Falklands* (London: Cecil Woolf Publishers, 1982), p. 51. Italics in the original.

11 John Nott, *Here Today, Gone Tomorrow: Recollections of an Errant Politician* (London: Politico's Publishing, 2002), pp. 245–6.

12 Hansard, HL Deb, 5th Series, v. 430 c. 1176, 26 May 1982. Lord Molloy was on the Left of the Labour Party who had served with the Royal Engineers during the Second World War. A fluent German speaker, he gave help to resistance movements across Europe and was later granted the freedom of Amsterdam. Obituary: Lord Molloy, *Daily Telegraph*, 5 January 2001.

13 Moore, *Margaret Thatcher*, pp. 18–19.

14 Margaret Thatcher, *The Autobiography* (London: HarperCollins, 2013), p. 22.

15 On Thatcher's confrontational political rhetoric, see Jonathan Charteris-Black, *Politicians and Rhetoric: the Persuasive Power of Metaphor* (Basingstoke:

Palgrave Macmillan, 2nd edn, 2011), pp. 168–78. For an excellent portrait of Thatcher as a maker of foreign policy, see George R. Urban, *Diplomacy and Disillusion at the Court of Margaret Thatcher: An Insider's View* (London: I.B. Tauris, 1996).

16 *Hansard*, HC Deb, 6th Series, v. 21, c. 644, 3 April 1982.

17 Diary entry: London, 8 April 1982. Thatcher Archive (Churchill Archive Centre): 'James Rentschler's Falklands diary 1 April–25 June 1982', p. 4. Rentschler was a National Security Council (NSC) official responsible for European matters. He handled the Falklands for the White House throughout the crisis. Italics in the original.

18 Alexander M. Haig, Jr., *Caveat: Realism, Reagan, and Foreign Policy* (New York: Scribner, 1984), pp. 272–3. Quote at p. 272. A former general and a veteran of the Korean and Vietnam wars, Haig responded to Argentine Admiral Jorge Anaya's enthusiasm for war by responding: 'You know, when you see the body bags, it's different.' The *Sunday Times* Insight Team, *The Falklands War* (London: Sphere Books, 1982), p. 133.

19 Moore, *Margaret Thatcher*, p. 752.

20 Michael Jopling MP to Pym ('Reaction within the Parliamentary Party to Falklands Situation'), 6 April 1982. Thatcher MSS (Churchill Archive Centre): THCR 1/20/3/5 f13.

21 Laurio H. Destefani, *Malvinas, Georgias y Sandwich del Sur ante el conflicto con Gran Bretaña* (Buenos Aires: Edipress, 1982), pp. 91–2.

22 The 'temporary provision' reads: 'The Argentine Nation ratifies its legitimate and non-prescribing sovereignty over the Malvinas, South Georgia and the South Sandwich Islands and over the corresponding maritime and insular zones, as they are an integral part of the National territory.' Argentina's 'Constitución Nacional', www.senado.gov.ar/web/interes/constitucion/cuerpo1.php.

23 In February 2010, Foreign Minister Jorge Taiana typically stated, with regard to the Argentine claims against the British: 'We will continue to take all necessary steps in the legal and diplomatic spheres to preserve our rights', *Información para la prensa*, 055/10, 11 February 2010, 'El canciller argentino Jorge Taiana recibió esta tarde a Fabiana Ríos, Gobernadora de Tierra del Fuego, Antártida e Islas del Atlántico Sur'.

24 David Cameron, 'Falklands Christmas Message', broadcast on 23 December 2011, www.number10.gov.uk/news/falklands-christmas-message/.

25 On a turnout of 92%, 99.8% of the islanders voted to remain a British territory. Only three voted against. 'Falklands Vote 98.8% Yes', *Falkland Islands News Network*, 12 March 2013.

26 The *Sunday Times* Insight Team, *The Falklands War*, p. 40.

27 Lowell S. Gustafson, *The Sovereignty Dispute over the Falkland (Malvinas) Islands* (New York: Oxford University Press, 1988), p. 32.

28 The *Sunday Times* Insight Team, *The Falklands War*, pp. 40–1. The 1940 file is, unsurprisingly, referred to in numerous Argentine publications. See, for example, Enrique Ferrer Vieyra, *Segunda cronología legal anotada sobre las Islas Malvinas (Falkland Islands)* (Córdoba, Argentina: Lerner, 1992), p. 194.

29 This offer, and De Valera's rejection of it, was first revealed in 1970. On this, see Earl of Longford and T.P. O'Neill, *Éamon de Valera* (London: Hutchinson, 1970), pp. 365–8.

30 Hugh Bicheno, *Razor's Edge: The Unofficial History of the Falklands War* (London: Phoenix, 2007), p. 43.

31 Douglas Kinney, 'Anglo-Argentine Diplomacy and the Falklands Crisis' in Alberto R. Coll and Anthony C. Arend (eds), *The Falklands War: Lessons for Strategy, Diplomacy and International Law* (Boston, MA: Allen & Unwin, 1985), p. 83.

32 Lord Carrington, *Reflect on Things Past: the Memoirs of Lord Carrington* (London: Collins, 1988), pp. 349, 350.

33 TNA: PRO: CAB/195/11/14, CC 6(53), Cabinet notebook, 3 February 1953; TNA: PRO: CAB/128/26, C.C. (53), 24th Conclusions, 1 April 1953; Freedman, *The Official History of the Falklands Campaign, 1*, p. 19.

34 This consisted of the nuclear submarine HMS *Dreadnought*, two frigates, HMS *Alacrity* and HMS *Phoebe*, and the support vessels RFA *Resource* and RFA *Olwen*. On this, see Freedman, *The Official History of the Falklands Campaign, 1*, pp. 76–88.

35 *Hansard*, HC Deb, 6th Series, v. 21, c. 168, 30 March 1982.

36 *Hansard*, HC Deb, 6th Series, v. 27, c. 482, 8 July 1982; Morgan, *Callaghan*, p. 725.

37 Kenneth O. Morgan, *Callaghan: A Life* (Oxford: Oxford University Press, 1997), p. 594. Morgan repeats this in his *Michael Foot: A Life* (London: Harper Perennial, 2008), p. 410. Denis Healey, chancellor of the exchequer in 1977, concurs with this account and states: 'This deterrent was sufficient. There was no invasion.' Denis Healey, *The Time of My Life* (London: Michael Joseph, 1989), p. 494. Healey also made a similar claim to the British ambassador, Sir Nicholas Henderson, during a visit to Washington, DC, at the time of the Falklands Crisis. Henderson, diary entry 24 April 1982. Nicholas Henderson, *Mandarin: The Diaries of Nicholas Henderson* (London: Weidenfeld & Nicolson, 1995), p. 455.

38 James Callaghan, *Time and Chance* (London: Collins, 1987), p. 375.

39 Richard Deacon, *British Secret Service* (London: Grafton Books, 3rd edn 1991), p. 436.

40 Denys Blakeway, *The Falklands War* (London: Sidgwick & Jackson/Channel 4, 1992), pp. 7–8. Freedman notes that Anaya was certainly keen to embark upon an invasion in 1982 *before* the British could deploy SSNs to the South Atlantic. Freedman, *The Official History of the Falklands Campaign, 1*, p. 85. Note: SSN: nuclear-powered general-purpose attack submarine; SSK: diesel-electric general-purpose attack submarine.

41 David Owen, *Time to Declare* (London: Michael Joseph, 1991), p. 349.

42 Ibid., p. 350.

43 Peter Hennessy, *The Prime Minister: The Office and Its Holders since 1945* (London: Penguin, 2001), p. 390. In support of this view Hennessy quotes an (anonymous) SIS source: 'This kind of personal involvement was right up Maurice's street. The message would certainly have got through' (p. 390).

44 Freedman, *The Official History of the Falklands Campaign, 1*, p. 85.

45 Owen, *Time to Declare*, p. 349.

46 Ibid., p, 350.

47 Lord Owen, question-and-answer session, Aberystwyth University, 16 April 2013. Owen nevertheless asserted that had a similar deployment been undertaken in 1982 there would have been no invasion.

48 Freedman, *The Official History of the Falklands Campaign, 1*, p. 84.

49 Owen, *Time to Declare*, p. 349.

50 Private email from Hugh Bicheno to author, 3 March 2013.

51 This fact, Bicheno observes, is established by the documentation already declassified and released to the National Archives. Private email from Hugh Bicheno to author, 3 March 2013. Nigel West concludes that the SSN, HMS *Dreadnought*, was was ordered not to expose itself to any Argentine vessel. Nigel West, *The Secret War for the Falklands: SAS, MI6 and the War Whitehall nearly Lost* (London: Little Brown and Company, 1997), pp. 220–2. Freedman concurs here: 'I have seen no suggestion in any official papers of such a move.' Freedman, *The Official History of the Falklands Campaign, 1*, p. 232(n).

52 Bicheno, *Razor's Edge*, p. 25(n). Italics added. In his memoirs, Carrington also stated that there was no evidence that knowledge of the 1977 deployment was ever communicated to Buenos Aires. Carrington, *Reflect on Things Past*, p. 351. Carrington testified to the Franks Committee: 'It is perfectly true that those three ships that Dr Owen sent were kept secret, and I must say that this is the biggest mystery of all time how it was kept secret' given the ease with which anyone could find out which vessels had sailed. Carrington testimony, 29 December 1982. TNA: PRO: CAB 292/62.

53 Private email from Hugh Bicheno to author, 3 March 2013.

54 Freedman, *The Official History of the Falklands Campaign, 1*, p. 86

55 TNA: PRO: PREM 16/ 734, Callaghan to Sir Derick Ashe, Buenos Aires, 21 March 1975.

56 Carrington, *Reflect on Things Past*, pp. 348–52; Ian Gilmour, *Dancing with Dogma: Britain under Thatcherism* (London: Pocket Books, 1993), pp. 296–7

57 Hugo Young, *One of Us* (London: Pan, 1990), p. 173; Henderson, *Mandarin*, p. 5.

58 Carrington, *Reflect on Things Past*, p. 352; Kinney, 'Anglo-Argentine Diplomacy and the Falklands Crisis', p. 86; Gilmour, *Dancing with Dogma*, p. 296.

59 Ian Gow MP, parliamentary private secretary to the prime minister, notes on a 1922 Committee Meeting on the invasion of the Falkland Islands, 3 April 1982. Thatcher MSS (Churchill Archive Centre): THCR 2/6/2/67 Part 1 f213.

60 Gilmour, *Dancing with Dogma*, p. 300.

61 'Argentina and the Falkland Islands', Ridley minute for Carrington, 4 June 1979. Thatcher MSS (Churchill Archive Centre): ALW 040/325/1 (Part B). Documents released to the Margaret Thatcher Foundation per FOI request 0181–12.

62 Carrington, *Reflect on Things Past*, p. 353.

63 Bicheno, *Razor's Edge*, pp. 93–4.

64 Gilmour, *Dancing with Dogma*, p. 300.

65 Moore, *Margaret Thatcher*, p. 639.

66 TNA: PRO: PREM 19/ 656, PM 79/81, Carrington to Thatcher, 20 September 1979; TNA: PRO: PREM 19/ 656, 'Falkland Islands', OD (79)31, Carrington memorandum for Defence and Oversea Policy Committee of the Cabinet, 17 October 1979.

67 TNA: PRO: PREM 19/ 656, PM 80/6, Carrington to Thatcher, 24 January 1980.

68 On this, see Carrington, *Reflect on Things Past*, pp. 354–6.

69 *Hansard*, HC Deb, 5th Series, v. 995, c. 128–9, 2 December 1980.

70 Young, *One of Us*, p. 260.

71 Bicheno, *Razor's Edge*, p. 94; Carrington, *Reflect on Things Past*, pp. 356–7.

72 *Hansard*, HC Deb, 5th Series, v. 995, c. 130, 2 December 1980.

73 Max Hastings and Simon Jenkins, *The Battle for the Falklands* (London: Pan, 1983), p. 48.

74 Young, *One of Us*, p. 259.

75 Gilmour, *Dancing with Dogma*, p. 302; Carrington, *Reflect on Things Past*, pp. 357–8; *Falkland Islands Review*, paras. 90, 96, 98–9.

76 Hastings and Jenkins, *The Battle for the Falklands*, p. 325.

77 Gilmour, *Dancing with Dogma*, p. 298.

78 Ibid., p. 302. See also Cmnd. 8787, *Falkland Islands Review: Report of a Committee of Privy Counsellors* (London: HMSO, 1983), para. 104.

79 Carrington, 'Farewell Message to the FCO', 6 April 1982. Thatcher MSS (Churchill Archive Centre): THCR 1/20/3/5 f6.

80 Carrington to Thatcher, 6 April 1982. Thatcher MSS (Churchill Archive Centre): THCR 1/20/3/5 f3.

81 Carrington, *Reflect on Things Past*, p. 369.

82 Bicheno, *Razor's Edge*, p. 83.

83 *Hansard*, HC Deb, 5th Series, v. 249, c. 997, 21 January 1981.

84 Callaghan, *Time and Chance*, pp. 375–6.

85 Carrington, *Reflect on Things Past*, pp. 359–62; Young, *One of Us*, p. 261. Ridley and Gilmour supported Carrington's opposition to the scrapping of HMS *Endurance*. Gilmour, *Dancing with Dogma*, pp. 300–2.

86 TNA: PRO: FCO 7/ 4924 (FCS/82/55), 'Falkland Islands: HMS Endurance', Carrington to Nott, 24 March 1982. For similar protests, see also Carrington to Nott, 17 February 1982 (FCS/82/26); Carrington to Nott, 22 January 1982 (FCS/82/14).

87 TNA: PRO: FCO 7/ 4924, (MO 26/9/1), Nott to Carrington, 3 February 1982. This was in reply to Carrington's letter of 22 January 1982 (FCS/82/14). Nott later conceded 'with the wisdom of hindsight', that he was wrong to deny Carrington's pleas for a reprieve. On this, see Nott, *Here Today, Gone Tomorrow*, p. 255.

88   TNA: PRO: FCO 7 /4924 [91/82], Jerry Wiggin MP, under-secretary of state for the armed forces, to Carrington, 26 March 1982.

89   TNA: PRO: FCO 7/ 4924, Richard Luce MP, minister of state at the FCO, to Russell Johnston MP, 12 March 1982; Lord Trefgarne, parliamentary under-secretary of state at the FCO, to Dr Rhodes Boyson MP, 18 January 1982; Briefing paper no. 18 for Anglo-Argentine Talks, New York, 26–7 February 1982.

90   *Hansard*, HC Deb, 6th Series, v. 21, c. 856, 9 February 1982. See also Callaghan, *Time and Chance*, p. 376.

91   *Hansard*, HC Deb, 6th Series, v. 21, c. 857, 9 February 1982. Thatcher also asserted this in a response to a letter from a member of the public. TNA: PRO: FCO 7/ 4490, Thatcher to M. Nicholls, 3 February 1982. Thatcher told Franks that while HMS *Endurance* reassured the islanders, it was not a deterrent against Argentine action. Thatcher testimony, 25 October 1982. TNA: PRO: CAB 292/47.

92   Callaghan, *Time and Chance*, p. 376.

93   Keith Speed, *Sea Change: The Battle for the Falklands and the Future of Britain's Navy* (Bath: Ashgrove Press, 1982), p. 111.

94   *Falkland Islands Review*, para. 116.

95   Cmnd 8288, *The United Kingdom Defence Programme: The Way Forward* (London: HMSO, 1981).

96   Eric J. Grove, *The Royal Navy since 1815: A New Short History* (Basingstoke: Palgrave Macmillan, 2005), pp. 243–6.

97   For Nott's account of his controversial proposals and opposition to them, see Nott, *Here Today, Gone Tomorrow*, pp. 203–44.

98   Speed complained: 'I do not know how these financial decisions and air, military and naval force directives were arrived at.' Speed, *Sea Change*, p. 102.

99   Gilmour, *Dancing with Dogma*, p. 298.

100 Owen Bowcott, 'Thatcher Warned of Defence Cuts Dangers before Falklands War', *The Guardian*, 30 December 2011.

101 TNA: PRO: PREM 19/ 416, meeting between the first sea lord, the prime minister and the secretary of state for defence, 10 Downing Street. Clive Whitmore, principal private secretary to the prime minister, to B. M. Norbury, MoD, 8 June 1981.

102 *Hansard*, HC Deb, 6th Series, v. 21, c. 27, 29 March 1982.

103 *Hansard*, HC Deb, 6th Series, v. 21, c. 658–9, 3 April 1982.

104 Moore, *Margaret Thatcher*, p. 673.

105 *Hansard*, HC Deb, 6th Series, v. 21, c. 641, 3 April 1982.

106 Jopling to Pym, 7 April 1982. Thatcher MSS (Churchill Archive Centre): THCR 1/20/3/5 f17.

107 Morgan, *Michael Foot*, pp. 413, 410–15. Quote at p. 413.

108 Healey, *The Time of My Life*, p. 496.

109 In addition to the material assistance from Washington, this ensured that, unlike 1956, the British were in no danger of being brought to their knees

by economic pressure. Robin Harris, *The Conservatives: A History* (London: Bantam Press, 2011), p. 491.

110   *Hansard*, HC Deb, 6th Series, v. 21, c. 643, 3 April 1982.

111   In the wake of the Falklands War Sir Anthony Parsons (ambassador to the UN) highlighted the manner in which the United Kingdom had mobilized support for UNR 502. In the same despatch he was less than complimentary about the United States and its obsession with the Cold War and its 'subservience' to the Israeli government. TNA: PRO: FCO 58/ 2750, Sir Anthony Parsons to Francis Pym, Valedictory Despatch, 'Britain at the United Nations', New York, 22 June 1982.

112   The *Sunday Times* Insight Team, *The Falklands War*, p. 108.

113   Sir Anthony Parsons later recalled: 'Resolution 502 was a kind of basis for our diplomacy and it also, I think, helped to unify the House of Commons.' BDOHP: Sir Anthony Parsons, interviewed by Jane Barder, 22 March 1996, p. 25. Panama voted against while Red China, the Soviet Union, Poland and Spain abstained. UN Security Council Resolution 502, adopted on 3 April 1982, was unambiguous, stating that the UNSC '[d]emands an immediate withdrawal of all Argentine forces from the Falkland Islands'. Lawrence Freedman, *The Official History of the Falklands Campaign, Volume 2: War and Diplomacy* (London: Routledge, rev. edn 2007), p. 43.

114   The *Sunday Times* Insight Team, *The Falklands War*, pp. 116–18.

115   *Hansard*, HC Deb, 6th Series, v. 21, c. 960, 7 April 1982.

116   For Pym's views on foreign policy, see Francis Pym, *The Politics of Consent*, rev. edn (London: Sphere Books, 1985), pp. 38–57.

117   *Hansard*, HC Deb, 6th Series, v. 22, c. 274–5, 21 April 1982.

118   *Hansard*, HC Deb, 6th Series, v. 22, c. 275, 21 April 1982.

119   *Hansard*, HC Deb, 6th Series, v. 23, c. 983, 13 May 1982.

120   Pym came from the more conciliatory wing of the Conservative Party. Thatcher had been forced to turn to him when Carrington resigned. She dismissed him after the general election victory of June 1983. Mark Stuart, 'Francis Pym: Foreign Secretary, 1982–83' in Kevin Theakston (ed.), *British Foreign Secretaries since 1974* (London: Routledge, 2004), p. 152.

121   Margaret Thatcher, *The Downing Street Years* (London: HarperCollins, 1993), p. 187.

122   On Thatcher and the 'Special Relationship', see James Cooper, *Margaret Thatcher and Ronald Reagan: A Very Political Special Relationship* (Basingstoke: Palgrave Macmillan, 2012).

123   Louise Richardson, *When Allies Differ: Anglo-American Relations during the Suez and Falklands Crises* (New York: St. Martin's Press, 1996), p. 183.

124   Julian Borger, 'US feared Falklands war would be "close-run thing", documents reveal: Declassified cables show US felt Thatcher had not considered diplomatic options, and feared Soviet Union could be drawn in', *The Guardian*, 1 April 2012.

125   On 29 April the Senate passed a pro-British resolution by 79 votes to 1. The House Foreign Affairs Committee passed a similar resolution. Freedman,

The Official History of the Falklands Campaign, 2, p. 179; Moore, *Margaret Thatcher*, p. 708. The latter resolution was endorsed by the full House of Representatives on 4 May. TNA: PRO: PREM 19/ 624, Henderson to FCO, telegram no. 1610, 5 May 1982.

126 'Discussions in London', Haig memo for the president, 9 April 1982. White House, Top Secret Situation Room flash cable, www.documentcloud.org/documents/329522–19820409-memo-to-the-president-discussions-in.html.

127 Thatcher to Reagan, 16 April 1982 (CAB/WH 1/16). Thatcher MSS (Churchill Archive Centre): THCR 3/1/20 f88 (T77/82).

128 Ronald Reagan, *An American Life: The Autobiography* (New York: Simon & Schuster, 1990), pp. 357–8.

129 Richard Aldous, *Reagan and Thatcher: The Difficult Relationship* (London: Hutchinson, 2012), pp. 69–94.

130 Moore, *Margaret Thatcher*, p. 683–4.

131 Richard Norton-Taylor and Owen Bowcott, 'Thatcher was ready for Falkland Islands deal, National Archives papers show', *The Guardian*, 28 December 2012.

132 Moore, *Margaret Thatcher*, pp. 690–6.

133 Robin Renwick, *A Journey with Margaret Thatcher: Foreign Policy under the Iron Lady* (London: Biteback, 2013), pp. 57, 73.

134 Henderson, *Mandarin*, p. 446.

135 Moore, *Margaret Thatcher*, p. 685.

136 Renwick, *A Journey with Margaret Thatcher*, p. 53. Kirkpatrick famously argued: 'Communist elites are more repressive than traditional dictatorships' because 'maintaining a culture requires less repression than does the effort to radically alter it by administrative decision'. Gary Wills, *Reagan's America: Innocents at Home* (New York: Penguin 2000), pp. 539(n), 413.

137 TNA: PRO: PREM 19/ 633, 'Falkland Islands: FCO Siterep', P. R. Fearn, FCO 'Emergency Unit', 5 June.

138 Diary 10 April 1982. Henderson, *Mandarin*, pp. 451–2.

139 TNA: PRO: PREM 19/ 647, R. L. Wade-Grey, deputy secretary (Foreign Affairs) Cabinet Office to prime minister and Cabinet Secretary Sir Robert Armstrong, 'Falklands: OD(SA) on 16th May', 14 May 1982.

140 Moore, *Margaret Thatcher*, p. 704(n). One US commentator remarked that the Bohemian Henderson looked like 'a broken-down old English country house'.

141 Henderson, *Mandarin*, pp. 442–4; Aldous, *Reagan and Thatcher*, pp. 92–3.

142 Henderson, *Mandarin*, p. 443.

143 Renwick, *A Journey with Margaret Thatcher*, pp. 51–2. The offer was politely declined.

144 Caspar Weinberger, *Fighting for Peace: Seven Critical Years in the Pentagon* (New York: Warner, 1990), p. 205. The United States provided the United Kingdom with intelligence as well as a wide range of military equipment ranging from

airfield matting to 100 of the latest model of the Sidewinder air-to-air missile (the AIM9-L). On this, see TNA: PRO: PREM 19/ 943 (MO 5/21), David B. Omand, private secretary to Nott, to A. J. Coles, private secretary to Thatcher, 'Annex: Main features of US material and other assistance in the Falklands context', 4 June 1982. Robin Renwick, British embassy in Washington in 1982, gives a figure of 105 Sidewinder AIM9-Ls. Renwick, *A Journey with Margaret Thatcher*, p. 63. See also Caspar Weinberger (with Gretchen Roberts), *In the Arena: A Memoir of the Twentieth Century* (Washington, DC: Regnery, 2001), pp. 205–6, 374. A high degree of Anglo-American naval cooperation had been established in the 1950s. On this, see A. P. Dobson, 'Informally Special? The Churchill-Truman Talks of January 1952 and the State of Anglo-American Relations', *Review of International Studies*, 23.1 (1997), p. 46. Such close relations did not, however, preclude the US Sixth Fleet from attempting to impede the progress of the Anglo-French seaborne armada towards Suez in 1956. At the time of the Falklands War John Lehman, US secretary of the navy, could say: 'One has to understand the relationship of the United States Navy to the Royal Navy – there's no other relationship, I think, like it in the world between two military services . . . There was no need to establish a new relationship . . . it was really just turning up the volume . . . almost a case of not being told to stop rather than crossing a threshold to start.' David Dimbleby and David Reynolds, *An Ocean Apart: The Relationship between Britain and America in the Twentieth Century* (London: Hodder & Stoughton, 1988), pp. 314–15.

145 Henderson, *Mandarin*, p. 443; Reagan, *An American Life*, p. 359. This was confirmed in 2012. Carlos Osorio, Sarah Christiano and Erin Maskell (eds), 'Reagan on the Falkland/Malvinas: "Give [] Maggie enough to carry on. . ."', *National Security Archive Electronic Briefing Book*, No. 374, 1 April 2012, www.gwu.edu/~nsarchiv/NSAEBB/NSAEBB374/.

146 US Embassy, London to US Embassy, Buenos Aires, report of Haig-Thatcher meeting, 8 April 1982. www.documentcloud.org/documents/329527–19820410-secretarys-meeting-with-prime-minister.html.

147 TNA: PRO: PREM 19/ 943, Thatcher–Reagan meeting, 10 Downing Street, 9 June 1982.

148 Moore, *Margaret Thatcher*, p. 708.

149 At one stage Pym stated: 'Maybe we should ask the Falklanders how they feel about a war.' Lawrence Freedman and Virginia Gamba-Stonehouse, *Signals of War: The Falklands Conflict of 1982* (London: Faber and Faber, 1990), p. 171.

150 Nott, *Here Today, Gone Tomorrow*, p. 287.

151 This consisted of: Prime Minister Margaret Thatcher; Deputy Prime Minister and Home Secretary William Whitelaw; Secretary of State for Foreign and Commonwealth Affairs Francis Pym; Secretary of State for Defence John Nott; Chief of the Defence Staff Admiral Sir Terence Lewin; Attorney General Michael Havers. Thatcher chose not to include any representation of Her Majesty's Treasury on the advice of Harold Macmillan, so as to avoid the war effort being hampered for financial reasons. Macmillan had been in the Suez 'War Cabinet' in 1956. At that time Macmillan was chancellor of the

exchequer. Moore, *Margaret Thatcher*, pp. 679–80; Renwick, *A Journey with Margaret Thatcher*, p. 60.

152   TNA: PRO: CAB 148/212, OD (SA) (82) 25, Defence and Overseas Policy Committee: Sub-Committee on the South Atlantic and the Falkland Islands, 'Falkland Islands: Washington discussions with Mr Haig', Memo by Pym, 24 April 1982.

153   Thatcher, *The Downing Street Years*, p. 205.

154   Renwick, *A Journey with Margaret Thatcher*, p. 60.

155   Thatcher, *The Downing Street Years*, pp. 205–6.

156   Ibid., p. 206.

157   In a speech in 1981 Thatcher stated: 'To me consensus seems to be – the process of abandoning all beliefs, principles, values and policies in search of something in which no-one believes, but to which no-one objects – the process of avoiding the very issues that have to be solved, merely because you cannot get agreement on the way ahead. What great cause would have been fought and won under the banner "I stand for consensus"?' Margaret Thatcher, speech at Monash University (1981 Sir Robert Menzies Lecture), Melbourne, 6 October 1981. Margaret Thatcher Foundation, www.margaretthatcher.org/document/104712.

158   Thatcher, *The Downing Street Years*, p. 206.

159   Ibid., p. 207.

160   Ronald Reagan Library, Simi Valley, CA: Executive Secretariat, NSC: Meeting File, Box 91284: NSC meeting, White House, 30 April 1982.

161   Renwick, *A Journey with Margaret Thatcher*, pp. 69–70.

162   Freedman, *The Official History of the Falklands Campaign*, 2, pp. 173–4; Moore, *Margaret Thatcher*, pp. 701–2.

163   Moore, *Margaret Thatcher*, p. 690.

164   Thatcher, *The Downing Street Years*, p. 208.

165   Moore, *Margaret Thatcher*, p. 703.

166   Pym asserted a real need for an 'alternative diplomatic solution'. TNA: PRO: CAB 148/212, OD (SA) (82) 35, Defence and Overseas Policy Committee: Sub-Committee on the South Atlantic and the Falkland Islands, 'Falkland Islands: Diplomatic Action Following the Failure of Mr Haig's Proposals', Memo by Pym, 29 April 1982.

167   TNA: PRO: CAB 148/212, (OD (SA) (82) 34 and OD (SA) (82) 37), Defence and Overseas Policy Committee: Sub-Committee on the South Atlantic and the Falkland Islands: Thatcher to Reagan, 29 April 1982; and Reagan to Thatcher, 29 April 1982. See also Reagan to Thatcher, 29 April 1982. Thatcher MSS (Churchill Archive Centre): THCR 1/20/3/12 f25; Reagan, *An American Life*, p. 359; Moore, *Margaret Thatcher*, p. 707–8.

168   Diary entry, 29 April 1982. *The Reagan Diaries*, ed. Douglas Brinkley (New York: HarperCollins, 2007), p. 80; Ronald Reagan Library, Simi Valley, CA: Executive Secretariat, NSC: Meeting File, Box 91284: NSC meeting, White House, 30 April 1982. At this meeting, true to form, while Weinberger pushed

the case for material support for the British, Kirkpatrick fretted about the potential humiliation of Argentina in any war against Britain.

169   Thatcher, *The Downing Street Years*, pp. 211–12.

170   After the Allied victory at El Alamein, Churchill had famously stated: 'Now this is not the end. It is not even the beginning of the end. But it is, perhaps, the *end of the beginning*.' W. S. Churchill, 'The End of the Beginning', speech at the Lord Mayor's Luncheon, Mansion House, London, 10 November 1942. Charles Eade (ed.), *The End of the Beginning: War Speeches by Right Hon. Winston S. Churchill C.H., M.P. 1942* (London: Cassell, 1946, 3rd edn), p. 214.

171   Most notably, the peace proposal made by Belaunde Terry, the president of Peru – although this plan foundered on the intransigence of Buenos Aires. Freedman, *The Official History of the Falklands Campaign*, 2, pp. 319–44. Pym, once again, strongly supported the plan. Stuart, 'Francis Pym', p. 146; Moore, *Margaret Thatcher*, pp. 715–17. Thatcher's official biographer questions whether or not in her positive response to the Peruvian plan, the prime minister was relying, once more, on Argentine intransigence to get her out of a tricky situation. Moore, *Margaret Thatcher*, pp. 721–2.

172   Moore, *Margaret Thatcher*, pp. 552–6.

173   Thatcher to Reagan, 29 April 1982. Thatcher MSS (Churchill Archive Centre): THCR 3/1/20 f121 (T89/82). For context, see Renwick, *A Journey with Margaret Thatcher*, p. 61.

174   TNA: PRO: PREM 19/ 624, Thatcher to Reagan, 5 May 1982.

175   Moore, *Margaret Thatcher*, p. 725.

176   Ibid., pp. 724–5.

177   Diary entry for 31 May 1982. *The Reagan Diaries*, p. 87.

178   Margaret Thatcher, 'Speech to Conservative Women's Conference', Royal Festival Hall, London, 26 May 1982. Margaret Thatcher Foundation, www.margaretthatcher.org/document/104948.

179   Margaret Thatcher, 'Speech to Mid-Bedfordshire Conservatives (Falklands)', 30 May 1982. Margaret Thatcher Foundation, www.margaretthatcher.org/document/104929; Moore, *Margaret Thatcher*, 710.

180   TNA: PRO: PREM 19/ 633, Pym, 'Falkland Islands: Some Current Issues', guidance telegram no. 118, 4 June 1982.

181   TNA: PRO: PREM 19/ 943 (MO 5/21), D. B. Omand to A. J. Coles, 4 June 1982. Thatcher expressed regret to Reagan with regard to the Latin American caveat. TNA: PRO: PREM 19/ 633, Thatcher–Reagan meeting, US Embassy, Paris, 10 Downing Street, 4 June 1982; TNA: PRO: PREM 19/ 943, Thatcher–Reagan meeting, 10 Downing Street, 9 June 1982.

182   Bicheno, *Razor's Edge*, pp. 79–80.

183   Thatcher to Foot, 11 June 1982. Thatcher MSS (Churchill Archive Centre): THCR 3/2/93 f28.

184   Hannah Kuchler, 'Reagan Pleaded with Thatcher Not to Retake Falklands', *Financial Times*, 28 December 2012.

185 TNA: PREM 19/ 633, A. J. Coles to Brian Fall, principal private secretary to the foreign secretary, 1 June 1982. Report of Thatcher–Reagan telephone conversation, 31 May 1982. Thatcher asked Reagan how he would feel if Alaska were to invaded and the British failed to show unequivocal support for the United States. Renwick, *A Journey with Margaret Thatcher*, p. 74; Moore, *Margaret Thatcher*, pp. 737–8.

186 *Hansard*, HC Deb, 6th Series, v. 27, c. 502–3, 8 July 1982.

187 On this, see M. Patricia Marchak, *God's Assassins: State Terrorism in Argentina in the 1970s* (Montreal and Kingston: McGill-Queen's Press, 1999).

188 TNA: PRO: FCO 7/ 4077 (ALA 014/3), Anthony Williams, Valedictory Address from Buenos Aires to FCO, 1 June 1982.

189 See, for example, Simon Winchester, 'Britain "given the invasion plans" 11 days ago', *The Times*, 5 April 1982; Kenneth Clarke, 'London "knew of attack plan 10 days ago"', *Daily Telegraph*, 6 April 1982.

190 TNA: PRO: FCO 7/ 4490, N. M. Fenn, News Department of the FCO, to Mr Ure, 8 April 1982.

191 *Falkland Islands Review*, para. 260.

192 Gilmour, *Dancing with Dogma*, p. 308.

193 Carrington to Nott, 5 June 1981. Thatcher MSS (Churchill Archive Centre): ALW 076/1 Part A1–50.

194 Nott, *Here Today, Gone Tomorrow*, p. 187.

195 Cmnd 8758, *The Falklands Campaign: The Lessons* (London: HMSO, 1982), para. 313.

196 Thatcher won a majority of 144 seats at the General Election of June 1983. Harris, *The Conservatives*, p. 491.

197 *Falkland Islands Review*, para. 339.

198 Hansard, HC Deb, 6th Series, v. 35, c. 939, 23 January 1983. On the Franks Report, see Freedman, *The Official History of the Falklands Campaign, 2*, pp. 721–7.

199 Owen, *Time to Declare*, p. 350–1.

200 Callaghan, *Time and Chance*, p. 378.

201 Malcolm Allsop, 'Foreign Office knew of likely Argentine invasion', letter to the *Daily Telegraph*, 31 December 2012. A few months before the invasion Allsop produced a documentary for ITV called *More British than the British*.

202 *Hansard*, HC Deb, 6th Series, v. 35, c. 916, 921, 23 January 1983 (Pym was referring to the *Falkland Islands Review*, para. 116).

203 Dayell was a vocal critic of the Falklands War (especially with regard to the sinking of the Argentine cruiser ARA *General Belgrano* on 3 May 1982). On this, see Tam Dayell, *Thatcher's Torpedo: Sinking of the 'Belgrano'* (London: Cecil Woolf, 1983) and Freedman, *The Official History of the Falklands Campaign, Volume 2*, pp. 743–53.

204 *Hansard*, HC Deb, 6th Series, v. 52, c. 384W, 23 January 1984.

205 Richard Gott, 'Argentina's claim on the Falklands is still a good one', *The Guardian*, 2 April 2007. Gott's infantile pro-Argentine stance is hardly

surprising given his past association with the KGB. On this, see Hugo Abedul and R. Gerald Hughes, 'The Comandante in His Labyrinth: Fidel Castro and His Legacy', *Intelligence and National Security*, 26.4 (2011), p. 557.

206 On this, see Patrick Finney, '"And I will tell you who you are": Historiographies of Munich and the Negotiation of National Identity' in Fritz Taubert (ed.), *Mythos München* (Munich: Oldenbourg, 2002), pp. 331–2.

207 Margaret Thatcher, 26 June 1982. Gill Bennett, *Six Moments of Crisis: Inside British Foreign Policy* (Oxford: Oxford University Press, 2013), p. 149.

208 Thatcher–Gorbachev meeting, Moscow, 1987. Pavel Striolov, 'The Iron Lady and the Iron Curtain: Soviet files reveal Margaret Thatcher to have been tougher with Gorbachev behind closed doors', *The Spectator*, 20 April 2013.

209 John Nott, *Haven't We Been Here Before? Afghanistan to the Falklands: A Personal Connection* (London: Discovered Authors, 2007), p. 106.

210 *Hansard*, HC Deb, 6th Series, v. 25, c. 1081, 17 June 1982; Thatcher MSS (Churchill Archive Centre): THCR 2/6/2/75 part 1 f19.

211 This event gave rise to the verb to *maffick* – meaning to celebrate wildly. Thomas Pakenham, *The Boer War* (London: Weidenfeld and Nicolson, 1979), p. 416.

212 Thomas Pakenham, 'Behind the Falklands Victory', *New York Times Magazine*, 11 July 1982.

213 Henderson, *Mandarin*, p. 445.

214 TNA: PRO: PREM 19/ 611, Frederick Forsyth to Thatcher, 15 June 1982.

215 Alexander Chancellor, 'The Falklands Victory', *The Spectator*, 19 June 1982.

216 Margaret Thatcher, 'Speech to Conservative Rally at Cheltenham', 3 July 1982. Margaret Thatcher Foundation, www.margaretthatcher.org/speeches.

217 Margaret Thatcher, 'Falklands: MT speech for Falklands Dinner at No.10', 11 October 1982. Thatcher MSS (Churchill Archive Centre): THCR 1/20/3/29 B f3.

Chapter 7

1 Bush private journal entry of 7 September 1990. George H. W. Bush, *All the Best, George Bush: My Life in Letters and Other Writings* (New York: Scribner, 1999), pp. 478–9.

2 *Hansard*, HC Deb, 6th Series, v. 178, c. 883, 30 October 1990.

3 James Baker III, *The Politics of Diplomacy: Revolution, War, and Peace 1989–1992* (New York: G. P. Putnam's, 1995), p. 332.

4 Diary entry for 18 July 1958. *The Macmillan Diaries, Volume II: Prime Minister and After, 1957–1966*, ed. Peter Catterall (London: Macmillan, 2011), p. 137.

5 TNA: PRO: CAB/129/105, 'Kuwait: Future Relations with the United Kingdom', C. (61) 77, Memorandum to Cabinet by the Lord Privy Seal Ted Heath MP, 9 June 1961.

6   Abdul-Reda Asiri, *Kuwait's Foreign Policy: City State in World Politics* (Boulder, CO: Westview Press, 1990), p. 7.

7   Harold Macmillan, *At the End of the Day 1961–1963* (London: Macmillan, 1973), pp. 252, 268. On this episode, see Nigel Ashton, 'Britain and the Kuwaiti Crisis, 1961', *Diplomacy & Statecraft*, 9.1 (1998), pp. 163–81.

8   TNA: PRO: CAB/129/106, 'Kuwait', C. (61) 140, Memorandum to Cabinet by the Lord Privy Seal Ted Heath MP, 2 October 1961.

9   TNA: PRO: CAB/128/35, C.C. (61) 37th Conclusions. This, of course, all rather glosses over Macmillan's own shady role at Suez. After his Treasury officials put before him the economic consequences of the Suez adventure, Macmillan lost his nerve. 'First in, first out' was the caustic, but accurate, view of Labour's Harold Wilson. Robert McNamara, *Britain, Nasser and the Balance of Power in the Middle East 1952–1967: From the Egyptian Revolution to the Six Day War* (London: Frank Cass, 2003), p. 65.

10 Diary entry for 8 July 1961. *The Macmillan Diaries, Volume II*, p. 398.

11 George C. Peden, *The Treasury and British Public Policy 1906–1959* (Oxford: Oxford University Press, 2000), pp. 499–502.

12 Aftab Kamal Pasha, *Iraq: Sanctions and Wars* (New Delhi: A.K. Pasha Sterling Publishers, 2003), pp. 10–11.

13 TNA: PRO: CAB/129/106, 'Kuwait', C. (61) 140, Memorandum to Cabinet by the Lord Privy Seal Ted Heath MP, 2 October 1961. On 22 November 1961 Sir William Luce, British political resident in the Gulf between 1961 and 1966, advised Lord Home that 'given Kuwait's geographical position . . . British and Western interest in her independence . . . is at the root of our present-day position and commitments to the Gulf as a whole'. Luce quoted in Helene von Bismarck, *British Policy in the Persian Gulf, 1961–1968: Conceptions of Informal Empire* (Basingstoke: Palgrave Macmillan, 2013), p. 55.

14 TNA: PRO: CAB/129/109, 'Intervention in Kuwait', C. (62) 63, Memorandum to Cabinet by Defence Secretary Harold Watkinson MP, 13 April 1962.

15 Peter J. Rowe, *The Gulf War 1990–91 in International and English Law* (London: Routledge, 1993), p. 41.

16 Douglas Hurd, *Memoirs* (London: Abacus, 2004), p. 439.

17 On this, see Hugo Young, *One of Us* (London: Pan, 1990), pp. 379–400.

18 Thatcher–Gorbachev telephone conversation, 1990. Pavel Striolov, 'The Iron Lady and the Iron Curtain: Soviet files reveal Margaret Thatcher to have been tougher with Gorbachev behind closed doors', *The Spectator*, 20 April 2013.

19 Striolov, 'The Iron Lady and the Iron Curtain'. In 1990, Thatcher stated: 'The pictures of [the Prague Spring] are etched on our memory and our inability to help remains a burden on the conscience of the free world.' Margaret Thatcher, Speech to Czechoslovak Federal Assembly, 18 September 1990. Margaret Thatcher Foundation, www.margaretthatcher.org/speeches.

20 Margaret Thatcher, Speech to Czechoslovak Federal Assembly, 18 September 1990. Margaret Thatcher Foundation, www.margaretthatcher.org/speeches.

21 Margaret Thatcher, *The Downing Street Years* (London: HarperCollins, 1993), p. 817.

22 Shibley Telhami, 'Did We Appease Iraq?', *New York Times*, 29 June 1992; Stephen R. Rock, *Appeasement in International Politics* (Lexington, KY: University Press of Kentucky, 2000), pp. 103–26; George H. W. Bush, 'Remarks and an Exchange with Reporters on the Iraqi Invasion of Kuwait', 2 August 1990, The American Presidency Project, www. presidency.ucsb.edu/index.php.

23 George Bush and Brent Scowcroft, *A World Transformed* (New York: Knopf, 1998), p. 315.

24 Baker, *The Politics of Diplomacy*, p. 2.

25 Bush and Scowcroft, *A World Transformed*, p. 315.

26 Experience had taught Thatcher to stand up to domestic, as well as foreign, enemies. On the Thatcher government and subversion, see Christopher Andrew, *The Defence of the Realm: The Authorized History of MI5* (London: Penguin, 2010), pp. 670–82. Examples of what Thatcher termed 'the enemy within' included the National Union of Mineworkers, the Campaign for Nuclear Disarmament and the National Council for Civil Liberties. In 2004 two authors wrote: 'Such operations against legal and generally harmless left-wing activities badly damaged [MI5's] reputation.' Peter Chalk and William Rosenau, *Confronting 'the Enemy Within': Security Intelligence, the Police, and Counterterrorism in Four Democracies* (Santa Monica, CA: Rand Corporation, 2004), p. 14. Partly as a result of this, one British politician opined in 1988: '[S]ince the war, MI5 has been one of the worst and most ridiculed security services in the western alliance'. Quoted in Mark Urban, *UK Eyes Alpha: The Inside Story of British Intelligence* (London: Faber and Faber, 1996), p. 48.

27 Margaret Thatcher, *The Downing Street Years* (New York: Harper Collins, 1993), p. 817.

28 See, for example, Khaled Bin Sultan, *Desert Warrior: A Personal View of the Gulf War by the Joint Forces Commander* (New York: HarperCollins, 1995), p. 261. Khaled Bin Sultan was a member of the ruling House of Saud and a Saudi army officer during the Gulf War.

29 Nicholas Ridley, *'My Style of Government': The Thatcher Years* (London: Fontana, 1992), p. 260; John Campbell, *The Iron Lady: Margaret Thatcher: From Grocer's Daughter to Iron Lady* (London: Vintage, 2012), p. 441.

30 Dilip Hiro, *Desert Shield to Desert Storm: The Second Gulf War* (London: Paladin, 1992), p. 116.

31 The memoirs of the then British ambassador to the UN, David Hannay, make it clear that, while certain questions remained unresolved, UNR 660 laid the foundations for coordinated international response to Iraq's invasion of Kuwait. David Hannay, *Britain's Quest for a Role: A Diplomatic Memoir from Europe to the UN* (London: I.B. Tauris, 2013), pp. 177–87.

32 Bush and Scowcroft, *A World Transformed*, pp. 303–4.

33 Gary R. Hess, *Presidential Decisions for War: Korea, Vietnam, the Persian Gulf and Iraq* (Baltimore, MD: John Hopkins University Press, 2nd edn 2001), p. 162.

34 Bernard Ingham, *Kill the Messenger* (London: HarperCollins, 1991), p. 262. Ingham was Thatcher's press secretary, 1979–90.

35 'Remarks by President Bush', Washington, DC, 5 August 1990, Margaret Thatcher Foundation, www.margaretthatcher.org/.

36 Bush and Scowcroft, *A World Transformed*, pp. 319–20.

37 Bob Woodward, *The Commanders* (New York: Simon and Schuster, 1991), p. 273; Hiro, *Desert Shield to Desert Storm*, p. 116.

38 Baker, *The Politics of Diplomacy*, p. 278.

39 Hiro, *Desert Shield to Desert Storm*, p. 116.

40 Thatcher, *Downing Street Years*, p. 826.

41 Colin L. Powell, *My American Journey* (New York: Random House, 1995); Baker, *The Politics of Diplomacy*, p. 279, p. 453

42 Baker, *The Politics of Diplomacy*, p. 279.

43 George H. W. Bush, 'Address to the Nation Announcing the Deployment of U.S. Armed Forces to Saudi Arabia', White House, 8 August 1990. George H. W. Bush, *Speaking of Freedom: The Collected Speeches* (New York: Scribner, 2009), p. 123; Stephen R. Graubard, *Mr. Bush's War Adventures in the Politics of Illusion* (New York: Hill and Wang, 1992), pp. 10–11.

44 Gary A. Donaldson, *America at War since 1945: Politics and Diplomacy in Korea, Vietnam, and the Gulf War* (Santa Barbara, CA: Praeger, 1996), p. 143.

45 Diary entry for 18 August 1990. Alan Clark, *Diaries* (London: Phoenix, 1994), p. 332; Bush and Scowcroft, *A World Transformed*, pp. 382–4.

46 George H. W. Bush, 'Remarks at a Ceremony Commemorating the End of Communist Rule', Wenceslas Square, Prague, 17 November 1990. Bush, *Speaking of Freedom*, pp. 149–50.

47 George H. W. Bush, 'Remarks to the Military Airlift Command in Dhahran, Saudi Arabia', 22 November 1990. Bush, *Speaking of Freedom*, p. 154.

48 *Hansard*, HC Deb, 6th Series, v. 177, c. 735, 6 September 1990.

49 Philip Ziegler, *Edward Heath: The Authorised Biography* (London: HarperPress, 2011), pp. 553–7; John Campbell, *Edward Heath: A Biography* (London: Jonathan Cape, 1993), p. 781.

50 Edward Heath, *The Course of My Life: My Autobiography* (London: Hodder and Stoughton, 1998), p. 655.

51 Interview with Margaret Thatcher. Charles Moore, *Margaret Thatcher: The Authorized Biography: Volume One: Not for Turning* (London: Allen Lane, 2013), p. 18.

52 *Hansard*, HC Deb, 6th Series, v. 178, c. 883, 30 October 1990.

53 Thatcher, *The Downing Street Years*, pp. 826–7. Thatcher later noted with pride that Primakov 'had reported back to Moscow that Mrs Thatcher is quite the most difficult and determined of them all'. Thatcher, *The Downing Street Years*, p. 827.

54 *Hansard*, HC Deb, 6th Series, v. 182, c. 842, 11 December 1990.

55 Barbara A. Spellman and Keith J. Holyoak, 'If Saddam Is Hitler Then Who Is George Bush? Analogical Mapping between Systems of Social Roles', *Journal of Personality and Social Psychology*, 62.6 (1992), p. 913.

56 Scot Macdonald, 'Hitler's Shadow: Historical Analogies and the Iraqi Invasion of Kuwait', *Diplomacy & Statecraft*, 13.4 (2002), p. 30. Reagan's adherents proclaimed the ghost of Vietnam exorcised after the US invasion of Grenada in 1983. On this, see Christopher D. O'Sullivan, *Colin Powell: American Power and Intervention from Vietnam to Iraq* (Lanham, MD: Rowman & Littlefield, 2009), pp. 29–30. Vietnam is omnipresent in histories of the Gulf War. See: Jeffrey Record, *Hollow Victory: A Contrary View of the Gulf War* (Washington, DC Brassey's, 1993), p. 75; James F. Dunnigan and Austin Bay, *From Shield to Storm* (New York: William Morrow & Co., 1992), p. 511; Bob Woodward, *The Commanders* (New York: Pocket Star Books, 1991), p. 211; and Richard Hallion, *Storm Over Iraq Air Power and the Gulf War* (Washington, DC Smithsonian Institution Press, 1992), p. 242.

57 Bush and Scowcroft, *A World Transformed*, p. 435; Bush, *All the Best, George Bush*, p. 497

58 Bush and Scowcroft, *A World Transformed*, pp. 303, 319, 375.

59 George Herring noted that: 'the lingering impact of the Vietnam War [meant] that the Persian Gulf conflict appeared at times as much a struggle with its ghosts as with Saddam Hussein's Iraq'. George C. Herring, 'America and Vietnam: The Unending War', *Foreign Affairs*, 70.5 (1991–2), p. 104. On the Vietnam syndrome and its enduring legacy, see Harry G. Summers, 'The Vietnam Syndrome and the American People', *American Journal of Culture*, 17.1 (1994), pp. 53–8; and Andrew Priest, 'From Saigon to Baghdad: The Vietnam Syndrome, the Iraq War and American Foreign Policy', *Intelligence and National Security*, 24.1 (2009), pp. 139–71.

60 Graubard, *Mr. Bush's War Adventures in the Politics of Illusion*, p. 4

61 Robert W. Tucker, and David C. Hendrickson, 'Thomas Jefferson and American Foreign Policy', *Foreign Affairs*, 69.2 (1990), p. 137.

62 Margaret Thatcher, *The Path to Power* (New York: Harper and Collins, 1995), pp. 510–11. Thatcher is quoting a Jan Smuts speech delivered in London, November 1943. Jan C. Smuts, *Smuts: A Biography* (New York: William Morrow and Company, 1952), p. 467.

63 Ridley, *'My Style of Government'*, p. 261.

64 Harris, *The Conservatives*, p. 493.

65 James Cooper, *Margaret Thatcher and Ronald Reagan: A Very Political Special Relationship* (Basingstoke: Palgrave Macmillan, 2012), p. 9.

66 Harris, *The Conservatives*, pp. 495–6.

67 Thatcher, *The Downing Street Years*, pp. 829, 855.

Chapter 8

1 Soviet Commissar for Foreign Affairs Maxim Litvinov, speech on the international situation, 27 November 1937. Quoted in J. Degas (ed.), *Soviet Documents on Foreign Policy, Volume 3, 1933–1941* (New York: Doubleday, 1978), p. 268.

2   *Hansard*, HC Deb, 6th Series, v. 223, c. 33, 19 April 1993.

3   Brendan Simms, *Unfinest Hour: Britain and the Destruction of Bosnia* (London: Penguin, 2002), p. 49.

4   John Major, *The Autobiography* (London: HarperCollins, 1999), p. 244.

5   Christopher Meyer, *Getting Our Way: 500 Years of Adventures and Intrigue: The Inside Story of British Diplomacy* (London: Phoenix, 2010), p. 249.

6   Ken Booth, 'Duty and Prudence' in Lawrence Freedman (ed.), *Military Intervention in European Conflicts* (Oxford: Blackwell, 1994), p. 60.

7   *Hansard*, HC Deb, 6th Series, v. 223, c. 34, 19 April 1993.

8   Douglas Hurd, *Memoirs* (London: Abacus, 2004), p. 431.

9   A 'witticism' from the US DoD on why the West was willing to intervene in Kuwait but not in Bosnia. Cited in John Fenske, 'The West and "The Problem from Hell"', *Current History*, 92.577 (1993), p. 354.

10   Hurd, *Memoirs*, p. 450. Major generously acknowledged Thatcher's work in laying the foundations of the victory in 1991. Major, *The Autobiography*, p. 220.

11   Brian C. Rathbun, *Partisan Interventions: European Party Politics and Peace Enforcement in the Balkans* (Ithaca, NY: Cornell University Press, 2004), p. 54. In 2012, Ed Vulliamy noted 'the [key] role of Britain in appeasing the Serbs diplomatically'. Ed Vulliamy, *The War is Dead, Long Live the War: Bosnia: the Reckoning* (London: The Bodley Head, 2012), p. 82.

12   Hurd, *Memoirs*, pp. 490–2.

13   Kenneth O. Morgan, 'The end of a foreign affair', *The Independent*, 31 October 2003.

14   In 1992 one commentator wrote: 'In the days of Mrs Thatcher leadership was no problem. A decision would be taken to punish a foreign aggressor . . . At least under Mrs Thatcher, whatever the merits of the decision, Britain entered into war at its own volition.' Martin Ivens, 'Whitehall at War', *The Times*, 30 December 1992.

15   Gyles Brandreth, 'Dictators I have known' (interview with Edward Heath), *Sunday Telegraph*, 14 November 1999.

16   Hurd, *Memoirs*, pp. 439, 491–2.

17   Rathbun, *Partisan Interventions*, p. 58.

18   Douglas Hurd, *Choose Your Weapons: The British Foreign Secretary – 200 Years of Argument, Success and Failure* (London: Phoenix, 2011), p. 309; Hurd quoted: Annika Savill, 'Diplomacy 'most effective' behind closed doors: Douglas Hurd tomorrow will deny charges of appeasement on Bosnia', *The Independent*, 8 September 1993; Joseph R. Biden Jr., 'More U.N. Appeasement on Bosnia', *New York Times*, 7 June 1993.

19   See, for example, Niall Ferguson, 'Europe Nervosa' (originally published 31 May 1993) in Nader Mousavizadeh (ed.), *The Black Book of Bosnia: The Consequences of 'Appeasement'* (New York: Basic Books, 1996), pp. 127–32.

20   Hurd, *Memoirs*, p. 495.

21 Warren Zimmermann, *Origins of a Catastrophe: Yugoslavia and Its Destroyers – America's Last Ambassador Tells What Happened and Why* (New York: Random House, 1999), pp. 1–9.

22 In 1995, Paul Addison said of Milošević: 'One could argue that it's Hitler within a Balkan context.' John Bosnall, Sian Griffiths, Gerard Kelly, Huw Richards and Simon Targett, 'Perspective: A Balkan Question in Search of an Answer', *The Times Higher Education Supplement*, 4 August 1995.On Serb expansionism, see James Gow, *The Serbian Project and Its Adversaries: A Strategy of War Crimes* (London: Hurst, 2003).

23 Robert J. McMahon, 'Credibility and World Power: Exploring the Psychological Dimension in Postwar American Diplomacy', *Diplomatic History*, 15.4 (1991), pp. 455–71. Quote at p. 455. See also Joseph Nye, *Bound to Lead: The Changing Nature of American Power* (New York: Basic Books, 1990), pp. 189–90; John G. Ikenberry, 'The Future of International Leadership', *Political Science Quarterly*, 111.3 (1996), pp. 389–91.

24 Richard W. Stevenson, 'Conflict in the Balkans: The British; New Casualty Fuels Debate in Britain', *New York Times,* 18 April 1994.

25 Malcolm Rifkind, 'Principles and Practice of British Foreign Policy', speech at The Royal Institute of International Affairs, 21 September 1995, www.fco.gov.uk/.

26 Simms, *Unfinest Hour*, p. 49.

27 James Gow, *Triumph of the Lack of Will: International Diplomacy and the Yugoslav War* (London: Hurst, 1997), p. 8.

28 *Hansard*, HC Deb, 6th Series, v. 223, c. 1168, 29 April 1993.

29 Hurd quoted in Major, *The Autobiography*, p. 548.

30 John Nott, *Haven't We Been Here Before? Afghanistan to the Falklands: A Personal Connection* (London: Discovered Authors, 2007), p. 240.

31 Major, *The Autobiography*, p. 535.

32 Simms, *Unfinest Hour*, pp. 24–5.

33 'Britannia Rules the Waverers', *Economist*, 15 August 1992.

34 Douglas Hurd, 'Making the World a Safer Place: Our Five Priorities', *Daily Telegraph*, 1 January 1992.

35 James Gow, 'British Perspectives' in Alex Danchev and Thomas Halverson (eds), *International Perspectives on the Yugoslav Conflict* (Basingstoke: Macmillan, 1996), p. 87.

36 *Hansard*, HC Deb, 6th Series, v. 199, c. 282, 20 November 1991.

37 *Hansard*, HC Deb, 6th Series, v. 198, c. 130, 1 November 1991.

38 'We have a formidable agenda in 1992 because the world will be a dangerous and complex place. In recent years Britain has punched above her weight in the world. We intend to keep it that way.' Hurd, 'Making the World a Safer Place: Our Five Priorities'.

39 Gow, 'British Perspectives', pp. 90–1.

40 Brendan Simms, *Yugoslavia: The Case for Intervention* (London: The Bow Group, 1994), pp. 4, 7.

41　Rathbun, *Partisan Interventions*, p. 55.

42　Senior foreign office official quoted in William Wallace, 'British Foreign Policy after the Cold War', *International Affairs*, 68.3 (1992), p. 442.

43　*Hansard*, HC Deb, 6th Series, v. 226, c. 858–9, 16 June 1993.

44　Rathbun, *Partisan Interventions*, pp. 55–7.

45　*Hansard*, HC Deb, 6th Series, v. 223, c. 30–1, 19 April 1993.

46　*Hansard*, HC Deb, 6th Series, v. 267, c. 659, 22 November 1995.

47　For a discussion of 'Realism' and British foreign policy see David Sanders, *Losing an Empire, Finding a Role* (Basingstoke: Macmillan, 1990), pp. 258–72.

48　One of six main realist propositions. Ibid., p. 262.

49　Gow, 'British Perspectives', p. 88.

50　Senior official of the US State Department quoted in Ed Vulliamy, 'Bosnia – The Secret War: Tragic Cost of Allies' Hidden Hostility', *The Guardian*, 21 May 1996.

51　Simms, *Unfinest Hour*, p. 65.

52　Wallace, 'British Foreign Policy after the Cold War', p. 442.

53　Hurd, *Memoirs*, p. 508; Ferguson 'Europa Nervosa', pp. 127–9.

54　The long-standing 'Eastern Question' revolved around the issue of what should happen to the Balkans if, and when, the Ottoman Empire collapsed. The reference here is to the international crisis that arose as a result of the brutal Ottoman suppression of the Bulgarian rebellion of 1875. Disraeli, the Conservative prime minister, favoured staying out of the crisis; Gladstone, his Liberal opponent, advocated intervention. Robert Blake, Disraeli's most accomplished biographer, observed of the bitter dispute between the two men and their followers: 'Few political issues have raise such venomous feelings.' For while 'Munich and Suez are nearest equivalents in recent times . . . on neither occasion did even the most vehement partisans' engage in the sort of public vituperation that the 'Eastern Question' inspired in the 1870s. Robert Blake, *Disraeli* (London: Methuen, 1969), p. 607. On the 'Eastern Question' and British politics in the 1870s, see Richard Aldous, *The Lion and the Unicorn: Gladstone vs. Disraeli* (New York: W.W. Norton, 2007), pp. 268–89; H. C. G. Matthew, *Gladstone: 1875–1898* (Oxford: Clarendon Press, 1995), pp. 1–40; and Miloš Ković, *Disraeli and the Eastern Question* (Oxford: Oxford University Press, 2011).

55　*Hansard*, HC Deb, 6th Series, v. 260, c. 1000, 31 May 1995.

56　Douglas Hogg, FCO Minister of State, to the Foreign Affairs Committee, *Central and Eastern Europe: Problems of the Post-Communist Era*, First Report, Volume II (London: HMSO, 1992), p. 58. Douglas Hogg was the son of Quintin Hogg, the former Conservative minister who had won the infamous Oxford 'Munich' by-election in October 1938.

57　Anthony Seldon, *Major: A Political Life* (London: Phoenix, 1998), p. 506.

58　Major, *The Autobiography*, p. 533.

59　Andy Marshall, 'What Could Die at Bihac', *The Independent*, 28 November 1994.

60 Robert Cooper and Mats Berdal, 'Outside Intervention in Ethnic Conflicts', *Survival*, 35.1 (1993), pp. 118–42.

61 On this, see the following articles by George C. Herring: 'American Strategy in Vietnam: The Postwar Debate', *Military Affairs*, 46.2 (1982), pp. 57–63; 'Vietnam Remembered', *The Journal of American History*, 73.1 (1986), pp. 152–64; 'America and Vietnam: The Debate Continues', *American Historical Review*, 92.2 (1987), pp. 350–62; and 'America and Vietnam: The Unending War', *Foreign Affairs*, 70.5 (1991–2), pp. 104–19.

62 Major, *The Autobiography*, pp. 539–41.

63 'Britannia and Bosnia', *Economist*, 15 August 1992.

64 Gow, 'British Perspectives', p. 89.

65 Major, *The Autobiography*, p. 538.

66 Ironically, given the British government's reluctance to intervene in Bosnia, it was British journalists who first uncovered some of the worst horror stories of 'ethnic cleansing'. Edgar O'Ballance, *Civil War in Bosnia 1992–94* (Basingstoke: Macmillan, 1995), p. 80.

67 Anne J. Lane, 'Coming to terms with Tito: Britain and Yugoslavia, 1945–49' in Richard J. Aldrich and Michael F. Hopkins (eds), *Intelligence, Defence and Diplomacy: British Policy in the Post-War World* (London: Frank Cass, 1994), p. 13.

68 E. Barker, *British Policy towards South-East Europe during the Second World War* (Basingstoke: Macmillan and SSEES, 1976), p. 136.

69 Lane, 'Coming to Terms with Tito', pp. 14–15.

70 TNA: PRO: FO 954/ 23, Eden to Churchill, 18 January 1945.

71 TNA: PRO: FO 371/ 48874 [R 19433/130/G] Sir Orme Sargent to Ambassador Sir Ralph Stevenson, Belgrade, 24 November 1945.

72 Steven L. Burg, 'Why Yugoslavia Fell Apart', *Current History*, 92.577 (1993), p. 360.

73 Hurd, *Memoirs*, p. 493.

74 *Hansard*, 6th Series, HC Deb, v. 212, c.119, 25 September 1992.

75 Two 1990 CIA reports, for instance, warned of war in Yugoslavia within 18 months. National Archives College Park (NACP), Washington, DC: CIA Reports, 'Yugoslavia: Army Ponders Its Role', 1 November 1990 and 'Yugoslavia: Army Interventions Rumblings Growing', 29 November 1990; Christopher Cviic, 'Perceptions of Former Yugoslavia: An Interpretative Reflection', *International Affairs*, 71.4 (1995), p. 823.

76 Jonathan Eyal, *Europe and Yugoslavia: Lessons from a Failure* (London: RUSI for Defence Studies, Whitehall Paper Series, 1993), p. 2.

77 Ibid. pp. 8–9.

78 See, for example, Editorial: 'No to Balkanisation', *The Times,* 8 May 1991.

79 Sabrina Petra Ramet, *Balkan Babel: The Disintegration of Yugoslavia from the Death of Tito to Ethnic War* (Boulder, CO: Westview Press, 1996), p. 259.

80 Jane Sharp, 'Appeasement, Intervention and the Failure of Europe' in Freedman (ed.), *Military Intervention in European Conflicts*, p. 48.

81 Eyal, *Europe and Yugoslavia*, p. 16.

82 Lenard J. Cohen, *Broken Bonds. Yugoslavia's Disintegration and Balkan Politics in Transition* (Boulder, CO: Westview Press, 2nd edn. 1995), p. 220.

83 Thomas Halverson, 'American Perspectives' in Alex Danchev and Thomas Halverson (eds), *International Perspectives on the Yugoslav Conflict* (Basingstoke: Macmillan, 1996), p. 6.

84 Eyal, *Europe and Yugoslavia*, pp. 24, 13.

85 Laura Silber and Allan Little, *The Death of Yugoslavia* (London: Penguin/ BBC books, 1995), pp. 211–12.

86 A Dutch source quoted in Boris Johnson, 'Douglas Hurd's Public Conscience', *The Spectator,* 17 April, 1993. Even had Britain favoured intervention it would never have favoured the WEU over NATO.

87 US government statement, 17 April 1992. Halverson, 'American Perspectives', p. 12

88 Graham Messervy-Whiting, *Peace Conference on Former Yugoslavia: The Politico-Military Interface* (London: Centre for Defence Studies, 1995).

89 On this, see Charalmbos Papasotiriou, *Liberal Idealism versus Realism: The Yugoslav Case* (Athens: Institute of International Relations, 1996).

90 Christopher Cviic, *Remaking the Balkans* (London: RIIA, 1995), p. 113.

91 Carrington had met Tito when he was minister of defence in the 1960s and was a fan of both his leadership and of Yugoslavia. Lord Carrington, *Reflect on Things Past: The Memoirs of Lord Carrington* (London: Collins, 1988), pp. 237–8.

92 Silber and Little, *The Death of Yugoslavia*, p. 209.

93 Gow, *Triumph of the Lack of Will*, p. 177.

94 Eyal, *Europe and Yugoslavia*, pp. 37–8.

95 There were four main initiatives: *viz.* Carrington–Cutileiro; Vance–Owen; Owen–Stoltenberg and the Contact Group. These, to a greater or lesser degree, accepted that ethnic separation was an essential precondition of any settlement. The Carrington–Cutileiro peace plan, named for its authors Lord Carrington and Portugal's José Cutileiro, resulted from the February 1992 EC Peace Conference designed to prevent war in Bosnia-Herzegovina. It was initialled on 18 March 1992 (by Alija Izetbegović for the Bosnians, Radovan Karadžić for the Bosnian Serbs and Mate Boban for the Bosnian Croats). Izetbegović withdrew his assent ten days later in an attempt to preserve a unitary state in Bosnia-Herzegovina. There were rumours that he had encouraged to do so by the then US ambassador to Yugoslavia, Warren Zimmermann. The Vance–Owen Peace Plan (VOPP) of 1993 – proposed by UN Special Envoy Cyrus Vance and EC representative Lord Owen – involved the division of Bosnia-Herzegovina into ten semi-autonomous regions. VOPP was seen as a modern-day Hoare–Laval Plan, it satisfied virtually no one and – much to the chagrin of the British government – was opposed by the Clinton administration before it collapsed. After Vance resigned, Norwegian Foreign Minister Thorvald Stoltenberg and Owen came up with the so-called

Owen-Stoltenberg plan. This would have created three ethnic mini-states, in which the Bosnian Serb would be given 52 per cent of Bosnia-Herzegovina's territory, the Muslims would be allotted 30 per cent and the Bosnian Croats would receive 18 per cent. The Bosnian government, supported by the United States, rejected this plan that would have given the Serbs nearly all that they wanted. Between February and October 1994, the Contact Group (consisting of the United States, Russia, France, Britain and Germany) tried, and failed, to find an acceptable formula for the future of Bosnia-Herzegovina. On these schemes, see James E. Goodby, 'When War Won Out: Bosnian Peace Plans before Dayton', *International Negotiation*, 1.3 (1996), pp. 501–23.

96   Editorial: 'Reinventing Bosnia', *Economist*, 22 August 1992.

97   Gow, 'British Perspectives', pp. 92–3.

98   Silber and Little, *The Death of Yugoslavia*, p. 218.

99   Hans-Dietrich Genscher, *Erinnerungen* (Berlin: Siedler Verlag, 1995), p. 958.

100   'The Arts of War and the Guiles of Peace', *Economist*, 15 August 1992.

101   FCO official quoted from a CSCE meeting in June 1991. Hella Pick, 'Doing the Splits over Belgrade: A Crisis that's Dividing Europe', *The Guardian*, 3 July 1991.

102   Misha Glenny, 'Germany Fans the Flames of War', *New Statesman and Society*, 20 December 1991; Craig R. Whitney, 'In the New Era, a New Realism: As Germany Flexes Its Muscles, the New Europe Goes Along ', *New York Times*, 29 December 1991.

103   Beverley Crawford, 'Explaining Defection from International Co-operation: Germany's Unilateral Recognition of Croatia', *World Politics*, 48.4 (1996), p. 496.

104   Misha Glenny, *The Third Balkan War* (London: Penguin Books, 1992), p. 180.

105   For Genscher's account, see Genscher, *Erinnerungen*, pp. 927ff. On the role of Germany in the dissolution of the former Yugoslavia, see Klaus Peter Zeitler, *Deutschlands Rolle bei der völkerrechtlichen Anerkennung der Republik Kroatien: unter besonderer Berücksichtigung des deutschen Außenministers Genscher* (Marburg: Tectum Verlag, 2000).

106   On this, see Richard Caplan, *Europe and the Recognition of New States in Yugoslavia* (Cambridge: Cambridge University Press, 2007).

107   *Hansard*, HC Deb, 6th Series, v. 201, c. 485, 19 December 1991.

108   Lord David Owen, *Balkan Odyssey* (London: Gollancz, 1995), p. 344.

109   Major, *The Autobiography*, p. 533.

110   Radovan Karadžić (president of *Republika Srpska*) quoted in *The Financial Times*, 23 December 1991.

111   O'Ballance, *Civil War in Bosnia 1992–94*, pp. 102–3.

112   Patrick Wintour, 'Rift Grows in Britain on Sending Troops', *The Guardian*, 14 August 1992.

113   Silber and Little, *The Death of Yugoslavia*, pp. 288–9.

114 O'Ballance, *Civil War in Bosnia 1992–94*, p. 102. Rifkind repeated this in January 1993: 'We have no intention of letting our ground forces in Bosnia be used for combat purposes.' Patrick Wintour, 'Rifkind Promises Withdrawal from Bosnia If Risks too High', *The Guardian*, 18 January 1993. Note: UNPROFOR – United Nations Protection Force.

115 Meyer, *Getting Our Way*, p. 249.

116 Michael White, 'Bosnia Crisis: Major Urges Caution', *The Guardian*, 19 December 1992.

117 Martin Bell, 'Conflict of Interest', *The Guardian*, 11 July 1996.

118 James Gow, 'Nervous Bunnies: The International Community and the Yugoslav War of Dissolution, the Politics of Military Intervention in Time of Change' in Freedman (ed.), *Military Intervention in European Conflicts*, p. 18.

119 For a recently published collection of documents, see David Owen (ed.), *Bosnia-Herzegovina: The Vance/Owen Peace Plan* (Liverpool: Liverpool University Press, 2013). Publicity for this book claimed that 'Sadly, Bosnia-Herzegovina is still deeply divided, a direct consequence of not imposing the VOPP.' See the relevant page on the Liverpool University Press web page at www.liverpooluniversitypress.co.uk/.

120 For a discussion of the problems associated with peacemaking in such situations, see Chaim Kaufmann, 'Possible and Impossible Solutions to Ethnic Civil Wars', *International Security*, 20.4 (1996), pp. 136–75.

121 ICFY Press Release, Geneva (mid) January 1993, 'Vance's Views on Moral Appeasement'. Owen (ed.), *Bosnia-Herzegovina*, pp. 256, 257.

122 Silber and Little, *The Death of Yugoslavia*, p. 300.

123 On this see, for example, Tom Fraser, 'Partitioning Ireland, India and Palestine' in Peter Collins (ed.), *Nationalism and Unionism: Conflict in Ireland, 1885–1921* (Belfast: Institute of Irish Studies, Queen's University Belfast, 1994), pp. 177–86.

124 On the problems associated with the 'panacea' of ethnic partition, see Radha Kumar, 'The Troubled History of Partition', *Foreign Affairs*, 76.1 (1997), pp. 22–34; Ray E. Johnston, 'Partition as a Political Instrument", *Journal of International Affairs*, 27.2 (1973), pp. 159–74; Norman J. G. Pounds, 'History and Geography: A Perspective on Partition', *Journal of International Affairs*, 18.2 (1964), pp. 161–72; Nicholas Sambinis, 'Partition as a Solution to Ethnic War: An Empirical Critique of the Theoretical Literature', *World Politics*, 52.4 (2000): 437–83; Stanley Waterman, 'Partitioned States', *Political Geography Quarterly*, 6.2 (1987), pp. 151–70; Stanley Waterman, 'Partition and Modern Nationalism', pp.117–32 in Colin H. Williams and Eleonore Kofman (eds), *Community Conflict: Partition and Nationalism* (London: Routledge, 1989), pp. 117–32.

125 Simms, *Unfinest Hour*, p. 153.

126 Patrick Wintour, 'Rift with US Alarms Britain', *The Guardian*, 1 April 1993. Owen accused the United States of letting the Muslims believe that 'Washington may come in on their side any day now'. Owen quoted in O'Ballance, *Civil War in Bosnia 1992–94*, p. 145.

127 Gow, *Triumph of the Lack of Will*, p. 175. Robin Renwick, the UK ambassador to Washington between 1991 and 1995, later recalled his frustration with the Americans: 'while they lectured us constantly on what we ought to do to deal with the problem i.e. be much tougher with the Bosnian Serbs, they were not themselves prepared to accept any of the risks on the ground.' BDOHP: Lord Renwick, interviewed by Malcolm McBain, 6 August 1998, p. 20. For Clinton's assessment of matters at the outset of his presidency, see Bill Clinton, *My Life* (London: Arrow Books, 2005), pp. 511–12. For a scathing critique of the inconsistencies and failures in Clinton's policy towards Bosnia between 1993 and 1995, see Donald Kagan and Frederick W. Kagan, *While America Sleeps: Self-delusion, Military Weakness, and the Threat to Peace Today* (New York: St. Martin's Press, 2000), pp. 400–15.

128 Rathbun, *Partisan Interventions*, p. 58.

129 Samantha Powers, *'A Problem from Hell': America and the Age of Genocide* (New York: HarperCollins, 2002), p. 326.

130 *Hansard*, HC Deb, 6th Series, v. 223, c. 1167, 29 April 1993.

131 *Hansard*, HC Deb, 6th Series, v. 223, c. 1170, 29 April 1993.

132 Clinton, *My Life*, p. 511.

133 Halverson, 'American Perspectives', p. 12; Gow, 'Nervous Bunnies', p. 30.

134 American official cited in Fenske, 'The West and "The problem from hell"', p. 355.

135 W. R. Smyser, *The Humanitarian Conscience: Caring for Others in the Age of Terror* (New York: Palgrave Macmillan, 1993), p. 134.

136 'Bosnia: US views', Robin Renwick, Washington, DC, to FCO 18 April 1993. Owen (ed.), *Bosnia-Herzegovina*, p. 388.

137 Jonathan Clarke, 'Rhetoric before Reality', *Foreign Affairs*, 74.5 (1995), p. 7. On US diplomatic failings during the Bosnian War, see Marshall, 'What Could Die at Bihac'.

138 Clinton, *My Life*, p. 512; Hurd, *Memoirs*, pp. 506–8. On US enthusiasm for this 'solution', see Susan Woodward, *The Balkan Tragedy: Chaos and Dissolution after the Cold War* (Washington, DC: The Brookings Institution, 1995), pp. 297, 499. Lord Owen later testified that the West should have use air strikes to prevent the flow of arms across the River Drina from Serbia proper so as to 'alter the balance' in Bosnia. Lord Owen, question-and-answer session, Aberystwyth University, 16 April 2013.

139 Major, *The Autobiography*, p. 542.

140 Norman Cigar, *Genocide in Bosnia: The Policy of 'Ethnic Cleansing'* (College Station, TX: Texas A&M University Press, 1995), p. 150.

141 Hurd, *Memoirs*, p. 505.

142 *Hansard*, HC Deb, 6th Series, v. 223, c. 1173, 29 April 1993. For similar, see Major, *The Autobiography*, pp. 541–2.

143 One UN source stated: 'The plan will freeze the military situation on the ground. The "safe areas" have no chance of becoming viable – already they are turning into permanent refugee camps. Politically it contradicts the Vance–Owen plan

for Bosnia. It is deeply unfair, as the Serbian side keep their arms while the Muslims will be disarmed. We are just setting the stage for a long-term war of skirmishes.' Marcus Tanner, 'Bosnia's "Safe Areas": West Sets the Stage for a Human Tragedy', *The Independent*, 8 June 1993.

144   Charles G. Boyd, 'Making Peace with the Guilty: The Truth about Bosnia', *Foreign Affairs*, 74.5 (1995), p. 33.

145   *Hansard*, HC Deb, 6th Series, v. 223, c. 1174, 29 April 1993.

146   O'Ballance, *Civil War in Bosnia 1992–94*, p. 149.

147   David Rieff, *Slaughterhouse: Bosnia and the Failure of the West* (London: Vintage, 1995), p. 14.

148   Owen, *Balkan Odyssey*, p. 173.

149   US official quoted in ibid., p. 170.

150   This was to be achieved by means of 'safe areas' and the sealing of Bosnia's borders to outside incursions. Silber and Little, *The Death of Yugoslavia*, p. 320.

151   Michael Foot, 'Another Hand, Another Piece of Paper: British policy on former Yugoslavia is similar to earlier shameful appeasements', *The Guardian*, 26 May 1993. On Spain, see Glyn Stone, 'Britain, Non-Intervention and the Spanish Civil War', *European History Quarterly*, 9.1 (1979), pp. 129–49; Glyn Stone, 'Neville Chamberlain and the Spanish Civil War, 1936–9', *International History Review*, 35:2 (2013), pp. 377–95. In 1938 George Orwell wrote: 'By a combination of meanness and hypocrisy that would take a lot of beating, Chamberlain and his friends have allowed the Spanish Republic to be slowly strangled.' (Review of Frank Jellinek, *The Civil War in Spain*, *New English Weekly*, 21 July 1938). George Orwell, *The Collected Essays, Journalism and Letters of George Orwell: Volume 1: An Age Like This 1920–1940*, ed. Sonia Orwell and Ian Angus (London: Penguin, 1970), p. 382. In 2011, during a Commons debate on British intervention in the civil war in Libya, Labour leader Ed Miliband stated: 'In 1936, a Spanish politician came to Britain to plead for support in the face of General Franco's violent fascism. He said: "We are fighting with sticks and knives against tanks and aircraft and guns, and it revolts the conscience of the world that that should be true." As we saw the defenceless people of Libya attacked by their own Government, it would equally revolt the conscience of the world to know that we could have done something to help them yet chose not to.' *Hansard*, HC Deb, 6th Series, v. 525, c. 715, 21 March 2011.

152   By December 1994, the German government had shifted firmly towards Washington's position. Owen, *Balkan Odyssey*, p. 300.

153   Nenad Ivankovic, *Vjesnik* (Zagreb), 23 May 1993. Cited in Sabrina Petra Ramet, 'The Bosnian War and the Policy of Accommodation', *Current History*, 93.586 (1994), p. 383.

154   Lawrence Freedman, 'Allies Stick Together to Contain Bosnia Conflict', *The Times*, 14 May 1993.

155   *Hansard*, HC Deb, 6th Series, v. 223, c. 1173, 29 April 1993.

156   Owen, *Balkan Odyssey*, p. 224.

157　This included the dispatch of some 500 US peacekeepers to Macedonia in July 1993. Ivankovic cited in Ramet, 'The Bosnian War and the Policy of Accommodation', p. 384.

158　Tristan Garel-Jones, minister of state, FCO. *Hansard*, HC Deb, 6th Series, v. 224, c. 285, 6 May 1993

159　*Hansard*, HC Deb, 6th Series, v. 233, c. 119, 19 November 1993.

160　In his memoirs Major casts doubt on the assertion that the Serbs fired the shell. Major, *The Autobiography*, p. 543.

161　Silber and Little, *The Death of Yugoslavia*, p. 345.

162　Hurd, *Memoirs*, p. 514.

163　'Decisions Taken at the Meeting of the North Atlantic Council in Permanent Session', 9 February 1994, www.nato.int/docu/comm/49–95/c940209a.htm.

164　Clinton, *My Life*, p. 534. On this, and Russia's subsequent involvement in Bosnia, see James Headley, *Russia and the Balkans: Foreign Policy from Yeltsin to Putin* (New York: Columbia University Press, 2008), pp. 167–210.

165　Deputy Foreign Minister Sergei Lavrov to the Duma quoted in Andrei Edemskii, 'Russian Perspectives' in Danchev and Halverson (eds), *International Perspectives on the Yugoslav Conflict*, p. 45.

166　Silber and Little, *The Death of Yugoslavia*, p. 362.

167　William Safire, 'Arm Muslim fighters and Bomb Serbian Positions', *New York Times*, 29 November 1994.

168　When the 'safe area' of Gorazde came under attack in April 1994 and the United States again called for air strikes, the British opposed this as being inconsistent with the UNPROFOR mandate. A US diplomat chided the British as 'really wet', while London asked why the Americans had no troops on the ground. Silber and Little, *The Death of Yugoslavia*, p. 369. In the event, the United States backed away from air strikes in order to preserve NATO and was to do so again over Bihać in November 1994.

169　Cohen, *Broken Bonds*, p. 311.

170　Silber and Little, *The Death of Yugoslavia*, pp. 378–9.

171　Brendan Simms, 'Why America Is Right about Bosnia; Appeasement Does not Work. Britain Should Pull Its Troops out and Allow the Arms Embargo to Be Lifted', *The Independent*, 2 December 1995; Clinton, *My Life*, p. 581; Hurd, *Memoirs*, p. 521.

172　Simms, *Unfinest Hour*, p. 211.

173　Marshall, 'What Could Die at Bihac'. In Bosnia, Marshall noted, while 'the Americans see Munich . . . [the] Europeans see Vietnam'.

174　Joseph Lepgold, 'British-American Relations after the Cold War: The End of the Special Relationship', *Brassey's Defence Yearbook* (London: Brassey's, 1996), p. 118.

175　Clinton, *My Life*, pp. 590–1.

176　US State Department official quoted in Vulliamy, 'Bosnia – The Secret War'.

177　Janusz Bugajski, 'Dayton's Impact on the US Presidential Election', *Transition*, 2.14 (1996), p. 17.

178   Owen, *Balkan Odyssey*, p. 253.

179   Albright aide quoted in Vulliamy, 'Bosnia – The Secret War'.

180   Vulliamy, 'Bosnia – The Secret War'.

181   Simon Serfaty, 'America and Europe beyond Bosnia', *The Washington Quarterly*, 19.3 (1996), p. 34.

182   Marie-Janine Calic, 'Bosnia-Hercegovinia after Dayton: Opportunities and Risks for Peace', *Aussenpolitik: German Foreign Affairs Review*, 47.2 (1996), pp. 128–9.

183   Nott, *Haven't We Been Here Before?*, p. 257.

184   Vernon Bogdanor, 'Srebrenica: The Silence over Britain's Guilt must Be Ended', *The Guardian*, 12 July 2012.

185   Ed Vulliamy, 'US "Gave Green Light to Croat offensive"', *The Guardian*, 31 July 1995.

186   Clinton, *My Life*, pp. 667, 684.

187   Quoted in Craig R. Whitney, 'With Ethnic Strife, NATO Finds the Enemy Is within', *New York Times*, 6 July 1997.

188   Jonathan Freedland, 'Congress Votes to Arm Bosnians', *The Guardian*, 2 August 1995.

189   Nott, *Haven't We Been Here Before?*, p. 257; Vulliamy, 'Bosnia – The Secret War'.

190   For Holbrooke's account fo the Dayton talks (1–21 November 1995), see Richard Holbrooke, *To End a War* (New York: Random House, 1998), pp. 231–312.

191   Ibid., pp. 321–22.

192   President Clinton, 'Remarks at the Harry S Truman Library Institute', Washington, DC, 25 October 1995, cited in 'Sustaining American Leadership through NATO', *US State Department Dispatch*, 6.45 (6 November 1995), pp. 813–15.

193   Clinton address to the nation, 27 November 1995. Alvin Z. Rubinstein, Albina Shayevich and Boris Zlotnikov (eds), *The Clinton Foreign Policy Reader: Presidential Speeches with Commentary* (New York: M.E. Sharpe, 2000), p. 175.

194   Christopher Dandeker and James Gow, 'The Future of Peace Support Operations: Strategic Peacekeeping and Success', *Armed Forces & Society*, 23.3 (1997), pp. 327–48.

195   Richard Holbrooke, 'America, a European Power', *Foreign Affairs*, 74.2 (1995), p. 40; Holbrooke, *To End a War*, p. 21.

196   The Dayton agreement provided for a Serb 'entity' (49% of Bosnia) and a Muslim-Croat Federation (51%) in a supposedly unitary state with a revolving presidency. See 'The Dayton Peace Accords: Text of Documents Related to the Dayton Peace Agreement which was initialled at Wright-Patterson Air Force Base in Dayton, Ohio on November 21, 1995 and signed in Paris on December 14, 1995', US State Department, www.state.gov/www/regions/eur/bosnia/bosagree.html.

197 Laura Silber and Allan Little accurately described the creation and structure of the so-called Contact Group as being 'reminiscent of [nothing so much as] nineteenth-century Great Power politics'. Silber and Little, *The Death of Yugoslavia*, p. 374.

198 George Orwell, 'Looking Back on the Spanish War' (1943) in *England, Your England and Other Essays* (London: Secker and Warburg, 1953), p. 169.

199 Pauline Neville-Jones, 'Dayton, IFOR and Alliance Relations in Bosnia', *Survival*, 38.4 (1996–7), pp. 45–65.

200 Ambrose Evans Pritchard, 'Will Clinton Keep It Special?', *Sunday Telegraph*, 21 February 1993.

201 Patricia Wynn Davies, 'Ashdown Accuses Government of "Worst Appeasement"', *The Independent*, 11 December 1992.

202 *Hansard*, HC Deb, 6th Series, v. 223, c. 1192, 29 April 1993.

203 Martin Bell, 'Conflict of Interest', *The Guardian*, 11 July 1996.

204 *Hansard*, HL Deb, 5th Series, v. 566, c. 375, 20 July 1995. Lord Dubs was born in December 1932 in Prague. He was one of the 669 Czech children rescued from the Nazis by English stockbroker Nicholas Winton.

205 Nott, *Haven't We Been Here Before?*, p. 261.

206 Philip Towle, 'The British Debate about Intervention in European Conflicts' in Freedman (ed.), *Military Intervention in European Conflicts*, p. 103–4.

207 *Hansard*, HC Deb, 6th Series, v. 225, c. 580, 24 May 1993.

208 R. D. Wilkinson, of FCO planning staff cited in Rieff, *Slaughterhouse*, pp. 28–9.

209 Douglas Hurd, June 1993. Quoted in Towle, 'The British Debate about Intervention in European Conflicts', p. 103.

210 *Hansard*, HC Deb, 6th Series, v. 267, c. 659, 22 November 1995.

211 Gow, 'Nervous Bunnies', pp. 25–6.

212 Fitzroy Maclean, *Eastern Approaches* (London: Jonathan Cape, 1949). For refutations of many of the myths about Yugoslavia in the Second World War, see Milovan Djilas, *Wartime*, trans. Michael B. Petrovitch (London: Secker & Warburg, 1977) and Rieff, *Slaughterhouse*, pp. 154–5.

213 Norman Stone, 'Shooting Down the Myth of Serbia's Mighty Guerrillas', *The Sunday Times*, 16 August 1992.

214 Catherine Bennett, 'Paralysed with Fear: We Agonise while Bosnia Burns. Should we try to end the slaughter? Could we? Might it go horribly wrong?', *The Guardian*, 23 October 1992.

215 David Hannay, *Britain's Quest for a Role: A Diplomatic Memoir from Europe to the UN* (London: I.B. Tauris, 2013), p. 212.

216 Statement by Major, London, 21 November 1995, www.johnmajor.co.uk/page1371.html.

217 Conor Cruise O'Brien, 'We Enter Bosnia at Our Peril', *The Independent*, 23 April 1993. David Rieff, a fierce critic of Western policy, opined: 'Comparisons between Milosevic and Hitler are foolish and unworthy – the knee-jerk

impulse of an age mired in rhetorical success which has to insist that good is the greatest and anything bad the worst'. Rieff, *Slaughterhouse*, p. 31.

218 Papasotiriou, *Liberal Idealism versus Realism*, p. 10.

219 John Bosnall, Sian Griffiths, Gerard Kelly, Huw Richards and Simon Targett, 'Perspective: A Balkan Question in Search of an Answer', *The Times Higher Education Supplement*, 4 August 1995.

220 *Hansard*, HC Deb, 6th Series, v. 260, c. 1029, 31 May 1995.

221 Charlotte Eagar, 'Foot Names Guilty Men of Bosnia', *The Observer*, 1 January 1995.

222 *Hansard*, HC Deb, 6th Series, v. 260, c. 1020, 31 May 1995.

223 Bennett, 'Paralysed with Fear'.

224 Editorial: 'Into Yugoslavia', *The Economist*, 15 August 1992.

225 Hurd, *Memoirs*, p. 492. For Hurd's take on appeasement and the civil war in Spain, see Hurd, *Choose Your Weapons*, p. 307.

226 Hugh Thomas, *The Spanish Civil War* (London: Penguin books, 1965), p. 289.

227 Hurd quoted in Noel Macolm, *Bosnia: A Short History* (London: Papermac, 1996), p. 244.

228 Stejpan G. Meštrović, 'Introduction' in Meštrović (ed.), *Genocide after Emotion: The Postemotional Balkan War* (London: Routledge, 1996), p. 14.

229 Cigar, *Genocide in Bosnia*, p. 173.

230 Gow, *Triumph of the Lack of Will*, p. 83.

231 Hannay, *Britain's Quest for a Role*, p. 212.

232 Meštrović, 'Epilogue' in *Genocide after Emotion*, p. 212.

233 Cigar, *Genocide in Bosnia*, p. 168.

234 Brankas Magaš, 'Bosnia: A very British Betrayal', *New Statesman and Society*, 10 September 1993.

235 Cigar, *Genocide in Bosnia*, p. 171.

236 Maisky to Cadogan, 10 August 1938. Jonathan Haslam, *The Soviet Union and the Struggle for Collective Security in Europe 1933–39* (Basingstoke: Macmillan, 1984), p. 117.

237 Cigar, *Genocide in Bosnia*, p. 168.

238 *Hansard*, HC Deb, 6th Series, v. 251, c. 321, 7 December 1994; *Hansard*, HC Deb, 6th Series, v. 251, c. 912, 14 December 1994; *Hansard*, HC Deb, 6th Series, v. 259, c. 637, 9 May 1995.

239 John Nott, 'America Is Right about Bosnia', *The Times*, 1 December 1994. See also, Nott, *Haven't We Been Here Before*, pp. 253–5.

240 Ed Vulliamy, 'Farewell, Sarajevo: As he steps down as the de facto ruler of Bosnia, Paddy Ashdown tells Ed Vulliamy that it has been "frightening to have so much power"', *The Guardian*, 2 November 2005.

241 Jane M. O. Sharp, *Bankrupt in the Balkans: British Policy in Bosnia* (London: Institute for Public Policy Research, 1992), pp. 19–20.

242 Douglas Hurd, 2 August 1993, interview on UK Channel 4 TV. Gow, 'Nervous Bunnies', p. 30.

243 Gow, 'British Perspectives', p. 94.

244 *Hansard*, HC Deb, 6th Series, v. 251, c. 322, 7 December 1994; *Hansard*, HC Deb, 6th Series, v. 251, c. 912, 14 December 1994; Hurd, *Memoirs*, pp. 492–3. Quote at p. 493.

245 *Hansard*, HC Deb, 6th Series, v. 223, c. 1169, 29 April 1993. The relevant passage from Tacitus reads: 'To robbery, butchery and rapine, they give the lying name of "government"; they create a desolation and call it peace'. Tacitus, *The Agricola*: 30 in *The Agricola and the Germania*, trans. H. Mattingly and S. A. Handford (London: Penguin, 1970), p. 81.

246 Henry Kissinger, *Diplomacy* (New York: Simon and Schuster, 1994), p. 471.

Chapter 9

1   Tony Blair, 'A New Generation Draws the Line', *Newsweek*, 19 April 1999.

2   Louise Richardson, 'A Force for Good in the World? Britain's Role in the Kosovo Crisis' in Marc Brawley and Pierre Martin (eds), *Alliance Politics, Kosovo and NATO'S War: Allied Force or Forced Allies?* (New York: Palgrave, 2000), p. 159.

3   Tony Blair, *A Journey* (London: Hutchinson, 2010), p. 99. For Thatcher's opinion of Blair's adoption of her mantle in certain respects, see Margaret Thatcher, *Statecraft: Strategy for a Changing World* (London: HarperCollins, 2003), p. 428.

4   Jonathan Powell, *The New Machiavelli: How to Wield Power in the Modern World* (London: Vintage, 2011), p. 262.

5   Dan Bulley, *Ethics as Foreign Policy: Britain, the EU and the Other* (London: Routledge, 2009), p. 51.

6   Blair, *A Journey*, pp. 228–9.

7   Powell, *The New Machiavelli*, p. 264.

8   Jackie Ashley and Ewen MacAskill, '"History Will Be My Judge": Tony Blair . . . says demos and rebels will not deflect him over Iraq', *The Guardian*, 1 March 2003.

9   Brian C. Rathbun, *Partisan Interventions: European Party Politics and Peace Enforcement in the Balkans* (Ithaca, NY: Cornell University Press, 2004), p. 74.

10 Blair, *A Journey*, pp. 223, 227.

11 Thatcher, *Statecraft*, p. 34.

12 On the significance of this, see Paul Latawski, 'NATO's Military Action over Kosovo: The Conceptual Landscape after the Battle' in Stephen Badsey and Paul Latawski (eds), *Britain, NATO and the Lessons of the Balkan Conflicts, 1991–1999*, intro. Geoffrey Hoon (London: Frank Cass, 2004), pp. 121–38.

13 Rathbun, *Partisan Interventions*, p. 75

14 Diary entry for 4 April 1999. Alan Clark, *The Last Diaries: In and Out of the Wilderness,* ed. Ion Trewin (London: Weidenfeld & Nicolson, 2002), p. 306.

15 Tony Blair, 'Doctrine of International Community', speech given at the Economic Club of Chicago, 22 April 1999. Rob D. Kaiser and Michael McGuire, 'Blair Unveils Bold Intervention Doctrine', *Chicago Tribune,* 23 April 1999.

16 Bill Clinton, *My Life* (London: Arrow Books, 2005), p. 851.

17 Anthony Seldon, *Blair: The Biography* (London: Free Press, 2004), p. 403; Andrew Marr *A History of Modern Britain* (London: Pan, 2008), p. 550; Blair, *A Journey,* pp. 236–8.

18 Powell, *The New Machiavelli,* p. 264

19 Thatcher, *Statecraft,* p. 309.

20 Margaret Thatcher, 'Speech to the International Free Enterprise dinner', London, 20 April 1999, Margaret Thatcher Foundation, www.margaretthatcher.org/document/108381.

21 Blair, 'Doctrine of International Community' in Michael Parsons, 'New Directions in British Foreign Policy?' in Mark McNaught (ed.), *Reflections on Conservative Politics in the United Kingdom and the United States: Still Soul Mates?* (Lanham, MD: Lexington Books, 2012), p. 54.

22 Ashley and MacAskill, '"History Will Be My Judge"'.

23 On Blair's rhetoric of 'good and evil', see Jonathan Charteris-Black, *Politicians and Rhetoric: the Persuasive Power of Metaphor* (Basingstoke: Palgrave Macmillan, 2nd edn, 2011), pp. 228–33; Blair, 'Doctrine of International Community'. Quoted in Anthony F. Lang Jr., 'Punitive Intervention: Enforcing Justice or Generating Conflict?' in Mark Evans (ed.), *Just War Theory: A Reappraisal* (Edinburgh: Edinburgh University Press, 2005), p. 56.

24 Tony Blair, 'The Kosovo Conflict: A Turning Point for South Eastern Europe', speech given at Sofia University, 17 May 1999. Quoted in Christopher Meyer, *Getting Our Way: 500 Years of Adventure and Intrigue: The Inside Story of British Diplomacy* (London: Phoenix, 2009), p. 199.

25 On this, see Andrew M. Dorman, *Blair's Successful War: British Military Intervention in Sierra Leone* (Farnham: Ashgate, 2009).

26 Marr, *A History of Modern Britain,* p. 551.

27 Blair, *A Journey,* p. 389.

28 Allan Little, 'The Brigadier Who Saved Sierra Leone', *From Our Own Correspondent,* BBC News, 10 May 2010, http://news.bbc.co.uk/1/hi/programmes/from_our_own_correspondent/8682505.stm.

29 Matt Seaton, 'Blast from the Past: Mark Mazower', *The Guardian,* 19 February 2003.

30 Seldon, *Blair,* p. 498.

31 James Pettifer, 'The Price of Appeasement', *The World Today,* 56.1 (2000), pp. 10–12; Paul R. Williams and Karina M. Waller, 'Coercive Appeasement: The Flawed International Response to the Serbian Rogue Regime', *New England Law Review,* 36.4 (2002), pp. 825–89.

32 Condoleezza Rice, *No Higher Honour: A Memoir of My Years in Washington* (London: Simon & Schuster, 2011), p. 40. This view of an instant rapport

between the two leaders was shared by Jonathan Powell. Powell, *The New Machiavelli*, p. 291.

33 George W. Bush, *Decision Points* (London: Virgin Books, 2010), p. 140. Bush also later compared Blair with Churchill in terms of his resolution (p. 246).

34 On 18 March 2003 Tony Blair secured the backing of Parliament to send British troops to war against Iraq when an anti-war motion was defeated in the Commons by 396 votes to 217. George Jones, 'Blair Wins Historic Vote for War', *Daily Telegraph*, 19 March 2003.

35 Philip Smith, *Why War? The Cultural Logic of Iraq, the Gulf War, and Suez* (Chicago, IL: University of Chicago Press, 2005), p. 185

36 *Hansard*, 6th Series, HC Deb, v. 401, c. 726, 17 March 2003. For Cook's critical account of Blair and his wars and the actions of the UK government, see Robin Cook, *Point of Departure: Diaries from the Front Bench* (London: Simon & Schuster, 2003).

37 Robin Cook, 'Why I Had to Leave the Cabinet', *The Guardian*, 12 March 2003. For background, see Tara McCormack, 'From "Ethical Foreign Policy" to National Security Strategy: Exporting Domestic Incoherence' in Oliver Daddow and Jamie Gaskarth (eds), *British Foreign Policy: The New Labour Years* (Basingstoke: Palgrave Macmillan, 2011), pp. 103–22.

38 Jack Straw, *Last Man Standing: Memoirs of a Political Survivor* (London: Macmillan, 2012), p. 363.

39 Rhiannon Vickers, *The Labour Party and the World: The Evolution of Labour's Foreign Policy 1900–1951* (Manchester: Manchester University Press, 2003), p. 193.

40 Blair, *A Journey*, p. 629.

41 D. Coates and J. Krieger, *Blair's War* (Cambridge: Polity Press, 2004), p. 20.

42 'Full text of Dick Cheney's speech: The US vice president, Dick Cheney, delivered this speech to the Veterans of Foreign Wars (VFW) national convention in Nashville, Tennessee', 26 August 2002. *The Guardian*, 27 August 2002, www.guardian.co.uk/world/2002/aug/27/usa.iraq.

43 For an instructive assessment of the political manipulation of rhetoric, see Jennifer Milliken, *The Social Construction of the Korean War: Conflict and Its Possibilities* (Manchester: Manchester University Press, 2001).

44 Paul A. Chilton, *Security Metaphors: Cold War Discourse from Containment to Common House* (Bern: Peter Lang, 1996), p. 413.

45 Hywel Williams, *Guilty Men: Conservative Decline and Fall 1992–1997* (London: Aurum Press, 1998), p. 14.

46 Diary entry for 27 August 1996. Alastair Campbell and Richard Stott (eds), *The Blair Years: Extracts from the Alastair Campbell Diaries* (London: Arrow Books, 2008), p. 129. On the main policy discourses of Blair and New Labour, see Norman Fairclough, *New Labour, New Language?* (Abingdon: Routledge 2000).

47 John Kampfner, *Blair's Wars* (London: Free Press, 2004), p. 9.

48 Blair, *A Journey*, p. 224.

49 Coates and Krieger, *Blair's War*, pp. 12, 14, 43–5, 50. David Cameron, Conservative prime minister from 2010, followed a very similar trajectory to Blair and was instrumental in initiating the intervention in Libya in 2011. Douglas Murray, 'Beware of the hawks', *The Spectator*, 31 August 2013.

50 Peter Hennessy, *The Prime Minister: The Office and Its Holders since 1945* (London: Penguin, 2001), p. 488.

51 Peter Mandelson, *The Third Man: Life at the Heart of New Labour* (London: HarperPress, 2010), pp. 352–4, 359–60.

52 Donald Rumsfeld, *Known and Unknown: A Memoir* (New York: Sentinel, 2012), pp. 441, 495. On the use of rhetoric in the modern political arena, see Paul Chilton, *Analysing Political Discourse: Theory and Practice* (Abingdon: Routledge, 2003), esp. pp. 92–109.

53 'Prime Minister's Speech at the TUC Congress', 10 September 2002, www.tuc. org.uk/the_tuc/tuc-5527-f0.cfm.

54 Straw nevertheless observes that because of the bloodletting of the First World War, 'Chamberlain's attempts in 1938 to "appease" Adolf Hitler were much acclaimed at the time'. Straw, *Last Man Standing*, p. 12. Ironically, Straw's pacifist father avoided military service during the Second World War as a conscientious objector. His mother was also a socialist and pacifist. Nick Assinder, 'Profile of Jack Straw', http://news.bbc.co.uk/1/hi/uk_politics/2950279.stm. Straw makes no secret of the fact that his father was imprisoned for his beliefs. Straw, *Last Man Standing*, p. 12.

55 'Prime Minister's Speech at the TUC Congress'.

56 Blair spoke of 'a history of UN will flouted, of lies told by Saddam about the existence of his chemical, biological and nuclear weapons programmes, and of obstruction, defiance and denial'. *Hansard*, 6th Series, HC Deb, v. 390, c. 3, 24 September 2002. Bush similarly stated in Cincinnati on 7 October: 'The entire world has witnessed Iraq's eleven-year history of defiance, deception and bad faith. We also must never forget the most vivid events of recent history.' Thomas R. Mockaitis, *The Iraq War: A Documentary and Reference Guide* (Santa Barbara, CA: Greenwood Press, 2012), p. 24.

57 'Remarks by the President in Address to the United Nations General Assembly', 12 September 2002, http://georgewbush-whitehouse.archives.gov/news/releases/2002/09/20020912–1.html.

58 'Prime Minister's Speech at the TUC Congress'. Less than a month later Bush concurred: 'Failure to act would embolden other tyrants . . . and make blackmail a permanent feature of world events.' Speech in Cincinnati, 7 October 2002. Mockaitis, *The Iraq War*, p. 28.

59 *Hansard*, 6th Series, HC Deb, v. 390, c. 5, 24 September 2002.

60 Bush speech in Cincinnati, 7 October 2002. Saddam Hussein, too, was ripe for historical analogy. In the same speech Bush noted that the 'the dictator of Iraq is a student of Stalin, using murder as a tool of terror and control, within his own cabinet, within his own army, and even within his own family'. John Ehrenberg, J. Patrice McSherry, José Ramón Sánchez and Caroleen Marji Sayej (eds), *The Iraq Papers* (New York: Oxford University Press, 2010), p. 90; Mockaitis, *The Iraq War*, p. 28.

61 Bush, *Decision Points*, p. 137. Throughout the 'War on Terror', both George W. Bush and Barack Obama have embraced Ronald Reagan's rhetoric of Vietnam as a 'noble cause'. On this, see Andrew Priest, 'The Rhetoric of Revisionism: Presidential Rhetoric about the Vietnam War since 9/11', *Presidential Studies Quarterly*, 43.3 (2013), pp. 538–61.

62 Jack Straw speech to International Institute for Strategic Studies, London, 11 February 2003, www.guardian.co.uk/politics/2003/feb/11/foreignpolicy.iraq2.

63 Matt Seaton, 'Blast from the Past', *The Guardian*, 19 February 2003.

64 *Hansard*, HC Deb, 6th series, v. 400, c. 276, 26 February 2003.

65 Paul McGeough, *Manhattan to Baghdad: Despatches from the Frontline in the War on Terror* (Crows Nest, Australia: Allen & Unwin, 2003), p. 49.

66 Bush, *Decision Points*, p. 244. See also Blair, *A Journey*, p. 433.

67 UNSC Resolution 1441, adopted unanimously on 8 November 2002, gave Saddam Hussein 'a final opportunity to comply with its disarmament obligations' (outlined in resolutions 661, 678, 686, 687, 688, 707, 715, 986, and 1284), http://www.un.org/depts/unmovic/documents/1441.pdf.

68 Straw, 'Iraq: Legal Basis for Use of Force', to Michael Wood, FCO legal adviser, 29 January 2003, http://www.iraqinquiry.org.uk/transcripts/declassified-documents.aspx.

69 'Iraq', Lord Goldsmith to Blair, 30 January 2003, http://www.iraqinquiry.org.uk/transcripts/declassified-documents.aspx.

70 'Iraqi use of chemical and biological weapons – possible scenarios' and 'An initial assessment of Iraq's WMD declaration' (JIC, 9 September and 18 December 2002), http://www.iraqinquiry.org.uk/transcripts/declassified-documents.aspx; Blair, *A Journey*, p. 433.

71 Joseph Nye, 'The American National Interest and Global Public Goods', *International Affairs*, 78.2 (2002), p. 236.

72 Rumsfeld, *Known and Unknown*, p. 441.

73 On this, see Raymond Aron, *The Imperial Republic: The United States and the World 1945–1973* (London: Weidenfeld & Nicolson, 1975).

74 Straw, *Last Man Standing*, p. 364.

75 John Dumbrell, 'The Neoconservative Roots of the War in Iraq' in James P. Pfiffner and Mark Phythian (eds), *Intelligence and National Security Policymaking on Iraq: British and American Perspectives* (College Station, TX: Texas A&M University Press, 2008), pp. 19–39.

76 'The President's State of the Union Address', The United States Capitol, Washington, DC, 29 January 2002, http://georgewbush-whitehouse.archives.gov/news/releases/2002/01/20020129–11.html.

77 Fred Anderson and Andrew Cayton, *The Dominion of War: Empire and Liberty in North America, 1500–2000* (New York: Viking, 2005), p. 421.

78 Warren I. Cohen, *America's Response to China: A History of Sino-American Relations* (New York: Columbia University Press, 5th edn 2010); and David S. Folksong, *The American Mission and the 'Evil Empire': The Crusade for a 'Free Russia' since 1881* (Cambridge: Cambridge University Press, 2007).

79 Andrew J. Acetic, *American Empire: The Realities and Consequences of U.S. Diplomacy* (Cambridge, MA: Harvard University Press, 2002), pp. 7–31. See also William O. Walker III, *National Security and Core Values in American History* (Cambridge: Cambridge University Press, 2009), pp. 259–92.

80 Powell, *The New Machiavelli*, p. 265.

81 Even Thatcher, Reagan's staunch ally, criticized the US invasion of Grenada in 1983 for lacking essential perspective with regard to the real threat posed to US security by that island's government. Hugo Abdul and R. Gerald Hughes, 'The Comandante in His Labyrinth: Fidel Castro and His Legacy', *Intelligence and National Security*, 26.4 (2011), p. 544.

82 Straw, *Last Man Standing*, p. 371.

83 Christopher Meyer, *DC Confidential: The Controversial Memoirs of Britain's Ambassador to the US at the Time of 9/11 and the Run-up to the Iraq War* (London: Weidenfeld & Nicholson, 2005), p. 1. Jonathan Powell later claimed that the desire for good relations with the United States was inspired by Machiavelli ('A prince is likewise esteemed who is a staunch friend and a thorough foe, that is to say, who, without reserve openly declares for one against another'). Powell, *The New Machiavelli*, p. 261. In the George Bull translation this is rendered as: 'A prince also wins prestige for being a true friend or a true enemy, that is, for revealing himself without reservation in favour of one side or another.' Niccolò Machiavelli, *The Prince*, trans. and intro. George Bull (London: Penguin, 1995), p. 71.

84 Straw says that after Powell told him that we had to 'get right up the arse of the Americans' the 'vulgar riposte from my office was 'Yes, but we don't need to clean their teeth from the inside.'' Straw, *Last Man Standing*, p. 371.

85 Mohamed ElBaradei, *The Age of Deception: Nuclear Diplomacy in Treacherous Times* (London: Bloomsbury, 2012), p. 67.

86 Hugh Beach, *The Concept of 'Preventive War': Old Wine in a New Wineskin* (London: Strategic and Combat Studies Institute, 2004), p. 69.

87 When Blair opened the debate Straw told his FCO ministers: 'If we lose tonight, we can't send in the troops, and the government has to resign.' Straw, *Last Man Standing*, p. 390.

88 *Hansard*, HC Deb, 6th series, v. 401, c. 767–8, 18 March 2003.

89 Blair, *A Journey*, p. 436.

90 On this, see Jason Ralph, 'A Difficult Relationship: Britain's 'Doctrine of International Community' and America's War on Terror' in Daddow and Gaskarth (eds), *British Foreign Policy*, pp. 123–38.

91 Bush famously repeatedly invoked Churchill in the wake of 11 September 2001. He later recalled: 'I told Tony [Blair] I admired Churchill's courage, principle and sense of humor – all of which I thought were necessary for leadership.' Bush, *Decision Points*, p. 108.

92 Seaton, 'Blast from the Past'. See also Andrew Roberts, 'This is only the beginning . . . unless we take our stand', *Scotland on Sunday*, 16 February 2003.

93 Straw prevailed upon Blair to allow vote for war, although there was no precedent for doing so throughout the twentieth century. Straw, *Last Man Standing*, p. 375.

Straw makes the point that parliament had made significant military decisions in the Napoleonic Wars and would now do so again (Straw, *Last Man Standing*, p. 375 (n)).

94 Blair to Powell, 17 March 2002, www.iraqinquiry.org.uk/transcripts/declassified-documents.aspx

95 Brian Jones, *Failing Intelligence: The True Story of How We Were Fooled into Going to War in Iraq* (London: Biteback, 2010); Robert Jervis, 'Reports, Politics and Intelligence Failures: The Case of Iraq', *Journal of Strategic Studies* 29.1 (2006) pp. 3–52; Philip H. J. Davies, 'Collection and Analysis on Iraq: A Critical Look at Britain's Spy Machinery', *Studies in Intelligence*, 49.4 (2005), pp. 41–54.

96 ElBaradei, *The Age of Deception*, p. 87. See also: Richard Norton-Taylor, 'Tony Blair's Promise to George Bush: Count on Us on Iraq War', *The Guardian*, 21 January 2011.

97 Riazat Butt and Richard Norton-Taylor, 'Tony Blair Admits: I Would Have Invaded Iraq Anyway', *The Guardian*, 12 December 2009. See also Blair, *A Journey*, pp. 378–9. Ten days before Bush's ultimatum to Iraq, Hans Blix, chair of the UN Monitoring, Verification and Inspection Commission (UNMOVIC), had totally contradicted the administration's claims about Iraq. Blix briefing for the UN Security Council, 7 March 2003. Ehrenberg, McSherry, Sánchez and Sayej (eds), *The Iraq Papers*, pp. 106–10.

98 Named for its chairman Sir John Chilcot, the inquiry was established to examine the United Kingdom's role in Iraq. Blair's successor, Gordon Brown, asserted that 'the primary objective of the committee will be to identify lessons learned. The committee will not set out to apportion blame or consider issues of civil or criminal liability'. *Hansard*, HC Deb, 6th Series, v. 494, c. 24, 15 June 2009. This assertion was to prove particularly contentious from the outset.

99 On Blair and 9/ 11, see *Blair, A Journey*, pp. 341–70.

100 Jack Straw minute to PM, 25 March 2002. Cited by Sir Roderic Lyne in cross-examination of Tony Blair, *The Iraq Inquiry*, 29 January 2010, www.iraqinquiry.org.uk/media/45139/20100129-blair-final.pdf.

101 'Rice Defends Decision to Go to War in Iraq', Associated Press/ CNN, 22 October 2004.

102 Tony Blair, oral evidence to *The Iraq Inquiry*, 29 January 2010, www.iraqinquiry.org.uk/media/45139/20100129-blair-final.pdf.

103 On this, see Colin Wastell, 'Cognitive Predispositions and Intelligence Analyst Reasoning', *International Journal of Intelligence and CounterIntelligence*, 23.3 (2010), p. 455.

104 Straw, *Last Man Standing*, p. 377.

105 Rice, *No Higher Honour*, p. 154.

106 George W. Bush, 'Ultimatum to Iraq', 17 March 2003. Ehrenberg, McSherry, Sánchez and Sayej (eds), *The Iraq Papers*, p. 113.

107 'Prime Minister's Speech at the TUC Congress', 10 September 2002, www.tuc.org.uk/the_tuc/tuc-5527-f0.cfm.

108 *Hansard*, HC Deb, 6th series, v. 390, c. 5, 24 September 2002.

109 False analogies abound with regard to the war in Iraq. For a refutation of the myths regarding the invasions of Iraq (in 2003) and Spain (in 1808), see Charles Esdaile, 'Spain 1808 – Iraq 2003: Some Thoughts on the Use and Abuse of History', *Journal of Military History*, 74.1 (2010), pp. 173–88.

110 Blair, *A Journey*, p. 436.

111 Michael Portillo, 'When Blair admits his errors, we can face the terror truth', *The Sunday Times*, 4 April 2004.

112 On Blair's use of language, see Norman Fairclough, 'Blair's Contribution to Elaborating a New Doctrine of "International community"', *Journal of Language and Politics*, 4.1 (2005), pp. 41–63.

113 Blair, *A Journey*, p. 248.

114 Thatcher, *Statecraft*, p. 35.

115 Douglas Hurd, *Choose Your Weapons: The British Foreign Secretary – 200 Years of Argument, Success and Failure* (London: Phoenix, 2011), p. 368. On this question, see the forceful critique of Blair by Jim Whitman: 'The Origins of the British Decision to Go to War: Tony Blair, Humanitarian Intervention, and the "New Doctrine of the International Community"' in Pfiffner and Phythian (eds), *Intelligence and National Security Policymaking on Iraq*, pp. 40–56.

116 Douglas Hurd, 'Half a Century on, the Ghosts of Suez Return', *The Spectator*, 22 July 2006.

117 Douglas Hurd, *Memoirs* (London: Abacus, 2004), p. 527.

118 Blair, *A Journey*, pp. 629–30.

Conclusion

1 Arthur M. Schlesinger, Jr., 'On the Inscrutability of History', *Encounter*, 27.5 (1966), p. 13.

2 James Callaghan, *Time and Chance* (London: Collins, 1987), p. 51.

3 Noel Annan, *Our Age: The Generation that Made Post-War Britain* (London: Fontana, 1991), p. 256.

4 Brian Harrison, *Seeking a Role: The United Kingdom 1951–1970* (Oxford: Clarendon Press, 2009), p. 535.

5 David Sanders, *Losing an Empire, Finding a Role* (Basingstoke: Macmillan, 1990), p. 283. For similar lessons drawn by US policy makers, see Jeffrey Record, 'Appeasement: A Critical Evaluation Seventy Years On' in Frank McDonough (ed.), *Origins of the Second World War: An International Perspective* (London: Continuum, 2011), pp. 223–5.

6 Paul M. Kennedy, 'The Tradition of Appeasement in British Foreign Policy, 1865–1939', *British Journal of International Studies*, 2.3 (1976), p. 215.

7 Robert J. Beck, 'Munich's Lessons Reconsidered', *International Security*, 14.2 (1989), p. 161. On the continuing relevance of appeasement to contemporary politics in the United States, see Fredrik Logevall and Kenneth Osgood, 'The Ghost of Munich: America's Appeasement Complex', *World Affairs*, 173.2 (2010), pp. 13–26.

8 Paul Kennedy, 'A Time to Appease', *The National Interest*, 108 (2010), p. 7.

9 Winston S. Churchill, *The Second World War: Volume I: The Gathering Storm* (London: Cassell, 8th edn, 1966 [1948]), p. 287.

10 Donald Cameron Watt, 'Churchill and Appeasement' in Robert Blake and Wm. Roger Louis (eds), *Churchill* (Oxford: Oxford University Press, 1993), p. 214.

11 *Hansard*, HC Deb, 5th Series, v. 339, c. 373, 5 October 1938.

12 Hans J. Morgenthau, *Politics among Nations: The Struggle for Power and Peace*, ed. Kenneth W. Thompson (New York: Alfred A. Knopf, 5th edn 1985), p. 6.

13 Lynne Olson, *Troublesome Young Men: The Rebels Who Brought Churchill to Power and Helped Save England* (London: Bloomsbury, 2007), p. 137.

14 Watt, 'Churchill and Appeasement', p. 214.

15 Robert Jervis, *Perception and Misperception in International Politics* (Princeton, NJ: Princeton University Press, 1976), p. 224.

16 *Hansard*, HC Deb, 5th Series, v. 558, c. 1708–9, 1 November 1956.

17 Lewis Namier, 'History' (1952) in Fritz Stern (ed.), *The Varieties of History: From Voltaire to the Present* (London: Macmillan, 2nd edn 1970), pp. 376–7.

18 'Statement by PM Netanyahu at meeting with Czech Republic PM Nečas', 5 December 2012, Israeli Ministry of Foreign Affairs, www.mfa.gov.il/MFA/Government/Speeches+by+Israeli+leaders/2012/PM_Netanyahu_meets_Czech_PM_Necas_5-Dec-2012.htm.

19 Isabel Kershner, 'Israeli Minister Vents Anger at Europe', *New York Times*, 12 December 2012.

20 Robert Tait, 'Israel Foreign Minister Risks Wrath of the West with Appeasement Claim', *Daily Telegraph*, 12 December 2012.

21 Speech in Margate, 1 October 1950. Alan Bullock, *Ernest Bevin: Foreign Secretary 1945–1951* (New York: W.W. Norton, 1983), p. 815.

22 Robert Pearce, 'Ernest Bevin' in Kevin Jefferys (ed.), *Labour Forces: From Ernest Bevin to Gordon Brown* (London: I.B. Tauris, 2002), pp. 13–14.

23 *Hansard*, HC Deb, 6th Series, v. 35, c. 937, 23 January 1983. Richard Luce was the son of Sir William Luce, British political resident in the Gulf between 1961 and 1966.

24 Anthony Lewis 'War Crimes' (originally published 20 March 1995) in Nader Mousavizadeh (ed.), *The Black Book of Bosnia: The Consequences of 'Appeasement'* (New York: Basic Books, 1996), p. 60.

25 John Adams to Thomas Jefferson, 2 February 1816. *The Writings of Thomas Jefferson*, Volume IV, ed. Henry Augustine Washington (New York: Derby & Jackson, 1859), p. 547.

26 Ed Vulliamy, 'Bosnia: The Crime of Appeasement', *International Affairs*, 74.1 (1998), p. 76. Vulliamy saw British policy in Bosnia as part of 'a long history of [the] appeasement of tyrants.' Ed Vulliamy, *The War is Dead, Long Live the War: Bosnia: the Reckoning* (London: The Bodley Head, 2012), p. xxxiii.

27 Brian C. Rathbun, *Partisan Interventions: European Party Politics and Peace Enforcement in the Balkans* (Ithaca, NY: Cornell University Press, 2004), p. 60. After he stood down as foreign secretary Hurd, along with Pauline Neville-Jones, was employed by the National Westminster Bank. In July 1996 the two Britons met Slobodan Miloševic in Belgrade to discuss the part-privatisation of Serbia's telecoms network. Francis Wheen, 'How our politicians helped keep the Butcher of the Balkans in power: Slobo's appeasers', *The Guardian*, 11 October 2000; Vulliamy, *The War is Dead, Long Live the War*, p. xxxviii. Of his business trip to Belgrade, Hurd later reflected: 'This was a legal and legitimate deal, but the visit was a mistake, [although] not interesting enough to justify the embarrassment it later caused.' Hurd, *Memoirs*, p. 526.

28 John Nott, *Haven't We Been Here Before? Afghanistan to the Falklands: A Personal Connection* (London: Discovered Authors, 2007), p. 240.

29 Margaret Thatcher, 'Speech to the International Free Enterprise dinner', London, 20 April 1999, Margaret Thatcher Foundation, www.margaretthatcher.org/document/108381.

30 Douglas Hurd, *Choose Your Weapons: The British Foreign Secretary – 200 Years of Argument, Success and Failure* (London: Phoenix, 2011), p. 309.

31 Hugo Young, 'Commentary: Double-Balk in the Balkans Leaves a Bigger Hurdle', *The Guardian*, 1 June 1993.

32 Hurd, *Memoirs*, pp. 504, 527.

33 Tony Blair, *A Journey* (London: Hutchinson, 2010), p. 207.

34 President Dwight D. Eisenhower, 'Annual Message to the Congress on the State of the Union', 2 February 1953. Dwight D. Eisenhower, *The White House Years: Mandate for Change 1953–1956* (London: Heinemann, 1963), p. 1.

35 Francis J. Gavin, *Nuclear Statecraft: History and Strategy in America's Atomic Age* (Ithaca, NY: Cornell University Press, 2012), p. 57.

36 *Hansard*, HC Deb, 5th Series, v. 437, c. 1951, 16 May 1947.

37 For a contemporary discussion of these issues, see George F. Kennan, *Russia, the Atom, and the West* (New York: Harper, 1958).

38 As an old man, Macmillan stated that only two things gave him nightmares: the trenches of the Great War and the Cuban Missile Crisis. Peter Hennessy, *The Prime Minister: The Office and Its Holders since 1945* (London: Penguin, 2001), pp. 102–3.

39 Stephen R. Rock, *Appeasement in International Politics* (Lexington, KY: University Press of Kentucky, 2000), p. 139.

40 Ibid. pp. 151–2.

41 Graham Allison, 'Lessons from JFK on Power, Diplomacy', *The Boston Globe*, 2 March 2007. Opponents of the appeasement of North Korea stressed that the government in Pyongyang had never halted its nuclear programme and could never be trusted. See, for example, Donald Rumsfeld, *Known and Unknown: A Memoir* (New York: Sentinel, 2011), pp. 641–2.

42 Walter Russell Mead, 'You Can Be Warriors or Wimps; or so say the Americans: The foreign-policy gap between Europeans and Americans is getting bigger again', *Economist*, 8 August 2002.

43 Rumsfeld, *Known and Unknown*, p. 444. Rumsfeld noted with satisfaction that the president of Latvia had told him: 'If Americans had listened to some European leaders during the last 50 years, we would still be in the Soviet Union.' Rumsfeld, *Known and Unknown*, p. 444(n). For an assessment of the notion outlined by Rumsfeld, see Peter Roter and Zlatko Šabič, '"New" and "Old Europe" in the Context of the Iraq War and Its Implications for European Security', *Perspectives on European Politics and Society*, 5.3 (2004), pp. 517–42.

44 One month after the terrorist attacks against the United States on 11 September 2001, Israeli Prime Minister Ariel Sharon issued the following statement: 'I call upon the United States not to commit again the terrible mistake made in Munich when Czechoslovakia was sacrificed for a temporary solution to German aggression. Do not try to appease Arab aggression at Israeli expense. It is unacceptable. Israel will not be another Czechoslovakia.' Press Conference, Tel Aviv, 4 October 2001. James Bennet, 'Sharon Invokes Munich in Warning U.S. on "Appeasement"', *New York Times*, 5 October 2001.

45 On the conceptual relationship between appeasement and détente, see Gordon A. Craig and Alexander L. George, *Force and Statecraft: Diplomatic Problems of Our Time* (New York: Oxford University Press, 3rd edn, 1995), pp. 80–5, 247, 253–6.

46 Jeffrey Record, 'The Use and Abuse of History: Munich, Vietnam and Iraq', *Survival*, 49.1 (2007), pp. 163–80.

47 Gerhard L. Weinberg, 'No Road from Munich to Iraq', *Washington Post*, 3 November 2002.

48 Keith Robbins, *Munich 1938* (London: Simon & Schuster, 2nd edn 1984), p. 6.

49 Evan Thomas, 'The Mythology of Munich', *Newsweek*, 23 June 2008.

50 The obvious parallels with Kennedy and Tuchman's *The Guns of August* are of note here. On the latter, see Richard E. Neustadt and Ernest R. May, *Thinking in Time: The Uses of History for Decision Makers* (New York: The Free Press, 1986), pp. 15, 244.

51 Jeffery Record, *The Specter of Munich: Reconsidering the Lessons of Appeasing Hitler* (Washington, DC: Potomac, 2007), p. 1. For a similar view from an earlier generation, see Charles O. Lerche, *Principles of International Politics* (New York: The Ronald Press Company, 1956), p. 375.

52 Lynne Olson, 'Why Winston Wouldn't Stand for W', *Washington Post*, 1 July 2007.

53 *Hansard*, HC Deb, 6th Series, v. 219, c. 774, 23 February 1993.

54 Disraeli to Lord Derby, foreign secretary, 8 September 1876. Dick Leonard, *The Great Rivalry: Gladstone & Disraeli* (London: I.B. Tauris, 2013) pp. 167–8. Quote at p. 168.

55 *Hansard*, HC Deb, 4th Series, v. 231, c. 1146–7, 11 August 1876.

56 Hurd, *Choose your Weapons*, p. 363. On the rivalry between the two men, see John Campbell, *Pistols at Dawn: Two Hundred Years of Political Rivalry from Pitt & Fox to Blair & Brown* (London: Jonathan Cape, 2009), pp. 57–89. Lord

Castlereagh (foreign secretary, 1812–22) and George Canning (foreign secretary, 1807–9, 1822–7) even fought a duel against each other in September 1809. Both survived after Canning was wounded in the thigh and the honour of all sides was deemed satisfied. John Bew, *Castlereagh: Enlightenment, War and Tyranny* (London: Quercus, 2011), pp. 260–2.

57 Alfred Duff Cooper, *Talleyrand* (London: Jonathan Cape, 1932), p. 252.

58 Allan. J. Lichtman and Valerie French, 'Past and Present: History and Contemporary Analysis' in Stephen Vaughn (ed.), *The Vital Past: Writings on the Uses of History* (Athens, GA: University of Georgia Press, 1985), p. 287.

59 'Rollback', its proposed successor policy, turned out to be far too dangerous to ever be seriously adopted as anything other than a rhetorical strategy. On this, see László Borhi, 'Rollback, Liberation, Containment, or Inaction? U.S. Policy and Eastern Europe in the 1950s', *Journal of Cold War Studies*, 1.3 (1999), pp. 67–110.

60 See, for example, Donald Kagan and Frederick W. Kagan, *While America Sleeps: Self-delusion, Military Weakness, and the Threat to Peace Today* (New York: St. Martin's Press, 2000); Michael Gove, *Celsius 7/ 7: How the West's Policy of Appeasement Has Provoked yet more Fundamentalist Terror – and What Has to Be Done Now* (London: Phoenix, 2007); Bruce Bawer, *While Europe Slept: How Radical Islam Is Destroying the West from Within* (New York: Anchor Books, 2007); and Bruce S. Thornton, *The Wages of Appeasement: Ancient Athens, Munich, and Obama's America* (New York: Encounter Books, 2011).

61 On 29 August 2013, the House of Commons debated whether or not to consider intervention in the Syrian civil war following the use of chemical weapons by government forces. Dr. Liam Fox, a former Conservative secretary of state for defence, stated: 'Let us be very clear that to do nothing will be interpreted in Damascus as appeasement of a dreadful regime and the dreadful actions it has carried out. Appeasement has never worked to further the cause of peace in the past, and it will not now, and it will not in the future.' Dr. Sarah Wollaston, a Conservative MP, disagreed: 'The country is almost unanimously opposed to unilateral western military intervention. That is not because we are a nation of appeasers and apologists; it is because the nation rightly has weighed up the risks of such action exploding into a wider military conflict with hundreds of thousands more deaths.' *Hansard*, HC Deb, 6th series, v. 566, c.1454, 1535, 29 August 2013. In the event, the government motion authorizing the use of force ('if necessary') was defeated by 285 votes to 272, as a number of Conservative MPs rebelled against Prime Minister David Cameron. Robert Winnett, 'Syria crisis: No to war, blow to Cameron', *Daily Telegraph*, 30 August 2013. During the debate David Anderson, a Labour MP, noted: 'The ghost of Tony Blair haunts this debate, but the ghost of Hans Blix haunts it even more. We should have listened to him in 2003.' *Hansard*, HC Deb, 6th series, v.566, c.1535, 29 August 2013. (Blix had been the head of the UN Monitoring, Verification and Inspection Commission (UNMOVIC) in Iraq). On 14 September 2013, the United States and Russia struck a deal under the terms of which the Syrian government would allow its stockpile of chemical weapons to be removed or destroyed by mid-2014. US Department of State, 'Framework for Elimination

of Syrian Chemical Weapons', http://state.gov/r/pa/prs/ps/2013/09/214247.htm. This deal eased the international tension arising from the threat of US military action and President Obama described the deal as 'an important concrete step' towards putting Syria's chemical weapons under international control. 'Statement by the President on U.S.-Russian Agreement on Framework for Elimination of Syrian Chemical Weapons', 14 September 2014. Charges of appeasement were inevitably made as the Syrian government hailed the US-Russia agreement, while the Syrian rebels were left feeling betrayed. The Syrian minister Ali Haidar told Russian news agency RIA Novosti: 'On the one hand, it helps Syria come out of the crisis and, on the other, it helps avoid the war against Syria depriving those who wanted to launch it of arguments to do so . . . It's a victory for Syria achieved thanks to our Russian friends.' 'Syria hails US-Russia deal on chemical weapons', BBC News, 15 September 2014, http://bbc.co.uk/news/world-middle-east-24100296. At a Syrian opposition news conference in Istanbul, General Salim Idris asserted: 'We feel let down by the international community. We don't have any hope.' Loveday Morris, 'Syrian rebels say U.S.-Russia agreement on chemical weapons leaves Assad unpunished', *Washington Post*, 14 September 2013. The US-Russia agreement had been concluded despite the fact that Secretary of State John Kerry had previously declared: 'This is really our Munich moment. This is our chance . . . to pursue accountability over appeasement. The United States . . . cannot be silent spectators to this slaughter. This is not the time to allow a dictator unfettered use of some of the most heinous weapons on Earth.' Secretary of State John Kerry and French Foreign Minister Laurent Fabius, press availability, Quai d'Orsay, Paris, 7 September 2013, http://state.gov/secretary/remarks/2013/09/213938.htm. Following the deal with Russia, Michael Portillo, the former British defence secretary, stated: 'I don't believe in intervention [in Syria] at all but if you've made the case that Obama has made, that Kerry has made, and then you settle for what Russia has given you, you are Neville Chamberlain.' *This Week*, broadcast on BBC1, 19 September 2013.

62 Herb Keinon, 'Weak world response on Syria boosts chance of strong Israeli action on Iran', *The Jerusalem Post*, 1 September 2013. After the US-Russia deal on Syria, and with the US apparently willing to engage in appeasement, at a memorial for the Yom Kippur War, Israeli Prime Minister Binyamin Netanyahu stated: 'Israel will have to be ready to defend itself, by itself, against all threats . . . That capacity is more important today than ever . . . and Israel is stronger today than ever. Editorial: 'Israel and the Syria deal', *Jerusalem Post*, 15 September 2013.

63 On the historical legacy of Munich and Czech political culture, see Karel Bartošek, 'Could We Have Fought? The "Munich Complex" in Czech Policies and Czech Thinking', in Norman Stone and Eduard Strouhal (eds), *Czechoslovakia: Crossroads and Crises, 1918–88* (New York: St. Martin's Press, 1989), pp. 101–19.

64 Josef Kopecký, 'Zeman podpořil preventivní úder na Írán, Fischer mírové řešení', *Dnes*, 15 October 2012. Bernd Kaussler argues that the opprobrium attached to the term 'appeasement' should not preclude the employment of a diplomacy of 'constructive engagement' between Iran and the West. Bernd Kaussler, *Iran's Nuclear Diplomacy: Power politics and conflict resolution* (Abingdon: Routledge, 2014), pp. 6–9. Such logic cuts little ice in Israel. In April 2013,

former foreign minister Avigdor Lieberman opined: 'The result of the latest round of talks between the powers and Iran . . . is a de facto acceptance by the West of an Iranian nuclear bomb, like the past acceptance of a nuclear North Korea and of the take over of Czechoslovakia by Hitler'. 'Lieberman: World appeasing Iran like Nazis in 1938', *Times of Israel*, 9 April 2013.

65 Edward Heath, *The Course of My Life: My Autobiography* (London: Hodder & Stoughton, 1998), p. 653. In the Oxford by-election of 1938 Heath (like Macmillan) had opposed Quintin Hogg, Chamberlain's pro-appeasement candidate. Heath, *The Course of My Life*, pp. 58–61. In 2008, echoing Heath, Correlli Barnett wrote: 'The word "appeasement" haunts us to this day. It confuses our political leaders who believe that not to stand up to any aggressor anywhere at any time is to be an "appeaser".' Correlli Barnett, 'We have learnt the wrong lessons from Munich', *The Times*, 29 September 2008.

66 Conversation between Walter Lippmann and Howard K, Smith, CBS broadcast, 15 June 1961. Walter Lippmann, intro. Edward Weeks, *Conversations with Walter Lippmann* (Boston, MA: Little, Brown & Co., 1965), p. 69.

67 E. H. Carr, *The Twenty Years' Crisis: An Introduction to the Study of International Relations* (London: Macmillan, 1940), p. 284. In line with such thinking, Hans J. Morgenthau noted that Carr had initially regarded the Munich Agreement 'as a great act of statesmanship, a concession made to a would-be conqueror for the sake of peace.' Hans J. Morgenthau, 'The Intellectual and Political Functions of Theory' [1964] in *Truth and Power: Essays of a Decade, 1960–70* (New York: Praeger, 1970), p. 256.

BIBLIOGRAPHY

Primary sources

Archives

National Archives, Public Record Office, Kew
House of Lords Library, London
US National Archives, Washington, DC
Harold Macmillan Papers and Diaries: Bodleian Library, Oxford
Neville Chamberlain Papers and Lord Avon Papers: University of Birmingham
Churchill Archives Centre, Cambridge
Labour Party Archive, Manchester
Hugh Gaitskell Papers: University College London
Thatcher Foundation Archive, Churchill Archives Centre, Cambridge
Harry S. Truman Presidential Library, Independence, MO
Dwight D. Eisenhower Library, Abilene, KS
John F. Kennedy Library, Boston, MA
Gerald R. Ford Library, Ann Arbor, MI
Jimmy Carter Library, Atlanta, GA
Ronald Reagan Library, Simi Valley, CA

Published Sources

Hansard, Parliamentary Debates (HC Deb and HL Deb)

Documents on British Foreign Policy 1919–1939

Series III

Volume 4: 1939, *The Aftermath of Munich, October 1938–March 1939*, London: HMSO, 1951.

Documents on British Policy Overseas (DBPO)

Series I

Volume 1: *The Conference at Potsdam, July–August 1945*, London: HMSO, 1984.

Volume 5: *Germany and Western Europe, 11 August–31 December 1945*, London: HMSO, 1990.

Volume 6: *Eastern Europe, August 1945–April 1946*, London: HMSO, 1991.

Series II

Volume 3: *German Rearmament, September–December 1950*, London: HMSO, 1989.

Volume 4: *Korea, June 1950–April 1951*, London: HMSO, 1991.

Series III

Volume 1: *Britain and the Soviet Union, 1968–1972*, London: HMSO, 1998.

Volume 2: *Conference on Security and Co-operation in Europe, 1972–1975*, London: HMSO, 1998.

Volume 3: *Détente in Europe, 1972–1976*, London: Whitehall Publishing/Routledge, 2001.

Volume 6: *Berlin in the Cold War, 1948–1990*, London: Whitehall Publishing/Routledge, 2009.

Volume 8: *The Invasion of Afghanistan and UK–Soviet Relations, 1979–1982*, London: Whitehall Publishing/Routledge, 2012.

Miscellaneous Diplomatic Documents

Cmd. 6115, Germany No. 1 (1939), *Final Report by the Right Honourable Nevile Henderson G.C.M.G. on the circumstances leading to the termination of his mission to Berlin, September 20, 1939*, London: HMSO, 1939.

Cmd. 6739, *Policy of His Majesty's Government in the United Kingdom in Regard to Czechoslovakia*, London: HMSO, 1942.

Cmd. 7087, *Protocol of the Proceedings of the Berlin Conference*, London: HMSO, 1947.

Cmd. 8571, *Convention on Relations between the Three Western Powers and the Federal Republic*, London: HMSO, 1952.

Documents on Germany under Occupation 1945–1954, selected and edited by Beate Ruhm von Oppen, Oxford: Oxford University Press/RIIA, 1955.

Cmd. 9543, *Documents Relating to the Meeting of Heads of Government of France, the United Kingdom, the Soviet Union, and the United States of America [Geneva 18–23 July 1955]*, London: HMSO, 1955.

Cmd. 8081, *Documents Relating to the Meeting of Heads of Government of France, the United Kingdom, the Soviet Union, and the United States of America*, London: HMSO, 1955.

Cmd. 124, *Defence: Outline of Future Policy*, London: HMSO, 1957.

Cmd. 1552, *Selected Documents on Germany and the Question of Berlin 1944–1961*, London: HMSO, 1961.

Cmnd. 6932, *Selected Documents Relating to Problems of Security and Cooperation in Europe 1954–77*, London: HMSO 1977.

Cmnd 8758, *The Falklands Campaign: The Lessons*, London: HMSO, 1982.

Cmnd. 8787, *Falkland Islands Review: Report of a Committee of Privy Counsellors*, London: HMSO, 1983.

Ross, Graham (ed.), *The Foreign Office and the Kremlin: British Documents on Anglo-Soviet Relations 1941–45*, Cambridge: Cambridge University Press, 1984.

Official History

Freedman, Lawrence, *The Official History of the Falklands Campaign, Volume 1: The Origins of the Falklands War*, London: Routledge, rev. edn 2007.

—, *The Official History of the Falklands Campaign, Volume 2: War and Diplomacy*, London: Routledge, rev. edn 2007.

Official Inquiry

The Iraq Inquiry (Chilcot Inquiry), http://www.iraqinquiry.org.uk/

Foreign Relations of the United States (FRUS)

1945

The Conference of Berlin (The Potsdam Conference), 1945 (2 volumes), Washington, DC: GPO, 1960.

1947

Volume 2: *Council of Foreign Ministers; Germany and Austria*, Washington, DC: GPO, 1972.

1948

Volume 2: *Germany and Austria*, Washington, DC: GPO, 1973.

Volume 3: *Council of Foreign Ministers; Germany and Austria*, Washington, DC: GPO, 1974.

1951

Volume 3 (2 parts): *European Security and the German Question*, Washington, DC: GPO, 1981.

1955-7

Volume 4: *Western European Security and Integration*, Washington, DC: GPO, 1963.

1958-60

Volume 7, pt. 1: *Western European Integration and Security*, Washington, DC: GPO, 1993.
Volume 7, pt. 2: *Western Europe*, Washington, DC: GPO, 1993.
Volume 8: *Berlin Crisis, 1958-1959*, Washington, DC: GPO, 1996.
Volume 9: *Berlin Crisis, 1959-1960; Germany; Austria*, Washington, DC: GPO, 1993.

1961-3

Volume 8: *National Security Policy*, Washington, DC: GPO, 1996.
Volume 14: *Berlin Crisis, 1961-62*, Washington, DC: GPO, 1993.
Volume 15: *Berlin Crisis, 1962-1963*. Washington, DC: GPO, 1994.

1964-8

Volume 15: *Germany and Berlin*, Washington, DC: GPO, 1996.

Other US

Public Papers of the Presidents of the United States, John F. Kennedy, 1961, Washington, DC: United States Government Printing Office, 1962.
Public Papers of the Presidents of the United States: Lyndon B. Johnson, 1965, Volume I, Washington, DC: Government Printing Office, 1966.

Other

Akten zur Auswärtigen Politik der Bundesrepublik Deutschland, 1973: I/II/III (Munich: Oldenbourg Verlag, 2004).
—, 1974: I/II (Munich: Oldenbourg Verlag, 2005).
—, 1975: I/II (Munich: Oldenbourg Verlag, 2006).
Bush, George H. W., *Speaking of Freedom: The Collected Speeches*, New York: Scribner, 2009.
Chamberlain, Neville, *In Search of Peace*, New York: G.P. Putnam's, 1939.
Churchill, Winston S., *The End of the Beginning: War Speeches by Right Hon. Winston S. Churchill C.H., M.P. 1942*, ed. Charles Eade, London: Cassell, 3rd edn, 1946.
—, *The Dawn of Liberation: War Speeches by the Rt. Hon. Winston S. Churchill, 1944*, ed. Charles Eade, London: Cassell, 1945.
Degras, J. (ed.), *Soviet Documents on Foreign Policy, Volume 3, 1933-1941*, New York: Doubleday, 1978.

Ehrenberg, John, McSherry, J. Patrice, Sánchez, José Ramón and Sayej, Caroleen Marji (eds), *The Iraq Papers*, New York: Oxford University Press, 2010.

Hanhimäki, Jussi M. and Westad, Odd Arne (eds), *The Cold War: A History in Documents and Eyewitness Accounts*, Oxford: Oxford University Press, 2003.

James, Robert Rhodes (ed.), *Winston Churchill: His Complete Speeches 1987–1963, Volume VIII, 1950–63*, London: Heinemann, 1974.

Mastny, Vojtech and Byrne, Malcolm (eds), *A Cardboard Castle? An Inside History of the Warsaw Pact 1955–1991*, Budapest: CEU Press, 2005.

Mockaitis, Thomas R., *The Iraq War: A Documentary and Reference Guide*, Santa Barbara, CA: Greenwood Press, 2012.

Münch, Ingo von (ed.), *Dokumente des geteilen Deutschland*, Stuttgart: Brentano, 1968.

Owen, David (ed.), *Bosnia-Herzegovina: The Vance/Owen Peace Plan*, Liverpool: Liverpool University Press, 2013.

Rubinstein, Alvin Z., Shayevich, Albina and Zlotnikov, Boris (eds), *The Clinton Foreign Policy Reader: Presidential Speeches with Commentary*, New York: M.E. Sharpe, 2000

Memoirs, autobiography, correspondence and diaries

Adenauer, Konrad, *World Indivisible*, London: George Allen & Unwin, 1956.

—, *Erinnerungen 1955–1959*, Stuttgart: DVA, 1967.

—, *Erinnerungen 1959–1963*, Stuttgart: DVA, 1968.

Amery, Leo, *The Empire at Bay: The Leo Amery Diaries 1929–1945*, eds. John Barnes and David Nicolson, foreword by Lord Stockton, London: Hutchinson, 1988.

Attlee, C. R., *As It Happened*, London: William Heinemann, 1954.

Baker III, James, *The Politics of Diplomacy: Revolution, War, and Peace 1989–1992*, New York: G. P. Putnam's, 1995.

Blair, Tony, *A Journey*, London: Hutchinson, 2010.

Boyle, Peter G. (ed.), *The Churchill–Eisenhower Correspondence, 1953–1955*, Chapel Hill, NC: University of North Carolina Press, 1990.

—, *The Eden–Eisenhower Correspondence, 1955–1957*, Chapel Hill, NC: University of North Carolina Press, 2005.

Brandt, Willy, *People and Politics: The Years 1960–1975*, trans. J. Maxwell Brownjohn, Boston, MA: Little, Brown & Co., 1978.

Brown, George, *In My Way*, London: Victor Gollancz, 1971.

Bundy, McGeorge, *Danger and Survival*, New York: Random House, 1988.

Bush, George H. W., *All the Best, George Bush: My Life in Letters and Other Writings*, New York: Scribner, 1999.

Bush, George H. W. and Scowcroft, Brent, *A World Transformed*, New York: Knopf, 1998.

Bush, George W., *Decision Points*, London: Virgin Books, 2010.

Butler, R. A., *The Art of the Possible*, London: Hamish Hamilton, 1971.

Cadogan, Sir Alexander, *The Diaries of Sir Alexander Cadogan 1938–45*, ed. David Dilks, London: Cassell, 1971.

Callaghan, James, *Time and Chance*, London: Collins, 1987.

Campbell, Alastair, *The Blair Years: Extracts from the Alastair Campbell Diaries*, ed. Richard Stott, London: Arrow Books, 2008.

Carrington, Lord (Peter), *Reflect on Things Past: the Memoirs of Lord Carrington*, London: Collins, 1988.

Castle, Barbara, *The Castle Diaries, 1964–1976*, London: Papermac, 1990.

Channon, Henry, *'Chips': The Diaries of Sir Henry Channon*, ed. Robert Rhodes James, London; Phoenix, 1996.

Churchill, Winston S., *Great Contemporaries*, London: Odhams Press, 1947.

—, *The Second World War: Volumes 1–6*, London: Cassell, 1948–52.

Ciechanowski, J., *Victory in Defeat*, London: Doubleday, 1947.

Clark, Alan, *Diaries*, London: Phoenix, 1994.

—, *Diaries: Into Politics 1972–1982*, ed. Ion Trewin, London: Phoenix, 2001.

—, *The Last Diaries: In and Out of the Wilderness*, ed. Ion Trewin, London: Weidenfeld & Nicolson, 2002.

Clinton, Bill, *My Life*, London: Arrow Books, 2005.

Colville, John, *The Fringes of Power: Downing Street Diaries: Volume I: 1939–October 1941*, London: Sceptre, 1986.

—, *The Fringes of Power: Downing Street Diaries, Volume II: 1941–April 1955*, London: Sceptre, 1987.

Cook, Robin, *Point of Departure: Diaries from the Front Bench*, London: Simon & Schuster, 2003.

Crossman, Richard, *The Backbench Diaries of Richard Crossman*, ed. Janet Morgan, London: Hamish Hamilton and Jonathan Cape, 1981.

Davenport-Hines, Richard (ed.), *Letters from Oxford: Hugh Trevor-Roper to Bernard Berenson*, London: Phoenix, 2007.

Djilas, Milovan, *Wartime*, trans. Michael B. Petrovitch, London: Secker & Warburg, 1977.

Dobrynin, Anatoly, *In Confidence: Moscow's Ambassador to Six Cold War Presidents*, New York: Times Books, 1995.

Duff Cooper, Alfred, *Old Men Forget: The Autobiography of Duff Cooper*, London: Rupert Hart-Davis, 1954.

—, John Julius Norwich (ed.), *The Duff Cooper Diaries 1915–1951*, London: Phoenix, 2006.

Eden, Anthony, *The Memoirs of Sir Anthony Eden: Full Circle*, London: Cassell, 1960.

—, *The Memoirs of Sir Anthony Eden: Facing the Dictators*, London: Cassell, 1962.

—, *The Memoirs of Sir Anthony Eden: The Reckoning*, London: Cassell, 1965.

—, *The Suez Crisis of 1956*, Boston, MA: Beacon Press, 1968.

Eisenhower, Dwight D., *The White House Years: Mandate for Change 1953–1956*, London: Heinemann, 1963.

—, *The White House Years: Waging Peace 1956–61*, London: Heinemann, 1966.

—, *The Eisenhower Diaries*, ed. Robert H. Ferrell, London: Norton, 1981.

de Gaulle, Charles, *Memoirs of Hope*, trans. Terence Kilmartin, London: Weidenfeld & Nicolson, 1971.

Gaitskell, Hugh, *The Diary of Hugh Gaitskell 1945–1956*, ed. Philip M. Williams, London: Jonathan Cape, 1983.

Genscher, Hans-Dietrich, *Erinnerungen*, Berlin: Siedler Verlag, 1995.

Gilmour, Ian, *Dancing with Dogma: Britain under Thatcherism*, London: Pocket Books, 1993.

Gladwyn, Lord (Gladwyn Jebb), *The Memoirs of Lord Gladwyn*, London: Weidenfeld & Nicolson, 1972.

Haig, Jr., Alexander M., *Caveat: Realism, Reagan, and Foreign Policy*, New York: Scribner, 1984.

Hailsham, Lord (Quintin Hogg), *A Sparrow's Flight: Memoirs*, London: Collins, 1990.

Halifax, *Lord, Fulness of Days*, London: Collins, 1957.

Hannay, David, *Britain's Quest for a Role: A Diplomatic Memoir from Europe to the UN*, London: I.B. Tauris, 2013.

Healey, Denis, *The Time of My Life*, London: Michael Joseph, 1989.

Heath, Edward, *The Course of My Life: My Autobiography*, London: Hodder & Stoughton, 1998.

Henderson, Nevile, *Failure of a Mission: Berlin 1937–1939*, London: Hodder and Stoughton, 1940.

Henderson, Nicholas, *Mandarin: The Diaries of Nicholas Henderson*, London: Weidenfeld & Nicolson, 1995.

Holbrooke, Richard, *To End a War*, New York: Random House, 1998.

Home, Lord, *The Way the Wind Blows*, London: Collins, 1976.

Hurd, Douglas, *Memoirs*, London: Abacus, 2004.

Ingham, Bernard, *Kill the Messenger*, London: HarperCollins, 1991.

Jefferson, Thomas, *The Writings of Thomas Jefferson*, Volume IV, ed. Henry Augustine Washington, New York: Derby & Jackson, 1859.

Johnson, Lyndon Baines, *The Vantage Point: Perspectives of the Presidency 1963–1969*, London: Weidenfeld and Nicolson, 1972.

Kellner, Friedrich, *'Vernebelt, verdunkelt sind alle Hirne': Tagebücher 1939–1945*, Sascha Feuchert, Robert Martin Scott Kellner, Erwin Leibfried, Jörg Riecke and Markus Roth (eds), 2 volumes, Göttingen: Wallstein Verlag, 2011.

Kennedy, Robert F., *Thirteen Days: A Memoir of the Cuban Missile Crisis*, New York: W.W. Norton, 1969.

Khrushchev, Nikita, *Khrushchev Remembers*, introduction, commentary and notes by Edward Crankshaw; trans. and ed. Strobe Talbott, London: Andre Deutsch, 1971.

—, *Khrushchev Remembers: The Glasnost Tapes*, foreword by Strobe Talbott, trans. and ed. Jerrold L. Schecter with Vyacheslav V. Luchkov, Boston, MA: Little, Brown & Co., 1990.

Kirkpatrick, Ivone, *The Inner Circle: The Memoirs of Ivone Kirkpatrick*, London: Macmillan, 1959.

Kissinger, Henry A., *The White House Years*, London: Weidenfeld & Nicolson and Michael Joseph, 1979.

—, *Years of Renewal*, New York: Simon and Schuster, 1999.

Lloyd, Selwyn, *Suez 1956: A Personal Account*, London: Jonathan Cape, 1978.

Loewenheim, Francis L., Langley, Harold D. and Jonas, Manfred (eds), *Roosevelt and Churchill: Their Secret Wartime Correspondence*, London: Barrie and Jenkins, 1975.

Maclean, Fitzroy, *Eastern Approaches*, London: Jonathan Cape, 1949.

Macmillan, Harold, *Winds of Change 1914–1939*, London: Macmillan, 1966.

—, *The Blast of War 1939–1945*, London: Macmillan, 1967.

—, *Tides of Fortune 1945–55*, London: Macmillan, 1969.

—, *Riding the Storm 1956–1959*, London: Macmillan, 1971.

—, *Pointing the Way 1959–1961*, London: Macmillan, 1972.

—, *At the End of the Day 1961–1963*, London: Macmillan, 1973.

—, *The Macmillan Diaries: The Cabinet Years 1950–1957*, ed. Peter Catterall, London: Pan, 2004.

—, *The Macmillan Diaries, Volume II: Prime Minister and after, 1957–1966*, ed. Peter Catterall, London: Macmillan, 2011.

Major, John, *The Autobiography*, London: HarperCollins, 1999.

Mandelson, Peter, *The Third Man: Life at the Heart of New Labour*, London: HarperPress, 2010.

McNamara, Robert S., *In Retrospect: The Tragedy and Lessons of Vietnam*, New York: Vintage, 1996.

Meyer, Christopher, *DC Confidential: The Controversial Memoirs of Britain's Ambassador to the US at the Time of 9/11 and the Run-up to the Iraq War*, London: Weidenfeld & Nicholson, 2005.

Nicolson, Harold, *The Harold Nicolson Diaries 1907–1964*, ed. Nigel Nicolson, London: Phoenix, 2005.

Nitze, Paul H., *From Hiroshima to Glasnost: At the Centre of Decision – A Memoir*, London: Weidenfeld and Nicolson, 1990.

Nott, John, *Here Today, Gone Tomorrow: Recollections of an Errant Politician*, London: Politico's Publishing, 2002.

—, *Haven't We Been Here Before? Afghanistan to the Falklands: A Personal Connection*, London: Discovered Authors, 2007.

Orwell, George, *England, Your England and Other Essays*, London: Secker and Warburg, 1953.

—, *The Collected Essays, Journalism and Letters of George Orwell*, 4 volumes, ed. Sonia Orwell and Ian Angus, London: Penguin, 1970.

Owen, David, *Time to Declare*, London: Michael Joseph, 1991.

—, *Balkan Odyssey*, London: Victor Gollancz, 1995.

Powell, Colin L., *My American Journey*, New York: Random House, 1995.

Powell, Jonathan, *The New Machiavelli: How to Wield Power in the Modern World*, London: Vintage, 2011.

Pym, Francis, *The Politics of Consent*, rev. edn, London: Sphere Books, 1985.

Raczyński, Edward, *In Allied London: The Wartime Diaries of the Polish Ambassador*, London: Weidenfeld and Nicolson, 1962.

Reagan, Ronald, *An American Life: The Autobiography*, New York: Simon & Schuster, 1990.

—, *The Reagan Diaries*, ed. Douglas Brinkley, New York: HarperCollins, 2007.

Rees, Goronwy, *Sketches in Autobiography*, ed. and intro. John Harris, Cardiff: University of Wales Press, 2001.

Rice, Condoleezza, *No Higher Honour: A Memoir of My Years in Washington*, London: Simon & Schuster, 2011.

Ridley, Nicholas, *'My Style of Government': The Thatcher Years*, London: Fontana, 1992.

Roberts, Frank, *Dealing with Dictators: The Destruction and Revival of Europe 1930–70*, London: Weidenfeld & Nicolson, 1991.

Rumsfeld, Donald, *Known and Unknown: A Memoir*, New York: Sentinel, 2012.

Rusk, Dean, *As I Saw It*, London: I.B. Tauris, 1991.

Shuckburgh, Evelyn, *Descent to Suez: Diaries, 1951–56*, ed. John Charmley, London: Weidenfeld & Nicolson, 1986.

Solzhenitsyn, Aleksandr, *Détente, Democracy, and Dictatorship*, Daniel J. Mahoney (Preface), Irving Louis Horowitz (Contributor), and Arthur Schlesinger, Jr. (Contributor), New York: Transaction Publishers, 3rd edn 2009.

Straw, Jack, *Last Man Standing: Memoirs of a Political Survivor*, London: Macmillan, 2012.

Taylor, A. J. P., *A Personal History*, London: Coronet, 1984.

Templewood, Viscount (Sir Samuel Hoare), *Nine Troubled Years*, London: Collins, 1954.

Thatcher, Margaret, *The Downing Street Years*, London: HarperCollins, 1993.

—, *The Path to Power*, London: HarperCollins, 1995.

—, *Statecraft: Strategy for a Changing World*, London: HarperCollins, 2003.

—, *The Autobiography*, London: HarperCollins, 2013.

Truman, Harry S., *Year of Decisions*, Memoirs: Volume One, New York: Doubleday, 1955.

—, *Years of Trial and Hope*, Memoirs: Volume Two, New York: Doubleday, 1956.

Urban, George R., *Diplomacy and Disillusion at the Court of Margaret Thatcher: An Insider's View*, London: I.B. Tauris, 1996.

Weinberger, Caspar, *Fighting for Peace: Seven Critical Years in the Pentagon* (New York: Warner, 1990.

Weinberger, Caspar (with Gretchen Roberts), *In the Arena: A Memoir of the Twentieth Century*, Washington, DC: Regnery, 2001.

Wilson, Harold, *The Labour Government 1964–70: A Personal Record*, London: Weidenfield and Nicolson and Michael Joseph, 1971.

—, *Final Term: The Labour Government 1974–76*, London: Weidenfeld & Nicolson/Michael Joseph, 1979.

Zimmermann, Warren, *Origins of a Catastrophe: Yugoslavia and Its Destroyers – America's Last Ambassador Tells What Happened and Why*, New York: Random House, 1999.

Secondary sources

Selected monographs and edited works

Aldous, Richard, *The Lion and the Unicorn: Gladstone vs. Disraeli*, New York: W.W. Norton, 2007.

—, *Reagan and Thatcher: The Difficult Relationship*, London: Hutchinson, 2012.

Andrew, Christopher, *The Defence of the Realm: The Authorized History of MI5*, London: Penguin, 2010.

Andrew, Christopher and Mitrokhin, Vasili, *The Sword and the Shield: The Mitrokhin Archive and the Secret History of the KGB*, New York: Basic, 1999.

Annan, Noel, *Our Age: The Generation that Made Post-War Britain*, London: Fontana, 1991.

Applebaum, Anne, *Iron Curtain: the Crushing of Eastern Europe, 1944–56*, London: Allen Lane, 2012.

Aron, Raymond, *The Imperial Republic: The United States and the World 1945–1973*, London: Weidenfeld & Nicolson, 1975.

Ashton, Nigel, *Kennedy, Macmillan and the Cold War: The Irony of Interdependence*, London: Palgrave Macmillan, 2002.

Aster, Sidney (ed.), *Appeasement and All Souls: A Portrait with Documents, 1937–1939*, Cambridge: Cambridge University Press for the Royal Historical Society, 2004.

Ball, Simon, *The Guardsmen: Harold Macmillan, Three Friends and the World They Made*, London: HarperCollins, 2004.

Bange, Oliver and Niedhart, Gottfried (eds), *Helsinki 1975 and the Transformation of Europe*, Oxford: Berghahn, 2008.

Bar-Noi, Uri, *The Cold War and Soviet Mistrust of Détente, 1951–1955*, Brighton: Sussex Academic Press, 2007.

Baxter, Christopher, Dockrill, Michael L. and Hamilton, Keith (eds), *Britain in Global Politics Volume 1: From Gladstone to Churchill*, Basingstoke: Palgrave Macmillan, 2013.

Baylis, John, *Anglo-American Defence Relations, 1939–1984*, London: Macmillan, 1984.

Bell, Coral, *Negotiation from Strength*, London: Chatto and Windus, 1962.

—, *The Diplomacy of Détente*, London: Martin Robertson, 1977

Bennett, Gill, *Six Moments of Crisis: Inside British Foreign Policy*, Oxford: Oxford University Press, 2013.

Bew, John, *Castlereagh: Enlightenment, War and Tyranny*, London: Quercus, 2011.

Bicheno, Hugh, *Razor's Edge: The Unofficial History of the Falklands War*, London: Phoenix, 2007.

Blake, Robert, *Disraeli*, London: Methuen, 1969.

—, *The Decline of Power 1915–1964*, London: Paladin Books, 1986.

Bremen, Christian, *Die Eisenhower-Administration und die zweite Berlin-Krise, 1958–1961*, Berlin: de Gruyter, 1998.

Brivati, Brian, *Hugh Gaitskell*, London: Richard Cohen Books, 1997.

Brown, David, *Palmerston: A Biography*, New Haven, CT: Yale University Press, 2010.

Bullock, Alan, *Ernest Bevin: Foreign Secretary 1945–1951*, New York: W.W. Norton, 1983.

Campbell, Duncan Andrew, *Unlikely Allies: America, Britain and the Victorian Beginnings of the Special Relationship*, London: Continuum, 2007.

Campbell, John, *Edward Heath: A Biography*, London: Jonathan Cape, 1993.

—, *The Iron Lady: Margaret Thatcher: From Grocer's Daughter to Iron Lady*, London: Vintage, 2012.

Carr, E. H., *The Twenty Years' Crisis: An Introduction to the Study of International Relations*, London: Macmillan, 1940.

Cato, *Guilty Men*, London: Victor Gollancz, 1940.

Cate, Curtis, *The Ides of August: The Berlin Wall Crisis 1961*, London: Weidenfeld & Nicolson, 1978.

Charlton, Michael, *The Eagle and the Small Birds: Crisis in the Soviet Empire: From Yalta to Solidarity*, London: BBC, 1984.

Charmley, John, *Chamberlain and the Lost Peace*, London: Curtis, 1989.

—, *Churchill: The End of Glory*, London: Hodder and Stoughton, 1993.

—, *Splendid Isolation? Britain and the Balance of Power 1874–1914*, London: Hodder and Stoughton, 1999.

Cigar, Norman, *Genocide in Bosnia: The Policy of 'Ethnic Cleansing'*, College Station, TX: Texas A&M University Press, 1995.

Clarke, Peter, *Mr Churchill's Profession: Statesman, Orator, Writer*, London: Bloomsbury, 2012.

Cohen, Lenard J., *Broken Bonds: Yugoslavia's Disintegration and Balkan Politics in Transition*. 2nd edn, Oxford: Westview Press, 1995.

Colvin, Ian, *None So Blind: A British Diplomatic View of the Origins of World War II*, New York: Harcourt, Brace & World, 1965.

Cornwall, Mark and Evans, R. J. W. (eds), *Czechoslovakia in a Nationalist and Fascist Europe, 1918–1948*, Oxford: Oxford University Press for the British Academy, 2007.

Cosgrave, Patrick, *R.A. Butler: An English Life*, London: Quartet Books, 1981.

Cowling, Maurice, *The Impact of Labour 1920–1924: The Beginning of Modern British Politics*, Cambridge: Cambridge University Press, 1971.

—, *The Impact of Hitler: British Politics and British Policy 1933–1940*, Cambridge: Cambridge University Press, 1975.

Crossman, R. H. S., *The Charm of Politics: and Other Essays in Political Criticism*, London: Hamish Hamilton, 1958.

Cubitt, Geoffrey, *History and Memory*, Manchester: Manchester University Press, 2007.

Cviic, Christopher, *Remaking the Balkans*, London: RIIA, 1995.

Daddow, Oliver and Gaskarth, Jamie (eds), *British Foreign Policy: The New Labour Years*, Basingstoke: Palgrave Macmillan, 2011.

Danchev, Alex and Halverson, Thomas (eds), *International Perspectives on the Yugoslav Conflict*, Basingstoke: Macmillan, 1996.

Deighton, Anne, *The Impossible Peace: Britain, the Division of Germany and the Origins of the Cold War*, Oxford: Oxford University Press, 1993

Dilks, David, (ed.), *Retreat from Power: Studies in Britain's Foreign Policy of the Twentieth Century* (2 volumes), London: Macmillan, 1981.

Dockrill, Michael and McKercher, Brian (eds), *Diplomacy and World Power: Studies in British Foreign Policy, 1890–1950*, Cambridge: Cambridge University Press, 1996.

Dockrill, Saki, *Britain's Policy for West German Rearmament, 1950–1955*, Cambridge: Cambridge University Press, 1991.

Duff Cooper, Alfred, *Talleyrand*, London: Jonathan Cape, 1932.

David Dutton, *Anthony Eden: A Life and Reputation* (London: Arnold, 1997).

—, *Neville Chamberlain*, London: Arnold, 2001.

Dyson, Keith, (ed.), *European Détente: Case Studies of the Politics of East–West Relations*, London: Frances Pinter, 1986.

Eade, Charles, (ed.), *Churchill by his Contemporaries*, London: Hutchinson, 1953.

Einzig, Paul, *Appeasement: Before, During and After the War*, London: Macmillan, 1942.

Esdaile, Charles, *Napoleon's Wars: An International History 1803–1815*, London: Allen Lane, 2007.

Eyal, Jonathan, *Europe and Yugoslavia: Lessons from a Failure*, London: Royal United Services Institute, 1993.

Ferguson, Niall, *The Pity of War*, London: Allen Lane, 1999.

Ferrell, Robert H., *Harry S. Truman and the Cold War Revisionists*, Columbia, MO/ London: University of Missouri Press, 2006.

Foot, Michael, *Aneurin Bevan 1897–1960*, ed. Brian Brivati, London: Indigo, 1997.

Foot, Michael and Jones, Mervyn, *Guilty Men, 1957*, London: Victor Gollancz, 1957.

Freedman, Lawrence (ed.), *European Intervention in European Conflicts*, Oxford: Blackwell publishers, 1994.

Gaddis, John L., *Strategies of Containment: A Critical Appraisal of Postwar American National Security Policy*, Oxford: Oxford University Press, 1982.

—, *George F. Kennan: An American Life*, London: Penguin, 2011.

Gaddis, John L., Gordon, Phillip H., May, Ernest R. and Rosenberg, Jonathon (eds), *Cold War Statesman Confront the Bomb: Nuclear Diplomacy since 1945*, Oxford: Oxford University Press, 1999.

Gearson, John P. S., *Harold Macmillan and the Berlin Wall Crisis, 1958–1962: The Limits of Interest and Force*, Basingstoke: Macmillan, 1998.

George, Margaret, *The Warped Vision: British Foreign Policy, 1933–1939*, Pittsburgh, PA: University of Pittsburgh Press, 1965.

Gilbert, Martin, *The Roots of Appeasement*, London: Weidenfeld and Nicolson, 1966.

—, *Road to Victory: Winston S. Churchill 1941–1945*, London: Heinemann, 1986.

—, *Never Despair: Winston S. Churchill 1945–1965*, London: Heinemann, 1988.

Gilbert, Martin and Gott, Richard, *The Appeasers*, London: Weidenfeld and Nicolson, 1963.

Glenny, Misha, *The Fall of Yugoslavia: The Third Balkan War*, London: Penguin Books, 1992.

Gossel, Daniel, *Briten, Deutsche und Europa: die Deutsche Frage in der britischen Außenpolitik, 1945–1962*, Stuttgart: Steiner, 1999.

Gow, James, *Triumph of the Lack of Will: International Diplomacy and the Yugoslav War*, London: Hurst, 1997.

Gutman, Roy, *A Witness to Genocide*, London: Element, 1993.

Haase, Christian (ed.), *Debating Foreign Affairs: The Public and British Foreign Policy since 1867*, Berlin: Philo, 2003.

Hague, William, *William Pitt the Younger*, London: HarperColllins, 2004.

Hakkarainen, Petri, *A State of Peace in Europe: West Germany and the CSCE, 1966–1975*, New York: Berghahn, 2011.

Hans J. Morgenthau, *Truth and Power: Essays of a Decade, 1960–70*, New York: Praeger, 1970.

—, *Politics among Nations: The Struggle for Power and Peace*, ed. Kenneth W. Thompson, New York: Alfred A. Knopf, 5th edn 1985.

Haslam, Jonathan, *The Soviet Union and the Struggle for Collective Security in Europe 1933–39*, London: Macmillan, 1984.

—, *Russia's Cold War: From the October Revolution to the Fall of the Wall*, New Haven, CT and London: Yale University Press, 2010.

Halbwachs, Maurice, *On Collective Memory*, trans. and ed. Lewis A. Coser, Chicago, IL: University of Chicago Press, 1992.

Harris, Kenneth, *Attlee*, London: Weidenfeld & Nicolson, 1995.

Hayter, Sir William, *The Kremlin and the Embassy*, London: Hodder & Stoughton, 1966.

Hegel, Georg Wilhelm Friedrich, *The Philosophy of History*, New York: Dover Publications, 1956 [1837].

Hennessy, Peter, *Never Again: Britain, 1945–51*, London: Jonathan Cape, 1992.

—, *The Prime Minister: The Office and Its Holders since 1945*, London: Penguin, 2001.

—, *Cabinets and the Bomb*, Oxford: Oxford University Press 2007.

—, *Having It so Good: Britain in the Fifties*, London: Penguin, 2007.

—, *Distilling the Frenzy: Writing the History of One's Own Times*, London: Biteback, 2012.

Hicks, Geoffrey (ed.), *Conservatism and British Foreign Policy: The Derbys and Their World*, Farnham: Ashgate, 2011.

Hinsley, F. H., *Power and the Pursuit of Peace: Theory and Practice in the History of Relations between States*, Cambridge: Cambridge University Press, 1963.

Horne, Alastair, *Macmillan 1894–1956*, London: Macmillan, 1988.

—, *Macmillan 1957–1986*, London: Macmillan, 1989.

—, *A Savage War of Peace: Algeria 1954–1962*, London: Papermac, 3rd edn 1996.

Howard, Anthony, *RAB: The Life of R.A. Butler*, London: Jonathan Cape, 1987.

Hucker, Daniel, *Public Opinion and the End of Appeasement in Britain and France*, Farnham: Ashgate, 2011.

Hughes, R. Gerald, *Britain, Germany and the Cold War: The Search for a European Détente, 1949–1967*, London: Routledge, 2007.

Hurd, Douglas, *The Search for Peace: A Century of Peace Diplomacy*, London: Warner Books, 1997.

—, *Choose Your Weapons: The British Foreign Secretary: 200 Years of Argument, Success and Failure*, London: Phoenix, 2011.

Jaksch, Wenzel, *Europe's Road to Potsdam*, trans. and ed. Kurt Glaser, New York: Praeger, 1963.

James, Robert Rhodes, *Anthony Eden*, London: Papermac, 1987.

Jeffery, Keith, *MI6: The History of the Secret Intelligence Service 1909–1949*, London: Bloomsbury, 2010.

Jenkins, Roy, *Churchill*, London: Pan, 2002.

Jervis, Robert, *Perception and Misperception in International Politics*, Princeton, NJ: Princeton University Press, 1976.

Johns, Andrew L., *Vietnam's Second Front: Domestic Politics, the Republican Party, and the War*, Lexington, KY: University Press of Kentucky, 2012.

Johnson, Paul, *The Suez War*, intro. Aneurin Bevan, London: MacGibbon and Kee, 1957.

Keeble, Curtis, *Britain, the Soviet Union and Russia*, London: Palgrave Macmillan, 2001.

Kennan, George F., *The Nuclear Delusion*, New York: Pantheon, 1982.

Kennedy, John F., *Why England Slept*, London: Hutchinson, 1940.

Kennedy, Paul M., *The Rise of the Anglo-German Antagonism, 1860–1914*, London: Allen & Unwin, 1980.

—, *The Realities Behind Diplomacy: Background Influences on British External Policy 1865–1980*, London: Fontana, 1981.

Khong, Yuen Foong, *Analogies at War: Korea, Munich, Dien Bien Phu, and the Vietnam Decisions of 1965*, Princeton, NJ: Princeton University Press, 1992.

Kipp, Yvonne, *Eden, Adenauer und die deutsche Frage: Britische Deutschlandpolitik im internationalen Spannungsfeld 1951–1957*, Paderborn: Ferdinand Schöningh, 2002.

Kissinger, Henry A., *The Troubled Partnership: A Reappraisal of the Atlantic Alliance*, Council on Foreign Relations, 1965.

—, *A World Restored: Metternich, Castlereagh and the Problems of Peace, 1812–1822*, Boston, MA: Houghton Mifflin, 1973 [1957].

—, *Diplomacy*, New York: Simon and Schuster, 1994.

Kochanski, Halik, *The Eagle Unbowed: Poland and the Poles in the Second World War*, London: Penguin, 2013.

Köhler, Henning, *Adenauer: Eine Politische Biographie*, Frankfurt aM: Propyläen, 1994.

Ković, Miloš, *Disraeli and the Eastern Question*, Oxford: Oxford University Press, 2011.

Kramer, Mark (ed.), *The Black Book of Communism: Crimes, Terror, Repression*, Cambridge, MA: Harvard University Press, 1999.

Kyle, Keith, *Suez: Britain's End of Empire in the Middle East*, London: I.B. Tauris, 2011 edn.

Lacoutre, Jean, *De Gaulle: The Ruler 1945–1970*, trans. Alan Sheridan, London: Harvill, 1993.

Lambert, Andrew, *The Crimean War: British Grand Strategy against Russia, 1853–56*, Farnham: Ashgate, 2nd edn, 2011.

Larres, Klaus, *Politik der Illusionen: Churchill, Eisenhower und die deutsche Frage, 1945–1955*, Göttingen: Vandenhoeck und Ruprecht, 1995.

—, *Churchill's Cold War: The Politics of Personal Diplomacy*, London: Yale University Press, 2002.

Leffler, Melvyn P., *A Preponderance of Power: National Security, the Truman Administration, and the Cold War*, Stanford, CA: Stanford University Press, 1992.

Lerche, Charles O., *Principles of International Politics*, New York: Oxford University Press, 1956.

Lewis, Terrance L., *Prisms of British Appeasement: Revisionist Reputations of John Simon, Samuel Hoare, Anthony Eden, Lord Halifax and Alfred Duff Cooper*, Brighton: Sussex Academic Press, 2009.

Louis, Wm. Roger (ed.), *The Origins of the Second World War: A.J.P. Taylor and His Critics*, New York: Wiley, 1972.

Louis, Wm. Roger and Bull, Hedley (eds), *The Special Relationship: Anglo-American Relations since 1945*, London: Clarendon Press, 1986.

Loth, Wilfried, *Overcoming the Cold War: A History of Détente, 1950–1991*, Basingstoke: Palgrave, 2002.

Machiavelli, Niccolò, *The Prince*, trans. and intro. George Bull, London: Penguin, 1995.

Martel, Gordon (ed.), The *Origins of the Second World War Reconsidered: The A.J.P. Taylor Debate after Twenty-Five Years*, London: Allen & Unwin, 1986.

—, *Origins of the Second World War Reconsidered: A.J.P. Taylor and the Historians*, London: Routledge, 1999.

Matthew, H. C. G., *Gladstone: 1875–1898*, Oxford: Clarendon Press, 1995.

May, Ernest R., *'Lessons' of the Past: The Use and Misuse of History in American Foreign Policy*, New York: Oxford University Press, 1973.

Mayer, Frank A., *Adenauer and Kennedy: A Study in German–American Relations, 1961–1963*, London: Macmillan: 1996.

McDonough, Frank, *Neville Chamberlain, Appeasement, and the British Road to War*, Manchester: Manchester University Press, 1998.

—, (ed.), *Origins of the Second World War: An International Perspective*, London: Continuum, 2011.

Medlicott, W. N., *British Foreign Policy since Versailles: 1919–1963*, London: Methuen, 1968.

MeGoldrick, Dominic, *From '9-11' to the 'Iraq War 2003': International Law in an Age of Complexity*, Oxford: Hart, 2004.

Mertsalov, Andrei, *Munich: Mistake or Cynical Calculation? Contemporary Non-Marxist Historians on the Munich Agreement of 1938*, Moscow: Novosti Press Agency, 1988.

Messervy-Whiting, Graham, *The Peace Conference on Former Yugoslavia: The Politico-Military Interface*, London: Centre for Defence Studies, 1995.

Meštrović, Stjepan G. (ed.), *Genocide after Emotion: The Postemotional Balkan War*, London: Routledge, 1996.

Meyer, Christopher, *Getting Our Way: 500 Years of Adventures and Intrigue: The Inside Story of British Diplomacy*, London: Phoenix, 2010.

Moore, Charles, *Margaret Thatcher: The Authorized Biography: Volume One: Not for Turning*, London: Allen Lane, 2013.

Morgan, Kenneth O., *Callaghan: A Life*, Oxford: Oxford University Press, 1997.

—, *Michael Foot: A Life*, London: Harper Perennial, 2008.

Mousavizadeh, Nader (ed.), *The Black Book of Bosnia: The Consequences of 'Appeasement'*, New York: Basic Books, 1996.

Müller, Jan-Werner (ed.), *Memory and Power in Post-War Europe*, Cambridge: Cambridge University Press, 2002.

Münger, Christof, *Die Berliner Mauer, Kennedy und die Kubakrise: Die westliche Allianz in der Zerreißprobe 1961–1963*, Paderborn: Schöningh, 2003.

Murray, Williamson, Sinnreich, Richard Hart, and Lacey, James (eds), *The Shaping of Grand Strategy: Policy, Diplomacy, and War*, Cambridge: Cambridge University Press, 2011.

Neustadt, Richard E. and May, Ernest R., *Thinking in Time: The Uses of History for Decision Makers*, New York: The Free Press, 1986.

New York Times (ed.), *Portraits of Power*, London: Octopus, 1979.

Namier, Lewis, *Diplomatic Prelude, 1938–1939*, London: Macmillan, 1948.

—, *Europe in Decay: A Study in Disintegration, 1936–40*, London: Macmillan, 1950.

Northedge, F. S., and Wells, A., *Britain and Soviet Communism*, London: Macmillan, 1982.

O'Ballance, Edgar, *Civil War in Bosnia 1992–1994*, London: Macmillan, 1995.

Olson, Lynne, *Troublesome Young Men: The Rebels who Brought Churchill to Power in 1940 and Helped Save Britain*, London: Bloomsbury, 2007.

Onslow, Sue, *Backbench debate within the Conservative Party and its influence on British Foreign Policy, 1948–57*, Basingstoke: Macmillan, 1997.

Otte, T. G., *The Foreign Office Mind: The Making of British Foreign Policy, 1865–1914*, Cambridge: Cambridge University Press, 2011.

Oudenaren, John van, *Détente in Europe: The Soviet Union and the West since 1953*, London: Duke University Press, 1991.

Ovendale, R. (ed.), *The Foreign Policy of the British Labour Governments 1945–51*, Leicester University Press, 1984.

Papasotiriou, Charalmbos, *Liberal Idealism versus Realism: The Yugoslav Case*, Athens: Institute of International Relations, 1996.

Parker, R. A. C., *Chamberlain and Appeasement: British Policy and the Coming of the Second World War*, London: Macmillan, 1993.

—, *Churchill and Appeasement*, London: Macmillan, 2000.

Peden, George C., *The Treasury and British Public Policy 1906–1959*, Oxford: Oxford University Press, 2000.

—, *Arms, Economics and British Strategy: From Dreadnoughts to Hydrogen Bombs*, Cambridge: Cambridge University Press, 2007.

Perica, Vjekoslav and Gavrilović, Darko (eds), *Political Myths about Yugoslavia in the Former Yugoslavia and Successor States: A Shared Narrative*, Institute for Historical Justice and Reconciliation, trans. Dana Todorović, Dordrecht: Republic of Letters Publishing, 2011.

Pfiffner, James P. and Phythian, Mark (eds), *Intelligence and National Security Policymaking on Iraq: British and American Perspectives*, College Station, TX: Texas A&M University Press, 2008.

Presseisen, Ernst L., *Amiens and Munich: Comparisons in Appeasement*, The Hague: Martinus Nijhoff, 1978.

Ramet, Sabrina Petra, *Balkan Babel: The Disintegration of Yugoslavia from the Death of Tito to Ethnic War*, Oxford: Westview Press, 1996.

Rathbun, Brian C., *Partisan Interventions: European Party Politics and Peace Enforcement in the Balkans*, Ithaca, NY: Cornell University Press, 2004.

Raymond, D. N., *British Policy and Opinion during the Franco-Prussian War*, New York: Columbia University Press, 1921.

Record, Jeffery, *The Specter of Munich: Reconsidering the Lessons of Appeasing Hitler*, Washington, DC: Potomac Books, 2007.

Reilly, Robin, *William Pitt the Younger: A Biography*, New York: Putnam, 1979.

Reynolds, David, *In Command of History: Churchill Fighting and Writing the Second World War*, London: Allen Lane, 2004.

—, *From World War to Cold War: Churchill, Roosevelt, and the International History of the 1940s*, Oxford: Oxford University Press, 2006.

—, *Summits: Six Meetings that Shaped the Twentieth Century*, New York: Basic Books, 2007.

Rieff, David, *Slaughterhouse: Bosnia and the Failure of the West*, London: Vintage, 1995.

Ritter, Gerhard, *The Schlieffen Plan: Critique of a Myth*, foreword by B. H. Liddell Hart, London: Wolff, 1958.

Robbins, Keith, *Munich 1938*, London: Cassell, 1968; London: Simon & Schuster, 1984.

—, *Appeasement*, Oxford: Wiley-Blackwell, 2nd edn 1997.

Roberts, Andrew, *'The Holy Fox': The Life of Lord Halifax*, London: Phoenix, 1997.

—, *Salisbury: Victorian Titan*, London: Weidenfeld & Nicolson, 1999.

Roberts, Geoffrey, *The Unholy Alliance: Stalin's Pact with Hitler*, London: I.B. Tauris, 1989.

—, *Stalin's Wars: From World War to Cold War, 1939–1953*, London: Yale University Press, 2006.

Robertson, Esmonde M. (ed.), *The Origins of the Second World War*, London: Macmillan, 1971.

Rock, W. R., *Appeasement on Trial: British Foreign Policy and Its Critics: 1938–1939*, North Haven, CT: Archon Press, 1966.

—, *Appeasement in International Politics*, Lexington, KY: University Press of Kentucky, 2000.

Rowse, A. L., *All Souls and Appeasement: A Contribution to Contemporary History*, London: Macmillan, 1961.

—, *Appeasement: A Study in Political Decline 1933–1939*, New York: W.W. Norton, 1961.

Rudman, Stella, *Lloyd George and the Appeasement of Germany, 1919–1945*, Newcastle upon Tyne: Cambridge Scholars Publishing, 2011.

Rystad, Göran, *Prisoners of the Past? The Munich Syndrome and Makers of American Foreign Policy in the Cold War*, Lund, Sweden: CWK Gleerup, 1982.

Sanders, David, *Losing an Empire, Finding a Role: British Foreign Policy Since 1945*, London: Macmillan, 1990.

Schlesinger, Arthur M., *A Thousand Days: John F. Kennedy in the White House*, London: André Deutsch, 1965.

—, *The Bitter Heritage: Vietnam and American Democracy, 1941–1968*, Greenwich, CT: Fawcett, 1968.

Self, Robert, *Neville Chamberlain: A Biography*, Farnham: Ashgate, 2006.

Sharp, Jane M. O., *Bankrupt in the Balkans: British Policy in Bosnia*, London: IPPR, 1993.

Shaw, Tony, *Eden, Suez and the Mass Media: Propaganda and Persuasion during the Suez Crisis*, London: I.B. Tauris, 2009.

Silber, Laura and Little, Allan, *The Death of Yugoslavia*, London: Penguin/BBC Books, 1995.

Simms, Brendan, *Unfinest Hour: Britain and the Destruction of Bosnia*, London: Penguin, 2002.

Smith, Simon C. (ed.), *Reassessing Suez 1956: New Perspectives on the Crisis and Its Aftermath*, Farnham: Ashgate, 2008.

Smyser, W. R., *From Yalta to Berlin: The Cold War Struggle over Germany*, London: Macmillan, 1999.

Smetana, Vít, *In the Shadow of Munich: British Policy towards Czechoslovakia from the Endorsement to the Renunciation of the Munich Agreement (1938–1942)*, Prague: Karolinum, 2008.

Soffer, Reba N., *History, Historians, and Conservatism in Britain and America: From the Great War to Thatcher and Reagan*, New York: Oxford University Press, 2009.

Sorensen, Theodore C., *Kennedy*, London: Pan, 1965.

Später, Jörg, *Vansittart: Britische Debatten über Deutsche und Nazis 1902–1945*, Göttingen: Wallstein Verlag, 2003.

Speed, Keith, *Sea Change: The Battle for the Falklands and the Future of Britain's Navy*, Bath: Ashgrove Press, 1982.

Steel, Ronald, *Walter Lippmann and the American Century*, Boston, MA: Little, Brown & Co., 1980.

Steininger, Rolf, *Der Mauerbau: Die Westmächte und Adenauer in der Berlinkrise 1958–1963*, Munich: Olzog, 2001.

Stewart, Bob, *Broken Lives: A Personal View of the Bosnian Conflict*, London: HarperCollins, 1993.

Steiner, Zara, *The Lights that Failed: European International History, 1919–1933*, Oxford: Oxford University Press, 2005.

Stirk, Peter M. R. and Willis, David (eds), *Shaping Postwar Europe: European Unity and Disunity 1945–1957*, London: Pinter Publishers, 1991.

Szkopiak, Zygmunt C. (ed.), *The Yalta Agreements: The White Book: Documents prior to, during and after the Crimea Conference 1945*, London: Polish Government in Exile, 1986.

Tanca, Antonio, *Foreign Armed Intervention in Internal Conflict*, Dordrecht: M. Nijhoff Publishers, 1993.

Taubert, Fritz (ed.), *Mythos München*, Munich: Oldenbourg, 2002.

Taubman, William, *Khrushchev: The Man and His Era*, New York: W.W. Norton, 2003.

Taylor, A. J. P., *The Origins of the Second World War*, London: Hamish Hamilton, 1961.

—, *English History 1914–1945*, Oxford: Oxford University Press, 2nd edn 1975.

—, *An Old Man's Diary*, London: Hamish Hamilton, 1984.

Taylor, Telford, *Munich: the Price of Peace*, Garden City, NY: Doubleday, 1979.

Theoharis, Athan G., *The Yalta Myths: An Issue in U.S. Politics, 1945–1955*, Columbia, MO: University of Missouri Press, 1970.

Thomas, Hugh, *The Spanish Civil War*, London: Penguin books, 1965.

—, *Armed Truce: The Beginnings of the Cold War, 1945–6*, London: Heinemann, 1987.

Thomas-Symonds, Nicklaus, *Attlee: A Life in Politics*, London: I.B. Tauris, 2012.

Thompson, Mark, *A Paper House: The Ending of Yugoslavia*, London: Hutchinson/Radius, 1992.

Thorpe, D. R., *Selwyn Lloyd*, London: Jonathan Cape, 1989.

—, *Alec Douglas-Home*, London: Sinclair-Stevenson, 1996.

—, *Eden: The Life and Times of Anthony Eden, First Earl of Avon 1897–1977*, London: Chatto, 2003.

—, *Supermac: The Life of Harold Macmillan*, London: Chatto and Windus, 2010.

Tolstoy, Nikolai, *Victims of Yalta*, London: Corgi, rev. edn 1979.

Towle, Philip, *Going to War: British Debates from Wilberforce to Blair*, Basingstoke: Palgrave Macmillan, 2009.

Toye, Richard, *The Roar of the Lion: The Untold Story of Churchill's World War II Speeches*, Oxford: Oxford University Press, 2013.

Trachtenberg, Marc, *A Constructed Peace: The Making of the European Settlement 1945–1963*, Princeton University Press, 1999.

Tuchman, Barbara, *The Guns of August*, New York: Macmillan, 1962.

Urban, G. R. (ed.), *Détente*, London: Temple Smith, 1976.

Vaughn, Stephen (ed.), *The Vital Past: Writings on the Uses of History*, Athens, GA: The University of Georgia Press, 1985.

Watt, Donald Cameron, *Succeeding John Bull: America in Britain's Place 1900–1975*, Cambridge: Cambridge University Press, 1984.

—, *How War Came: The Immediate Origins of the Second World War, 1938–1939*, London: William Heinemann, 1989.

Welch, David and Fox, Jo (eds), *Justifying War: Propaganda, Politics and War in the Modern Age*, Basingstoke: Palgrave Macmillan, 2012.

West, Richard, *Tito and the Rise and Fall of Yugoslavia*, London: Sinclair-Stevenson, 1994.

Wheeler-Bennett, John, *Munich: Prologue to Tragedy*, London: Macmillan, 1948.

White, Brian, *Britain, Détente and Changing East–West Relations*, London: Routledge, 1992.

Williams, Philip, *Hugh Gaitskell: A Political Biography*, London: Jonathan Cape, 1979.

Wilson, Keith (ed.), *Forging the Collective Memory: Government and International Historians Through Two World Wars*, Oxford: Berghahn, 1996.

Wiskemann, Elizabeth, *Germany's Eastern Neighbours: Problems Relating to the Oder-Neisse Line and the Czech Frontier Regions*, Oxford: Oxford University Press, 1956.

Wolfers, Arnold (ed.), *Alliance Policy in the Cold War*, Baltimore, MD: Johns Hopkins University Press, 1959.

Wolfers, Arnold, *Discord and Collaboration: Essays on International Politics*, Baltimore, MD: Johns Hopkins University Press, 1962.

Young, John W., Pedaliu Effie G. H. and Kandiah, Michael D. (eds), *Britain in Global Politics Volume 2: From Churchill to Blair*, Basingstoke: Palgrave Macmillan, 2013.

Zeitler, Klaus Peter, *Deutschlands Rolle bei der völkerrechtlichen Anerkennung der Republik Kroatien: unter besonderer Berücksichtigung des deutschen Außenministers Genscher*, Marburg: Tectum Verlag, 2000.

Ziegler, Philip, *Edward Heath: The Authorised Biography*, London: HarperPress, 2011.

Zimmer, Louis B., *The Vietnam War Debate: Hans J. Morgenthau and the Attempt to Halt the Drift into Disaster*, Lanham, MD: Lexington Books: 2011.

Zubok, Vladislav and Pleshakov, Constantine, *Inside the Kremlin's Cold War: From Stalin to Khrushchev*, Cambridge, MA: Harvard University Press, 1996.

Selected journal articles and chapters from books

Abedul, Hugo and Hughes, R. Gerald, 'The Comandante in His Labyrinth: Fidel Castro and His Legacy', *Intelligence and National Security*, 26.4 (2011), pp. 531–65.

Addison, Paul, 'The three careers of Winston Churchill', *Transactions of the Royal Historical Society*, 6th series, 11 (2001), pp. 183–200.

Amery, Julian, 'The Suez Group: A Retrospective on Suez' in S. I. Troen and M. Shemesh (eds), *The Suez-Sinai Crisis 1956*, London: Frank Cass, 1990.

Asselin, Pierre, '"We Don't Want a Munich": Hanoi's Diplomatic Strategy, 1965-1968', *Diplomatic History*, 36.3 (2012), pp. 547–81.

Aster, Sidney, 'Guilty Men: The Case of Neville Chamberlain' in Patrick Finney (ed.), *The Origins of the Second World War*, London: Bloomsbury Academic, 1997.

—, 'Appeasement: Before and After Revisionism', *Diplomacy & Statecraft*, 19.3 (2008), pp. 443–80.

Bartošek, Karel, 'Could We Have Fought? The "Munich Complex" in Czech Policies and Czech Thinking' in Norman Stone and Eduard Strouhal (eds), *Czechoslovakia: Crossroads and Crises, 1918–88*, New York: St. Martin's Press, 1989.

Beck, Robert J., 'Munich's Lessons Reconsidered', *International Security*, 14.2 (1989), pp. 161–91.

Bialer, Uri, 'Telling the Truth to the People: Britain's Decision to Publish the Diplomatic Papers of the interwar Period' in Keith Wilson (ed.), *Forging the Collective Memory: Government and International Historians Through Two World Wars*, Oxford: Berghahn, 1996.

Blaazer, David, 'Finance and the End of Appeasement: The Bank of England, the National Government and the Czech Gold', *Journal of Contemporary History*, 40.1 (2005), pp. 25–39.

Boyd, Charles G., 'Making Peace with the Guilty: The Truth about Bosnia', *Foreign Affairs*, 75.5 (1995), pp. 23–38.

Brown, Martin D., 'A Munich Winter or a Prague Spring? The evolution of British policy towards the Sudeten Germans from October 1938 to September 1939', in H. H. Hahn (ed.), *Hundert Jahre sudetendeutsche Geschichte: Eine völkische Bewegung in drei Staaten*, Frankfurt a.M: Peter Lang, 2007.

Bugajski, Janusz, 'Dayton's Impact on the US Presidential Election', *Transition*, 2.14 (1996), pp. 17–21.

Burg, Steven L., 'Why Yugoslavia Fell apart', *Current History*, 92.577 (1993), pp. 357–61.

Calic, Marie-Janine, 'Bosnia-Hercegovinia after Dayton: Opportunities and Risks for Peace', *Aussenpolitik*, 47.2 (1996), pp. 127–35.

Canfora, Luciano, 'Analogie et Histoire', *History and Theory*, 22.1 (1983), pp. 22–42.

Carlton, David, 'Churchill and the Two Evil Empires' in David Cannadine and Roland Quinault (eds), *Winston Churchill in the Twenty First Century*, Cambridge: Cambridge University Press, 2004.

Charmley, John, 'Neville Chamberlain and the Consequences of the Churchillian Hegemony' in Frank McDonough (ed.), *Origins of the Second World War: An International Perspective*, London: Continuum, 2011.

—, 'Traditions of Conservative Foreign Policy' in Geoffrey Hicks (ed.), *Conservatism and British Foreign Policy: The Derbys and Their World*, Farnham: Ashgate, 2011.

Chuter, David, 'Munich, or the Blood of Others' in Cyril Buffet and Beatrice Heuser (eds), *Haunted by History: Myths in International Relations*, Oxford: Berghahn Books, 1998.

Clarke, Jonathan, 'Rhetoric before reality', *Foreign Affairs*, 7.5 (1995), pp. 2–7.

Cowling, Maurice, 'Lytton, the Cabinet and the Russians, August–November 1878', *English Historical Review*, 76.298 (1961), pp. 59–79.

Craig, Gordon A., 'High Tide of Appeasement: The Road to Munich, 1937–38', *Political Science Quarterly*, 65.1 (1950), pp. 20–37.

Crawford, Beverley, 'Explaining Defection from International Co-operation: Germany's Unilateral Recognition of Croatia', *World Politics*, 48.4 (1996), pp. 482–521.

Crowson, N. J., 'Conservative parliamentary dissent over foreign policy during the premiership of Neville Chamberlain: myth or reality?', *Parliamentary History*, 14.3 (1995), pp. 315–36.

Cviic, Christopher, 'Perceptions of Former Yugoslavia: An Interpretative Reflection', *International Affairs*, 71.4 (1995), pp. 819–26.

Davy, Richard, 'Helsinki Myths: Setting the Record Straight on the Final Act of the CSCE, 1975', *Cold War History*, 9.1 (2009), pp. 1–22.

Douglas, Roy, 'Chamberlain and Eden, 1937–38', *Journal of Contemporary History*, 13.1 (1978), pp. 97–116.

—, 'Chamberlain and Appeasement' in Wolfgang J. Mommsen and Lothar Kettenacker (eds), *The Fascist Challenge and the Policy of Appeasement*, London: Allen and Unwin, 1983.

Dumbrell, John and Ellis, Sylvia, 'British Involvement in Vietnam Peace Initiatives, 1966–1967: Marigolds, Sunflowers, and "Kosygin Week"', *Diplomatic History*, 27.1 (2003), pp. 113–49.

Eyal, Jonathan, 'Managing the Balkans', *Brassey's Defence Yearbook 1992*, London: Brassey's, 1992, pp. 79–89.

Fenske, John, 'The West and "The problem from hell"', *Current History*, 92.577 (1993), pp. 353–6.

Finney, Patrick, '"And I will tell you who you are": Historiographies of Munich and the Negotiation of National Identity' in Fritz Taubert (ed.), *Mythos München*, Munich: Oldenbourg, 2002.

Foley, Robert T., 'The Origins of the Schlieffen Plan', *War in History*, 10.2 (2003), pp. 223–32.

Freedman, Lawrence, 'Bosnia: Does Peace Support Make any Sense?' *NATO Review*, 6 (1995), pp. 19–23.

Hall, Ian, 'Power Politics and Appeasement: Political Realism in British International Thought, c. 1935–1955', *British Journal of Politics and International Relations*, 8.2 (2006), pp. 174–92.

Herz, John H., 'The Relevancy and Irrelevancy of Appeasement', *Social Research*, 31.3 (1964), pp. 296–320.

Heuser, Beatrice, 'Modern Man's Myths: The Influence of Historical Memory on Policy-Making' in Fritz Taubert (ed.), *Mythos München*, Munich: Oldenbourg, 2002.

Hicks, Geoffrey, '"Appeasement" or Consistent Conservatism? British Foreign Policy, Party Politics and the Guarantees of 1867 and 1939', *Historical Research*, 84.225 (2011), pp. 513–34.

Holdich, P. G. H., 'A Policy of Percentages? British Policy in the Balkans after the Moscow Conference of October 1944', *International History Review*, 9.1 (1987), pp. 32–46.

Hucker, Daniel, 'The Unending Debate: Appeasement, Chamberlain and the Origins of the Second World War', *Intelligence and National Security*, 23.4 (2008), pp. 536–51.

Hughes, R. Gerald, '"We Are not Seeking Strength for Its Own Sake': The Labour Party and West Germany, 1951–64', *Cold War History*, 3.1 (2002), pp. 67–94.

—, 'Unfinished Business from Potsdam: Britain, West Germany, and the Oder-Neiße line, 1945–1962', *International History Review*, 27.2 (2005), pp. 259–94.

—, '"Possession is nine tenths of the law": Britain and the Boundaries of Eastern Europe since 1945', *Diplomacy and Statecraft*, 16.4 (2005), pp. 723–47.

—, '"Don't let's be beastly to the Germans': Britain and the German Affair in History', *Twentieth Century British History*, 17.2 (2006), pp. 257–83.

—, 'Of Revelatory Histories and Hatchet Jobs: Propaganda and Method in Intelligence History', *Intelligence and National Security*, 23.6 (2008), pp. 842–77.

—, 'A Coalition of "Compromise and Barter": Britain and West Germany in the Cold War, 1945–1975' in Matthew Grant (ed.), *The British Way In Cold Warfare: Intelligence, Diplomacy and the Bomb, 1945–75*, London: Continuum, 2009.

—, 'Britain, East–West Détente and the CSCE' in Vladimir Bilandžić, Dittmar Dahlmann and Milan Kosanović (eds), *From Helsinki to Belgrade: The First CSCE Follow-up Meeting and the Crisis of Détente*, Göttingen: Vandenhoeck and Ruprecht/Bonn University Press, 2012.

—, 'Truth Telling and the Defence of the Realm: History and the History of the British Secret Intelligence Service', *Intelligence and National Security*, 26.5 (2011), pp. 701–19.

—, 'Strategists and Intelligence' in Robert Dover, Michael S. Goodman and Claudia Hillebrand (eds), *Routledge Companion to Intelligence Studies* (Abingdon: Routledge, 2014).

—, 'The Ghosts of Appeasement: Britain and the Legacy of the Munich Agreement', *Journal of Contemporary History*, 48.4 (2013), pp. 688–716.

Hughes, R. Gerald and Robb, Thomas, 'Two Princes and their Adviser: Nixon, Ford and Kissinger', *The Journal of Peace Studies*, 13.2 (2012), pp. 49–75.

—, 'Kissinger and the Diplomacy of Coercive Linkage in the "Special Relationship" between the United States and Great Britain, 1969–1977', *Diplomatic History*, 37.4 (2013), pp. 861–905.

Hughes, R. Gerald and Stoddart, Kristan, 'Hope and Fear: Intelligence and the Future of Global Security a Decade after 9/11', *Intelligence and National Security*, 27.5 (2012), pp. 625–52.

Imlay, Talbot and Kennedy, Paul M., 'Appeasement' in Gordon Martel (ed.), *The Origins of the Second World War Reconsidered*, London: Unwin Hyman, 1999.

Jeszenszky, Geza, 'The lessons of appeasement', *RUSI Journal*, 139.1 (1994), pp. 6–8.

Kaiser, Wolfram, 'Against Napoleon and Hitler: Background Influences on British Diplomacy' in Kaiser Wolfram and Staerck, Gillian Staerck (eds), *British Foreign Policy 1955–64: Contracting Options*, Basingstoke: Macmillan, 2000.

Kennedy, Paul M., 'The Tradition of Appeasement in British Foreign Policy, 1865–1939', *British Journal of International Studies*, 2.3 (1976), pp. 195–215.

—, 'A Time to Appease', *The National Interest*, 108 (2010), pp. 7–17.

Klein, Ira, 'The Anglo-Russian Convention and the Problem of Central Asia, 1907–1914', *Journal of British Studies*, 11.1 (1971), pp. 126–47.

Küsters, Hanns Jürgen, 'Konrad Adenauer und Willy Brandt in der Berlin-Krise 1958–1963', *Vierteljahrshefte für Zeitgeschichte*, 40.4 (1992), pp. 483–542.

Lane, Anne J., 'Coming to Terms with Tito: Britain and Yugoslavia, 1945–49' in Richard J. Aldrich and Michael F. Hopkins (eds), *Intelligence, Defence and Diplomacy: British Policy in the Post-War World*, Frank Cass, 1994.

Laqueur, Walter, 'The Psychology of Appeasement' in *The Political Psychology of Appeasement : Finlandization and Other Unpopular Essays*, New Brunswick, NJ : Transaction Books, 1980.

Mayhew, Christopher, 'British Foreign Policy Since 1945', *International Affairs*, 26.4 (1950), pp. 477–86.

Mayer, Arno J., 'Vietnam Analogy: Greece, Not Munich', *Annals of International Studies*, 1 (1970), pp. 224–32.

Morgenthau, Hans J., 'Diplomacy', *The Yale Law Journal*, 55.5 (1946), pp. 1067–80.

—, 'The Twilight of International Morality', *Ethics*, 58.2 (1948), pp. 79–99.

—, 'Alliances in Theory and Practice' in Arnold Wolfers (ed.), *Alliance Policy in the Cold War*, Baltimore, MD: Johns Hopkins University Press, 1959.

—, 'The Roots of America's China Policy', *The China Quarterly*, 10 (1962), pp. 45–50.

—, 'To Intervene or Not to Intervene', *Foreign Affairs*, 45.3 (1967), pp. 425–36.

—, 'Remarks on the Validity of Historical Analogies', *Social Research*, 39.2 (1972), pp. 360–4.

Murray, Williamson, 'British Grand Strategy, 1933-1942' in Williamson Murray, Richard Hart Sinnreich and James Lacey (eds), *The Shaping of Grand Strategy: Policy, Diplomacy, and War*, Cambridge: Cambridge University Press, 2011.

Nicholls, Anthony J., '"Appeasement" or "Common Sense"? The British Response to the Building of the Berlin Wall, 1961' in Ursula Lehmkuhl, Clemens A. Wurm and Hubert Zimmermann (eds), *Deutschland Großbritannien, Amerika: Politik, Gesellschaft, und Internationale Geschichte im 20. Jahrhundert: Festschrift fur Gustav Schimdt zum 65. Geburtstag*, Wiesbaden/Stuttgart: Steiner, 2003.

Nicolson, Harold, 'Modern Diplomacy and British Public Opinion', *International Affairs*, 14.5 (1935), pp. 599–618.

—, 'Diplomacy Then and Now', *Foreign Affairs*, 40.1 (1961), pp. 39–49.

Peden, G. C., 'A Matter of Timing: The Economic Background to British Foreign Policy, 1937–1939', *History*, 69.225 (1984), pp. 15–28.

Pettifer, James, 'The Price of Appeasement', *The World Today*, 56.1 (2000), pp. 10–12.

Portes, Alejandro, 'Hazards of Historical Analogy', *Social Problems*, 28.5 (1981), pp. 517–9.

Ramet, Sabrina Petra, 'The Bosnian War and the Policy of Accommodation', *Current History*, 93.586 (1994), pp. 380–5.

Record, Jeffrey, 'The Use and Abuse of History: Munich, Vietnam and Iraq', *Survival*, 49.1 (2007), pp. 163–80.

Reynolds, David, 'Churchill's Writing of History: Appeasement, Autobiography and *The Gathering Storm*', *Transactions of the Royal Historical Society*, Sixth Series, 11 (2001), pp. 221–48.

Richardson, J. L., 'New Perspectives on Appeasement: Some Implications for International Relations', *World Politics*, 40.3 (1988), pp. 289–316.

Rifkind, Malcolm, 'Peacekeeping or Peacemaking? Implications and Prospects', *RUSI Journal*, 138.2 (1993), pp. 1–6.

—, 'Where is the Axis of Freedom? ', *RUSI Journal*, 147.3 (2002), pp. 15–9.

Rose, Norman, 'The Resignation of Anthony Eden', *Historical Journal*, 25.4 (1982), pp. 911–31.

Schroeder, Paul W., 'Munich and the British Tradition', *Historical Journal*, 19.1 (1976), pp. 223–43.

—, 'Napoleon's Foreign Policy: A Criminal Enterprise', *The Journal of Military History*, 54.2 (1990), pp. 147–62.

Schwartz, Thomas, 'The Berlin Crisis and the Cold War', *Diplomatic History*, 21.1 (1997), pp. 140–8.

Serfaty, Simon, 'America and Europe beyond Bosnia', *Washington Quarterly*, 19.3 (1996), pp. 31–44.

Sinnreich, Richard Hart 'About turn: British strategic transformation from Salisbury to Grey' in Williamson Murray, Richard Hart Sinnreich and James Lacey (eds), *The Shaping of Grand Strategy: Policy, Diplomacy, and War*, Cambridge: Cambridge University Press, 2011.

Skidelsky, Robert, 'Going to War with Germany: Between Revisionism & Orthodoxy', *Encounter*, 39.1 (1972), pp. 56–65.

Small, Melvin, 'Some Lessons of Munich' in Melvin Small (ed.), *Appeasing Fascism: Articles from the Wayne State University Conference on Munich after Fifty Years*, New York: University Press of America, 1991.

Stafford, Paul, 'Political Autobiography and the Art of the Plausible: R.A. Butler at the Foreign Office, 1938–1939', *Historical Journal*, 28.4 (1985), pp. 901–22.

Steiner, Zara, 'The Historian and the Foreign Office' in Pamela Beshoff and Christopher Hill (eds), *Two Worlds of International Relations: Academics, Practitioners and the Trade in Ideas*, London: Routledge, 1994.

Tebinka, Jacek, 'British Memoranda on Changing the Curzon Line in 1944', *Acta Poloniae Historica*, 80 (1999), pp. 167–94.

Trevor-Roper, H. R., 'A.J.P. Taylor, Hitler, and the War', *Encounter*, 17.1 (1961), pp. 88–96.

Urban, G. R., 'Co-existence without Sanctimony' in G. R. Urban (ed.), *Détente*, London: Temple Smith, 1976.

Varsori, Antonio, 'British Policy Aims at Geneva' in Gunther Bischof and Saki Dockrill (eds), *Cold War Respite: The Geneva Summit of 1955*, Baton Rouge, LA: Louisiana University Press, 2000.

—, 'Britain as a Bridge between East and West' in Wilfried Loth (ed.), *Europe, Cold War and Coexistence, 1953–1965*, London: Frank Cass, 2004.

Vertzberger, Yaacov Y. I., 'Foreign Policy Decisionmakers as Practical-intuitive Historians: Applied History and Its Shortcomings', *International Studies Quarterly*, 30.2 (1986), pp. 223–47.

Vulliamy, Ed, 'Bosnia and the Crime of Appeasement', *International Affairs*, 74.1 (1998), pp. 73–92.

Walker, Stephen G., 'Solving the Appeasement Puzzle: Contending Historical Interpretations of British Diplomacy during the 1930s', *Review of International Studies*, 6.3 (1980), pp. 219–46.

Watt, Donald Cameron, 'Appeasement: The Rise of a Revisionist School?', *Political Quarterly*, 36.2 (1965), pp. 191–213.

—, 'The Historiography of Appeasement' in Alan Sked and Chris Cook (eds), *Crisis and Controversy: Essays in Honour of A.J.P. Taylor* (London: Macmillan, 1976).

—, 'Churchill and Appeasement' in Robert Blake and Wm. Roger Louis (eds), *Churchill*, Oxford: Oxford University Press, 1993.

Webster, Charles, 'Munich Reconsidered: A Survey of British Policy', *International Affairs*, 37.1 (1961), pp. 137–54.

Williams, Beryl J., 'The Strategic Background to the Anglo-Russian Entente of August 1907', *Historical Journal*, 9.3 (1966), pp. 360–73.

Williams, Paul R. and Waller, Karina M., 'Coercive Appeasement: The Flawed International Response to the Serbian Rogue Regime', *New England Law Review*, 36.4 (2002), pp. 825–89.

Williams, Philip, 'Britain, Détente and the Conference on Security and Cooperation in Europe' in Keith Dyson (ed.), *European Détente: Case Studies of the Politics of East-West Relations*, London: Frances Pinter, 1986.

Wright, Louis B., 'Propaganda against James I's "Appeasement" of Spain', *Huntington Library Quarterly*, 6.2 (1943), pp. 149–72.

Young, John W., 'Cold War and Détente with Moscow' in John W. Young (ed.), *The Foreign Policy of Churchill's Peacetime Administration 1951–55*, Leicester University Press, 1988.

Zelikow, Philip, 'The Statesman in Winter: Kissinger on the Ford Years', *Foreign Affairs*, 78.3 (1999), pp. 123–8.

Zuber, Terence, 'The Schlieffen Plan Reconsidered', *War in History*, 6.3 (1999), pp. 262–305.

INDEX